Running IPv6

Iljitsch van Beijnum

Apress®

Running IPv6

Copyright © 2006 by Iljitsch van Beijnum

ISBN : 1-4302-1174-1

Library of Congress Cataloging-in-Publication data is available upon request.

Lead Editor: Jim Sumser
Technical Reviewers: Jordi Palet Martinez and Pim van Pelt
Editorial Board: Steve Anglin, Dan Appleman, Ewan Buckingham, Gary Cornell, Tony Davis,
     Jason Gilmore, Jonathan Hassell, Chris Mills, Dominic Shakeshaft, Jim Sumser
Project Manager: Laura Cheu and Richard Dal Porto
Copy Edit Manager: Nicole LeClerc
Copy Editor: Kristen Imler
Assistant Production Director: Kari Brooks-Copony
Production Editor: Lori Bring
Compositor: Linda Weidemann, Wolf Creek Press
Proofreader: Linda Seifert
Indexer: Michael Brinkman
Artist: Kinetic Publishing Services, LLC
Cover Designer: Kurt Krames
Manufacturing Director: Tom Debolski

For information on translations, please contact Apress directly at 2560 Ninth Street, Suite 219, Berkeley, CA 94710. Phone 510-549-5930, fax 510-549-5939, email info@apress.com, or visit http://www.apress.com.

The source code for this book is available to readers at http://www.apress.com in the Source Code section.

Contents at a Glance

Contents

About the Author

**ILJITSCH VAN BEIJNUM** is a self-employed network consultant in The Hague, Netherlands. He first got interested in unusual network protocols in the early 1990s when, working in a technical support job for the Dutch PTT, he discovered he could connect to a DECserver in the office basement that provided services with intriguing names such as LAT, MOP and X.25. He left this job to go to college, but a few years later, he found himself in the emerging Internet Service Provider business. There he learned about system administration, IP networking, and especially routing. After starting a small ISP with four others in 1997 and working as a senior network engineer for UUNET Netherlands in 1999, he became a freelance consultant in 2000. Not long after that, he started contributing to the IETF multihoming in IPv6 working group and wrote a book about the Border Gateway Protocol. All the while, Iljitsch continued his education at night and not too long ago received his Bachelor of Information and Communication Technology degree at the Haagse Hogeschool. When he can find the time, Iljitsch posts news and the occasional rant about BGP, IPv6, and related topics on his Web site, `http://www.bgpexpert.com/`.

About the Technical Reviewers

**JORDI PALET MARTÍNEZ** has experience with technical, marketing, and product management in several companies and is now working as CEO/ CTO at Consulintel, Madrid. He has been involved in the IPv6 Forum as chair of the Education & Awareness Working Group since the Forum foundation. He is a member of the Technical Directorate and IPv6 Logo Committee, which is responsible for the "IPv6 Ready" Program. He is a frequent lecturer and author of papers related to different technologies, specifically IPv6, in addition he has been involved in a number of R&D projects (such as Euro6IX, 6POWER, 6QM, Eurov6, IPv6 TF-SC, 6LINK, PlaNetS). He is involved in standardization for IETF (for example, he is a co-author of numerous documents) and other Internet-related organizations such as the RIRs. Jordi is an active member of nonprofit organizations for the dissemination of technologies and telecommunications and Internet. He is also an active member and a main contributor of the European Commission IPv6 Task Force (http://www.ipv6tf.org), Spanish IPv6 Task Force, and the IPv6 Task Force Steering Committee. He participates in several European and worldwide IPv6 Task Forces and related activities.

PIM VAN PELT is a network and (UNIX) system administrator and programmer based in the Netherlands. As a youngster, he lived in the U.S. and in England, and more recently, he has lived in Belgium. He got exposed to IPv6 in college and has been a well-known proponent of the new protocol since then. He also created the software used by the SixXS tunnel broker. Pim holds a Bachelor degree in Computer Science from the Fontys Hogeschool in Eindhoven, Netherlands, and currently works for Dutch ISP BIT.

Acknowledgments

First of all, I'd like to thank all the people at Apress, especially Laura, Richard, Kristen, Lori, and most of all Jim, who showed great patience. Without them, this book wouldn't exist. Another person who was instrumental in making this book possible, even though neither of us knew it at the time, is Hans Goes. Hans provided me with my first IPv6 tunnel many years ago. And thanks to Daniël, Michael, Bastiaan, and Laurens for letting me hone my IPv6 skills on their networks. Last but certainly not least, I owe the technical reviewers, Pim van Pelt and Jordi Palet Martínez, many thanks for the additional facts and viewpoints they brought to the project. And thanks to my brother Ernesto for introducing me to computers in the first place.

Introduction

This is a book about running the IPv6 protocol in heterogeneous environments. It will tell you how to enable the protocol on Windows, MacOS, FreeBSD, Linux, and Cisco routers, and, up to a point, on Juniper routers. The intent behind the book is to present a clear view of the aspects to IPv6 that are of interest to those who'll be running and administrating the protocol, not to bombard the reader with unnecessary details. This means that the book covers the IPv6 specifications to the degree necessary to successfully operate an IPv6 network; for a detailed discussion of the IPv6 protocol itself, see *IPv6 Essentials* by Silvia Hagen (O'Reilly & Associates, 2002) or *IPv6: The New Internet Protocol* (Second Edition) by Christian Huitema (Prentice Hall, 1998). Alternatively, you can get this information straight from the horse's mouth by reading the relevant Request For Comment documents that specify the IPv6 standards. See Appendix A for a list of IPv6-related RFCs and how to obtain RFCs.

This book is a little different from most technical books. Rather than explain IPv6 as a more or less self-contained technology, most chapters deal with the impact that IPv6 has on a particular aspect of IP networking, such as configuring hosts (Chapter 2), routing (Chapter 4), the DNS (Chapter 5), applications (Chapter 6), security (Chapter 9), and providing transit services if you're an ISP (Chapter 11). All these chapters address two audiences: people who already know the chapter's subject and just need to know what's different in IPv6, and people who have some TCP/IP background but aren't all that familiar with the subject discussed in the chapter, let alone with how it relates to IPv6. So all these chapters have some background information that experts already know, but the chapters quickly proceed into more complex territory, so non-experts may find it hard to follow the entire chapter.

Many chapters build on information from earlier chapters, so reading the book from the beginning to the end is not a bad idea. However, there are frequent pointers to other chapters, so don't be afraid to start in the middle of the book if that's your thing.

Throughout the book, you'll find configuration examples for FreeBSD versions 4.9 and 5.4, Red Hat 9 Linux and Red Hat Enterprise ES4 Linux, Windows XP (mostly Service Pack 2), Apple MacOS X Panther (10.3) and Tiger (10.4), and Cisco IOS. The Windows XP examples should also work on Windows 2003 Server, but this wasn't tested. The IPv6 features vary greatly between IOS releases, versions, trains, images, and so on. Use a fairly recent IOS version and consult the Cisco documentation if a feature you want to use isn't available. Chapter 4 (routing) also has some examples for Juniper routers. You need basic system or router administration skills on the system in question to be able to use the examples.

Sometimes, sentences end in URLs, addresses, or commands. In these cases, a period denotes proper grammar and isn't part of the URL, address, or command. This can happen with a comma, too. URLs and commands appear in this font. Sometimes listings contain examples with lines that are longer than will fit on a single line in the book. In that case, the character ➥ indicates that the next line is a continuation of the current one. Numbers preceded by 0x, such as 0x800, are in hexadecimal.

Throughout the book, a "system" or "node" is any device that connects to the network and implements IP (IPv4 and/or IPv6). A "router" is a system that forwards packets that it didn't generate itself from one system to the next. All IP-capable devices that aren't routers are "hosts."

CHAPTER 1

■ ■ ■

IPv6

The Internet Protocol (IP) is the most successful network protocol in the history of network protocols. Not only is all the information that flows over the Internet contained in packets that conform to the Internet Protocol, IP has also driven out of the marketplace the other protocols that were used in private networks during the last two decades of the previous century. Today, a non-IP computer network is almost unthinkable. So what kind of new protocol could possibly challenge IP's supremacy?

A new version of IP, of course.

And that's exactly what IPv6 (Internet Protocol version 6) is: the next step in the natural evolution of the Internet Protocol. In case a new version of IP was ever needed, the designers of the original IP included a field that contains a version number in the packet layout. This way, there would never be a risk that the contents of a data packet would be misinterpreted, because the receiver assumes a different version of the Internet Protocol than the one used by the sender. Today's IP sets the version number in each packet to 4, making it IPv4. Version numbers 1, 2, and 3 were left unused. The lowest and highest possible values (0 and 15 for the IP version number) are traditionally reserved. IP version number 5 was allocated to a non-IP protocol that had to coexist with IP under some circumstances, so 6 was the logical choice for the next-generation IP.[1]

IPv6—Why?

In the mid-1980s, the Internet Engineering Task Force (IETF) was created to provide a setting where the people who built and ran Internet-related networks or network equipment could interact. Over the years, the IETF has evolved into a standards organization, but it's still very different from other standards organizations such as the ANSI, IEEE, ITU-T, or ETSI. The most fundamental difference is that other standards organizations charge for membership and for the standards documents themselves. Within the IETF, on the other hand, anyone can participate through email and obtain RFC documents for free. Most of the work is done through email, so even those who can't afford traveling to the IETF meetings that are held three times a year can participate. This directly leads to another peculiar aspect of the IETF: because membership is open, it makes little sense to arrive at decisions through voting, so the IETF works by "rough consensus." Nobody really knows for sure what "rough consensus" means, but the rough consensus is that it's somewhere between a majority and unanimity. As the IETF

---

1. See http://www.iana.org/assignments/version-numbers for details on IP version numbers.

motto, coined by Dave Clark, puts it: "We reject presidents, kings, and voting; we believe in rough consensus and running code."

Work inside the IETF is done in working groups (wgs). The working groups are organized into areas such as Routing, Security and Operations, and Management. Each area has two area directors, and the area directors, together with the IETF chair, make up the Internet Engineering Steering Group (IESG). The IESG is the IETF's governing body. There is also the Internet Architecture Board (IAB), which has close ties to the IETF and overlooks the Internet architecture. The Internet Assigned Numbers Authority (IANA) keeps track of protocol numbers, and the RFC Editor publishes IETF standards and other documents as "RFCs" (see Appendix A for more information). The IESG and IAB members don't receive compensation for their work, but the IETF has a small secretariat that provides administrative support to the IESG.

In the early 1990s, the IETF realized that the IPv4 address space was running out at a dangerous rate. Around 1990, about one-eighth of the 3.7 billion usable IPv4 addresses was given out, a number that doubled every five years. At this rate, the last IP address would be used up in 2005. This apparently impending doom prompted the IETF to start work on "IP next generation" (IPng), which eventually led to the creating of the IPv6 standard. The first IPv6 RFC was published in 1995 (with many more to come). The main difference between IPv4 and IPv6 is that IPv6 uses addresses that are 128 bits, rather than the 32 bits in IPv4, allowing no less than 3.4×10^{38} individual addresses.

See Appendix A for an overview of the IETF standards process and a list of IPv6-related RFCs.

IPv6 Benefits

When the IETF set out to create "IPng," the Internet Protocol next generation, it took advantage of this opportunity to improve on IPv4 wherever possible.

More Address Space

Still, the most obvious and most important advantage of IPv6 is that the addresses are longer, which makes for a much, much larger address space. The actual number of individual addresses that is possible with 128 bits goes beyond numbers anyone except astronomers and particle physicists is familiar with:

340,282,366,920,938,463,463,374,607,431,768,211,456

The number of possible IPv4 addresses seems mundane by comparison:

4,294,967,296

The 128-bit address space is large enough to have 155 billion IPv4 Internets on every square millimeter of the Earth's surface, including the oceans. In U.S. measurements, the figure is even bigger: it's enough to supply every square inch of the Earth's surface with the equivalent of a hundred trillion IPv4 Internets. Or what if the amount of address space used would really have doubled every five years for years to come, rather than level off around the turn of the millennium? Even at this incredible exponential rate, the IPv6 address space would last until the year 2485.

The original goal of providing more address space to avoid running out of addresses altogether isn't as urgent as it once was, because IPv4 addresses are no longer used up at an exponential rate. There may even be enough IPv4 addresses for decades to come, although that's certainly a dangerous assumption to make. On the other hand, there aren't even enough IPv4 addresses for each person on Earth to have just one, and North America and Europe already use many more than a single address per person. So while the exact moment when the IPv4 address space will run out remains a topic for heated debate, it's obvious that at some point it will.

Innovation

One reason why IPv4 addresses aren't running out as fast as predicted 10 years ago is that many, if not most, IP-capable systems today use private address space and connect to the Internet using Network Address Translation (NAT). However, NAT is a double-edged sword. On the one hand, it allows for simple extension of IP connectivity to large numbers of hosts and IP-enabled devices everywhere where a single address is available, but the downside is that NAT gets in the way of many applications, especially those that don't adhere to a simple client/server model. Because with NAT in effect, several hosts share the translated IP address, and having hosts elsewhere on the Net connect to one of the NAT'ed hosts becomes a problem. This is similar to the situation where several phones are connected to a single line: for outgoing calls, there isn't much of a problem, but there is no easy way to get incoming calls delivered to the right phone.

For services such as the Web and email, there isn't much of a problem: the Web browser or email client always contacts the server. For these services, only a limited number of servers need to receive incoming connections. However, with other types of applications, everyone is a server. This is the case with Voice over IP (VoIP), where IP-enabled phones connect directly to each other, to similar applications such as video conferencing, and to any type of peer-to-peer application. NAT is a real stumbling block when it comes to adopting these new technologies. IPv6 can solve this by giving each IP-enabled system its own address, allowing for renewed innovation.

Stateless Autoconfiguration

IPv4 hosts typically use the Dynamic Host Configuration Protocol (DHCP) to obtain an address from a server or router. This generally works well, but it has two downsides: a server of some kind is required, and there is no guarantee that a host will receive the same address when repeating the request at some later time. IPv6 adds "stateless autoconfiguration" as a means for hosts to be configured with an address. With stateless autoconfiguration in effect (and it usually is), a host listens for routers to tell it which 64 bits to use for the top half of the IPv6 address. All hosts connected to the same network share these 64 bits. Hosts then derive the bottom 64 bits from their Ethernet MAC address to arrive at a full 128-bit IPv6 address. If there are several routers that advertise different 64-bit prefixes, hosts simply create multiple addresses by combining each of those prefixes with the MAC-derived 64-bit values. This means that unless there are special circumstances, *a host will always have the same address(es) without any per-host configuration of any kind*. In IPv4, client hosts that can stand to have their IP address changed mostly use DHCP, but servers still almost always receive their IP address through manual configuration to avoid nasty surprises when the DHCP server gets confused. With IPv6, manually configuring server addresses is no longer necessary, as there is no longer any "state" (configuration information) that can get lost or corrupted.

Of course, the router advertisements also tell hosts which routers they can use to reach the rest of the Internet.

Renumbering

Changing IP addresses for a group of hosts becomes a lot easier now, as all that's required is for routers to stop advertising the old prefix and to start advertising a new one. Hosts will automatically create new addresses for themselves and notice that the old addresses are no longer "refreshed." To avoid interruptions in ongoing sessions when the old addresses are suddenly removed, the old addresses are only "deprecated" at first, meaning they may still be used in existing communication sessions but for new sessions are set up using non-deprecated addresses.

Efficiency

IPv6 processing is more efficient than IPv4 processing in many ways. This boost in efficiency is illustrated by the fact that while the address fields are now four times as big as in IPv4, the total size of the IPv6 header that precedes all packets is only 40 bytes, twice as big as the typical 20-byte IPv4 header. Efficiency improvements in IPv6 include the following:

- The IPv6 header has a fixed length.

- The IPv6 header is optimized for processing up to 64 bits at a time (32 in IPv4).

- The IPv4 header checksum that is calculated every time a packet passes a router was removed from IPv6.

- Routers are no longer required to fragment oversized packets; they can simply signal the source to send smaller packets.

- All broadcasts for discovery functions were replaced by multicasts. Only hosts that are actively listening for multicasts are interrupted, rather than all hosts, as with broadcasts.

See Chapter 7 for additional details on IPv6 advantages and transition issues and Chapter 8 for more information on how IPv6 works internally.

Myths

A number of myths surround IPv6. Some are simple misinformation, but others are more persistent because they have small kernel of truth to them, which is then blown out of proportion.

Security

Probably the most persistent myth surrounding IPv6 is that it would be more secure than IPv4. This myth is probably fed by the fact that IPv6 has "mandatory" support for IPsec. IPsec provides authentication and encryption at the IP level, making it possible for any application that runs over IP to be protected against having its data intercepted or modified en route. However, IPsec is also available in many IPv4 implementations today, while the fact that it's supposed to be included in IPv6 doesn't mean that it's available to applications by default: IPsec requires extensive configuration efforts.

In practice, however, running IPsec over IPv4 is a challenge because NAT often gets in the way. The IPsec option that is designed to protect the entire packet will detect the modifications to packets introduced by NAT and throw those packets away. Other IPsec options aren't fundamentally incompatible with NAT but are hampered by the fact that the negotiation mechanism that sets up IPsec security associations gets confused when the two ends don't agree on each other's IP address (because it was translated in the middle). Although these issues are addressed in IPv4, it's still easier to run IPsec in IPv6.

IPv6 does have one security advantage over IPv4, though: in IPv6, an Ethernet usually gets 64 bits to number hosts. With IPv4, this is never more than 16 bits and is often much less. This means that an attacker or a worm looking for something to hack or infect has a much harder time scanning even a single Ethernet subnet in IPv6 than scanning the entire IPv4 Internet. See Chapter 9 for a detailed discussion of IPv6 security, including IPsec.

Mobility

Like IPsec, support for mobility is required for IPv6. In this context, mobility means that a host may connect to the network at different places at different times, receiving different IP addresses each time but retaining communications sessions to its "home address" all the while. However, fully functioning, if not terribly efficient, mobility support is also available for some IPv4 implementations, while it's often still lacking in IPv6 implementations because the Mobile IPv6 standard hasn't quite settled yet.

Quality of Service

It is often said that IPv6 has better support to provide for additional "quality of service" (QoS), or in other words, mechanisms to prioritize certain traffic over other traffic. This is not the case. IPv4 and IPv6 both support traffic prioritization by using a small field in the header that used to hold "type of service" and priority information. This field has since been redefined for use with "differentiated services" (diffserv). However, IPv6 also has a field that IPv4 doesn't have: the flow label. The flow label isn't really used today, and its only use is to recognize different communications sessions, something that is also easily done by looking at the TCP or UDP port numbers. IPv6 may gain QoS advantages over IPv4 when the flow label is put to good use in the future.

Routing

It has been said that routing would be improved in IPv6. Unfortunately, it's exactly the same as in IPv4, except that the addresses are bigger and we get to avoid some of the mistakes that were made with assigning IPv4 address space.

The Transition Will Be Too Expensive

In the cases where existing hardware can't be upgraded to support IPv6, the transition to IPv6 will indeed be expensive. However, having to replace hardware is a problem mostly with very big routers used by Internet Service Providers and large enterprises. If these routers have special hardware support for routing IPv4 that isn't compatible with IPv6, the router is either completely useless for IPv6 or performance is dramatically lower because IPv6 must be processed in software without any hardware acceleration. However, cutting-edge routing hardware has a fairly short economic lifespan, so this problem should go away by itself in a few years. (Unless people continue to keep buying IPv4-only hardware, of course.)

For small devices that can't be upgraded, either the price is so low that replacing them isn't an issue, or they can continue to run IPv4 without much trouble with transition mechanisms (see Chapter 7) picking up the slack. Regular computers don't pose a problem in this area because all the major operating systems already support IPv6. The only costs that remain are those for operating dual-stack networks and training personnel. But these costs should be measured against continued use of IPv4 and having to comply with address allocation policies that continue to get stricter.

IPv6—When?

IPv6 has been under development for the better part of 10 years, so the question when it is going to claim its place under the sun isn't easily answered. Some people say that if the protocol was going to succeed, it would have done so by now. That doesn't explain the incredible amount of activity surrounding IPv6 that has only increased in the past years, though. Vendors that had adopted a wait-and-see attitude before are now implementing the protocol into their products. The adoption of IPv6 in the Internet community at large seems to be on the rise as well, but not yet to the degree that IPv6 is becoming even close to mainstream, except maybe in Japan and Korea.

The way things are going now, it looks like IPv6 isn't going to run out of steam on its own any time soon. Given enough time, it should fairly naturally ease into wider deployment. How wide? Hard to say. IPv6 could quite possibly end up in a similar situation to that of the metric system in the U.S.: it's not something the general population knows or cares about, but certain groups, such as scientists, doctors, and engineers, would be lost without it. On the other hand, all the non-IP network protocols that are mentioned later in this chapter were very much in use 10 to 15 years ago, but IPv4 has replaced them all. So we can't rule out that IPv4 in turn will be replaced by IPv6 over the course of the next 10 to 15 years.

Differences Between IPv4, IPv6, and Other Protocols

It has been said[2] that the IP protocol family looks like an hourglass. The hourglass is wide at the top, where there are many application protocols, and narrows down to a much smaller set of transport protocols that are used between the two systems that take part in any particular communication session, such as TCP and UDP. A single Internet Protocol layer that is responsible for getting the packets across the underlying infrastructure forms the narrow middle of the hourglass. Below IP, the glass gets wider again to accommodate the different link layer protocols that know how to get packets from one IP router to the next, such as Ethernet, ATM, and PPP. Each datalink protocol can typically run over a variety of physical protocols that are responsible for getting the individual bits across a wire.

---

2. By Steve Deering, one of the authors of the IPv6 specification.

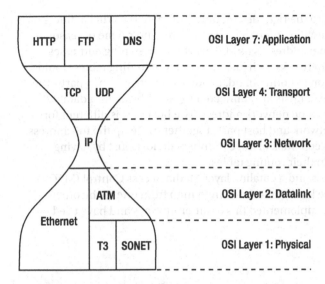

HTTP	FTP	DNS	OSI Layer 7: Application
	TCP	UDP	OSI Layer 4: Transport
		IP	OSI Layer 3: Network
		ATM	OSI Layer 2: Datalink
Ethernet	T3	SONET	OSI Layer 1: Physical

Figure 1-1. *The IP hourglass model*

The hourglass model puts IP squarely in the middle of the protocol family, sitting between the low-level protocols that are different at each hop along the way on the one hand, and the high-layer protocols that function end-to-end on the other hand. This model makes IP the only part of the protocol family that *must* be supported on all hosts and all routers. This isn't true for any other layer. For instance, when two hosts want to use the new SCTP protocol on top of IP rather than TCP, they can just go ahead and do so: the routers along the way don't have to understand SCTP. Conversely, a connection between two routers may be upgraded, for instance from Ethernet to Packet over SONET (POS), without any impact to the hosts that communicate over this link through the routers in question, as the lower layer protocols are removed and reapplied every time a packet passes a router.

The job of the Internet Protocol and alternative network layer protocols (that occupy the same place in different hourglasses) is to make the packets flow from the source to their destination and to accommodate the requirements of the different lower-layer protocols encountered along the way. IP implements an "unreliable datagram service," which means that packets ("datagrams") can be sent from one host connected to the network to another host that is also connected to the network without first having to set up a connection. In most cases, the datagram will be delivered to the destination, but there are no guarantees. For the network to deliver these datagrams to their destination, the packet must be completely self-contained and include at the very least source and destination addresses and the higher-layer protocol to which the packet is addressed. Routers along the way look at the address to decide which way the packet should go. Routers make these decisions with the aid of the routing table, which is nothing more than a long list of destination address ranges along with pointers to neighboring routers that are willing to forward packets for these addresses into the right direction. When the destination address can't be found in the routing table, or there is another problem, routers send back Internet Control Message Protocol (ICMP) messages to inform the source of the offending packet of the problem.

At first glance, there is significant overlap between what happens at the network layer in IP and the datalink layer in protocols such as Ethernet. Ethernet switches also use address information in the packet to forward it to the right destination. But there is a crucial difference: Ethernet addresses are burned into the Ethernet chip, so there is no rhyme or reason to where on the planet a particular Ethernet address is used. This way of assigning addresses makes it impossible to build really big networks with just Ethernet: the routing tables would get too large. Network layer protocols, on the other hand, divide the address in two parts: the network part and the host part. Whenever hosts are connected together by using a datalink layer network, all those hosts share the same network address. The host part is different for each host (or router), of course. The network and host parts together make up the full address, which makes it possible for routers to keep track of huge numbers of hosts just by having a limited number of network addresses in their routing tables.

Having both a network layer address and a datalink layer Media Access Control (MAC) address means that there must be some kind of mechanism to map from one to the other. Different network layer protocols have implemented this in different ways and have used wildly different address lengths.

IPX

Internetwork Packet Exchange (IPX) is a network layer protocol developed by Novell based on work by Xerox. It uses 80-bit addresses, with 32 bits for the network part of the address and 48 bits for the host part. The host part of the address simply contains the 48-bit Ethernet MAC address, so mapping from an IPX address to an Ethernet address is extremely simple. A host creates an IPX address for itself by taking the network address that routers periodically broadcast and filling in its Ethernet MAC address in the host part of the address. Figure 1-2 shows how an IPX address is created and how the Ethernet MAC address is found in the IPX when required.

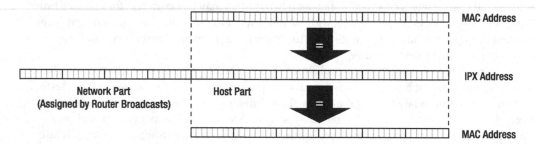

MAC Address

IPX Address

Network Part
(Assigned by Router Broadcasts)

Host Part

MAC Address

Figure 1-2. *The IPX address and the Ethernet MAC address*

When an IPX host wants to communicate with another host, it first checks if the intended correspondent is on the local Ethernet by checking whether the network parts of the local host's and the remote host's addresses are the same. If they are, the packet can be transmitted directly to the remote host because it's connected to the same Ethernet as the local host. If it is not, the packet is sent to a router.

DECnet Phase IV

Digital Equipment's DECnet Phase IV uses addresses that are only 16 bits long: 6 bits for the network part and 10 for the host part. DECnet solves the mapping problem the other way around: the Ethernet chip is reprogrammed to ignore its burned-in address and instead uses a special MAC address that includes the full DECnet address. DECnet Phase IV addresses must be manually configured. Figure 1-3 shows how the DECnet address fits inside the Ethernet MAC address.

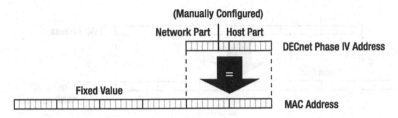

Figure 1-3. *The DECnet Phase IV address and the Ethernet MAC address*

AppleTalk

AppleTalk by Apple uses addresses that aren't much longer than DECnet addresses: 24 bits, with 16 bits for the network and 8 bits for hosts. As with IPX, the network address is learned from routers, but unlike IPX and DECnet Phase IV, AppleTalk doesn't use fixed information such as the Ethernet MAC address or a manually configured value to arrive at a host address. Instead, a host simply picks an address and checks if it's already in use by sending a message to this address. If there is no answer, the address is free, and the host may start using it. If there is an answer, the address is already in use, so the new host picks another address and retries. AppleTalk uses an address resolution protocol similar to that of IP (discussed later this chapter) to find Ethernet MAC addresses for other AppleTalk hosts it only knows the AppleTalk address for. Figure 1-4 shows how the AppleTalk address is created and how it's resolved into an Ethernet MAC address.

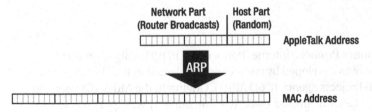

Figure 1-4. *The AppleTalk address and the Ethernet MAC address*

OSI CLNP

In the 1980s, the Open Systems Interconnection (OSI) protocol family was created by the International Organization for Standardization (ISO) and the International Telecommunication Union (ITU). The Connectionless Network Protocol (CLNP) provides a datagram service. In true OSI spirit, where even the most mundane details are carefully specified, there is a different name for the Connectionless Network *Service* (CLNS) and the actual CLNP *protocol* that is used to provide this service. However, this nuance is only appreciated by connoisseurs, so

CLNP and CLNS are often used interchangeably. Some people even simply say "OSI," disregarding the connection-oriented part of the protocol family (the X.25 protocol). CLNP addresses may vary in length, with a maximum of 160 bits, and include a system identifier that must be the same length for all systems inside a CLNP network. This means that in practice, the Ethernet MAC address is often used here, as shown in Figure 1-5.

Figure 1-5. *The variable length CLNP address and the Ethernet MAC address*

Unlike IPX, AppleTalk, IP, and IPv6, CLNP hosts don't try to figure out which addresses are reachable locally without involving a router. A CLNP host simply sends the packet to a router. The router then may or may not send a redirect message to inform the host on which MAC address it can use to communicate with the other host.

> ## OSI JARGON
>
> For people who are used to IP and the terminology that comes with it, OSI jargon can be quite baffling. For instance, a host is called an End System (ES) and a router is an Intermediate System (IS). A MAC address is a Subnetwork Point of Attachment (SNPA), and even the word "address" is deemed no good, so Network Service Access Point (NSAP) is used instead. To confuse matters even more, routers are generally addressed with a Network Entity Title (NET) rather than an NSAP.

TCP/IP

Then there is the Transport Control Protocol/Internet Protocol (TCP/IP) family of protocols. TCP/IP, or simply "IP" for short, was developed by researchers connected to the U.S. Department of Defense Advanced Research Projects Agency (DoD ARPA). Originally, the ARPANET used a single Network Control Protocol (NCP), but around 1980, NCP functionality was split up between the IP and TCP protocols. As the name suggests, the Internet Protocol was intended to be a protocol that could connect or internetwork different types of networks. As such, the IP address was fairly short at only 32 bits, so to accommodate both a large number of individual networks and large numbers of hosts per network, the designers of IP came up with a trick: rather than use a fixed boundary between the network and host parts of the address, they created three "classes." Class A networks have 7 bits for numbering networks and 24 bits for numbering hosts, class B networks have 14 network bits and 16 host bits, and class C networks have 21 bits to number networks and 8 for numbering hosts. (One to three bits are used to keep the classes apart.) This system with three different address classes allows IP to interconnect a small number of very large networks and also a very large number of small networks, along with a not very large number of medium-sized networks.

Unfortunately, the class B networks turned out to be the most popular choice, as very few organizations need to connect more than 65,536 hosts (which requires a class A net), while most organizations could see themselves using more than 256 hosts, the maximum for a class C network. This meant the class B networks started to run out rather quickly in the early 1990s. For a while, this impending shortage was fixed by giving out ranges of class C networks rather than a single class B network. However, this solution had the unfortunate side effect of using much more memory and processing capacity in routers: instead of keeping track of a single class B network, routers now had to know about, for instance, 16 individual class C networks. This problem was in turn fixed in 1993 by adopting classless interdomain routing (CIDR). With CIDR, the original class distinction was no longer relevant, and a value that indicated the division between the network and host bits was explicitly carried in routing protocols. This characteristic makes it possible to use the lowest possible number of bits to number hosts, using both the IPv4 address space and router resources as efficiently as possible.

Because there is no relation between the IP address and the factory-assigned Ethernet MAC address, IP uses the Address Resolution Protocol (ARP) to find out the MAC addresses for neighboring systems. A host that has an IP packet that it wants to transmit to another host or a router connected to the same Ethernet simply broadcasts a message asking for the owner of the IP address in question to respond. The target system sees its address in the broadcast and answers, and the original host learns the MAC address it was looking for from the reply. After that, the host knows which Ethernet MAC address to use for packets destined for this IP address. This process is shown in Figure 1-6.

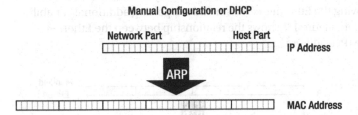

Figure 1-6. *The IP address is mapped to the Ethernet MAC address with ARP.*

CIDR—AN EXAMPLE

In 1988, an organization that needed 3,000 addresses would have received a class B net, wasting some 62,500 addresses but only using a single entry in the "global routing table" that is present in the large routers at Internet Service Providers. Three years later, in 1991, an organization that needed the same number of addresses would have received 12 class C nets, not wasting any IP addresses to speak of, but using 12 entries in routing tables worldwide. Another three years later, in 1994, a request for 3,000 IP addresses would have resulted in a /20 address assignment, which equals 16 class C nets or 1/16th of a class B net (4,096 addresses). However, these addresses could easily have come from class A space, as the old class distinction is no longer relevant and former class A space holds the most unused addresses. Using 12 bits to number hosts makes for a block of 4,096 addresses, which is more than 1,000 in excess of the 3,000 that are required. This situation is still much better than that with a full class B net, and only a single entry in the routing table is required.

IP Version 6

Last but not least, there is IPv6. There are many differences between IPv4 and IPv6, but it's important to recognize that IPv6 is still IP. Any and all protocols that run over IPv4 can also run over IPv6, assuming the necessary changes are made to accommodate the larger addresses. IPv6 addresses are 128 bits (16 bytes) long and fully classless. Well, in theory at least. In practice, in almost all cases, 64 bits are used to number networks and the remaining 64 bits are host bits. The 64 host bits are by default filled in with an Extended Unique Identifier (EUI-64), which is simply a 64-bit MAC address. Regular 48-bit Ethernet MAC addresses can easily be turned into EUI-64s by filling up the missing bits in the middle with 15 ones and a zero. The network part of the address is filled in with a network address that is periodically broadcast by routers. So it would seem that IPv6 adopts the IPX/CLNP approach by including the MAC address in the network layer address. However, this isn't the whole story. IPv6 also borrows from AppleTalk by performing a Duplicate Address Detection (DAD) procedure over the address, which means the actual address used may not contain a valid EUI-64. Just to be sure, IPv6 also supports the traditional IPv4 ways to assign addresses: through manual configuration and using an IPv6 version of the Dynamic Host Configuration Protocol (DHCP).

Because the host bits in the IPv6 address don't necessarily contain a MAC address, IPv6 includes an ARP-like mechanism to discover MAC addresses. But ARP is a fairly Ethernet-specific protocol, and it uses broadcasts, which IPv6 doesn't support. Instead, IPv6 uses multicasts extensively. Multicasts are like targeted broadcasts: packets are delivered to all hosts that are subscribed to a certain multicast group address. There are different group addresses for different purposes. Neighbor Discovery (ND), which is IPv6's replacement for ARP, is entirely multicast-based and is also more generic than ARP, removing the Ethernet-centrism and supporting additional capabilities such as dead neighbor detection. Figure 1-7 shows the relationship between the Ethernet MAC address, the EUI-64, and the IPv6 address.

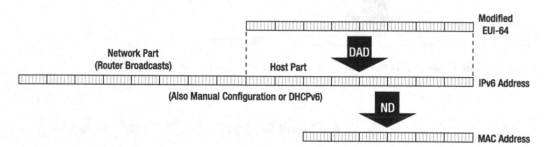

Figure 1-7. *The IPv6 address, the EUI-64, and the Ethernet MAC address*

This short overview may give you the impression that IPv6 is unnecessarily complex, but in my opinion, that's not the case. Yes, of the six network layer protocols, IPv6 is the most complex (or maybe it's a tie with CLNS), but as you read the rest of the book, you'll find out that IPv6 takes the best features from its direct and less direct predecessors, adds a few new ones of its own, and melds them into something elegant and powerful.

CHAPTER 2

■ ■ ■

Getting Started

Later in this chapter, we'll be enabling IPv6, but before that, it's important to understand IPv6 addressing. This subject is somewhat more complex than IPv4 addressing. First of all, IPv6 addresses are written differently: as eight 16-bit hexadecimal values separated by colons rather than as four 8-bit decimal values separated by periods. A typical IPv6 address looks like this:

2001:db8:31:1:20a:95ff:fef5:246e

Note that leading zeros are usually left out. To cut down on unnecessary zeros even more, one (and only one) sequence of zero values separated by colons may be removed. So the address 2001:db8:31:0:0:0:0:1 may also be written as 2001:db8:31::1. The fact that the address is now composed of only four values indicates that four zero values were removed at the place of the double colon, so they can easily be reinstated when the address must be converted to the internal 128-bit representation. This "zero compression" makes the following shorthand perfectly legal:

:: (0:0:0:0:0:0:0:0), which is the unspecified address.

::1 (0:0:0:0:0:0:0:1), which is the IPv6 loopback address.

2001:db8:31:: (2001:db8:31:0:0:0:0:0), which is (almost) a regular address.

However, something like 2001:db8:31::5900::1 isn't allowed, as there is no way to see that it is supposed to mean 2001:db8:31:0:5900:0:0:1 and not 2001:db8:31:0:0:5900:0:1. In this case, you should use either 2001:db8:31::5900:0:0:1 or 2001:db8:31:0:5900::1.

To accommodate the cases where the bottom 32 bits of an IPv6 address represent an IPv4 address (see Chapter 6), an IPv6 address may be expressed as six hexadecimal values separated by colons followed by the last 32 bits in the shape of an IPv4 address, for instance: 2001:db8:31:0:5900:0:172.31.45.60.

IPv6 doesn't use netmasks (a few exceptions prove the rule), but instead it uses the prefix notation that's common in IPv4 routing as well. So when an Ethernet has the IPv6 address range 2001:db8:31:1:: to 2001:db8:31:1:ffff:ffff:ffff:ffff assigned to it, this is written as 2001:db8:31:1::/64. The "/64" means that the first (upper or left) 64 bits of the address are assigned by an authority of some sort, and the contents of the remaining bits (also 64 in this case) are assigned locally. The address part in a prefix must be a valid IPv6 address with all the bits that aren't part of the prefix set to zero. So 2001:db8:31:1::/64 and 2001:db8:31:1::/127 are valid prefixes, but 2001:db8:31:1/64 or 2001:db8:31:1::/48 aren't. In the first case, the address part isn't a valid 128-bit IPv6 address; in the second case the ":1::" part falls outside the 48 prefix bits, so it should have been zero: 2001:db8:31::/48. However, even though it isn't

a valid prefix, 2001:db8:31:1:20a:95ff:fef5:246e/64 is shorthand for "address
2001:db8:31:1:20a:95ff:fef5:246e in subnet 2001:db8:31:1::/64."[1] An address without
a slash and a prefix value is always just an address, never a prefix or an address range. So
2001:db8:31::/48 is a prefix, but 2001:db8:31:: is an address that just happens to end in
a lot of zero bits.

See RFC 3513 for more information. Appendix A has more information on RFCs and how
to obtain them.

■**Tip** Because the colon character is already used to separate the port number from the hostname or
address in URLs, IPv6 addresses can't be used in URLs (and many other places such as configuration files)
as-is. Enclosing IPv6 addresses in brackets solves this problem. For example, a URL that points to the literal
IPv6 address 2001:db8:31:2::1 would be http://[2001:db8:31:2::1]/ (RFC 2732). You may also
encounter IPv4 addresses in this form, such as http://[192.0.2.1]/.

HEXADECIMAL AND BINARY REPRESENTATION

Numbers are stored in binary representation in computer memory; in other words, as strings of zeros and
ones. These binary values can easily be converted back and forth to our regular decimal representation when
necessary. But when such numbers become sufficiently large, the conversion between binary and decimal
becomes inconvenient because the decimal numbers get too large. In IPv4, this inconvenience is avoided by
converting the 32-bit address to decimal as four groups of 8 bits. This solution has the additional benefit that
it allows us to easily determine that 192.168.0.69 and 192.168.0.95 fall within the same address
range. Doing the same for 3221291245 and 3221291271 (the same 32-bit addresses converted to decimal
numbers) would be much harder. IPv6, on the other hand, takes advantage of the fact that hexadecimal digits
represent an even number of bits, as shown in the following table.

Binary	Hexadecimal	Decimal	Binary	Hexadecimal	Decimal
0000	0	0	1000	8	8
0001	1	1	1001	9	9
0010	2	2	1010	A	10
0011	3	3	1011	B	11
0100	4	4	1100	C	12
0101	5	5	1101	D	13
0110	6	6	1110	E	14
0111	7	7	1111	F	15

In hexadecimal, it's also easier to see that the two IP addresses share a common first part or prefix:
C0A80045 and C0A8005F. Whether they are really part of the same subnet, of course, depends on the
subnet size.

---

1. A "subnet" or "link" is a part of the network where the connected systems share an address range and
   can communicate with each other without involvement from a router. The most common example is
   an Ethernet network with one or more switches or hubs.

IPv6 Addressing

IPv6 has three types of addresses: unicast, multicast, and anycast. Unicast addresses are regular addresses used for one-to-one communication. Multicast addresses are "group addresses"; packets sent to such an address are delivered to all the systems that are interested and have joined the group. All functions that were performed by broadcasts in IPv4 are performed by using multicasts in IPv6. This type has the advantage that systems that aren't interested in certain information aren't forced to spend CPU cycles receiving it anyway, like they are with broadcasts. With multicasts, the network interface ignores packets addressed to groups that weren't joined at the hardware level. Anycasts are similar to multicasts, the difference being that packets sent to an anycast address are only delivered to *one* system in the anycast group rather than all of them.

At the highest level, the 128-bit IPv6 address space is divided into six parts, as shown in Table 2-1.

Table 2-1. *Overview of the IPv6 Address Space*

Start bits	IPv6 prefix notation	Use
000	::/3	Special addresses types
001	2000::/3	Allocated global unicast addresses
01 - 1111 1110 0	4000::/2 - FE00::/9	Reserved global unicast addresses
1111 1110 10	FE80::/10	Link-local unicast addresses
1111 1110 11	FEC0::/10	Site-local unicast addresses
1111 1111	FF00::/8	Multicast addresses

The special address types in the ::/3 include two special addresses (discussed later this chapter), IPv6-mapped IPv4 addresses (discussed in Chapter 6), and IPv6-encoded NSAP/CLNP addresses and IPX addresses.

Link-local addresses are for use on a single subnet; they are discussed later this chapter. In a similar vein, site-local addresses are meant for use within a single site. The site-local address range is somewhat similar to the RFC 1918 address ranges in IPv4 (10.0.0.0/8, 172.16.0.0/12, and 192.168.0.0/16). However, the IETF has identified a number of concerns regarding the use of site-local addresses. See Chapter 4 for a more detailed discussion.

Missing from Table 2-1 are anycast addresses, because anycast addresses are "syntactically indistinguishable" from unicast addresses. In other words, anycast addresses look the same as unicast addresses and share the same address space, and a host has no way of knowing whether it's sending a packet to a regular unicast address or to an anycast group address. A system that is set up to receive anycast packets must be explicitly configured so it knows it's dealing with an anycast address in order to enable the required special link layer behavior.

█Caution Multicast and anycast addresses may be used as destination addresses in packets, but only unicast addresses may be used as source addresses. Also, only routers may be configured with an IPv6 any- cast address.

This means strictly speaking, anycasting services such as the DNS isn't compatible with RFC 3513. After all, for anycast DNS to work, the anycast address must be present on more than one DNS server (which pre- sumably are hosts and not routers), and the responses to DNS queries are sent back with the destination address of the query (the anycast address) as the source address. The host that sent the query wouldn't recognize the response if it came from a different address. However, anycasting services is rarely done using the actual IPv6 anycast link-level mechanism, where several systems configured with the same any- cast address are connected to the same subnet.

Interface Identifiers

All unicast addresses, except those starting with three zero bits (prefix ::/3), are supposed to use a 64-bit interface identifier in the lower 64 bits of the IPv6 address. As mentioned in Chapter 1, an interface identifier is usually derived from a hardware MAC address. In turn, MAC addresses and EUI-64 Extended Unique Identifiers are made up of a 24-bit Organizationally Unique Iden- tifier (OUI), or "company_id," as administered by the Institute of Electrical and Electronics Engineers (IEEE), along with 24 or 40 bits that the owner of the OUI assigns. Although the IEEE habitually refers to the OUI as being 24 bits long, in reality, it's only 22 bits long, as two bits are used to indicate whether a MAC address or EUI-64 is globally unique (the universal/local bit)[2] and whether the MAC address is a group (multicast) address or a regular unicast address (the group bit).

Even in the cases where no hardware address is available or the address is set manually, the step from interface identifier to IPv6 address is still conceptually present. In this case, the univer- sal/local bit in the EUI-64 is set to one, indicating that the address isn't globally unique and thus not universally usable. However, to avoid complexity when manually configuring addresses, the universal/local bit (u/l bit) is flipped when creating an IPv6 address from a routing prefix and an interface identifier. An EUI-64 with the universal/local bit flipped is referred to as the "modified EUI-64." Figure 2-1 shows the relationship between the OUI, the MAC address, the EUI-64, and the modified EUI-64.

---

2. The IETF counts bits from left to right (most significant to least significant). The IEEE counts bits the way they are transmitted over the wire, which can differ between protocols. So, to the IEEE, the group bit in an Ethernet MAC address is bit number 0 and the universal/local bit is bit number 1, but to the IETF, they are bits 7 and 6, respectively. Someone trained in computer science would probably num- ber them 40 and 41.

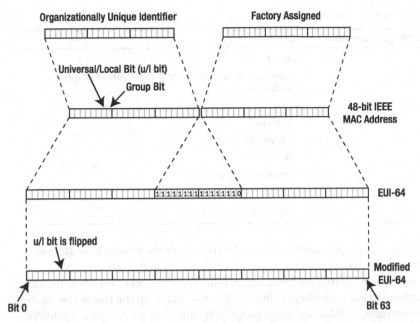

Figure 2-1. *The relationship between the OUI, MAC address, EUI-64, and modified EUI-64*

For example, the MAC address 00:0A:95:F5:E9:6E contains OUI 000A95, which is regis-tered to Apple. This 48-bit MAC address is turned into an EUI-64 by inserting the hexadecimal value FFFE between the OUI and the organization-assigned bits, which makes for the 64-bit value 00:0A:95:FF:FE:F5:E9:6E. By flipping bit 6 and adding a 64-bit prefix, for example, 2001:db8:31:1::/64, this makes for a full address: 2001:db8:31:1:20a:95ff:fef5:e96e in this case.

Another example: manually configuring the address 2001:db8:31:1::1. Because the inter-face identifier is mandatory for addresses in this range, this means there is a hidden EUI-64 with the value 02:00:00:00:00:00:00:01. Note that this doesn't mean that the Ethernet hardware will respond to this address (nor could it, as this 64-bit value doesn't translate into a 48-bit MAC address).

Multicast Scoping

More often than not, it's necessary to limit the propagation of multicast packets. For instance, it wouldn't be good if all routers connected to the Internet were to receive *all* the hello packets that OSPF routers use to find their neighbors. These packets are for use on the local subnet only. And the speech by the CEO should probably only be multicast throughout the company, rather than Internet-wide. Restrictions on the propagation of multicast packets are encoded in the multicast address in the form of a 4-bit scope value, as listed in Table 2-2.

Table 2-2. *IPv6 Multicast Scope Values*

Value (binary)	Value (hexadecimal)	Scope
0000	0	Reserved
0001	1	Interface-local (for the transmission of loopback multicast packets)
0010	2	Link-local
0011	3	Reserved
0100	4	Admin-local
0101	5	Site-local
1000	8	Organization-local
1110	E	Global
1111	F	Reserved

The remaining scope values (6, 7, and 9 - C) may be used by network administrators to define additional scopes where necessary.

The four scope bits in the address are preceded by four "flag" bits. RFC 3513 only defines the use of the last of these to indicate whether the 112 bits that make up the rest of the multicast address are a permanent, well-known value assigned by the Internet Assigned Numbers Authority (IANA), or some locally determined value. If the bit is set to zero, the 112-bit value is IANA-assigned. If the bit is set to one, the multicast address is "transient." So ff12::/16 is the prefix for transient link-local multicast use, while ff0e::/16 is the prefix for a permanent global multicast addresses.

Special Addresses

IPv6 has a significant number of special addresses. Some of these addresses are fixed and easily identifiable, while others depend on the interface identifier and are therefore harder to pin down:

:: is the unspecified address. This address is used in places where an address isn't yet known. For instance, as the source in DHCPv6 requests when the host requests an address from the DHCP server. Routers don't forward packets with unspecified addresses for a source or destination. (Relaying of DHCP packets doesn't count as regular forwarding.)

::1 is the local host or loopback address, which can be used by hosts to send packets to themselves, like the 127.0.0.1 address in IPv4. As with the unspecified address, routers ignore packets with the local host address in them.

fe80::/10 contains link-local addresses. All systems must create a link-local address for each of their IPv6-enabled network interfaces by combining their link (MAC) address with the prefix fe80::/64. Because the link-local prefix isn't tied to just one interface at a time, it is usually necessary to specify the intended interface when using link-local addresses. For instance, fe80::201:2ff:fe29:2640%xl0 refers to a link-local address that is reachable over the xl0 interface, while fe80::201:2ff:fe29:2640%fxp1 refers to the same address but now over the fxp1 interface. The %interface convention isn't universal. It's mostly seen on KAME-derived IPv6 stacks and utilities (see the section "FreeBSD" later this chapter), but it's also seen on some Linux systems. Even when the system supports specifying an interface in this way, applications may not recognize such an IPv6 address. Some utilities such as ping6 allow setting the output interface with a command line option.

fec0::/10 is the prefix for site-local addresses. These addresses are intended for use within a single site, similar to RFC 1918 addresses in IPv4 (10.0.0.0/8, 172.16.0.0/12, and 192.168.0.0/16). See Chapter 4 for more information on site-local addresses.

ff02::1 is the most common form of the all-hosts multicast address. This address, the closest thing that IPv6 has to a broadcast address, is usually found with link-local scope (ff02::1) but many hosts also implement it with interface-local scope (ff01::1), where it functions very similarly to the loopback address. Routers address the periodic router advertisement messages they send out for the benefit of all hosts on a link to ff02::1.

ff02::2 is the all-routers multicast address. It's similar to the all-hosts address, except that (of course) only routers join this multicast address. Apart from the usual link-local scope (ff02::2), this address may also be encountered with interface-local and site-local scope, ff01::2 and ff05::2, respectively.

ff02:0:0:0:0:1:ff00::/104 is the prefix for solicited node addresses. The solicited node address is a multicast address used for neighbor discovery (ND), the mechanism that replaced ARP. This address is created by replacing the top 104 bits in an IPv6 unicast or anycast address with the solicited node prefix. IPv6 systems are required to join the solicited node multicast groups that correspond to all the unicast and anycast addresses that are active on an interface (including the link-local address). This allows other IPv6 systems to inquire about the MAC address associated with a certain IPv6 address by multicasting a neighbor discovery query to the solicited node address that goes with the IPv6 address they're interested in.

The all-zeros multicast address for any scope (for instance, ff02:: for link-local scope) is reserved and may not be used.

The all-zeros address in any subnet (for instance, 2001:db8:31:1::) is the subnet all-routers anycast address. However, there is no real use for this anycast address, and some router vendors (such as Cisco) don't implement it. However, use this address at your peril, as it won't work reliably if there is a router on the subnet that *does* implement the all-routers anycast address correctly.

The highest 128 interface identifiers with the universal/local bit set to one or the highest 128 addresses for subnet addresses that don't use interface identifiers (i.e., they fall within ::/3) are reserved for well-known anycast addresses (RFC 2526).

Multicast addresses, especially those with interface-local or link-local scope, can be present on more than one interface; so when sending multicast packets, it's often also necessary to specify an interface by using the %interface syntax or through other means. However, some systems assume a default interface if one wasn't specified.

■**Note** Technically, using the %interface syntax to indicate a "scope zone" doesn't specify an *interface*, but a *link*, as two or more interfaces can be connected to the same link.

Address Allocation and Assignment

Formally, the IP address space falls under the responsibility of the Internet Corporation for Assigned Names and Numbers (ICANN). However, the ICANN's focus is on domain names, so management of the IP address space is left to the IANA, which in turn delegates the day-to-day allocation of IPv4 and IPv6 addresses to five Regional Internet Registries (RIRs):

- The African Network Information Centre (AfriNIC, http://www.afrinic.net/), serving Africa and the Indian Ocean.

- The Asia Pacific Network Information Centre (APNIC, http://www.apnic.net/), serving Australia, Oceania, and most of Asia.

- The American Registry for Internet Numbers (ARIN, http://www.arin.net/), serving North America.

- The Latin American and Caribbean Internet Addresses Registry (LACNIC, http://www.lacnic.net/), serving Latin America and the Caribbean.

- The Réseaux IP Européens Network Coordination Centre (RIPE NCC, often just called "RIPE," which isn't entirely correct, http://www.ripe.net/), serving Europe, the former Soviet Union, and the Middle East.

The RIRs then allocate blocks of IP address space to Local Internet Registries (LIRs), sometimes through an intermediate National Internet Registry (NIR) step. In nearly all cases, a LIR is an Internet Service Provider. Until not too long ago, the requirements for obtaining a block of IPv6 address space for ISPs boiled down to actually being an ISP and not an end-user organization, being a LIR (i.e., paying a membership fee to the RIR), and meeting the requirement to further assign IPv6 address space to at least 200 customers within two years. However, these policies have started to diverge recently and may change even further in the future. See Chapter 11 for a more detailed discussion.

An ISP that requests an IPv6 address block and meets these requirements is given a /32 allocation, from which assignments to end-users can be made. (ISPs that expect to connect really large numbers of IPv6 users may receive an allocation that's bigger than a /32.) The difference between an allocation and assignment is that the holder of an allocation can't start using the addresses at will; they're just holding them to be further assigned to the organization that will be using them. The RIRs allocate /32 prefixes to ISPs to limit the number of individual entries in the global IPv6 routing table that determines the flow of packets between ISPs.

Because there is an ample supply of IPv6 addresses, the policies for assigning address space to end users are much more relaxed in IPv6 than in IPv4: everyone gets a /48, unless they are absolutely, positively, never going to need more than a single subnet, in which case they get a /64, or are never going to need more than a single address, in which case they get—a single address. A /48 prefix allows for 65,536 /64 subnets, which should be enough for everyone except the largest corporations in the world. However, /48 prefixes are available to everyone, even just for home use. There is one important point to be aware of: when IP addresses are allocated or assigned, they do not become the property of the receiver. If there is no good faith effort to use the addresses as indicated at the time of request, the RIRs reserve the right to reclaim the address space. In theory, the RIRs could even reclaim allocations and assignments that meet the policies that were in effect at the time of the request but don't meet updated policies. In practice, RIRs are quite reluctant to reclaim address space even in IPv4, and the only issue that nonfraudulent end-user organizations need to be concerned about is that they can't take their address space with them when changing ISPs. A document outlining the IPv6 allocation and assignment policies is available at (among others) the RIPE Web site: http://www.ripe.net/ripe/docs/ipv6-policies.html.

In older IPv6 documentation, the terms Top-Level Aggregator (TLA), Next-Level Aggregator (NLA), Site-Level Aggregator (SLA), and sub-TLA often come up. These terms refer to the notion that the IPv6 address space should be distributed in a fixed, hierarchical manner. As of the publication of RFC 3587, this terminology is obsolete; IPv6 address space is distributed as outlined above, which is very similar to IPv4 except for the fixed minimum ISP allocation size of 32 bits and the also as good as fixed assignment size for end users of 48 bits.

The 6bone was established by the IETF as a global IPv6 testbed in 1996. Because the RIRs now provide "production" IPv6 address space, the 6bone and its 3ffe::/16 prefix will be phased out. However, in the meantime, 6bone address space may show up in various places alongside RIR address space as 6bone and production networks interconnect or even overlap in many places. The suggested date for putting the 6bone to rest is June 6, 2006.

Note The 6bone equivalent for a RIR /32 allocation is a /24 or /28 "pseudo TLA" (pTLA).

6to4 address space is a bit unusual: every /48 in this block corresponds to an IPv4 address. The mapping is very simple: the 48-bit prefix consists of 2002::/16 followed by the 32-bit IPv4 address as two 16-bit hexadecimal values, properly colon-separated as usual. A /48 in 6to4 space may be used by the host that is holding the corresponding IPv4 address at that particular time. 6to4 is not just a convenient way to distribute IPv6 addresses; its main function is to provide easy IPv6 connectivity to hosts and networks that otherwise only have IPv4 connectivity. This connectivity is accomplished by using tunneling mechanisms, as explained in Chapter 3.

Enabling IPv6

Because IPv6 contains extensive features for autoconfiguration, just enabling the protocol makes a host reachable over IPv6. If no IPv6 routers are available on the local subnet, the host will still create a link-local address for itself (on every interface), which is enough to allow other hosts that live on the same subnet to connect to it over IPv6. This means that it is important to use an IPv6 firewall where appropriate when IPv6 is enabled.

Caution As a rule, regular (IPv4) firewalls don't block IPv6 traffic, so a separate IPv6 firewall must be used to firewall IPv6-enabled applications that need protection. See Chapter 9 for more information on filtering and firewalling IPv6.

Windows

Real IPv6 support in Windows started with Windows XP.[3] In the initial release, IPv6 wasn't available through the graphical user interface but only by using a somewhat hidden command that must be entered using the command line:

```
ipv6 install
```

Removing IPv6 is done with `ipv6 uninstall`. The `ipv6.exe` command is now deprecated, and Microsoft encourages you to use `netsh interface ipv6 install` or `...uninstall` instead. Because `ipv6.exe`'s syntax is completely unfathomable, it's best to use `netsh interface ipv6` for all other purposes, but it's hard to beat the succinct elegance of "`ipv6 install`."

As of Service Pack 1, IPv6 can also be installed and removed as an additional protocol called "Microsoft IPv6 Developer Edition" in the network setup. In April 2003, Microsoft released the Advanced Networking Pack for Windows XP, which includes additional IPv6 features. The update is distributed through Windows Update, but if you're not sure you have it installed, you can go to `http://support.microsoft.com/` and select "Knowledge Base Article ID Number Search" (the URL is too hideous to repeat in print) and enter article number 817778. The Knowledge Base article discusses the update at length and includes instructions on downloading and installing it (but these pretty much boil down to "Use Windows Update"). After installing the update, IPv6 is available as an additional protocol under the name "Microsoft TCP/IP version 6." You can install it by selecting Start ➤ Control Panel ➤ Network and Internet Connections ➤ Network Connections and then right-clicking any network interface and selecting Properties, which will open the window shown in Figure 2-2.

In this window, click the Install... button and select installing an additional protocol. Then choose "Microsoft TCP/IP version 6," as shown in Figure 2-3.

■Note When Internet sharing is configured, which is almost unavoidable if you allowed Windows to "set up or change your home or small office network," some network interfaces may be bridged. In that case, the IPv6 protocol can't be added to the bridged interfaces themselves, only to the "Network Bridge" virtual bridging interface.

After installing the IPv6 protocol for any interface, the system will configure link-local addresses and also try to configure global addresses on all interfaces. (See Chapter 3 for details.) If you don't want to have IPv6 enabled on one or more interfaces, it is possible to disable the protocol on a per-interface basis by clearing the checkbox in the "this connection uses the following items" part of the Properties window for an interface.

Further configuration or monitoring of the protocol isn't possible by using the graphical user interface. You must use the `ipv6.exe` command or the newer, more general `netsh` command. To use these tools, select Start ➤ All Programs ➤ Accessories ➤ Command Prompt to open a command prompt window. Listing 2-1 shows how to start the `netsh` command and its use to see which addresses are configured. (Some additional output has been left out for brevity.)

---

3. IPv6 is available as a downloadable preview for Windows 2000, and an IPv6-capable version of Trumpet Winsock is available for Windows 98.

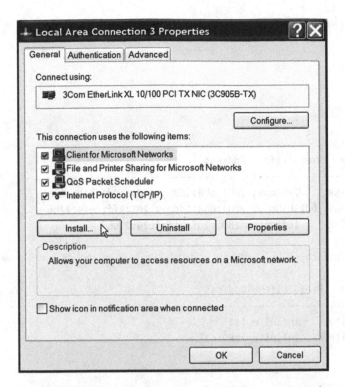

Figure 2-2. *The Windows XP network interface setup window*

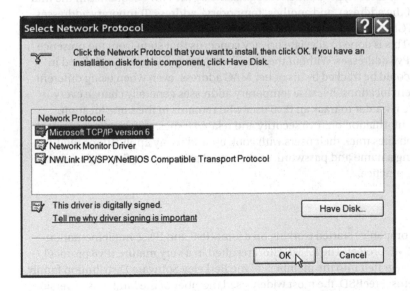

Figure 2-3. *The Windows XP network interface setup window*

Listing 2-1. *Monitoring IPv6 Addresses with the* netsh *Command*

```
C:\>netsh
netsh>interface ipv6
netsh interface ipv6>show addres

Querying active state...

Interface 6: Local Area Connection 3
Addr Type  DAD State   Valid Life    Pref. Life   Address
---------  ----------  ------------  ------------ ----------------------------
Temporary  Preferred    6d23h38m55s     23h36m8s  2001:db8:1dde:1:6d16:9d1:b1ec:2245
Public     Preferred   29d23h59m30s  6d23h59m30s  2001:db8:1dde:1:201:2ff:fe29:23b6
Link       Preferred       infinite     infinite  fe80::201:2ff:fe29:23b6

Interface 1: Loopback Pseudo-Interface

Addr Type  DAD State   Valid Life    Pref. Life   Address
---------  ----------  ------------  ------------ ----------------------------
Loopback   Preferred       infinite     infinite  ::1
Link       Preferred       infinite     infinite  fe80::1
```

Address Privacy

In this example, the computer has three addresses: a link-local address (address type "link"), a regular EUI-64 derived address (type "public," recognizable by the FF:FE sequence in the middle of the second half of the address), and another "temporary" address. Temporary addresses are used for outgoing TCP connections, while a stable public address is available to receive incoming connections. This is done to alleviate privacy concerns that stem from the presence of the MAC address in IPv6 addresses. Without the use of temporary addresses as defined in RFC 3041, an IPv6 user could be tracked by his or her MAC address, even when using different IPv6 addresses in different locations. Because temporary addresses generally change every 24 hours, they also make it harder to track an IPv6 user who remains in the same location. See Chapter 9 for more information on IPv6 security and related issues.

Of course, most Web sites track their users with cookies, and many applications require the user to log in by using a name and password, so the actual privacy benefits of temporary addresses are limited in practice.

FreeBSD

Several large Japanese companies started working on a joint IPv6 and IPsec implementation in 1998 as part of the KAME project. The KAME effort resulted in a very mature IPv6 protocol stack, which has been integrated into the members of the Berkeley Software Distribution family of UNIX operating systems: FreeBSD, the most widely used member of the family, as of version 4.0, NetBSD in version 1.5, and OpenBSD and BSD/OS in versions 2.7 and 4.2, respectively.

FreeBSD systems with IPv6 support in the kernel (which is the default for recent versions) have IPv6 processing and the creation of link-local addresses enabled by default, but auto-configuration of global scope addresses that use router advertisements is disabled. To enable autoconfiguration, add the lines

```
ipv6_enable="YES"
ipv6_network_interfaces="auto"
```

to the file /etc/rc.conf and reboot. This syntax is confusing, because IPv6 is enabled by default, so ipv6_enable="YES" doesn't enable it, nor does ipv6_enable="NO" disable it. Also, the list of IPv6 interfaces doesn't really do anything under FreeBSD 5.x, but, if the previous line is also present, it tricks the FreeBSD 4.x startup scripts into setting the sysctl variable net.inet6.ip6.accept_rtadv to 1, as IPv6 processing is enabled on all interfaces regardless of whether it's listed or not. With the new sysctl setting, global IPv6 addresses are configured for all interfaces that receive router advertisements. The most likely explanation for this way of configuration would be that at some point, functionality that used to be provided by startup scripts was moved to the kernel, but the startup scripts remained.

The creation of IPv6 addresses can be monitored by using the ifconfig command, as shown in Listing 2-2. It's not necessary to be root to run ifconfig in this way.

Listing 2-2. *Using* ifconfig *to Monitor IPv6 Addresses on FreeBSD*

```
# ifconfig xl0
xl0: flags=8843<UP,BROADCAST,RUNNING,SIMPLEX,MULTICAST> mtu 1500
        inet 192.0.2.123 netmask 0xffffff00 broadcast 192.0.2.255
        inet6 fe80::201:2ff:fe29:2640%xl0 prefixlen 64 scopeid 0x1
        inet6 2001:db8:31:2:201:2ff:fe29:2640 prefixlen 64 autoconf
        ether 00:01:02:29:26:40
        media: Ethernet autoselect (100baseTX <full-duplex>)
        status: active
```

The scopeid value is just a numerical reference for an interface, and it's listed to indicate that the link-local address is only valid within the scope of this particular interface. The autoconf keyword indicates that the listed global address was autoconfigured.

Triggering Router Solicitations

Router solicitation messages are still sent by a startup script or an external program, so when IPv6 connectivity changes, it may take a while before new global IPv6 addresses are config-ured, as the system waits for periodic unsolicited router advertisements. In these cases, it's a good idea to run rtsold, the router solicitation daemon. This can be done in one-shot mode by using the following syntax:

```
rtsold -f1a
```

The -f flag prevents rtsold from becoming a daemon and running in the background, the -1 flag makes the program quit after sending one router solicitation message and receiving a reply, and the -a flag is used to automatically find the interface to use, which only works if there is just one non-loopback and non-point-to-point network interface. Note that `rtsold` must be run as root. The program can also be run as a daemon:

```
rtsold xl0
```

The xl0 argument is the interface to be used for transmitting router solicitation messages.

Address Privacy

Address privacy isn't enabled by default on FreeBSD and other KAME-derived IPv6 implementations (including MacOS X). You can enable it with the following `sysclt` setting (as root):

```
sysctl -w net.inet6.ip6.use_tempaddr=1
```

The new setting may not take effect until after an interface is reconfigured, for instance, after a reboot or when a previously unconnected interface is connected to a network with an IPv6 router.

Linux

IPv6 first became available in the Linux kernel version 2.1.8 in 1998. Since that time, the Linux IPv6 implementation has advanced, and now many, but certainly not all, Linux distributions have IPv6 support built in the kernel. In this book, we'll cover the IPv6 specifics of the Red Hat 9 and Red Hat Enterprise Linux ES4 distributions. Because the IPv6 implementation itself is found in the kernel, a lot of the information supplied also pertains to other Linux distributions, but obviously the supporting programs are different from distribution to distribution. Note that in addition to the "regular" Linux IPv6 implementation, there is another Linux IPv6 implementation by the USAGI (Universal Playground for IPv6, http://www.linux-ipv6.org/) project, which works together closely with KAME.

The Red Hat distribution has supported IPv6 since version 7.1, and in ES4, it's enabled by default. Under Red Hat 9 (and at least a few other Linuxes), enabling IPv6 is done by adding the line

```
NETWORKING_IPV6="yes"
```

to the file /etc/sysconfig/network. After a reboot, the system then automatically configures link-local addresses and sends out router solicitation messages so it can autoconfigure global addresses for interfaces that connect to IPv6 routers that reply with a router advertisement. Linux sends a router solicitation only on startup, and a router solicitation utility isn't available. As with FreeBSD, the `ifconfig` command can be used to find out which IPv6 addresses were configured. This is shown in Listing 2-3. The path to the `ifconfig` command (/sbin/) is given because this directory isn't in the default search path for non-root users.

Listing 2-3. *Using* ifconfig *to Monitor IPv6 Addresses on Linux*

```
# /sbin/ifconfig eth0
eth0      Link encap:Ethernet  HWaddr 00:01:02:29:23:B6
          inet addr:192.0.2.8  Bcast:192.0.2.255  Mask:255.255.255.0
          inet6 addr: fe80::201:2ff:fe29:23b6/64 Scope:Link
          inet6 addr: 2001:db8:1dde:1:201:2ff:fe29:23b6/64 Scope:Global
          UP BROADCAST RUNNING MULTICAST  MTU:1500  Metric:1
          RX packets:226 errors:0 dropped:0 overruns:0 frame:0
          TX packets:76 errors:0 dropped:0 overruns:0 carrier:0
          collisions:0 txqueuelen:100
          RX bytes:27348 (26.7 Kb)  TX bytes:13251 (12.9 Kb)
          Interrupt:10 Base address:0xd000
```

■**Note** ifconfig is generally not the tool of choice to manipulate network settings under Linux, as the ifconfig command is rather limited. The ip package discussed in the next chapter is more powerful.

The Linux kernel version 2.4 doesn't support RFC 3041 temporary addresses. The 2.6 kernel, however, does: it's enabled with sysctl -w net.ipv6.conf.all.use_tempaddr=2 or one of several other tempaddr sysctls. (2 means that the temporary addresses are preferred, 1 indicates that regular addresses are preferred, and 0 turns temporary addresses off.) However, Red Hat ES Linux doesn't seem to generate temporary addresses.

MacOS

Under MacOS X, IPv6 has been available since version 10.2 Jaguar. MacOS differs from other operating systems in that IPv6 is enabled by default. However, because MacOS X doesn't expose any services to the network by default, there is little need for an IPv6 firewall. IPv6 support in Jaguar is fairly marginal as there is no way to enable/disable and configure the protocol by using the regular (graphical) system configuration tools. This was changed in MacOS 10.3 Panther, where IPv6 is controlled with the Network preference pane in the System Preferences. Select the appropriate interface and click TCP/IP, which brings up a window where both IPv4 and IPv6 can be configured, as shown in Figure 2-4. If IPv6 is enabled and the interface is active, an IPv6 address will be present at "IPv6 Address." This can be a global address if one could be configured from router advertisements or a link-local address if a global address isn't available.

IPv6 can be disabled or manually configured by clicking the Configure IPv6... button. Additionally, it is possible to turn off IPv4 and use IPv6 exclusively by selecting Off at Configure IPv4. In this case, it's important to list one or more IPv6 addresses for DNS servers that are available over IPv6 because otherwise, the system can't resolve names as there is currently no way to discover IPv6 DNS servers automatically. The graphical MacOS tools don't believe in compressing unnecessary zeros in IPv6 addresses, so the addresses may look a bit different than usual. You can find out where the listed IPv6 address came from by hovering the mouse pointer over it.

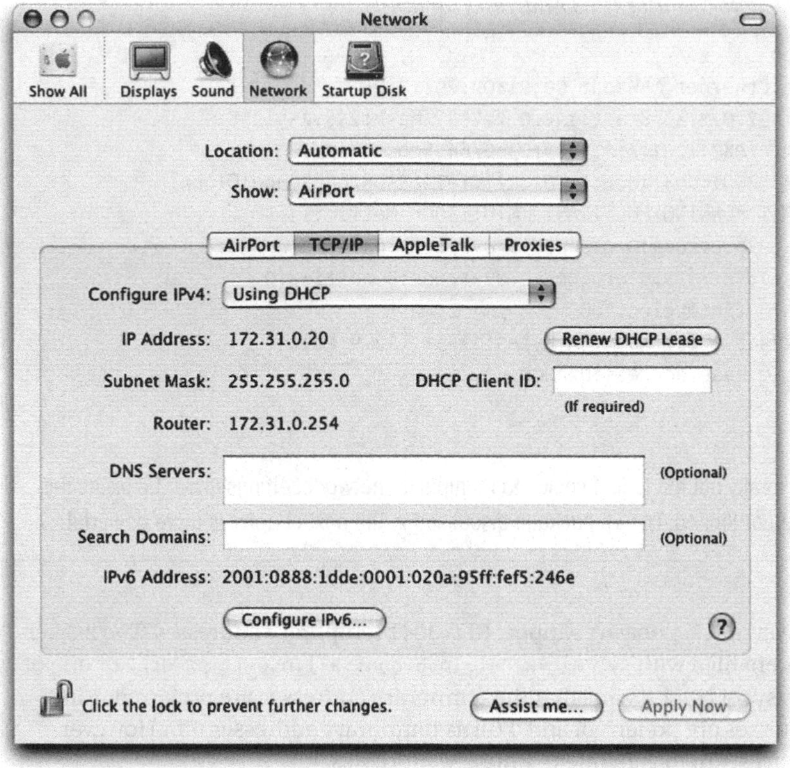

Figure 2-4. *The MacOS 10.3 network preference pane, TCP/IP section*

Because the System Configuration tool will only show a single IPv6 address and it doesn't always reflect the most current information, it can be useful to run the ifconfig command in the Terminal (located in Applications ➤ Utilities), as shown in Listing 2-4.

Listing 2-4. *Using* ifconfig *to Monitor IPv6 Addresses on MacOS*

```
% ifconfig en1
en1: flags=8863<UP,BROADCAST,SMART,RUNNING,SIMPLEX,MULTICAST> mtu 1500
     inet6 fe80::20a:95ff:fef5:246e prefixlen 64 scopeid 0x5
     inet6 2001:db8:1dde:1:20a:95ff:fef5:246e prefixlen 64 autoconf
     inet 172.31.0.20 netmask 0xffffff00 broadcast 172.31.0.255
     ether 00:0a:95:f5:24:6e
     media: autoselect status: active
     supported media: autoselect
```

Under MacOS X, the built-in Ethernet interface is usually en0, while the Airport (802.11b) or Airport Extreme (802.11g) interface is en1. Without arguments, ifconfig shows information for all interfaces. Because much of the MacOS UNIX core is derived from FreeBSD, many UNIX commands work almost identically to their FreeBSD counterparts. So for more information about the ifconfig output, see the explanation for the FreeBSD version of the command earlier.

The DNS Problem

Just like IPv4, IPv6 uses the Domain Name System (DNS) to resolve host names into addresses that make the desired communication possible. Requesting information from a DNS server is also nearly identical in IPv4, except for one problem: in IPv6, there aren't really any mechanisms to automatically discover the addresses of the local DNS servers. In theory, IPv6 hosts can auto-configure addresses and other information in two ways: stateless and stateful (see Chapter 8). Stateless autoconfiguration is the mechanism defined in RFC 2462 we've been discussing so far. But rather than supply the address prefixes themselves, routers can also indicate that hosts should use a stateful mechanism to configure addresses and/or other configuration information by setting the "managed address configuration" and "other stateful configuration" flags. The stateful mechanism in question is the Dynamic Host Configuration Protocol modified for IPv6 (DHCPv6), defined in RFC 3315. This RFC was published only in July 2003, and at the time of this writing, DHCPv6 hadn't found its way into the operating systems that are discussed here, except for Red Hat ES 4. See Chapter 8 for examples of how to use DHCPv6. Because DHCPv6 is currently the only way that is defined for automatically configuring IPv6 DNS addresses, current OSs simply lack this capability. And, as working with addresses exclusively isn't unlike cruel and unusual punishment, an IPv6 hosts must either also run IPv4 and discover IPv4 DNS addresses through DHCP(v4) or the IPv6 DNS addresses must be configured manually. In MacOS X Panther, the graphical TCP/IP configuration panes accept IPv6 addresses, as mentioned earlier. Under FreeBSD and Linux, this is done by adding a line like the following to the file /etc/resolv.conf:

```
nameserver 2002:a00:1:5353:20a:95ff:fef5:246e
```

Note that the above isn't the address for a functioning nameserver (and an illegal 6to4 address to boot). Under MacOS, the resolv.conf file is a symbolic link to the file /var/run/resolv.conf. You can modify this file, but it's removed and overwritten by the system whenever network connectivity changes. Under Windows XP, it's possible to configure a nameserver with the netsh interface ipv6 add dns command, but this doesn't result in Windows actually querying the thus configured IPv6 DNS servers.

See Chapter 5 for more information on putting IPv6 information in the DNS and running an IPv6-capable nameserver.

Diagnostics

The best test to see if your IPv6 configuration efforts were successful is to fire up a Web browser and visit an IPv6-enabled Web site. A good choice is the Web site for the KAME project at http://www.kame.net/. When using IPv6, you should see the famous "dancing kame" (turtle). You'll be told whether you're using IPv4 or IPv6 as seen by the remote server at the bottom of the page. The supplied Web browsers for all operating systems support and prefer IPv6 when available: Windows (Internet Explorer), Linux and FreeBSD (Firefox, Mozilla, Konqueror, or Lynx), and MacOS 10.4 (Safari). Older versions of Apple's Web browser Safari will connect to IPv6-only servers over IPv6 but prefer IPv4, so the KAME won't dance. See Chapter 6 for more information on IPv6-enabled Web browsers and other applications.

Ping and Traceroute

Time-tested network debugging tools ping and traceroute are of course also available for IPv6. However, on most systems, there is no integrated IPv4/IPv6 ping or traceroute, so pinging and tracerouting in IPv6 must be done with separate commands: ping6 and traceroute6. Under Windows, traceroute is "tracert" and the IPv6 version is "tracert6." The regular tracert also supports IPv6, and tracert6 is now deprecated under Windows though. On all systems, ping6 and traceroute6 are command line utilities. Under Windows, start a command prompt by choosing Start ➤ All Programs ➤ Accessories ➤ Command Prompt, and under MacOS, use the Terminal application in Applications ➤ Utilities. Listing 2-5 shows output from the traceroute6 command under FreeBSD.

Listing 2-5. traceroute6 *on FreeBSD*

```
% traceroute6 www.ipv6forum.com
traceroute6 to www.ipv6forum.com (2001:630:d0:131:a00:20ff:feb5:ef1e) from
2001:db8:31:2:201:2ff:fe29:2640, 30 hops max, 12 byte packets
 1  46.ge-0-2-0.xr1.pbw.xs4all.net  0.984 ms  0.967 ms  0.798 ms
 2  2001:db8:0:106::2  0.959 ms  0.93 ms  1.04 ms
 3  0.ge-1-3-0.xr1.tc2.xs4all.net  1.35 ms  1.199 ms  1.125 ms
 4  eth10-0-0.xr1.ams1.gblx.net  3.345 ms  1.299 ms  1.637 ms
 5  2001:798:2014:20dd::5  19.015 ms  16.712 ms  17.752 ms
 6  de.nl1.nl.geant.net  24.046 ms  23.325 ms  22.973 ms
 7  nl.uk1.uk.geant.net  33.594 ms  31.715 ms  30.407 ms
 8  janet-gw.uk1.uk.geant.net  29.726 ms  31.023 ms  28.623 ms
 9  po3-0.lond-scr3.ja.net  28.85 ms  33.616 ms  28.204 ms
10  po6-0.lond-scr.ja.net  28.483 ms  28.863 ms  28.46 ms
11  po0-0.london-bar1.ja.net  29.143 ms  29.582 ms  28.813 ms
12  fe0-1-0.ulcc.ipv6.ja.net  24.845 ms  24.751 ms  24.918 ms
13  fa1-0.rtr1.ipv6.ja.net  24.844 ms  24.966 ms  24.565 ms
14  po2-0.rtr2.ipv6.ja.net  24.841 ms  24.639 ms  26.232 ms
15  zaphod.6core.ecs.soton.ac.uk  33.2 ms  32.621 ms  35.53 ms
16  2001:630:d0:131:a00:20ff:feb5:ef1e  32.953 ms  31.756 ms  30.08 ms
```

Unlike its IPv4 counterpart, traceroute6 as implemented in FreeBSD, MacOS, and Linux doesn't by default show both hostnames and addresses for each hop, as the lines get too long that way. Instead, the command shows a hostname if one is available, and an address otherwise. With the -l option, traceroute6 shows both hostnames and addresses, and as usual, the -n option shows only addresses. Even more than with IPv4, it's common that traceroute6 probes don't receive an answer because the destination host or a router in the middle is rate limiting the number of ICMP messages it is prepared to return. Older IPv6 implementations tend to limit the number of ICMP messages they send to one per second; newer implementations often have a limit of one per 100 or 200 milliseconds. When traceroute6 doesn't receive an answer, it prints an asterisk to the screen instead of a time in milliseconds.

The ping6 command is mostly very similar to the IPv4 ping. Listing 2-6 shows the output of the Windows XP ping6 command.

Listing 2-6. *The Windows XP* ping6 *Command*

```
C:\>ping6 www.hitachi.co.jp

Pinging www.hitachi.co.jp [2001:240:400::101]
from 2001:db8:1dde:1:59eb:57:32ff:b6f4 with 32 bytes of data:

Reply from 2001:240:400::101: bytes=32 time=395ms
Reply from 2001:240:400::101: bytes=32 time=396ms
Reply from 2001:240:400::101: bytes=32 time=398ms
Reply from 2001:240:400::101: bytes=32 time=397ms

Ping statistics for 2001:240:400::101:
    Packets: Sent = 4, Received = 4, Lost = 0 (0% loss),
Approximate round trip times in milli-seconds:
    Minimum = 395ms, Maximum = 398ms, Average = 396ms
```

The system will show the available options for traceroute6 (or tracert6) and ping6 commands by typing the command without any arguments. Under Linux, FreeBSD, and MacOS, more detailed information is available in the man pages; to access it, type man ping6 or man traceroute6.

CHAPTER 3

■■■

Tunnels

In the previous chapter, we enabled IPv6 autoconfiguration, which works very well when there are IPv6 routers on the local Ethernet or when there is some other type of "native" IPv6 connectivity over a different type of connection than Ethernet. Unfortunately, large parts of the Internet are still IPv4-only. Rather than gloomily sit around and wait for the last IPv4 router to be upgraded to be able to run IPv6, the IETF standardized several tunneling mechanisms. This chapter discusses automatic 6to4 tunneling and manually configured tunnels.

A tunnel is a mechanism whereby one protocol is encapsulated into another protocol to be transported through a part of the network where the original protocol wouldn't normally be supported or would have been processed in some undesirable way. Tunneling IPv6 in IPv4 is usually done by simply adding an IPv4 header before the IPv6 packet. The resulting packet is then forwarded to the destination address listed in the IPv4 header. At this destination, the outer header is stripped away, and the packet is processed as if it had been received over a regular IPv6-enabled interface. Figure 3-1 shows what happens to a tunneled packet as it travels from the IPv6 network on the left through the IPv4 network in the middle toward the IPv6 network on the right.

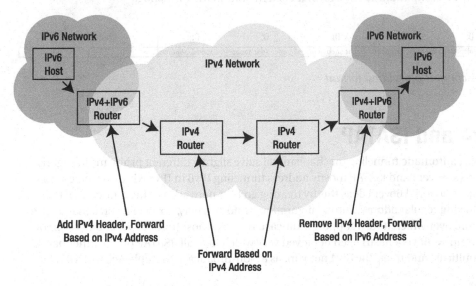

Figure 3-1. *Tunneling of IPv6 packets through an IPv4 network*

Tunnels come in two flavors: tunnels where each end has the other end's address manually configured and tunnels where the remote tunnel endpoint is determined automatically. Manually configured tunnels suffer from the downside that they must be manually configured on both ends, but apart from that, they're nice and simple, and the path tunneled packets follow through the network is predictable. While the internals of automatic tunneling mechanisms are more complex, their operation is usually very simple. Currently at least five different mechanisms are defined that allow automatic tunneling of IPv6 over IPv4:

- "Automatic Tunneling," using IPv4-compatible addresses (RFC 2893).

- 6over4: "Transmission of IPv6 over IPv4 Domains without Explicit Tunnels" (RFC 2529).

- ISATAP: "Intra-Site Automatic Tunnel Addressing Protocol." At the time of this writing, ISATAP had not been published as an RFC yet.

- 6to4: "Connection of IPv6 Domains via IPv4 Clouds" (RFC 3056).

- Teredo: "Tunneling IPv6 over UDP through NATs." Teredo was formerly known as Shipworm. There is no RFC as of yet.

"Automatic Tunneling"

The first automatic tunneling mechanism was simply called "automatic tunneling," which is unfortunate because it is now one of many such mechanisms. "Automatic tunneling" is very similar to 6to4, except that it suffers from the limitation that a single IPv4 address maps to just a single IPv6 address. These IPv6 addresses are called "IPv4-compatible" and consist of 96 zero bits (the prefix ::/96) followed by the 32-bit IPv4 address. Although not formally deprecated by an IETF standards action, "automatic tunneling" should be considered obsolete. Figure 3-2 shows the IPv4-compatible address format used in "automatic tunneling."

Figure 3-2. *The IPv4-compatible address format*

6over4 and ISATAP

The different automatic tunneling mechanisms all solve slightly different problems in slightly different ways. 6over4 and ISATAP mostly address tunneling IPv6 in IPv4 within a single organization or site network.[1] 6over4 does this by treating an IPv4 network as a fully functional IPv6 subnet, allowing regular address autoconfiguration. Unfortunately, 6over4 requires that the IPv4 infrastructure over which it runs support multicast. Because most IPv4 networks don't support multicast routing, 6over4 hasn't been deployed very widely, if at all. ISATAP on the other hand, foregoes multicast and treats the IPv4 network as a Non-Broadcast, Multiple Access (NBMA)

---

1. The word "site" comes up regularly in IPv6 specifications, but it is by no means well defined. Examples of a site are a home, an office, or a campus.

network. Without multicasts, autoconfiguration and neighbor discovery don't work, so ISA-TAP encodes the IPv4 address into the interface identifier part of the IPv6 address. This way, systems implementing ISATAP can easily determine which IPv4 host tunneled packets must be addressed to. The bottom 32 bits of an ISATAP interface identifier contain the IPv4 address, the top 32 bits are set to 02005EFE in hexadecimal when the IPv4 address is a regular, globally routable one and 00005EFE if the IPv4 address is a private address from one of the RFC 1918 ranges, thus preserving the meaning of the universal/local bit in the interface identifier. Figure 3-3 shows the relationship between the IPv4 and IPv6 addresses in ISATAP.

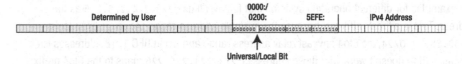

Figure 3-3. *The ISATAP address format*

Teredo

The idea behind Teredo is to allow hosts behind Network Address Translators to tunnel IPv6 in IPv4, much the same way as non-NATed hosts can do using 6to4. Although some Teredo implementations are available, the protocol is still in somewhat of a state of flux, and the required server and relay infrastructure hasn't materialized yet. There isn't even an address range assigned by IANA for use with Teredo.

6to4

6to4 is similar to ISATAP (or rather, the other way around), except that while ISATAP allows for automatic tunneling *within* a site, 6to4 makes it possible to tunnel IPv6 over IPv4 *between* sites. Every system that holds a valid, routable IPv4 address can automatically create a 6to4 prefix for itself by combining its IPv4 address with the 16-bit value 2002 (hexadecimal), as shown in Figure 3-4. The resulting prefix is 48 bits long, leaving enough bits for 65536 64-bit subnets.

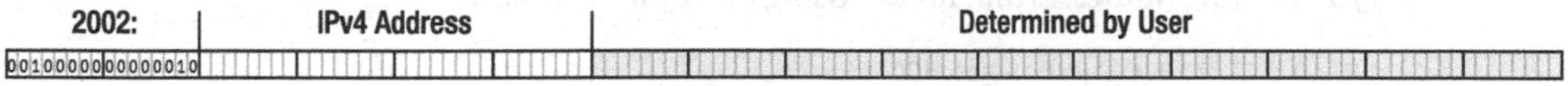

Figure 3-4. *The 6to4 address format*

When a 6to4-capable system wants to send a packet to another 6to4-capable system, it encapsulates the IPv6 packet in an IPv4 packet and addresses this packet to the IPv4 address encoded in the 6to4 destination address. Upon reception, the destination IPv4 host removes the IPv4 header and continues to process the IPv6 packet. Communication between the 6to4 world and the regular IPv6 Internet is facilitated by relays. It is possible to run a 6to4 relay at an arbitrary address, but RFC 3068 defines 192.88.99.1 as a 6to4 anycast relay router address. Don't confuse this type of anycasting with actual IPv6 anycast addressing. People who run a public 6to4 relay announce to the rest of the world that they're prepared to handle traffic toward the IPv4 prefix 192.88.99.0/24 and the IPv6 prefix 2002::/16.[2] This way, packets automatically find their way to one of the relays without the need for any relay-specific configuration. Anyone interested in using such a relay can enter 2002:c058:6301:: as a default gateway address. Packets from a 6to4 user to the regular IPv6 Internet are then tunneled in IPv4 to the nearest 6to4 gateway. The gateway decapsulates the packet and sends it on its way over IPv6. Packets in the other direction flow to one of the relays because of the 2002::/16 route. The relay encapsulates the packet in IPv4 and transmits it to the IPv4 address encoded in the 6to4 address.

Note In the examples for different operating systems that follow, I'll use 223.224.225.226 as the public IPv4 address. This is a "real" address, because the example address range 192.0.2.0/24 looks too similar to 192.88.99.0/24, the 6to4 anycast relay address range and using RFC 1918 addresses isn't appropriate, because 6to4 doesn't work with those addresses. 223.224.225.226 maps to the 6to4 prefix 2002:dfe0:e1e2::/48.

6to4 Under Windows

There is no need to specifically enable 6to4 under Windows XP. When IPv6 is installed, the system automatically sets up a 6to4 pseudo interface if a public (non-RFC 1918) IPv4 address is available. So packets to 6to4 addresses are directly tunneled to their destination in IPv4, as long as the system has a regular IPv4 address. Additionally, if there is no other IPv6 connectivity, Windows installs one or more IPv6 default routes that point to 6to4 relays. Rather than blindly installing a default route toward the RFC 3068 anycast address, Windows looks up the name 6to4.ipv6.microsoft.com in the DNS, transforms the resulting IPv4 addresses into 6to4 addresses, and pings them. Default routes and accompanying metrics ("Met" in the example below) are installed, depending on the replies to these ping packets. (Although it seems that any ICMP message, not just an ICMP Echo Reply, will do.) The default route with the lowest metric is used. A metric of 2147483648 (2^{31}) means the relay router is unreachable and the route can't be used. Listing 3-1 shows the relevant netsh output with a 6to4 prefix based on the IPv4 address 223.224.225.226.

Listing 3-1. *Listing Addresses and Routes Using the* netsh *Command*

```
C:\>netsh interface ipv6 show address

Interface 3: 6to4 Tunneling Pseudo-Interface

Addr Type DAD State Valid Life  Pref. Life  Address
--------  ---------  -----------  -----------  -----------------------
Other     Preferred  infinite     infinite     2002:dfe0:e1e2::dfe0:e1e2

C:\>netsh interface ipv6 show routes
```

---

2. Assuming that the relay works in both directions, which is often but not always the case.

```
Querying active state...

Publish Type    Met  Prefix    Idx  Gateway/Interface Name
------- ------- ---- --------  ---  ---------------------
yes     Manual  1191 ::/0       3   2002:836b:213c:1:e0:8f08:f020:8
yes     Manual  1041 ::/0       3   2002:c058:6301::c058:6301
yes     Manual  1001 2002::/16  3   6to4 Tunneling Pseudo-Interface
```

The netsh command can also be used to change the name and settings for the 6to4 relay (type netsh, interface ipv6 6to4, and then help for more information), but the mechanism whereby Windows uses a domain name to determine the 6to4 relays can't be turned off.

6to4 Under MacOS

Unlike Windows XP, MacOS X doesn't automatically enable 6to4. If you want to use 6to4 tunneling, you must create a new network port. Do so by selecting Network Port Configurations in the Network pane of the System Preferences, as shown in Figure 3-5, clicking the New button, typing a name for the new port, and selecting Port: 6to4.

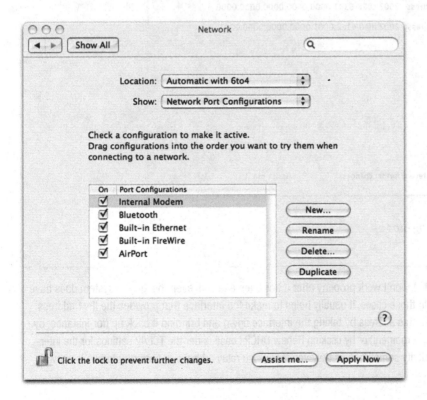

Figure 3-5. *Adding a 6to4 network port*

The new port must be activated by clicking the Apply Now button. With a 6to4 port configured, MacOS will automatically create a 6to4 address and install a default route toward the anycast relay address as soon as it has IPv4 reachability with a public, non-RFC 1918 address. The relay address can be changed in the 6to4 port configuration in the network settings, which are shown in Figure 3-6. The 6to4 address assigned to the 6to4 port can't be changed; this is always address 1 in subnet 1 of the 6to4 prefix derived from the current IPv4 address.

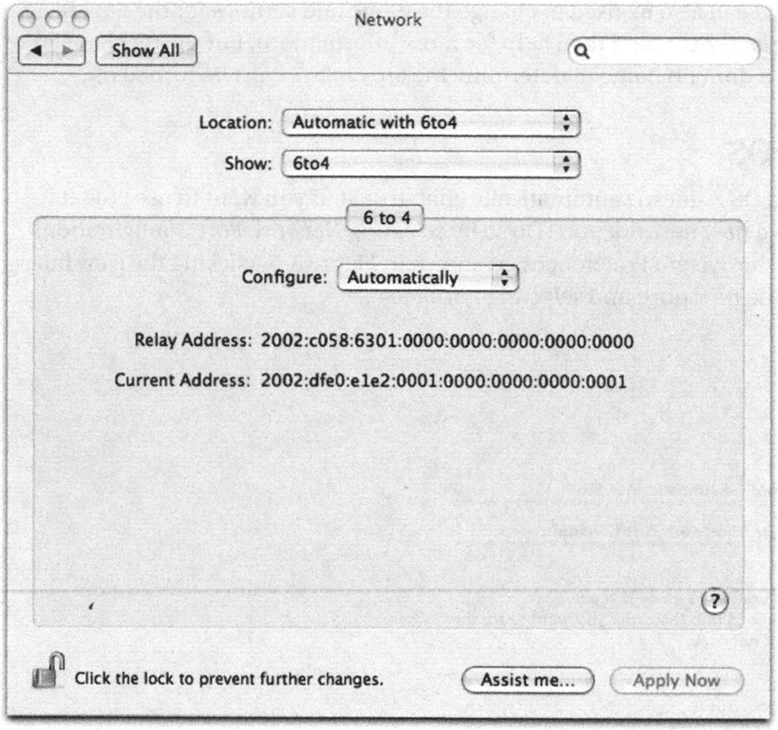

Figure 3-6. *Configuring 6to4*

Note Sometimes 6to4 won't work properly after it has been enabled, even though the system does have a public IPv4 address. In those cases, it usually helps to make the interface that provides the IPv4 address that 6to4 uses reacquire this address by taking the interface down and bringing it back up (for instance, by unplugging the cable for a moment) or by clicking Renew DHCP Lease under the TCP/IP settings for the interface. Also, 6to4 connectivity sometimes works even though no relay address or current address is shown.

Under the graphical configuration tool, MacOS uses the same stf tunneling device as FreeBSD. Only the root (the UNIX super-user or system administrator) may manipulate network interfaces, but MacOS doesn't have the user root enabled by default. The easiest way to use the FreeBSD-derived command line utilities that need root privileges under MacOS is with sudo, as shown in Listing 3-2. However, changing settings that are normally controlled by the Preferences program may lead to unpredictable results.

Listing 3-2. *Using* sudo *to Execute Commands as Root*

```
% sudo ifconfig stf0 inet6 2002:dfe0:e1e2:1::1/16

We trust you have received the usual lecture from the local System
Administrator. It usually boils down to these two things:

    #1) Respect the privacy of others.
    #2) Think before you type.

Password:
```

When it's used for the first time, sudo will display a warning. It then asks for the user's password and then runs the intended command (ifconfig in this case) as user root. Subsequent uses of sudo within a few minutes don't require retyping the password. Only users with admin privileges may use sudo.

6to4 Under FreeBSD

FreeBSD uses the stf pseudo device for 6to4 tunneling. Unfortunately, this device isn't included in the generic kernel in FreeBSD 4.9, so if you want to run 6to4 under FreeBSD, you'll have to build a custom kernel. The procedure for doing this is explained in Chapter 9 of the FreeBSD Handbook, "Configuring the FreeBSD Kernel." The handbook is available on the FreeBSD website at http://www.freebsd.org/. The line that needs to be added to the kernel configuration file is

```
pseudo-device    stf
```

After installing the new kernel, a new network interface named stf0 should be available. Under FreeBSD 5.4, there is no need to compile a custom kernel: you can simply create an stf interface with the command ifconfig stf create. The stf interface is enabled by giving it an IPv6 address that is a valid 6to4 address that corresponds to one of the host's IPv4 addresses. An online tool for calculating the 6to4 prefix that corresponds to a given IPv4 address is available at http://www.bgpexpert.com/ipv6tools/. After this, the system is able to communicate with other hosts that run 6to4. By adding a default route to a 6to4 relay, all non-local IPv6 traffic will be sent through 6to4. Listing 3-3 sets both the address (based on the IPv4 address 223.224.225.226) and a default route toward the anycast relay address. These commands must be executed as root.

Listing 3-3. *Enabling 6to4*

```
# ifconfig stf0 inet6 2002:dfe0:e1e2:1::1/16
# route add -inet6 default 2002:c058:6301::
```

With IPv6, setting a new address for an interface with ifconfig doesn't remove the existing address. Listing 3-4 removes the address and the default route again. In this case, the prefix length (/16 in Listing 3-3) shouldn't be included in the `ifconfig` command. Removing a route will also work without specifying the destination address argument, if there is only a single matching route.

Listing 3-4. *Removing an Address and a Default Route*

```
# ifconfig stf0 inet6 -alias 2002:dfe0:e1e2:1::1
# route delete -inet6 default 2002:c058:6301::
```

Alternatively, 6to4 can be enabled by the system startup scripts by setting the necessary parameters in the `/etc/rc.conf` file, as outlined in Listing 3-5.

Listing 3-5. *Enabling 6to4 in* `/etc/rc.conf`

```
stf_interface_ipv4addr="223.224.225.226"
stf_interface_ipv6_ifid="0:0:0:1"
stf_interface_ipv6_slaid="0"
ipv6_defaultrouter="2002:c058:6301::"
```

If `stf_interface_ipv6_ifid` isn't defined, the interface identifier part of the local 6to4 address will be set to 1. Note that the address must be specified as listed in the listing; `::1` doesn't work. It's also possible to specify `AUTO`, in which case a MAC address–derived interface identifier will be used. (The MAC address will be borrowed from an interface that has one.) Without specifying `stf_interface_ipv6_slaid`, the subnet number will be 0. The file `/etc/defaults/rc.conf` contains additional configuration options for `rc.conf` and brief explanations.

6to4 Under Linux

Under Red Hat 9 Linux,[3] you can enable 6to4 during system startup by making sure that the following lines are present in the file `/etc/sysconfig/network`:

```
NETWORKING_IPV6="yes"
IPV6_DEFAULTDEV="tun6to4"
```

Additionally, the contents of the file that determines the behavior of the interface supplying the IPv4 address (such as `/etc/sysconfig/network-scripts/ifcfg-eth0` in the case of the eth0 interface) must have these lines in it:

```
IPV6INIT=yes
IPV6TO4INIT=yes
```

You need to be root to change these files. With these settings, the system will use the IPv4 address that has been configured or discovered by using DHCP for the interface in question to construct a 6to4 prefix and install a semi-default route over the anycast 6to4 relay address. Many additional settings are possible, and they are listed in the file `sysconfig.txt`, which is in the directory `/usr/share/doc/initscripts-7.14/` or one ending in a slightly different version number.

---

3. The scripts that do this aren't unique to Red Hat, so you may very well encounter them in other distributions as well. However, the paths could be different than those listed here.

Wait a minute—"semi-default"? That's right. Listing 3-6 shows the IPv6 routing table when 6to4 has been enabled by the system startup scripts.

Listing 3-6. *Output of the* netstat *Command*

```
# netstat -rn --inet6
Kernel IPv6 routing table
Destination             Next Hop         Flags Metric Ref Use Iface
::1/128                 ::               U     0      0   0 lo
::/96                   ::               U     256    0   0 tun6to4
2002:dfe0:e1e2:1::1/128 ::               U     0      0   0 lo
2002::/16               ::               UA    256    0   0 tun6to4
::/0                    ::               UDA   256    0   0 eth0
2000::/3                ::192.88.99.1    UG    1      0   0 tun6to4
```

At first glance, the default route seems to point at the eth0 interface (which is because of the "on-link assumption" discussed later this chapter). However, there is also a route for 2000::/3, which is the entire IPv6 global unicast address space as currently defined by the IANA: the initial RIR block (2001::/16), the 6bone block (3ffe::/16), and the 6to4 block (2002::/16) are all part of this larger block. The 2000::/3 route points toward the 6to4 anycast relay address. Because the 2000::/3 route is more specific than the ::/0 default, this one takes precedence.

■Note I was unable to get Red Hat's Enterprise Linux ES4 to enable 6to4 by using the preceding configuration. However, setting up 6to4 manually as in Listing 3-7 worked without problems, except that the (IPv4) iptables filter blocked most of the tunneled packets. (See later in this chapter and also Chapter 9 for more information on filters.)

THE LONGEST MATCH FIRST RULE

In IPv4 and IPv6, overlapping routes are always resolved by using the "longest match first" rule: the route that covers the smallest block of address space always wins. The route that covers less address space is therefore said to be "more specific," and the number of bits in the prefix is higher (so the prefix is longer), making it the "longest match." Suppose the routing table holds three routes:

- 2001:db8::/32 over interface eth0.

- 2001:db8:31:1::/64 over interface eth1.

- 2001:db8:31:::/48 over interface eth2.

A packet for 2001:db8:31:1:20a:95ff:fef5:246e would potentially match any (or all) of these three entries, but the longest match first rule mandates that the middle one is "longest" at 64 bits, so the packet will be forwarded over interface eth1.

The longest match first rule makes fact that the metric is better (lower) for the 2000::/3 route in Listing 3-6 irrelevant: even with a lower metric, the ::/0 route would be ignored because of the difference in prefix length.

Using 2000::/3 rather than ::/0 when a default route is called for is somewhat of a tradition under Linux. It appears that there are even some older versions of Linux that won't accept a ::/0 route and require a 2000::/3 route instead when the system is configured as an IPv6 router. However, hard-coding the fact that the Internet Assigned Numbers Authority has so far only allocated 2000::/3 for use as unicast address space into systems isn't a good idea, as other parts of the IPv6 address space may be used for unicast in the future as well. After listing the multicast and special-purpose address blocks, RFC 3513 states:

"Future specifications may redefine one or more sub-ranges of the global unicast space for other purposes, but unless and until that happens, implementations must treat all addresses that do not start with any of the above-listed prefixes as global unicast addresses."

Should you desire to make your Red Hat Linux system RFC 3513-compliant, you can do this by changing all three occurrences of 2000::/3 to ::/0 in the file /etc/sysconfig/network-scripts/network-functions-ipv6.

Manual manipulation of the 6to4 functionality is best done by using the iproute package that comes with Red Hat. Most Linux distributions have this package on board, but some distributions don't or even lack support for netlink sockets in the kernel, which are used by iproute (and, optionally, by Zebra). If you're the adventurous type, you could install iproute yourself and compile a kernel with netlink support. Listing 3-7 creates a 6to4 tunneling interface and a default route toward the anycast 6to4 relay address. These commands must be executed as root.

Listing 3-7. *Manual 6to4 Configuration*

```
# ip tunnel add tun6to4 mode sit ttl 64 remote any local 223.224.225.226
# ip link set dev tun6to4 up
# ip -6 address add 2002:dfe0:e1e2:1::1/16 dev tun6to4
# ip -6 route delete ::/0
# ip -6 route add ::/0 via ::192.88.99.1
```

FreeBSD and Cisco IOS make packets flow to the 6to4 relay router by pointing a route to the IPv6 relay address, but with Linux, the route to the 6to4 relay must be specified in IPv4-compatible form, hence the ::192.88.99.1. Deleting the default route in the second to last line is necessary to remove a default route that is installed at boot time in order to generate "destination unreachable" messages.

For more information on the iproute package and the ip command, have a look at the file ip-cref.ps that should be available in the /usr/share/doc/iproute-2.4.7/ directory, or one with a name based on a slightly different version number. This is a PostScript file, so you need a PostScript printer to print it or software that can display PostScript, such as Ghostscript.

TUNNEL TTL

In Listing 3-7, the tunnel Time to Live (TTL) value is supplied explicitly. Without this value, the new IPv4 header that is added when an IPv6 packet is tunneled will inherit the Time to Live value from the one in the IPv6 header (where it's called Hop Limit). In theory, this is good, as it makes sure that the TTL can only get lower so when there are routing loops or tunneling loops, the TTL in looping packets will eventually reach zero and the packet is destroyed. However, when the TTL is inherited, traceroutes look very strange. `traceroute` works by first sending out packets with a TTL of one. Because routers always decrement the TTL by one for packets they forward, the TTL will reach zero in the first router, which means that the router won't forward the packet but sends back an ICMP "Time to Live exceeded in transit" message. The `traceroute` program now knows the address of the first router on the path to the destination in question, so it sends a packet with a TTL of 2. This packet will go through the first router unharmed, but its TTL will reach zero in the second router, which then sends back an ICMP message. This continues until the packet reaches its destination.

The problem with an inherited TTL value in tunneled packets is that the TTL in the IPv4 packet will now reach zero on one of the hidden IPv4 hops, which is invisible in IPv6. This results in one or more lines with asterisks that indicate lost packets. However, there is no impact on regular packets as these generally start out with a Hop Limit/Time to Live of 60 or higher.

6to4 on a Cisco Router

Configuring 6to4 on a Cisco router under IOS is very simple, as shown in Listing 3-8. However, this configuration isn't all that useful without setting up another interface for IPv6 and enabling IPv6 forwarding, because without that, only the router itself can use the 6to4 tunnel. Examples for that are given in the next chapter, which covers routing.

Listing 3-8. *Enabling 6to4 on a Cisco Router*

```
!
interface Tunnel2002
 ipv6 address 2002:dfe0:e1e2:1::1/16
 tunnel source 223.224.225.226
 tunnel mode ipv6ip 6to4
!
ipv6 route ::/0 2002:c058:6301::
!
```

The IPv4 address listed as the tunnel source must be an address configured on another interface, over which the router is reachable from the rest of the Internet. It is also possible to supply this address indirectly by pointing the tunnel source toward the interface that supplies the address in question rather than specify the address directly. The tunnel source address then automatically tracks any changes in the address of the tunnel source interface. However, because the 6to4-derived IPv6 address for the tunnel interface (and possibly other interfaces) must also be changed manually when this happens, there is little advantage in onfiguring a 6to4 interface this way. The `ipv6 route` command sets up a default route toward the anycast

6to4 relay address. Without this command, the router will still use 6to4 to reach 6to4 addresses, as those are "directly connected" to the tunnel interface, but destinations with regular non-6to4 addresses will then be unreachable if there isn't another default route or a suitable more specific route.

6to4 Security Issues

In theory, hosts should be able to handle all possible incorrect and even intentionally harmful packets that they receive. Unfortunately, this isn't always the case in practice, so more often than not, it's necessary to have filters or firewalls in place to filter out unwanted packets. Chapter 9 has more information about security issues and packet filtering in particular. However, there are some security issues that are specific to 6to4 tunneling that are best discussed here.

It is currently considered "best current practice" (BCP)[4] by the IETF for Internet Service Providers to make sure they only forward packets from their customers to the rest of the Internet if those packets have a source address that actually belongs to the customer in question. This is called "anti-spoofing" or "ingress" filtering. With anti-spoofing filters in effect, a customer can still attack hosts elsewhere on the Internet (either by choice or because their computer has been turned into a "zombie" after being infected with malicious software), but the packets involved in such an attack are simple to trace back and relatively straightforward to filter out. 6to4 allows people to create packets with spoofed IPv6 addresses and encapsulate them in legitimate IPv4 packets, thereby bypassing anti-spoofing filters that may be in effect. (However, many ISPs don't have anti-spoofing filters in place.) An attacker can do this either by addressing packets directly to the IPv4 address of the target, or by routing them over a 6to4 relay.

To reject the most obvious attacks that use 6to4, most systems filter out several ranges of invalid 6to4 addresses (see Listings 3-9 and 3-10). Additionally, it's conceivable that in the future 6to4 hosts, routers and/or relays will start rejecting 6to4 packets where the IPv4 address in the outer header doesn't match the embedded IPv4 address in the 6to4 IPv6 address in the inner header. So when using 6to4, make sure there is always a one-to-one relationship between the 48-bit 6to4 prefix and the IPv4 address used for 6to4 to avoid problems in this area.

Monitoring 6to4

Listing 3-9 shows how the `ifconfig` and `netstat` commands can be used to monitor the behavior of the FreeBSD or MacOS X `stf0` interface and the IPv6 routing table.

Listing 3-9. *Monitoring 6to4 Under FreeBSD or MacOS*

```
# ifconfig stf0
stf0: flags=1<UP> mtu 1280
        inet6 2002:dfe0:e1e2:1::1 prefixlen 16
# netstat -rnf inet6
Destination        Gateway              Flags      Netif Expire
::/96              ::1                  UGRSc       lo0 =>
default            2002:c058:6301::     UGSc        stf0
```

4. See RFC 2827 (which is also known as BCP 38).

```
::1                     ::1                  UH       lo0
::ffff:0.0.0.0/96       ::1                  UGRSc    lo0
2002::/24               ::1                  UGRSc    lo0 =>
2002::/16               2002:dfe0:e1e2:1::1  Uc       stf0
2002:7f00::/24          ::1                  UGRSc    lo0
2002:dfe0:e1e2::1       link#7               UHL      lo0
2002:e000::/20          ::1                  UGRSc    lo0
2002:ff00::/24          ::1                  UGRSc    lo0
```

The netstat flags are -r to list the routing table, -n to suppress looking up network names in the DNS, and -f allows us to specify the address family, where "inet6" means IPv6. The netstat output is rather extensive, even without the link local information that has been left out in the example. The ::/96 route allows special handling of IPv4-compatible addresses for the purpose of automatic tunneling, and the localhost address (::1) route points to the loopback interface. The ::ffff:0.0.0.0/96 route is linked to special addresses that make it possible for programs using the IPv6 socket API to communicate over IPv4 (see Chapter 6). The 2002::/24, 2002:7f00::/24, 2002:e000::/20, and 2002:ff00::/24 routes correspond to the 0.0.0.0/8, 127.0.0.0/8, 224.0.0.0/4, and 255.0.0.0/8 prefixes, respectively. These are IPv4 address blocks that aren't valid sources or destinations of 6to4 packets.

The 2002:dfe0:e1e2::1 route corresponds to the local 6to4 address. The 2002::/16 route makes sure that all packets with 6to4 destinations are handled by the stf0 interface in order to tunnel them directly to their destination over IPv4. Last but not least, the default route directs all remaining packets to the 6to4 anycast relay address 2002:c058:6301:: for relaying.

Listing 3-10 lists the IPv6 routing table under Linux with the ip command. This provides much more information than the netstat command.

Listing 3-10. *Monitoring 6to4 Under Red Hat 9 Linux*

```
# ip -6 route
::/96 via :: dev tun6to4  metric 256  mtu 1480 advmss 1420
unreachable ::/96 dev lo  metric 1024  error -101 mtu 16436 advmss 16376
unreachable ::ffff:0.0.0.0/96 dev lo  metric 1024  error -101 mtu 16436 advmss 16376
unreachable 2002:a00::/24 dev lo  metric 1024  error -101 mtu 16436 advmss 16376
unreachable 2002:7f00::/24 dev lo  metric 1024  error -101 mtu 16436 advmss 16376
unreachable 2002:a9fe::/32 dev lo  metric 1024  error -101 mtu 16436 advmss 16376
unreachable 2002:ac10::/28 dev lo  metric 1024  error -101 mtu 16436 advmss 16376
unreachable 2002:c0a8::/32 dev lo  metric 1024  error -101 mtu 16436 advmss 16376
unreachable 2002:e000::/19 dev lo  metric 1024  error -101 mtu 16436 advmss 16376
2002::/16 dev tun6to4  proto kernel  metric 256  mtu 1480 advmss 1420
unreachable 3ffe:ffff::/32 dev lo  metric 1024  error -101 mtu 16436 advmss 16376
default via ::192.88.99.1 dev tun6to4  metric 1024  mtu 1480 advmss 1420
```

Another difference from FreeBSD is that the Linux 6to4 implementation filters out even more invalid IPv4 prefixes: 10.0.0.0/8, 169.254.0.0/16, 172.16.0.0/12, 192.168.0.0/16, and 224.0.0.0/3. Note that these routes/filters don't show up in either the netstat -r output or the iptables firewall rules. Apparently, the Linux developers also found it necessary to filter out 3ffe:ffff::/32, the last /32 block in the 6bone prefix, which is often used in examples. However, Red Hat ES4 doesn't install any of the unreachable routes.

TUNNEL MTU

If you paid close attention to the listings, you may have noticed a difference in MTU for the tunnel interfaces on different systems: Windows, FreeBSD, and MacOS use the IPv6 standard minimum packet size of 1280 bytes on tunnel interfaces, while Linux and Cisco IOS make the tunnel MTU as large as will fit in the parent interface's MTU. This generally means 1480 bytes, as the Ethernet MTU is 1500 bytes and the extra IPv4 header takes up 20 bytes.

Using a 1280 byte MTU for tunnels has the advantage that there won't be any need for any further fragmentation, as this is the minimum MTU for IPv6. On the other hand, the 1480 byte MTU allows for an extra 200 bytes of payload per packet, so it's more efficient.

Under FreeBSD and MacOS, the tunnel MTU is easily changed with `ifconfig gif0 mtu 1480` or something along similar lines. Under IOS, you can set the IPv6 MTU (as opposed to the actual interface MTU) with the `ipv6 mtu ...` command in interface configuration mode.

In theory, when (for instance) a FreeBSD and a Linux host communicate over a tunnel and both use their default tunnel MTU, reliable communication shouldn't be possible, as the Linux host will at some point send packets that are larger than the FreeBSD host's MTU. Fortunately, this isn't an issue in practice, as all the mentioned systems accept tunneled packets that are larger than their MTU.

However, all bets are off when ICMP Packet Too Big messages are filtered out somewhere along the way, so that Path MTU Discovery can't work. See the next chapter for more on that.

Manually Configured Tunnels

6to4 has the advantages that it's easy to configure and there is no need to obtain IPv6 address space. However, 6to4 also has some disadvantages: whenever the IPv4 address changes, the IPv6 addresses must also change, and communication with users of regular IPv6 address space often incurs detours through remote relays in the absence of relays closer by. Also, the relay service isn't always very reliable, and the traffic flow is generally asymmetric (that is, packets in both directions follow different paths through the network). On the other hand, the fact that the remote endpoint is known for manually configured tunnels makes it easier to reject fake packets. Last but not least, unlike 6to4 tunnels, manually configured or point-to-point tunnels can transport multicast packets. Apart from allowing the use of multicast applications, this also makes it possible to use regular IPv6 autoconfiguration mechanisms and routing protocols, if desired.

Windows

Because the Windows graphical user interface lacks the capability to configure IPv6, creating a tunnel must be done by using the `netsh` command. Listing 3-11 shows how to create and configure a manual tunnel.

Listing 3-11. *Creating and Configuring a Manual Tunnel*

```
C:\>netsh
netsh>interface ipv6
netsh interface ipv6>add v6v4tunnel interface=tun0 localaddress=192.0.2.1
remoteaddress=223.224.225.226
netsh interface ipv6>add address interface=tun0 address=2001:db8:31:1::2
Ok.

netsh interface ipv6>add route prefix=2001:db8:31:1::/64 interface=tun0
Ok.

netsh interface ipv6>add route prefix=::/0 interface=tun0 nexthop=2001:db8:31:1::1
Ok.

netsh interface ipv6>quit
```

When netsh is started without any arguments, it waits for commands. Commands are available in several "contexts," most notably the interface ipv6 context. After switching to this context, the first order of business is to create the tunnel. The interface option takes the tunnel name as its argument; in this case, tun0. The localaddress and remoteaddress specify the local and remote addresses that will be used for this tunnel (the endpoints). The next command sets up an address for the new interface. Unlike most other systems, Windows doesn't automatically create a "directly connected" route that makes systems on the same subnet reachable, so we must configure this route ourselves. This explains why the add address command doesn't take an argument that specifies the prefix length. After creating the subnet route, which does include the subnet prefix length, it's possible to set up a default route toward the router on the other end of the tunnel. Although the nexthop option with the IPv6 address of the remote router as its argument is optional here, without this, the default route won't work. Depending on the service pack that's installed, the system may now respond when another system tries to ping6 it: with Service Pack 1, Windows XP doesn't reply to IPv6 pings or traceroutes. With Service Pack 2, it responds to pings but not to traceroutes. See Chapter 9 for more information on how to modify firewall settings to change this behavior.

■**Note** Commands that create new interfaces, addresses, and routes with netsh generally allow the option store, which can either be active or persistent. With store=active, the changes don't survive a reboot, but with store=persistent, they become permanent until another command removes them again. If the store option isn't provided, the default is persistent.

In many cases, the keyword preceding an argument (such as interface=) can be left out, as the order of the arguments for any command is fixed so that netsh doesn't need to be told which argument is which.

Listing 3-12 shows how to delete the routes, address, and interface created in Listing 3-11.

Listing 3-12. *Removing a Manual Tunnel*

```
C:\>netsh
netsh>interface ipv6
netsh interface ipv6>delete route prefix=::/0 interface=tun0 nexthop=2001:db8: ➥
31:1::1
Ok.

netsh interface ipv6>delete route prefix=2001:db8:31:1::/64 interface=tun0
Ok.

netsh interface ipv6>delete address interface=tun0 address=2001:db8:31:1::2
Ok.

netsh interface ipv6>delete interface interface=tun0
Ok.
```

FreeBSD

Under FreeBSD, manual tunnels run over the gif virtual interfaces. A gif interface must be configured with two IPv4 addresses: the tunnel source and the tunnel destination. This can be done with the ifconfig command but also with the special gifconfig command. Apart from the tunnel source and destination and the fact that the interface is virtual, a gif interface is configured like any other interface. Listing 3-13 shows how to create a gif interface and how to configure the tunnel endpoint addresses.

Listing 3-13. *Creating a gif Interface and Setting Up Tunnel Endpoints*

```
# ifconfig gif create
gif2
# ifconfig gif2 tunnel 192.0.2.1 223.224.225.226
```

After creating a new gif interface, the system will echo back the full interface name. If an unused gif interface already exists, creating a new one is, of course, unnecessary. The first argument following the tunnel keyword is the address for the local tunnel endpoint; the second, the address for the remote endpoint. It's fairly easy to forget the tunnel keyword, in which case the gif interface won't work. Unfortunately, the resulting output from ifconfig is very similar to that with the tunnel keyword, as shown in Listing 3-14.

Listing 3-14. *Tunnel Configuration Mistakes*

```
# ifconfig gif3
gif3: flags=8010<POINTOPOINT,MULTICAST> mtu 1280
# ifconfig gif3 tunnel 192.0.2.1 223.224.225.227
# ifconfig gif4 192.0.2.1 223.224.225.228
# ifconfig
gif3: flags=8050<POINTOPOINT,RUNNING,MULTICAST> mtu 1280
        tunnel inet 192.0.2.1 --> 223.224.225.227
gif4: flags=8011<UP,POINTOPOINT,MULTICAST> mtu 1280
        inet 192.0.2.1 --> 223.224.225.228 netmask 0xffffff00
        inet6 fe80::201:2ff:fe29:2640%gif4 prefixlen 64 scopeid 0xc
```

After creation, gif interfaces aren't automatically brought up, so they also don't have a link-local address yet. But there is no need to bring up tunnel interfaces explicitly with the ifconfig gif0 up command, as this happens automatically as soon as the interface is configured with an address, as shown in Listing 3-15.

Listing 3-15. *Configuring an IPv6 Address for a* gif *Interface*

```
# ifconfig gif0
gif0: flags=8010<POINTOPOINT,MULTICAST> mtu 1280
# ifconfig gif0 up
# ifconfig gif0 inet6 2001:db8:31:1:: eui64
# ifconfig gif0
gif0: flags=8051<UP,POINTOPOINT,RUNNING,MULTICAST> mtu 1280
        tunnel inet 192.0.2.1 --> 223.224.225.226
        inet6 fe80::201:2ff:fe29:2640%gif0 prefixlen 64 scopeid 0x9
        inet6 2001:db8:31:1:201:2ff:fe29:2640 prefixlen 64
```

We first need to set the interface to the "up" state, or setting an address in the next line will be rejected with the error message "Could not determine link local address." In the next line, the eui64 keyword tells the system to fill in the bottom 64 bits in the address with a modified EUI-64 interface identifier. It's also possible to specify the full address, in which case a prefix length may be supplied, either affixed to the address with a slash in between or preceded by the keyword prefixlen. Listing 3-16 shows how to remove an IPv6 address and tunnel endpoint addresses from a gif interface and how to remove the interface from the system.

Listing 3-16. *Removing Tunnel Settings and a Tunnel Interface*

```
# ifconfig gif0 inet6 delete 2001:600:8:34::2
# ifconfig gif0 deletetunnel
# ifconfig gif0 destroy
```

Although gif tunnel interfaces will happily autoconfigure if the router on the other side sends out router advertisements, this is rare, so configuring the tunnel interface and setting up a default route is usually done manually or through a startup script. Listing 3-17 shows how to do it manually, along with the shortened output of the netstat -r command that shows the effect on the routing table.

Listing 3-17. *Setting Up a Default Route Toward a Tunnel*

```
# route add -inet6 default 2001:db8:31:1::1
# netstat -rnf inet6
Routing tables

Internet6:
Destination                      Gateway          Flags     Netif Expire
default                          2001:db8:31:1::1  UG1c      gif1
2001:db8:31:1::/64               link#9            UC        gif1
2001:db8:31:1::1                 link#9            UHLW      gif1
2001:db8:31:1:201:2ff:fe29:2640  link#9            UHL       loo
```

In this example, the local system has address 2001:db8:31:1:201:2ff:fe29:2640, and the other side has the 1 address within the same subnet. This is where the default route points. It's also possible to have the FreeBSD system set up one or more tunnels during startup. Listing 3-18 shows the necessary additions to the /etc/rc.conf file.

Listing 3-18. *Configuring an IPv6 Tunnel at System Startup by Using /etc/rc.conf*

```
cloned_interfaces="gif0"
gif_interfaces="gif0"
gifconfig_gif0="192.0.2.1 223.224.225.226"
ipv6_ifconfig_gif0="2001:db8:31:1::2 prefixlen 64"
ipv6_defaultrouter="2001:db8:31:1::1"
```

MacOS X

The MacOS system preferences only support 6to4 tunneling, so manual tunnels must be configured with the ifconfig command. However, creating new tunnel interfaces on the fly isn't possible under MacOS X, so the lone gif0 interface that's supplied by default will have to do. Don't forget to use sudo, as changing interfaces with ifconfig requires root privileges.

Even though the ifconfig commands are largely identical to those used under FreeBSD, making MacOS enable the tunnel at system startup is very different. To do this, you must create a startup script of your own. See Appendix B for information on how to do that.

Linux

Although there are several ways to set up a manual tunnel in Linux, only one consistently produces the intended result: the ip command. Listing 3-19 creates and configures a new tunnel device tun0 with ip.

Listing 3-19. *Creating a Manual Tunnel Under Linux*

```
# ip tunnel add name tun0 mode sit local 192.0.2.1 remote 223.224.225.226 ttl 64
# ip link set dev tun0 up
# ip address add 2001:db8:31:1::2/64 dev tun0
```

The mode is set to sit, which stands for Simple Internet Transition. The sit tunnel type is used for all IPv6-in-IPv4 tunnels, including 6to4. The difference between a 6to4 tunnel and a manual tunnel is just the remote address: this is any for 6to4 tunnels, while it is (of course) set to a specific value for manually configured tunnels. In theory, it's also possible to create tunnels with the ifconfig command, but it's not possible to specify a local address this way, so it makes more sense to stick to ip when managing tunnels. To be able to use the tunnel, it's necessary to add a default route pointing to the new tun0 interface. This, along with showing the routing table using the ip command, is done in Listing 3-20.

Listing 3-20. *Adding a Default Route and Displaying the Routing Table with* ip

```
# ip route add default via 2001:db8:31:1::1 metric 15
# ip -6 route show
2001:db8:31:1::/64 via :: dev tun0  proto kernel  metric 256  mtu 1480 advmss 1420
fe80::/64 dev eth0  proto kernel  metric 256  mtu 1500 advmss 1440
fe80::/64 via :: dev tun0  proto kernel  metric 256  mtu 1480 advmss 1420
default via 2001:db8:31:1::1 dev tun0  metric 15  mtu 1480 advmss 1420
default dev eth0  proto kernel  metric 256  mtu 1500 advmss 1440·
unreachable default dev lo  metric -1  error -101
```

Although the syntax is a bit different, the ip route add command that sets up the default route isn't all that different from the commands that add routes to the routing table on other systems, except for one thing: the metric. A metric is a preference value that makes it possible for the system to select the best route if there are several toward the same destination prefix. In the example, the ip -6 route show command shows that there are actually two default routes in the IPv6 routing table: the one specified just before in the example and another one pointing toward the eth0 (Ethernet) interface, with no next hop address specified. This extra default route exists to meet the on-link assumption as explained in the sidebar. However, the metric for this route is 256, while the default metric for routes created with ip is 1024. Because a lower metric is better, it's necessary to specify a metric that's lower than 256 when adding a default route, to make sure that the system doesn't use the existing route toward the eth0 interface. (A third default route with a strange -1 metric is used to generate "unreachable" messages in the absence of any other routing information.) Again, in Red Hat ES4, these special-purpose routes are no longer there, which means that ES4 doesn't implement the on-link assumption. The reason there is no need to use the -6 flag when configuring the route though -6 is required when listing routes is that the supplied next hop address allows ip to determine that we're talking about IPv6; but nothing in route show hints toward a specific IP version, so without the -6 flag, IPv4 is assumed.

Note The error "RTNETLINK answers: Network is down" means that the interface wasn't properly brought up by using the ip link ... up command. Also, ip has the unpleasant habit of accepting certain incorrect commands without complaining but without executing them, either.

MISSING IPV6 DEFAULT ROUTE

When an IPv6 host doesn't have a default route, RFC 2461 specifies that it is should consider the entire IPv6 address space to be "on-link." This means that the host assumes that these addresses are reachable on the local subnet. The advantage the on-link assumption is that this way, any systems connected to the same physical or logical network (such as a large Ethernet) are able to communicate in the absence of any routers, even if they have addresses in different subnet prefixes. However, many systems don't implement the on-link assumption. The problem is that the on-link assumption makes it hard to ignore IPv6 when there is no IPv6 connectivity. Most systems that support IPv6 will immediately return a "host unreachable" error when an application tries to connect to an IPv6 address, so the application can retry over IPv4 without delay. However, if all IPv6 destinations are considered on-link, the system must try to connect to any given IPv6 destination locally and wait for a time out when this (surprisingly) doesn't work. There are also security issues, because local systems could pretend to hold arbitrary IPv6 addresses. It's likely that the on-link assumption will be removed in a new version of RFC 2461.

Adding and displaying routes can also be done by using the route and netstat commands, as shown in Listing 3-21.

Listing 3-21. *Adding a Default Route and Displaying the Routing Table with* route *and* netstat

```
# route -A inet6 add default gw 2001:db8:31:1::1
# netstat -rnA inet6
Kernel IPv6 routing table
Destination              Next Hop            Flags Metric Ref Use Iface
::1/128                  ::                  U     0      0   0   lo
2001:db8:31:1::2/128     ::                  U     0      0   0   lo
2001:db8:31:1::/64       ::                  UA    256    1   0   tun0
fe80::/64                ::                  UA    256    0   0   eth0
fe80::/64                ::                  UA    256    0   0   tun0
::/0                     2001:db8:31:1::1    UG    1      0   0   tun0
::/0                     ::                  UDA   256    0   0   eth0
```

Both the route and the netstat commands take a -A inet6 flag that specifies the IPv6 "address family." The gw argument indicates that the next value is the Next Hop address. The default route makes sure that all packets are delivered to the router with this address. With route, there is no need to specify a metric, as routes created with this command receive a metric of 1 by default. Two additional flags are specified for netstat: -r and -n. The former tells netstat to show the routing table (the default is to show current TCP, UDP, and UNIX sockets), and the latter disables DNS lookups for the routing table entries.

The differences between the ip route show and the netstat -r output is mostly of little consequence (and undocumented), except that netstat also shows host routes that are created for individual addresses the system needs to keep track of. Listing 3-22 shows how to remove a route, an IPv6 address, and a tunnel interface.

Listing 3-22. *Removing a Default Route and a Manual Tunnel Under Linux*

```
ip route delete default via 2001:db8:31:1::1
ip address del 2001:db8:31:1::2/64 dev tun0
ip tunnel del name tun0
```

Just as with 6to4, Red Hat Linux (including ES4) is able to configure a manual tunnel automatically on startup. This behavior is controlled by two files: /etc/sysconfig/network and /etc/sysconfig/network-scripts/ifcfg-sit1. Listing 3-23 shows the manual tunnel–related contents of the /etc/sysconfig/network file, and Listing 3-24 shows the full contents of the /etc/sysconfig/network-scripts/ifcfg-sit1 file.

Listing 3-23. *The Contents of* /etc/sysconfig/network

```
NETWORKING_IPV6="yes"
IPV6_DEFAULTDEV=sit1
IPV6_DEFAULTGW=2001:db8:31:1::1
```

Listing 3-24. *The Contents of* /etc/sysconfig/network-scripts/ifcfg-sit1

```
DEVICE=sit1
BOOTPROTO=none
ONBOOT=yes
IPV6INIT=yes
IPV6TUNNELIPV4=192.0.2.1
IPV6TUNNELIPV4LOCAL=223.224.225.226
IPV6ADDR=2001:db8:31:1::2
```

Note that the name of the tunnel interface must be sit and then a digit, but not sit0, and IPV6TUNNELIPV4 specifies the remote tunnel endpoint address.

■**Caution** Be careful when changing Linux tunnel interface settings, as the system may no longer be able to shut down properly when the shutdown scripts want to shut down a tunnel that's not there.

IFCONFIG: FRIEND OR FOE

People often assume that when someone has written a book about something, he or she knows a lot about the subject in question. I'm glad to say that this is generally indeed the case. *After* writing the book, at least. Authors discover many an interesting tidbit of information only during the writing process, which can be a humbling experience for those of us who think we knew everything already.

What I will take away from writing this book is knowledge of the proper ifconfig syntax. The first day at my first job in the Internet business, I impressed my new boss by reconfiguring an Ethernet interface on a SunOS machine with a new MAC address. Not all that impressive in and of itself, but the SunOS operating system had the strange habit of reprogramming all the Ethernet interfaces in a machine with the same MAC address. Because the server in question was connected to the same Ethernet with two interfaces, this meant that it would receive every packet twice (once on each interface), which didn't exactly help performance. With different MAC addresses on both interfaces, the speed increased significantly.

That day was probably the last time that I consulted the `ifconfig` man page, because I've been struggling with the command's syntax ever since. I can never remember the order of the inet6 (no, not *-inet6*) argument and the add, delete, alias, -alias parameters and the like on various UNIX-like systems. So imagine my surprise when, after scrutinizing a rough draft of this chapter, Pim van Pelt (one of the two invaluable technical reviewers for this book) pointed out that the proper order is as follows:

```
ifconfig [-L] [-m] interface [create] [address_family]
         [address[/prefixlength] [dest_address]] [parameters]
```

So the correct syntax in Listing 3-16 wouldn't be `ifconfig gif0 inet6 delete 2001:600:8:34::2` (or `ifconfig gif0 inet6 -alias 2001:600:8:34::2`) but `ifconfig gif0 inet6 2001:600:8:34::2 delete`. I think I can remember that.

The moral of the story is that commands such as `ip`, `ifconfig`, `route`, and `netstat` are sufficiently complex and different between various operating systems that it pays to have a look at the man page when you need to do things that fall outside your everyday routine. Whether allowing different ways to achieve the same result is a good idea is a philosophical question. It is certainly confusing from time to time.

Note I'm not going to change the listings as a result of my new insight, both to keep them as a reminder and because editing examples is a surefire way to introduce errors.

Cisco

Using a manually configured tunnel comes very natural to Cisco's Internetwork Operating System (IOS), and it's very easy to configure, as shown in Listing 3-25. However, this example only allows the router itself to use the tunnel, just as with the examples for Windows, FreeBSD, MacOS X, and Linux. See Chapter 4 for more information on routing IPv6.

Listing 3-25. *Configuring a Tunnel Interface and an IPv6 Default Route Under Cisco IOS*

```
!
interface Tunnel0
 ipv6 address 2001:DB8:31:1::2/64
 ipv6 enable
 tunnel source 192.0.2.1
 tunnel destination 223.224.225.226
 tunnel mode ipv6ip
!
ipv6 route ::/0 2001:DB8:31:1::1
!
```

The tunnel interface is created and put in the "up" state as soon as the interface tunnel0 command is given. (Deleting the interface again is done with no interface tunnel0.) IPv6 is enabled for the interface as soon as an IPv6 address is configured, so the ipv6 enable command isn't really necessary here. When configuring the address, the router won't accept the address without a prefix length, which is usually /64, as in the example. The tunnel source command also accepts an interface as its argument. In that case, the primary IPv4 address for that interface is used as the tunnel source. Because IOS supports a number of different tunneling mechanisms, it is necessary to specify IPv6 in IP encapsulation explicitly with the tunnel mode ipv6ip command.

The other tunneling mechanisms aren't appropriate for IPv6, with the exception of Generic Route Encapsulation (GRE). GRE is a tunneling protocol developed by Cisco that allows the transport of many protocols other than just IPv6 over IP tunnels. GRE also offers additional features, such as having a checksum over the tunneled packets or enforcing that packets aren't delivered out of order. However, GRE adds a few more housekeeping bytes on top of the new IPv4 header, so if the additional GRE features aren't needed, simple IPv6 in IP is the best choice.

Note Both manually configured tunnels (RFC 2893) and all automatic tunneling mechanisms except Teredo set the "protocol" field in the IPv4 header to 41 (decimal) to indicate that the content of the IPv4 packet is an IPv6 packet. The protocol number for GRE is 47. Teredo uses UDP port 3544. Be sure, if you run a firewall or other filter, that your tunnel protocol is allowed through. For instance, Red Hat ES4 with the default firewall configuration filters out protocol 41 so that 6to4 or manual tunnels don't work reliably. See Chapter 9 for more information on packet filters, including the Linux ip(6)tables filter.

SOURCE ADDRESS PROBLEMS

Most of the systems discussed here check whether the local address for a tunnel is indeed a valid address for the local system when a tunnel source address is configured. FreeBSD 4.9, MacOS, and Cisco will happily send out packets with the configured tunnel source as the source address, regardless of whether this is indeed an address that is present on the system. FreeBSD 5.4, Linux, and Windows, on the other hand, accept the configuration but don't transmit the packets.

Manually Configured Tunnels and NAT

Manually configured tunnels themselves can deal with Network Address Translation (NAT) without problems if the configuration on both ends is changed to reflect the idea each end has about its own address and the remote end's address. For instance, let's assume a tunnel between 192.0.2.1 and 223.224.225.226. Now the host that used to have the address 223.224.225.226 is moved behind a NAT and given the new (private) address 10.0.0.203. The old address is given to the NAT box. To keep the tunnel working, the configuration on the host behind the NAT box must now reflect that it has a private address, so the tunnel source becomes 10.0.0.203. But the configuration on the other host remains the same.

However, many NAT implementations can deal with only TCP and UDP and fail to handle IP packets with a protocol 41 payload. A larger class of NATs can handle forwarding protocol

41 packets toward a fixed internal address, which would of course be the host that's the local tunnel endpoint. This configuration item is often called "default host," or "DMZ." A small class of NATs can handle IPv6-in-IPv4 tunneling without any configuration. Unfortunately, there is no good way to find out what kind of NAT is implemented in a particular device other than just seeing what happens.

It's better to set up the default host or DMZ anyway, as otherwise the NAT limitation that external systems can't initiate communications toward internal systems also applies to the tunneled IPv6 connectivity. But the effect is slightly different than in IPv4: when an internal system connects to the outside world over IPv6, the appropriate NAT state is set up so that incoming tunnel packets are delivered to the system that terminates the tunnel. External systems can now connect to internal systems. When the tunnel is idle for some time, the NAT removes the mapping, and after that, systems elsewhere on the Internet can no longer reach IPv6 systems behind the tunnel that crosses the NAT device. You can solve this by periodically generating some traffic over the tunnel, for instance, by starting a one-packet `ping` to a remote system from the cron every minute.

Very much the same thing happens when there is a stateful IPv4 filter that allows incoming protocol 41 packets only after there have been outgoing protocol 41 packets.

Getting a Tunnel

After all the examples of how to create a manually configured tunnel, just one ingredient is missing for a successful tunnel setup: the other side. In this regard, there is good news and bad news. The good news is that many places around the Net offer tunnel connections. The bad news is that many of them are hard to find. This is especially true for ISPs that offer tunnels, as IPv6 isn't exactly big business (yet) for ISPs. Still, a tunnel from an ISP has considerable advantages. First, because your traffic flows over their network anyway, there is no detour for IPv6 traffic. Second, they know you, so it's usually possible to get a fixed tunnel without the need for authentication systems. Third, getting IPv6 traffic from your ISP doesn't cost them any extra bandwidth. Getting it from a third party means that all IPv6 traffic to and from you needs to flow over their network, and giving this away for free isn't a sustainable business model in the long run.

However, if your ISP doesn't support IPv6, you'll have to get a tunnel somewhere else. The 6bone is being phased out, so the old advice of connecting to the 6bone with a tunnel that still floats around the Net is no longer very useful. Your best bet is one of the tunnel brokers. Most, if not all, tunnel brokers give out IPv6 tunnels to the general public for free. However, they all approach this task differently. Most require some kind of registration, and some use special client software to set up the tunnel. The amount of address space they give out greatly varies, from a single address to a full /48. Table 3-1 lists some well-known tunnel brokers. It is well worth the time to find one that suits your needs rather than to pick just a random one.

Table 3-1. *Tunnel Brokers*

Name	URL	Location
Hurricane Electric IPv6 Tunnel Broker	http://www.tunnelbroker.net/	Fremont, California
Hexago Freenet6	http://www.hexago.com/	Quebec, Canada
Consulintel Tunnel Broker	http://tb.consulintel.euro6ix.org/	Madrid, Spain
SixXS Tunnel Broker	http://www.sixxs.net/	Various locations in Europe

CHAPTER 4

■ ■ ■

Routing

"Ah, yes. It's a lot like Star Trek: The Next Generation. In many ways, it's superior but will never be as recognized as the original."

—Wayne Campbell in the movie *Wayne's World*

For IPv6 packets to reach remote destinations, they must generally pass through several IPv6 routers. This chapter explains how to set up IPv6 routing, both in a simple end-user environment and in an ISP or enterprise environment, where one or more routing protocols are deployed. Most residential gateways and small office/home office routers that are sold these days don't support IPv6, so it's common for a simple end-user network to use a regular computer as an IPv6 router. Routing/forwarding IPv6 packets is supported on Windows XP and all UNIX-like operating systems such as Linux, the BSD family, and MacOS, which sort of married into the BSD family as of version "X."

Figure 4-1 shows the layout of the example network we'll be discussing in the rest of this chapter. A router sits between the host and the IPv6 Internet. The Ethernet link between the router and the host is depicted somewhat archaically as some length of coaxial Ethernet cable with terminators at both ends. This avoids any possible confusion that could be the result of including switches in the network diagram.

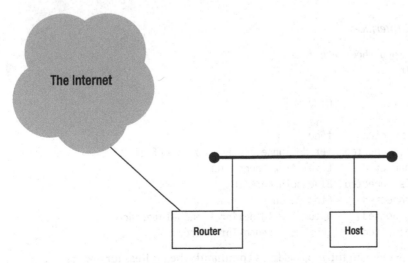

Figure 4-1. *A simple example network with a router and a host*

Routing IPv6

There is a difference between routing and forwarding a protocol. *Routing* is the process of maintaining a routing table, usually (but not necessarily) aided by routing protocols. With a routing table in place, any packets that come in that aren't addressed to the router can be *forwarded* to their destination, or to another router closer to that destination. Not everyone cares to make the distinction between the two, so "routing" is sometimes used to describe both.

In IPv6, there is more to being a router than just routing and forwarding. The host in Figure 4-1 not only depends on the router to forward packets to and from the Internet on its behalf; it also needs the router to provide an address prefix so it can autoconfigure an IPv6 address. So the router in Figure 4-1 must, like all well-behaved IPv6 routers, listen on the all-routers multicast address (ff02::2) for incoming router solicitation packets. When it receives one of those, it replies with a router advertisement (to the all-hosts group address, ff02::1) that contains the desired configuration information. Routers also send out router advertisements periodically to let hosts know that previously learned information is still valid.

In IPv4, routers often supply configuration information to hosts by using the Dynamic Host Configuration Protocol (DHCP), but there is no requirement that DHCP runs on a router: the DHCP service can be provided by a regular server, if desired. Stateless autoconfiguration, on the other hand, is closely tied to routing functionality, and therefore supplying the information that clients need to autoconfigure themselves *must* be done on actual routers. There is also DHCP for IPv6 (DHCPv6), but it's not widely supported yet, and it's doubtful that it ever will as a mechanism for hosts to configure their IPv6 addresses. See Chapter 8 for more information on DHCPv6.

Routing on Windows XP

Although Windows can forward IPv6 packets between any two IPv6-capable interfaces that happen to be present, we'll assume connectivity to the IPv6 Internet over a tunnel, as configured in Chapter 3. Listing 4-1 shows that the tunnel interface configured in Listing 3-11 is still present.

Listing 4-1. *Listing IPv6 Interfaces*

```
C:\>netsh interface ipv6 show interface
Querying active state...

Idx  Met  MTU    State          Name
---  ---- -----  ------------   -----
  7    1  1280   Connected      tun0
  6    2  1280   Disconnected   Teredo Tunneling Pseudo-Interface
  5    0  1500   Connected      Local Area Connection 3
  4    0  1500   Disconnected   Bluetooth Network
  3    1  1280   Connected      6to4 Pseudo-Interface
  2    1  1280   Connected      Automatic Tunneling Pseudo-Interface
  1    0  1500   Connected      Loopback Pseudo-Interface
```

Addresses can be listed with the show address command. The address for our tun0 interface is 2001:db8:31:1::2. The Windows machine will be acting as a router and will share the

connectivity it has to the IPv6 Internet over its IPv6 tunnel with another host on the local
Ethernet (see Figure 4-1). The necessary commands are shown in Listing 4-2.

Listing 4-2. *Configuring Windows XP as an IPv6 Router*

```
C:\>netsh
netsh>interface ipv6
netsh interface ipv6>add address interface="local area connection 3" address=2001:➥
db8:31:2::1
Ok.

netsh interface ipv6>add route prefix=2001:db8:31:2::/64 interface=5 publish=yes
Ok.

netsh interface ipv6>set interface interface=5 forwarding=enabled advertise=enabled
Ok.

netsh interface ipv6>set interface interface=7 forwarding=enabled
Ok.
```

In the first step, interface Local Area Connection 3 (or interface 5 for short; see Listing 4-1)
gets an address in a previously unused subnet. The second line adds the new subnet to the routing
table, and the keyword publish=yes tells Windows that this address prefix is eligible for inclusion
in router advertisements. After that, forwarding and router advertisements are enabled for the
Ethernet interface (5), and forwarding is enabled on the tunnel interface (7). In Windows, enabling
forwarding on an interface allows packets that are received on this interface to be forwarded.
So, to make Windows forward packets coming in from the Internet over the tunnel interface
to the Ethernet subnet and from the Ethernet subnet to the Internet, forwarding must be
enabled on both interfaces. Because there are no hosts that require configuration information
on the tunnel subnet, sending router advertisements isn't appropriate on this interface (nor
does Windows allow it). See http://www.microsoft.com/resources/documentation/WindowsServ/
2003/standard/proddocs/en-us/netsh_int_ipv6.asp for more information on the netsh command's interface ipv6 context. Navigating this page may not work on browsers other than
Internet Explorer.

In the days before Service Pack 2, this would be the end of it. However, as of SP2, Windows
will no longer touch Internet Control Message Protocol (ICMP) packets with a 10-foot pole. This
creates two problems for hosts sitting behind a Windows IPv6 router: the Windows router doesn't
show up in traceroutes, and Path MTU Discovery (PMTUD) doesn't work. While the former is a
minor inconvenience, the latter is absolutely fatal (see sidebar), especially because the default
Maximum Transmission Unit (MTU) for tunnel interfaces is 1280, so any 1500-byte packets
received over an Ethernet interface can't be forwarded over a tunnel. Listing 4-3 solves both these
problems by enabling the appropriate sending of ICMP messages types 2 and 11. Type 2 "Time
Exceeded" is used by traceroute, and type 11 "Packet Too Big" is used for PMTUD. Because these
settings govern the *sending* of ICMP packets, there shouldn't be any security risks.

Listing 4-3. *Enabling* traceroute *and PMTUD ICMP Messages*

```
netsh interface ipv6>firewall
netsh firewall>set icmpsetting type=11 mode=enable
Ok.

netsh firewall>set icmpsetting 2 enable
Ok.
```

PATH MTU DISCOVERY IN IPV6

IP allows packets to be up to nearly 64 kilobytes, but most of the link layer technologies it runs over support much smaller maximum packet sizes (Maximum Transmission Unit, or MTU). For instance, in IP over Ethernet, the maximum size of IP packets that may traverse an Ethernet network is 1500 bytes. Link layers that are newer than the original Ethernet, but that have subsequently been made obsolete by Ethernet's more recent incarnations, typically have larger MTUs, as bigger packets make for more efficient communication. For instance, FDDI, Token Ring, ATM, and Packet over SONET have (default) MTUs around the 4.5-kilobyte mark. The original ARPANET, on the other hand, used a 1006 byte MTU. Different kinds of tunneling, such as IPv6 in IP or PPP over Ethernet, reduce the "standard" 1500 byte MTU, and with Gigabit Ethernet, it's often possible to use "jumbo frames" (generally up to 9000 bytes).

To be able to route packets from one type of link layer to another, routers must accommodate for the MTU differences. In IPv4, this is done by "fragmenting" packets that are too large to be transmitted whole over a certain link. However, fragmenting takes extra work for the router that performs the fragmentation and for the destination host, which must reassemble the fragments into the original packet again. Enter Path MTU Discovery (PMTUD). The idea behind PMTUD is to discover the smallest MTU in a path toward a given destination so that it's possible to send the largest possible packets that the various links along the path can support without fragmentation. This works by setting the "don't fragment" bit in the IPv4 header. When a router encounters a packet that's too big to be transmitted over the link where it needs to go, the router drops (destroys) the packet and sends back a "packet too big" ICMP message containing the MTU of the offending link. The source host can now reduce the size of packets that it sends, so there is no need for fragmentation. This process is illustrated in Figure 4-2.

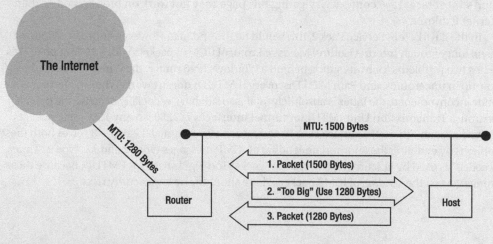

Figure 4-2. *Path MTU discovery*

In IPv6, Path MTU Discovery works exactly the same. However, there is an important difference when PMTUD isn't desired: in IPv4, PMTUD can be disabled and packets are sent with the "don't fragment" bit set to zero, so they can be fragmented when necessary. Not so in IPv6, as routers don't get to fragment packets. In essence, IPv6 behaves as if the "don't fragment" bit is always set. But unlike IPv4, IPv6 has a reasonable minimum MTU of 1280 bytes. So a host that isn't prepared to perform PMTUD can limit itself to sending packets of 1280 bytes or fewer. Routers, on the other hand, don't get to choose: they *must* send back "packet too big" ICMP messages when they encounter a packet that's too large for the link MTU. If they don't, communication becomes impossible, as the source host keeps sending oversized packets. This is already a problem with IPv4, and it's worse with IPv6 because it can't be fixed like in IPv4 by fragmenting the packets anyway, despite the value of the DF bit. The mandatory minimum MTU of 1280 bytes in IPv6 means that "legacy" links with smaller MTUs (576 or even 296 were once common for dial-up) must be upgraded, or special measures must be taken to make the smaller physical MTU invisible to IPv6. See the discussion of IPv6 over IEEE 1394 in Chapter 8.

FreeBSD

FreeBSD is very easy to configure as an IPv6 router. All that's needed, in addition to (for instance) IPv6 connectivity over a tunnel as shown in Listing 3-18 in Chapter 3, are some extra lines in the /etc/rc.conf file, as shown in Listing 4-4.

Listing 4-4. *Enabling IPv6 Routing Under FreeBSD*

```
ipv6_ifconfig_xl0="2001:db8:31:2:: eui64 prefixlen 64"
ipv6_gateway_enable="YES"
rtadvd_enable="YES"
rtadvd_interfaces="xl0"
```

The first line configures an IPv6 address for the xl0 Ethernet interface, with the eui64 keyword instructing the system to use a MAC address–derived modified EUI-64 for the lower 64 bits of the address. If the interface itself doesn't have a MAC address, one is borrowed from another interface. The second line enables IPv6 forwarding on all interfaces. The last two lines enable and configure rtadvd, the router advertisement daemon.

MacOS

The MacOS startup scripts don't provide the same IPv6 configurability that the FreeBSD ones do, so setting up a Mac as an IPv6 router requires a homegrown script, like the one in Appendix B. The easiest way to make one is to take Listings B-4 and B-5 from the appendix and add lines similar to those in Listing 4-5.

Listing 4-5. *Enabling IPv6 Routing Under MacOS*

```
ifconfig en0 inet6 2001:db8:31:2::1/64
sysctl -w net.inet6.ip6.forwarding=1
rtadvd en0
```

All these commands must be run as root. So if they're not part of a script that runs with root privileges, execute them with sudo. The first line specifies an address for the en0 (Ethernet) interface. Note that this can also be done by using the GUI. Because, unlike its FreeBSD counterpart, the MacOS ifconfig command doesn't support FreeBSD's eui64 keyword, you must supply the full address and accept the annoyance of having to keep track of which address is assigned to which system. It is of course possible to take the MAC address and specify an EUI-64–derived address manually, but that's not really worth the effort, especially as, presumably, this Mac is the only router on the subnet; so, the address ending in ::1 is a natural choice. The next line enables IPv6 forwarding in the kernel, and the last one starts the router advertisement daemon.

Note The rtadvd daemon will silently fail unless IPv6 forwarding is enabled.

On systems like FreeBSD, the sysctl net.inet6.ip6.accept_rtadv determines whether the system accepts router advertisements (1) or not (0). This setting changes the behavior of all interfaces. Under MacOS, the System Preferences allow the user to configure the IPv6 status of individual interfaces as autoconfiguring, manually configured, or disabled, so even though net.inet6.ip6.accept_rtadv is present, it's ignored. Unfortunately, this means that there is no easy way to stop the system from listening for router advertisements from a script. This becomes rather embarrassing when the MacOS router sees its own router advertisements and sets up a default route toward itself, breaking IPv6 connectivity to the rest of the world in the process. The best way to solve this is with a firewall rule, as in Listing 4-6. See Chapter 9 for more information on filtering IPv6 packets and other security issues.

Listing 4-6. *Filtering Out Incoming Router Advertisements*

```
ip6fw add 65000 drop ipv6-icmp from any to any icmptypes 134 in
```

Linux

Like FreeBSD, setting up Red Hat Linux for routing IPv6 is pretty straightforward when using the system startup scripts. Assuming connectivity to the IPv6 Internet through the sit1 tunnel interface, as per Listings 3-23 and 3-24 in Chapter 3, all that's needed are some changes to /etc/sysconfig/network and /etc/sysconfig/network-scripts/ifcfg-eth0. Listing 4-7 lists the former; Listing 4-8 the latter.

Listing 4-7. *Enabling IPv6 Routing in* /etc/sysconfig/network

```
NETWORKING_IPV6=yes
IPV6FORWARDING=yes
```

Listing 4-8. *Manual Configuration of the* eth0 *Interface*

```
IPV6INIT=yes
IPV6ADDR=2001:db8:31:2::1/64
```

With IPv6 forwarding enabled, several settings now have different defaults. For instance, in the absence of other instructions, incoming router advertisements are ignored, as routers are expected to have their IPv6 addresses configured manually. The term "manual configuration" may seem out of place here, but it just means that the address configuration doesn't happen automatically. In the previous FreeBSD example, the first 64 bits were configured manually, and the lower 64 bits were derived from the EUI-64. Strictly speaking, that would be a hybrid manual/automatic configuration, but I still call it "manual" because the address isn't configured fully automatically like it is with stateless autoconfiguration or DHCPv6.

Even though all Red Hat variations come with all the necessary scripts, one thing is lacking from the workstation distributions: a router advertisement daemon. A radvd daemon (as opposed to rtadvd under FreeBSD) can be installed by using various packages. Some packages and the source can be downloaded at http://v6web.litech.org/radvd/. Don't forget to set up a configuration file for radvd. When you compile the daemon from the source yourself, the default place for this file is /usr/local/etc/radvd.conf, but Red Hat may expect to see the file in /etc. Listing 4-9 is a very basic radvd configuration. You may also need to add a startup script (see Appendix B) for radvd.

Listing 4-9. *An* radvd *Configuration File*

```
interface eth0
  {
    AdvSendAdvert on;
    prefix 2001:db8:31:2::/64 { };
  };
```

Static Routes

If your IPv6 network is more complex, you may need to set up static routes to get packets from one router to the next. For instance, the host in the subnet 2001:db8:31:c03::/64 in Figure 4-3 may be reachable through Router 2, which has, for instance, the address 2001:db8:31:2::abf.

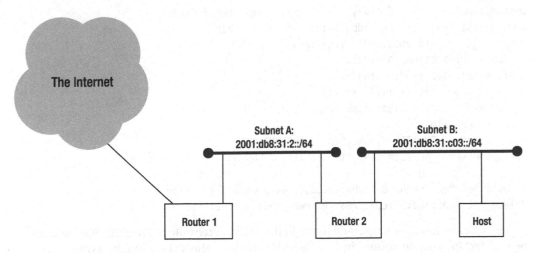

Figure 4-3. *A host behind two routers*

Listings 4-10 to 4-13 show how to create, inspect, and remove a static route for the extra sub-net under Windows, FreeBSD, MacOS, and Linux, respectively.

Listing 4-10. *A Static Route Under Windows*

```
C:\>netsh
netsh>interface ipv6
netsh interface ipv6>add route prefix=2001:db8:31:c03::/64 interface=5 ➥
nexthop=2001:db8:31:2::abf
Ok.

netsh interface ipv6>show routes
Querying active state...

Publish  Type    Met  Prefix                  Idx  Gateway/Interface Name
-------  ------  ----  --------------------    ---  ------------------
no       Manual   0   2001:db8:31:c03::/64      5   2001:db8:31:2::abf

netsh interface ipv6>delete route prefix=2001:db8:31:c03::/64 interface=5 ➥
nexthop=2001:db8:31:2::abf

Ok.
```

Listing 4-11. *A Static Route Under FreeBSD*

```
# route add -inet6 2001:db8:31:c03::/64 2001:db8:31:2::abf
add net 2001:db8:31:c03::/64: gateway 2001:db8:31:2::abf
# netstat -rnf inet6
Routing tables

Internet6:
Destination             Gateway             Flags  Netif Expire
2001:db8:31:c03::/64    2001:db8:31:2::abf  UGSc   xl0
# route get -inet6 2001:db8:31:c03::/64
   route to: 2001:db8:31:c03::
destination: 2001:db8:31:c03::
      mask: ffff:ffff:ffff:ffff::
   gateway: 2001:db8:31:2::abf
 interface: xl0
     flags: <UP,GATEWAY,DONE,STATIC,PRCLONING>
 recvpipe sendpipe ssthresh rtt,msec rttvar hopcount   mtu  expire
        0        0        0        0        0        0  1500        0
# route delete -inet6 2001:db8:31:c03::/64 2001:db8:31:2::abf
delete net 2001:db8:31:c03::/64: gateway 2001:db8:31:2::abf
```

It's also possible to set up static routes in the /etc/rc.conf file in FreeBSD. See the examples under "ipv6_static_routes" in /etc/defaults/rc.conf. However, I find this syntax to be confusing, and the trouble with setting anything up in rc.conf is that you need to reboot the system to see if it works correctly. I recommend having the static routes set up in a shell script and then calling this script at system boot time, as explained in Appendix B. The ability to execute the script manually makes for much easier testing.

Listing 4-12. *A Static Route Under MacOS*

```
% sudo route add -inet6 2001:db8:31:c03:: -prefixlen 64 2001:db8:31:2::abf
% netstat -rnf inet6
Routing tables

Internet6:
Destination              Gateway              Flags  Netif Expire
2001:db8:31:c03::/64  2001:db8:31:2::abf UGSc   en0
% route -n get -inet6 2001:db8:31:c03:: -prefixlen 64
   route to: 2001:db8:31:c03::
destination: 2001:db8:31:c03::
       mask: ffff:ffff:ffff:ffff::
    gateway: 2001:db8:31:2::abf
  interface: en0
      flags: <UP,GATEWAY,DONE,STATIC,PRCLONING>
 recvpipe sendpipe ssthresh rtt,msec rttvar hopcount    mtu  expire
        0        0        0        0      0        0   1500       0
% sudo route delete -inet6 2001:db8:31:c03:: -prefixlen 64 2001:db8:31:2::abf
delete net 2001:db8:31:c03::: gateway 2001:db8:31:2::abf
```

Listing 4-13. *A Static Route Under Linux*

```
# route --inet6 add 2001:db8:31:c03::/64 gw 2001:db8:31:2::abf
# route --inet6
Kernel IPv6 routing table
Destination              Next Hop             Flags Metric Ref Use Iface
2001:db8:31:c03::/64  2001:db8:31:2::abf UG    1       0   0 eth0
# route --inet6 delete 2001:db8:31:c03::/64 gw 2001:db8:31:2::abf
```

> **Note** Alternatively, you may want to use the `ip` package to set up static routes under Linux, like in Listing 3-20 in Chapter 3.

Windows and Linux only allow listing the entire IPv6 routing table (only the route that was just added is shown in the listings), while FreeBSD and MacOS also support looking up individual routes. The MacOS syntax is somewhat different than that of FreeBSD: the prefix length must be specified by using the -prefixlen option (purists feel that -prefixlen should be used on FreeBSD as well), and the route get command needs the -n option to turn off DNS lookups, or the "route to" and "destination" will be listed as "invalid" if they're not in the DNS. Note that manipulating the routing table (route add and route delete) requires root privileges, but just looking at the table doesn't.

Dynamic Routing

In a simple two- or three-router setup, using static routes isn't a problem. However, at some point, static routing becomes unmanageable. Currently four routing protocols work with IPv6:

- RIPng: the IPv6 version of RIP.

- OSPFv3: the IPv6 version of OSPF.

- Integrated IS-IS: the OSI IS-IS routing protocol extended for IPv6.

- BGP-4 with Multiprotocol Extensions.

The Routing Information Protocol (RIP) is an old and very simple routing protocol for small to medium-sized networks. It basically broadcasts the content of the routing table periodically and incorporates these broadcasts from other routers in its own table. A simple "hop count" makes sure that the most direct route is preferred. RIP suffers from two downsides: it doesn't work too well in large networks because of all the broadcasts, and it takes very long (several minutes) to detect outages and reroute traffic around the failure. These are fundamental problems caused by the way RIP works, so they're also present in RIPng.

Open Shortest Path First (OSPF) is a much more advanced routing protocol, which keeps maps of the entire network topology. OSPF sends out "hello" packets to see if neighboring routers are still reachable and to find new neighbors. Apart from that, it only sends out updates when there is a change in the network. In this case, all routers execute the Shortest Path First algorithm, and traffic immediately starts taking the new best path. Its quick reaction to outages and mechanisms to contain routing information to a subset of the network make OSPF suitable for networks of all sizes. Apart from the obsolete version 1, there are currently two versions of OSPF: OSPFv2 (for IPv4) and OSPFv3 (for IPv6). They are completely separate protocols that don't interact when both are enabled.

Intermediate System to Intermediate System[1] (IS-IS) is the OSI CLNS routing protocol for use within a single network or organization. It was later extended to carry IPv4 routing information as well as OSI CLNS routing information. The extended version is referred to as integrated IS-IS. The integrated version is very popular with large Internet Service Providers, because although its basic architecture is very similar to OSPF, its implementation makes it better capable of handling very large networks. In addition to CLNS and IPv4, IS-IS can also carry IPv6 routing information. Until not very long ago, this came with the caveat that every link or subnet that runs IPv4 must also run IPv6, and vice versa. However, there is now "multitopology" support for IS-IS, which removes this limitation when it's not desired. Because of its OSI background, IS-IS is not for the faint of heart: once it's up and running, IS-IS isn't too difficult to manage, but it does require that you to set up CLNS/CLNP addresses and routing and suffer the OSI jargon that comes with it. For small to medium-sized networks, IS-IS provides very few, if any, advantages over OSPF.

Unlike the other three routing protocols, the Border Gateway Protocol (BGP) is used between the networks of different organizations. BGP makes it possible for packets to find their way from one ISP to the other. BGP is also used by organizations that connect to two or more ISPs.[2] The current version of BGP is version 4. Multiprotocol extensions allow BGP4 to be used for different address families, such as IPv4 multicast or IPv6.

---

1. "Intermediate System" is OSI-speak for "router."

2. For more information on BGP, see my book, *BGP* (O'Reilly & Associates, 2002).

Routing protocol support on Cisco routers depends very much on the model and the software image. Larger models such as the Cisco 7200 support all IPv6 routing protocols. (One of the technical reviewers tells me a Cisco 7200 is no longer considered a "large" model. Obviously he never had to carry one from one end of a big building to another!) Smaller models such as the ancient Cisco 2500 support RIPng and BGP (even though it's not really powerful enough to do much with BGP), often but not always OSPF (depending on the IOS release train and version), and never IS-IS. The small SOHO/DSL models only support RIPng.

A Linux or FreeBSD machine (or even a MacOS one) can be turned into a full-fledged IPv6 router by installing the right software. In the beginning, there was Zebra, which implements RIP, OSPF, and BGP each for both IPv4 and IPv6. The makers of Zebra later started working on a commercial version, sold by IP Infusion. The commercial ZebOS has many more features, including IS-IS, IPv4 and IPv6 multicast routing, MPLS, and VLAN switching. Zebra progress slowed down significantly, and eventually, another group took advantage of the fact that Zebra was released under the GNU Public License and started developing its own version under the name Quagga. Quagga also supports IS-IS. See http://www.bgpexpert.com/hardsoft.php for a more extensive list of BGP implementations. The rest of the chapter will have examples for Zebra because it's very similar to Cisco and the configuration commands aren't subject to change to the degree they are in Quagga. The examples may or may not work with Quagga.

Installing Zebra

Zebra (or Quagga) is probably available as a package or RPM for your system, but compiling the source yourself is no trouble at all (for the routing protocol daemons, at least). The source is available from the Zebra website at http://www.zebra.org/. Listing 4-14 lists the commands for building and installing Zebra version 0.94. However, Zebra 0.95 was released in early 2005. The output of the commands in question is left out.

Listing 4-14. *Compiling Zebra*

```
# gunzip zebra-0.94.tar.gz
# tar xvf zebra-0.94.tar
# cd zebra-0.94
# ./configure
# make
# make install
```

The code compiles under Linux, FreeBSD, and MacOS. Under MacOS, it's usually a good idea to install UNIX software under a special prefix, for instance, with ./configure --prefix=/sw. This way, the binaries will be installed in /sw/sbin and the configuration files in /sw/etc rather than in /usr/local/sbin and /usr/local/etc, respectively, so they don't get in the way of the MacOS system. Zebra consists of a collection of different daemons:

- zebra, the daemon that ties it all together, on port 2601.

- ripd, the daemon that implements RIP for IPv4, on port 2602.

- ripngd, the daemon that implements RIPng for IPv6, on port 2603.

- ospfd, the daemon that implements OSPF for IPv4, on port 2604.

- bgpd, the daemon that implements BGP for both IPv4 and IPv6, on port 2605.

- ospf6d, the daemon that implements OSPF for IPv6, on port 2606.

The right way to start each of the daemons is to execute it with the option -d so it runs in the background. The daemons will start even if they're not run as root, but they may not work as desired because they may need access to privileged network services. It's generally best to start zebra first, as this daemon manages the communication between the different daemons on the one hand and the kernel on the other hand. If zebra is already running, it can provide bgpd, ospfd, and/or ospf6d with a router identifier. Each of these protocols requires a router identifier to identify the local system. Almost always, this is one of the IPv4 addresses configured on the system. If the zebra daemon isn't running and a router identifier isn't specified in the configuration file, routing protocols can't determine the router identifier, and they won't work. Other than zebra itself, there is no need to run any of the other daemons unless the routing protocol they provide is desired.

Configuring the daemons is generally done by connecting to it using telnet (hence the port numbers listed previously), even though the configuration is kept in a file on disk. But editing the file directly has a big downside: the daemon must be restarted for the changes to take effect. Restarting routing protocols is less than desirable, as it interrupts the flow of traffic through the router. Before you can type telnet localhost 2601 for the first time, however, it's necessary to create basic configuration files. Listing 4-15 shows a configuration file for the zebra daemon, although the same configuration can be used for all the daemons.

Listing 4-15. *A Basic* zebra *Configuration*

```
!
hostname zebra
password easy-to-guess
enable password hard-to-guess
!
access-list zebra-access permit 127.0.0.1/32
!
ipv6 access-list zebra-access-ipv6 permit ::1/128
!
line vty
 access-class zebra-access
 ipv6 access-class zebra-access-ipv6
 exec-timeout 60
!
```

If you're used to Cisco routers, this won't look a million miles removed from something familiar. However, note the small but important differences, such as the lack of numbers after the line vty configuration command. This configuration sets the hostname to "zebra," which is useful to be able to keep the daemons apart later. The password line sets the first password the daemon asks for when you telnet to it, and the enable password sets the password that's required to enter privileged mode, which is required to view or change the configuration. The remaining lines set up an access list that limits incoming telnet connections to those coming from the IPv4 or IPv6 localhost addresses. Without this, anyone can telnet to your routing daemons. Note that the configuration is stored in clear text. However, you can scramble the passwords in the configuration file somewhat by specifying service password-encryption in the configuration. The exec-timeout 60 command specifies a timeout of 60 minutes rather than the default of five minutes for virtual terminal sessions.

Tip Under Linux and FreeBSD, you can run the configure script with the options --enable-vtysh and --with-libpam to build the additional vtysh utility. vtysh makes it possible to communicate with the various Zebra daemons as a single entity, mimicking the Cisco user interface more closely. However, some configuration commands don't work in vtysh. Should you wish to use vtysh, you have to create a vtysh.conf file in the appropriate directory. If you add lines like username iljitsch nopassword to this file, then the user in question doesn't have to provide a password when starting vtysh. If vtysh asks for a password (which it may or may not do), it wants to hear the current user's login password.

Listing 4-16 shows how to connect to the zebra daemon, list the configuration, and make a small change. Changing configuration for the different routing protocols all happens in a similar vein, so this example should function as a very short introduction to the Zebra/Cisco command line. Have a look at a Cisco tutorial if you want to know more about how this command line interface works. It's not all that hard, as long as you remember that the Cisco command line has several modes or contexts, and each one accepts different commands. The prompt always shows the current mode.

Listing 4-16. *Connecting to the* zebra *Daemon for the First Time*

```
# telnet localhost 2601
Trying 127.0.0.1...
Connected to localhost.
Escape character is '^]'.

Hello, this is zebra (version 0.94).
Copyright 1996-2002 Kunihiro Ishiguro.


User Access Verification

Password:
zebra-t> enable
Password:
zebra-t# show running-config
```

```
Current configuration:
!
hostname zebra-t
password 8 U2uZd3cGSy89g
enable password 8 OqFtOGjdVxDwI
service password-encryption
!
interface lo
!
interface eth0
 ipv6 nd suppress-ra
!
interface sit1
 ipv6 nd suppress-ra
!
access-list zebra-access permit 127.0.0.1/32
!
!
line vty
 access-class zebra-access
!
end
zebra-t# configure terminal
zebra-t(config)# interface eth0
zebra-t(config-if)# description First Ethernet interface
zebra-t(config-if)# exit
zebra-t(config)# exit
zebra-t# show interface eth0
Interface eth0
  Description: First Ethernet interface
  index 3 metric 1 mtu 1500 <UP,BROADCAST,RUNNING,MULTICAST>
  HWaddr: 00:01:02:29:23:b6
  inet 172.16.1.5/24 broadcast 255.255.255.255
  inet6 fe80::201:2ff:fe29:23b6/64
  inet6 2001:db8:31:2::1/64
    input packets 9624, bytes 1142979, dropped 0, multicast packets 0
    input errors 0, length 0, overrun 0, CRC 0, frame 0, fifo 0, missed 0
    output packets 5549, bytes 1042517, dropped 0
    output errors 0, aborted 0, carrier 0, fifo 0, heartbeat 0, window 0
    collisions 0
zebra-t# quit
Connection closed by foreign host.
```

Note Zebra keeps a watchful eye on the kernel, so when interfaces acquire new addresses or new routes get added to the kernel routing table, the zebra daemon incorporates this information in its interface status or master routing table. However, this information is not added to the Zebra configuration file. And, of course, routing information and addresses in Zebra are communicated to the kernel.

Enabling IPv6 on Cisco and Zebra

On Cisco routers, IPv6 must be enabled per-interface either by explicitly specifying `ipv6 enable` or by assigning an IPv6 address to the interface. In addition, IPv6 routing must be enabled by using the `ipv6 unicast-routing` configuration command. On Zebra, this isn't necessary: the interface IPv6 status is inherited from the kernel and startup scripts, and Zebra enables IPv4 and IPv6 forwarding when the `zebra` daemon starts, although it doesn't disable forwarding when the daemon exits. Setting up routing between a tunnel interface and an Ethernet interface is very simple by using Zebra or a Cisco router, as shown in Listing 4-17. This example builds on Listing 3-25. A static route as in Listings 4-10 to 4-13 is thrown in for good measure.

Listing 4-17. *Routing IPv6 on a Cisco Router*

```
!
ipv6 unicast-routing
!
interface Ethernet0
 ipv6 address 2001:db8:31:2::/64 eui-64
!
ipv6 route 2001:db8:31:c03::/64 2001:db8:31:2::abf
!
```

Caution If you have access restrictions on (among others) telnet access to a Cisco router, you need to set up similar restrictions for IPv6, or the router will be accessible from every possible IPv6 address.

On a Cisco router, this is enough to make the router send out router advertisements. Zebra on the other hand, adds the line `ipv6 nd suppress-ra` to the configuration of each interface, which, unsurprisingly, stops the sending of router advertisements. (The nd part of the command refers to neighbor discovery, which is the more general mechanism router advertisements are part of.) So the Zebra version of Listing 4-17 would be Listing 4-18. These settings are for the zebra daemon (telnet to port 2601).

Listing 4-18. *Routing IPv6 on a Zebra Router*

```
!
interface eth0
 ipv6 address 2001:db8:31:2::1/64
 no ipv6 nd suppress-ra
!
ipv6 route 2001:db8:31:c03::/64 2001:db8:31:2::abf
!
```

Unlike Cisco IOS, Zebra doesn't support the `eui-64` keyword, so the full address must be specified. Listing 4-19 lists the IPv6 routing table on a Cisco router.

Tip It's always a good idea to use the `eui-64` keyword to fill in the lowest 64 bit in a router's address from a MAC address when possible. This is especially beneficial on interfaces between two or more routers: because these interface configurations now don't contain any information that is specific to the individual router, it's very easy to copy and paste an interface configuration between routers, and it's no longer necessary to keep records about which router holds which address in a subnet.

A slight downside is that it's a bit harder to populate the reverse DNS with long EUI-64–based addresses rather than much shorter manually assigned addresses.

Listing 4-19. *Listing the IPv6 Routing Table*

```
Cisco#show ipv6 route
IPv6 Routing Table - 4 entries
Codes: C - Connected, L - Local, S - Static, R - RIP, B - BGP
       U - Per-user Static route
       I1 - ISIS L1, I2 - ISIS L2, IA - ISIS interarea, IS - ISIS summary
       O - OSPF intra, OI - OSPF inter, OE1 - OSPF ext 1, OE2 - OSPF ext 2
       ON1 - OSPF NSSA ext 1, ON2 - OSPF NSSA ext 2
S   ::/0 [1/0]
     via 2001:DB8:31:1::1
C   2001:DB8:31:1::/64 [0/0]
     via ::, Tunnel0
L   2001:DB8:31:1::2/128 [0/0]
     via ::, Tunnel0
C   2001:DB8:31:2::/64 [0/0]
     via ::, Ethernet0
L   2001:DB8:31:2:260:70FF:FE35:AA5E/128 [0/0]
     via ::, Ethernet0
L   FE80::/10 [0/0]
     via ::, Null0
L   FF00::/8 [0/0]
     via ::, Null0
```

There is one static route (the default route), two "connected" routes for the subnets of directly connected interfaces, and several "local" routes. The first two local routes point toward the router's own addresses, and the last two encompass the link-local and multicast address blocks, which require special treatment. The Zebra routing table looks somewhat different, but this depends greatly on the host operating system. The main difference is that Zebra also lists "kernel" routes, which were added to the system routing table manually or through a routing process other than Zebra. Additionally, the routes that are actually used for forwarding traffic (i.e., which are in the "Forwarding Information Base") are listed with an asterisk. On most routers, there is a RIB and one or more FIBs. The Routing Information Base (RIB) is simply the routing table, as shown in the example. The Forwarding Information Base (FIB) is a copy of the RIB in a format that's highly optimized for packet forwarding. On Cisco routers, the most common form of a FIB is the Cisco Express Forwarding (CEF) table. Listing 4-20 turns on CEF for IPv6 and displays the CEF table. (Very small models such as SOHO routers don't support CEF.)

Listing 4-20. *Cisco Express Forwarding for IPv6*

```
RouterE#show ipv6 cef
%IPv6 CEF not running
RouterE#conf t
Enter configuration commands, one per line.  End with CNTL/Z.
RouterE(config)#ipv6 cef
%Must enable IPv4 CEF first
RouterE(config)#ip cef
RouterE(config)#ipv6 cef
RouterE(config)#^Z
RouterE#show ipv6 cef
2001:DB8:31:2:260:70FF:FE35:AA5E/128
  Receive
2001:DB8:31:2::/64
    attached to Ethernet0
2001:DB8:31:1::2/128
  Receive
2001:DB8:31:1::/64
    attached to Tunnel0
FE80::/10
  Receive
FF00::/8
  Receive
::/0
    attached to Tunnel0
```

For IPv6 CEF to work, IPv4 CEF must be enabled, too. The CEF table is similar to the routing table, except that it focuses more on what should actually happen to packets toward a certain prefix. In this example, there are two variants: "receive" means that the router processes the packet locally, and "attached to ..." means that the packets should go to the indicated interface. Also, the default route resolves to an "attached to Tunnel0" route in the CEF table, even though it points toward a specific neighbor address in the regular routing table. You can find out more detailed information with the show ipv6 cef detail command.

■Warning Zebra *really* doesn't like it when the clock is adjusted significantly. Because most PC hardware is hampered by enthusiastically drifting clocks, synchronizing the time over the network is almost a necessity. When this is done periodically with a program like ntpdate, the clock will often jump many seconds, which may cause erratic behavior by the Zebra daemons, such as broken BGP sessions. A better alternative is to run the ntpd daemon, which will speed up or slow down the clock by a fraction when needed.

It's a good idea to read about RIPng even if you only plan to use OSPFv3 and read about RIPng and OSPFv3 if you only plan to use BGP, as some more general routing concepts and IPv6 peculiarities aren't repeated for the other protocols.

RIPng

Because of its wide availability across the Cisco product line (and elsewhere), the Routing Information Protocol Next Generation is very well suited to replace a relatively small number of static routes in an environment where the network is expected to be stable and failure survivability isn't the number-one priority. Examples of such a network would be a SOHO (small office/home office) or residential network with just a few routers. (In a network with only one router, there is little need for routing protocols.) Listing 4-21 shows the Zebra `ripngd` (port 2603) configuration to enable RIPng.

Listing 4-21. *Enabling RIPng on Zebra*

```
!
router ripng
 default-information originate
 redistribute static
 network xl0
!
```

In this example, RIPng is enabled on the xl0 interface. It's also possible to specify and address range, and Zebra will find interfaces with addresses in that range and enable RIPng on those interfaces; in other words, the behavior of most IPv4 routing protocols. The `default-information originate` command instructs `ripngd` to broadcast a default route, and the `redistribute static` command allows static routes to be inserted into RIPng. These routes, along with any routes learned from other routers through RIPng, are entered into the RIPng database, which is shown in Listing 4-22.

Listing 4-22. *Displaying the RIPng Database on Zebra*

```
ripngd# show ipv6 ripng

Codes: R - RIPng

   Network                 Next Hop                  If Met Tag Time
R  ::/0                    ::                        0  1   0
R  2001:db8:31:1::/64      fe80::260:70ff:fe35:aa5e  3  2   0 02:59
S  2001:db8:31:2::/64      ::                        3  1   0
R  3ffe:9500:3c:600::/56   fe80::204:27ff:fefe:249f  3  2   0 02:54
```

The default route has the unspecified address as its next hop, meaning that the route is generated locally and the next hop address is outside of RIPng's view. The same is true for the redistributed static route (indicated with an S). The two other RIP routes (lines starting with an R) have link-local addresses for their next hops, so RIPng routing is independent of the global scope IPv6 addresses that the routers participating in the protocol happen to have. This is a fairly significant departure from IPv4, where it's a common problem for routing protocols to fail to initialize properly because two or more routers have different ideas about the address range used for a certain physical subnet. "If" is a pointer to the next hop interface, and "Met" is the metric, which in RIP equals the hop count or number of routers between the local system and the destination prefix. When several RIP routes are available from different routers, the one with the lowest metric (which is the hop count in RIP) is used. When two routes have the same hop count, they're both installed into the routing table for load balancing purposes. The tag is used in more complex setups, and the time shows how long the route has to live before it's considered unreachable and removed. The default life time of a route is three minutes, and RIP updates come along every 30 seconds, so under normal circumstances, the life time counts down to 2:30 and then reinitializes to 3:00 because of a RIP update.

The Cisco configuration for RIPng is quite different, as shown in Listing 4-23.

Listing 4-23. *Enabling RIPng on a Cisco Router*

```
!
interface Ethernet0
 ipv6 rip my-rip enable
 ipv6 rip my-rip default-information originate
!
ipv6 router rip my-rip
 redistribute connected
!
```

Unlike with Zebra, and unlike nearly all IPv4 routing protocols, RIPng is enabled for an interface in the configuration for that interface. In Cisco IOS, it's possible to have several instances of the RIP protocol active on a single router, making it necessary to name each instance. In the listing, this name is "my-rip." The name is only meaningful within this router; there is no requirement that other routers use the same name for their RIPng instance.

Whether or not a default route is broadcast through RIPng is also determined per interface. It's also possible to specify default-information only, in which case a default route and nothing else will be sent out over the interface in question. In this example, static routes aren't redistributed in RIPng, but connected routes are. Connected routes are routes that exist because the route has an interface configured with the prefix in question. Apart from static and connected routes (and in Zebra, kernel routes), it's also possible to redistribute routes learned from other routing protocols, but this can be dangerous. It is possible to redistribute selectively by applying a route map (examples of those, but in other contexts, are included later this chapter) to the redistribution. Listing 4-24 displays the RIPng database Cisco-style.

Listing 4-24. *Displaying the RIPng Database on a Cisco Router*

```
#show ipv6 rip database
RIP process "my-rip", local RIB
 2001:DB8:31:2::/64, metric 2, installed
     Ethernet0/FE80::204:27FF:FEFE:249F, expires in 155 secs
 3FFE:9500:3C:600::/56, metric 2, installed
     Ethernet0/FE80::201:2FF:FE29:23B6, expires in 173 secs
```

Notice the different take Cisco has on displaying the RIPng database: it only displays routes *received* through RIPng, unlike Zebra, which also displays static and connected routes that are being *transmitted* through RIP. Currently, there is no way to determine whether Cisco IOS includes a certain route in RIPng updates, other than turning on RIPng debugging with debug ipv6 rip and terminal monitor to display the debugging output. These are turned off with undebug ipv6 rip (or undebug all) and terminal no monitor, respectively.

■Note RIPng "broadcasts" are sent to the `ff02::9` multicast group address, UDP port 521.

OSPFv3

OSPF for IPv6 is an extensive and complex protocol, and it's impossible to do it justice in a few pages. However, the complexities are as good as identical to those of OSPF for IPv4, so if you want to know the gory details about running OSPF over non-broadcast links, connecting non-backbone areas through virtual links, or about the use of not-so-stubby areas (NSSAs), then read up on OSPF in general. The following information should be enough to enable those familiar with OSPF in the IPv4 world to apply their knowledge to IPv6 and those unfamiliar with OSPF to start running OSPF in most small to medium-sized networks. Listing 4-25 enables OSPFv3 on a Cisco router.

Listing 4-25. *OSPFv3 on a Cisco Router*

```
!
interface FastEthernet2/0
 ipv6 ospf 230 area 0.0.0.0
!
```

The number 230 designates the OSPFv3 process, which is required as it's possible to have several OSPFv3 instances running concurrently on a router. As with a RIPng instance name, the process number only has local meaning inside the router.

Areas and Metrics

Apart from major differences "under the hood" because OSPF is a link-state routing protocol while RIP is a distance-vector protocol, the two things that make OSPF much better suited for larger networks are the use of areas and a much better metric. When the original OSPF was developed around 1990, there were significant concerns about whether the routers would be able to run the heavy SPF algorithm that determines the best path. By allowing the network to be split up in different "areas" and containing the SPF calculations to a single area, it was possible to build much larger OSPF networks. However, this simplification requires that all the traffic between different areas only flows through a special "backbone" area. The backbone area is area 0. In a small network of 25 routers or fewer, it's best to stick with just a backbone area.

■Note Area numbers are 32 bits long and can be written either as a regular number or in IPv4 addresses format (not IPv6 addresses format), so the backbone area may also show up as `0.0.0.0`. Cisco routers accept both, but Zebra wants to see only the IPv4-like notation.

The difference between the OSPF metric and the RIP hop count is illustrated in Figure 4-4. There are two ways to get from router 1 to router 2: one 10 Mbps hop or three 100 Mbps hops. To RIP this is a no-brainer (although this can be tweaked somewhat): one hop is better than three. OSPF, on the other hand, takes the bandwidth of the links in to account and decides that three 100 Mbps hops are better than one 10 Mbps hop. OSPF does this by assigning a "cost" to each interface. Under Cisco IOS, the default cost is a hundred million divided by the interface speed in bits per second. So for a 1544 kbps T1 circuit, that would be 64, for 10 Mbps Ethernet 10, and for 100 Mbps or faster interfaces 1. So in the example in Figure 4-1, the direct link between routers 1 and 2 has a cost of 10, and the path through routers 3 and 4 has total cost of 3. The cost for an interface can be modified with the `ipv6 ospf cost ...` interface mode command (`ipv6 ospf6 cost ...` under Zebra; note the extra 6), where the cost is a number from 1 to 65535. On a Cisco router, changing the cost for an interface can be useful or even necessary when there are Gigabit Ethernet links, because by default, both 100 Mbps and 1000 Mbps Ethernet have a cost of 1. On Zebra, changing the default is always a good idea, as Zebra doesn't have good access to interface bandwidth information (assuming it bothers to look at this information at all).

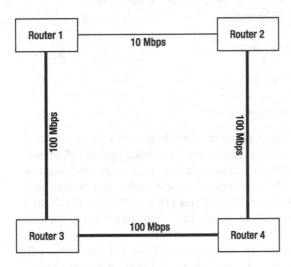

Figure 4-4. *An example OSPF network*

Although Listing 4-25 enables OSPF on an interface and creates an OSPFv3 process with number 230, it doesn't enable any redistribution, so any routes that show up in OSPF are routes for the address prefixes present on interfaces for which OSPF is configured.

Redistribution

Listing 4-26 enables redistribution of static and connected routes so that all static routes and connected routes from interfaces that don't run OSPFv3 are injected into the protocol. In addition to this, a default route is injected into OSPF, and the `log-adjacency-changes` command makes the router write a message to the logging buffer (and all other places the router is configured to log to) when an OSPFv3 neighbor appears or disappears. Listing 4-27 displays the resulting OSPF routes in the IPv6 routing table.

Listing 4-26. *Enabling Redistribution in OSPF*

```
!
ipv6 router ospf 230
 log-adjacency-changes
 default-information originate
 redistribute connected
 redistribute static
!
```

Listing 4-27. *The OSPF Routes in the IPv6 Routing Table*

```
#show ipv6 route ospf
IPv6 Routing Table - 644 entries
Codes: C - Connected, L - Local, S - Static, R - RIP, B - BGP
       U - Per-user Static route
       I1 - ISIS L1, I2 - ISIS L2, IA - ISIS interarea, IS - ISIS summary
       O - OSPF intra, OI - OSPF inter, OE1 - OSPF ext 1, OE2 - OSPF ext 2
       ON1 - OSPF NSSA ext 1, ON2 - OSPF NSSA ext 2
O   2001:7F8:1::/64 [110/2]
     via FE80::290:6902:EE02:E43E, FastEthernet2/0
O   2001:DB8:31:2::/64 [110/2]
     via FE80::212:1E02:EE05:58DB, FastEthernet2/0
OE2 3FFE:9500:3C:600::/56 [110/0]
     via FE80::212:1E02:EE05:58DB, FastEthernet2/0
```

The first two routes are "real" OSPF routes, as opposed to redistributed ones. As with RIPng, the next hop points toward a link-local address and an output interface, isolating OSPFv3 from potential address instability. The [110/2] information indicates that the routes have an "administrative distance" of 110 and a metric of 2. The administrative distance is a value that determines the preference between routing protocols. For instance, OSPF has 110 and RIP 120. So if both OSPF and RIP supply a route toward the same destination, the OSPF route is preferred because of the lower "distance."

The third route is an "external type 2" route, which means that it was redistributed. Redistributed routes may also take the shape of "external type 1" routes, but only when this is configured explicitly. There is a slight difference in the metric handling between type 1 and type 2: with type 1, the metric is updated at each router hop; with type 2, the metric set by the router that does the redistribution stays the same throughout the network. OSPF routes are of course also included when listing all IPv6 routes with the show ipv6 route command.

Neighbors

Because unlike RIP(ng), OSPF explicitly creates neighbor relationships with other routers, it's useful to list all the neighbors for a router in order to see what's going on. This is done with the show ipv6 ospf neighbor command, as shown in Listing 4-28.

Listing 4-28. *Displaying Active OSPFv3 Neighbors*

```
#show ipv6 ospf neighbor
Neighbor ID  Pri  State          Dead Time   Interface ID  Interface
192.0.2.91   128  FULL/BDR       00:00:38    3             FastEthernet2/0
192.0.2.17   128  FULL/DROTHER   00:00:35    2             FastEthernet2/0
192.0.2.19     1  FULL/DROTHER   00:00:30    8             FastEthernet2/0
```

Under Zebra, the command is `show ipv6 ospf6 neighbor`, and there can't be any further arguments. IOS accepts an interface name or `detail` as an additional argument. The neighbor ID is the router identifier for the neighbor. "Pri" is the priority of a router. Rather than have every router on a subnet communicate with every other router on the subnet, a "designated router" (DR) and a "backup designated router" (BDR) are selected to coordinate the communication between OSPF routers in a subnet. The routers with the highest priority become DR and BDR. The priority can be set by using the `ipv6 ospf priority ...` command for an interface (`ipv6 ospf6 priority ...` under Zebra). Priority values range from 0 to 255, with 1 being the default and 0 meaning that the router isn't eligible to become a DR or BDR. Stable states for a neighbor are FULL or 2WAY. FULL is to/from a DR or BDR, and 2WAY between two non-DR/non-BDR routers. DR or BDR under state indicate that the router in question is the DR or BDR, and DROTHER means it's neither. In Listing 4-28, no DR is listed, which means that the local router is the designated router. This also explains why the state for the DROTHER routers is FULL rather than 2WAY. The dead time counts down the time until the neighbor is considered "dead." OSPF routers send out "hello" packets every 10 seconds to find new neighbors and let existing neighbors know they're still alive. After missing four hellos, a neighbor is considered "dead." So under normal circumstances, the dead time counts down from 40 seconds to 30 and then a hello is received, so it jumps back to 40 again.

■**Note** Hello and dead time intervals can be changed by using `ipv6 ospf` / `ipv6 ospf6` interface mode commands, but the values *must* be the same for all routers on a subnet for OSPF to work properly.

As with RIPng, the Zebra approach to configuring OSPFv3 is more traditional, with most of the configuration commands grouped under the `router ospf6` heading rather than under an interface heading. Also, the Zebra implementation of OSPFv3 isn't nearly as complete as the Cisco implementation. For instance, Zebra doesn't support external type 1 or 2 routes in OSPFv3, even though it does in OSPFv2. Listing 4-29 enables OSPFv3 under Zebra. These commands are for the `ospf6d` daemon, which lives on port 2606.

Listing 4-29. *Enabling OSPFv3 Under Zebra*

```
!
interface xl0
 ipv6 ospf6 cost 10
!
router ospf6
 router-id 192.0.2.18
 redistribute static
 interface xl0 area 0.0.0.0
!
```

Note Zebra's ospf6d isn't capable of learning the router ID from the zebra daemon, so the router ID must always be set with the router-id command in the router ospf6 context.

Listing the OSPF routes in the IPv6 routing table works the same way as on a Cisco router with show ipv6 route ospf (on the zebra daemon), and listing OSPFv3 neighbors is done with show ipv6 ospf6 neighbor (on the ospf6d).

Note OSPFv3 hello packets are sent to the ff02::5 multicast address. OSPF doesn't use UDP (or TCP), but runs directly on top of IP, using protocol number 89.

Note Neither Cisco IOS nor Zebra implement authentication for RIPng or OSPFv3.

BGP

The Border Gateway Protocol is very different from all other current routing protocols, both in purpose and in the way it's configured and subsequently operates. RIP, OSPF, and IS-IS are all Interior Gateway Protocols (IGPs), which is a fancy way of saying that they operate within a single organization's network. BGP, on the other hand, is an External Gateway Protocol (EGP), and is used to communicate *between* networks from different organizations. BGP makes it possible for packets to find their way from one Internet Service Provider to the next. This means that all ISPs that are big enough to connect to two or more other ISPs run BGP. In fact, even end users who connect to two or more ISPs and want to use the different connections together (i.e., use the same address space over both connections) must run BGP. Doing this allows them to dynamically reroute existing sessions over another connection and thereby isolate themselves from most problems that may occur in the network of an upstream ISP. This is called "multihoming."

To keep the BGP protocol somewhat manageable, it doesn't concern itself with individual routers. Rather, BGP works with "autonomous systems." What an autonomous system (AS) is isn't easy to define. Generally, it's a set of routers operated by a single organization. However, ISPs generally don't operate their customer's routers, but still customers are part of their ISP's AS, because they don't do BGP routing themselves and therefore can't express a "routing policy" of their own. A routing policy determines which packets go where. With only one connection to the Internet, a routing policy obviously doesn't amount to much: locally generated packets are transmitted to the ISP, and incoming packets always find their way through the same ISP. However, even very small organizations with just a single router can be an AS if they connect to two or more ISPs and talk BGP with those ISPs.

Listing 4-30 shows an excerpt of the IPv4 "global routing table," which is what the full set of BGP routing information for the entire Internet is called. (The shorter addresses make the IPv4 information easier to look at than the equivalent IPv6 information.)

Listing 4-30. *Part of the IPv4 BGP Global Routing Table*

```
     Network         Next Hop     Metric LocPrf    Weight Path
*    4.0.0.0         62.9.194.3      40             0 646 335 i
*                    80.31.82.129    50             0 645 335 i
*>                   23.248.72.89           105     0 129 335 i
*> 64.86.28.0/24    80.31.82.129    50             0 645 3047 i
*                    62.9.194.3      40             0 646 645 3047 i
*                    23.248.72.89    60             0 129 645 3047 i
*>i145.52.0.0        195.69.14.34     0     110     0 110 i
*                    62.9.194.3      40             0 646 110 i
*                    23.248.72.89    60             0 129 354 110 i
*                    80.31.82.129    50             0 645 354 110 i
```

The example lists four destination prefixes or networks, each of them reachable over three or four different paths. The next hop address is simply the address where the packets go to (the next router). Three main "path attributes" determine which path is selected for each destination: the local preference, the AS path, and the metric, or Multi Exit Discriminator (MED). The local preference is the "strongest" path attribute: the highest local preference always wins. This is clear for the first and last prefixes in the listing, as indicated by the greater-than sign on the lines that sport a local preference value. The other lines don't have a local preference, which is equal to having one of 100. For the middle prefix, the local preference is the same for all paths, so the choice is determined by the AS path length. The first AS path only has two ASes in it, so it is preferred over the other two routes which both have three ASes in the path. In cases where the local preference and the AS path length are the same, the choice comes down to the MED metric, for which lower is better.

Address Families

Unlike with RIP and OSPF, there isn't a separate BGP protocol for IPv6. BGP operation for both IPv4 and IPv6 may even overlap. And, generally, after enabling IPv6 in BGP, the IPv4 configuration will look different. If you're familiar with BGP in IPv4, you'll expect to see a configuration like the one in Listing 4-31.

■**Note** In Zebra, BGP commands go to the bgpd daemon on port 2605.

Listing 4-31. *A Simple IPv4 BGP Setup*

```
!
router bgp 65500
 no synchronization
 bgp log-neighbor-changes
 network 192.0.2.0
 neighbor 172.16.1.242 remote-as 65500
 neighbor 172.16.1.242 prefix-list outfilter out
 no auto-summary
!
ip route 192.0.2.0 255.255.255.0 Null0
!
ip prefix-list outfilter seq 5 permit 192.0.2.0/24
!
```

This configuration sets up a BGP session toward a router with IP address 172.16.1.242 in AS 65500. The network 192.0.2.0/24 is advertised in BGP, and the prefixlist outfilter only allows this prefix and nothing else (by virtue of the "implicit deny" in Cisco filters) in outgoing updates toward the peer (neighboring router). The route to the Null0 interface makes sure that 192.0.2.0/24 is in the routing table so that BGP will actually advertise it to its neighbors. The no synchronization command avoids trouble when there are more BGP routers in the AS and there is also an interior routing protocol active, and bgp log-neighbor-changes makes sure that neighbors coming up and going down are logged. The no auto-summary command is a default setting that finds its way into the configuration automatically and keeps the router from exhibiting some very old and generally undesirable behavior. Listing 4-32 is a similar configuration for IPv6.

Listing 4-32. *A Simple IPv6 BGP Setup*

```
!
router bgp 65500
 bgp log-neighbor-changes
 neighbor 3ffe:9500:3C:74::10 remote-as 64900
 no neighbor 3ffe:9500:3C:74::10 activate
 !
 address-family ipv6
 neighbor 3ffe:9500:3C:74::10 activate
 neighbor 3ffe:9500:3C:74::10 prefix-list outfilter-ipv6 out
 network 2001:DB8:31::/48
 no synchronization
 exit-address-family
!
ipv6 prefix-list outfilter-ipv6 seq 5 permit 2001:DB8:31::/48
ipv6 route 2001:DB8:31::/48 Null0
!
```

The `no neighbor ... activate` line makes sure the IPv4 "address family" is disabled for the IPv6 neighbor. Other than this, the IPv6 configuration is pretty much identical to the IPv4 one, except that all the IPv6 settings are stored under the `address-family ipv6` heading. Don't forget to add a `no synchronization` line to the IPv6 address family, or IOS will wait for iBGP routes (internal BGP, discussed later this chapter) to show up in the interior routing protocol, which isn't going to happen as redistributing BGP routes into an IGP went out of style before the first IPv6 RFC saw the light of day. Zebra is more advanced than Cisco in this regard and doesn't support synchronization, so there is no need to turn it off.

Note that it's necessary to leave the address family configuration mode explicitly by using the `exit-address-family` command, which is unusual for IOS. In most cases, after adding IPv6 information to and existing BGP setup, the IPv4 part of the BGP configuration stays the same. However, without any prior warning, the IPv4 settings may move to an `address-family ipv4` heading. Because it's almost impossible to keep this from happening by itself at some point and there is no way back, short of removing the full BGP configuration and re-entering it, it's best to make this happen immediately, as shown in Listing 4-33.

Listing 4-33. *The IPv4 Address Family Configuration Grouping*

```
Cisco#conf t
Enter configuration commands, one per line.  End with CNTL/Z.
Cisco(config)#router bgp 65500
Cisco(config-router)#address-family ipv4
Cisco(config-router-af)#^Z
Cisco#show running-configuration | begin router bgp
router bgp 65500
 bgp log-neighbor-changes
 neighbor 3ffe:9500:3C:74::10 remote-as 64900
 neighbor 172.16.1.242 remote-as 65500
 !
 address-family ipv4
 no neighbor 3ffe:9500:3C:74::10 activate
 neighbor 172.16.1.242 activate
 neighbor 172.16.1.242 prefix-list outfilter out
 no auto-summary
 no synchronization
 network 192.0.2.0
 exit-address-family
 !
```

The router will continue to accept old-style IPv4 BGP configuration commands without problems. Zebra works the same, except that it sticks with a hybrid configuration that shows an old-style IPv4 BGP configuration (no `address-family` heading for IPv4) and new-style IPv6 BGP configuration (`address-family` heading for IPv6) longer.

In most cases, IOS add an extra line to the configuration that explicitly disables the IPv4 address family for a neighbor with an IPv6 address. However, sometimes an IPv6 neighbor may inadvertently have the IPv4 address family enabled, with puzzling results: IPv4 routes from the neighbor show up, but they aren't usable because of nonsensical next hop addresses. This can happen because with the introduction of the multiprotocol extensions in RFC 2858, BGP can exchange routing information for a great number of "address families."[3] BGP runs over TCP, and TCP generally runs over IPv4 or IPv6. So it's possible to exchange IPv6 routing information over an IPv4 TCP session, or the other way around. In theory, exchanging IPv4 routing information over an IPv6 TCP session isn't a problem, but in practice, it is. When exchanging IPv4 routes over an IPv4 session or IPv6 routes over an IPv6 session, the BGP router knows which next hop address it should include in the BGP updates: usually, the local address for the BGP TCP session. But when it has to transmit IPv4 routes over an IPv6 BGP TCP session (or the other way around), determining which next hop address it should include suddenly becomes a problem, because it doesn't know which of the local addresses share a subnet with the other router. For this reason and because of easier debugging, it's common practice to set up an IPv4 TCP session to exchange IPv4 routing information and a separate IPv6 TCP session to exchange IPv6 routing information between routers in different autonomous systems (in other words, when using external BGP or eBGP).

iBGP

However, for iBGP (internal BGP between the routers in the same AS), having one session for both is often beneficial. Unlike with eBGP (toward a router in another AS), in iBGP the next hop address isn't changed: it's communicated to the other routers within the AS as-is. As a result, there is no issue with exchanging IPv6 routes over an IPv4 TCP session for iBGP, so reusing the existing IPv4 session for this makes a lot of sense. Listing 4-34 does this, and more.

Listing 4-34. *IPv6 iBGP Routes over an IPv4 TCP Session*

```
!
router bgp 65500
 neighbor rrclients peer-group
 neighbor rrclients remote-as 65500
 neighbor 172.16.1.5 peer-group rrclients
 !
 address-family ipv4
 neighbor rrclients activate
 neighbor rrclients route-reflector-client
 neighbor 172.16.1.5 peer-group rrclients
 no synchronization
 network 192.0.2.0
 exit-address-family
 !
 address-family ipv6
 neighbor rrclients activate
 neighbor rrclients route-reflector-client
```

---

3. Some of these address families, such as E.164 phone numbers, aren't tied to a specific protocol, so RFC 2858 talks about "address families" rather than "protocol families." Protocols like IPv4 and IPv6 support both unicast and multicast routing, which are different members of the IPv4 and IPv6 address families.

```
neighbor 172.16.1.5 peer-group rrclients
neighbor 172.16.1.5 activate
network 2001:DB8:31::/48
no synchronization
exit-address-family
!
```

The neighbor 172.16.1.5 activate line shouldn't be necessary, as the peer group is already activated for IPv6 (although that doesn't initially happen when entering the neighbor rrclients activate line, but only when entering the next one). Still, what *should* happen and what *does* happen aren't always the same in these cases, and explicitly activating the neighbor doesn't do any harm in cases where it isn't needed.

The example defines a peer group named rrclients. Peer groups are an easy way to configure several peers with the same settings: every peer that is assigned to the group inherits all the settings. Additionally, peer groups make BGP processing more efficient because the router can generate a single update message and send it to all members of the group, rather than generate a separate update message for each individual neighbor. In this case, two settings are defined for rrclients: the AS number 65500 and the route-reflector-client setting. Because 65500 is the local AS number, all sessions toward BGP neighbors that have this AS number are iBGP sessions. Route reflection is a mechanism to make iBGP more scalable. Without it, every BGP router in the AS is required to have a BGP session with every other BGP router in the AS. With route reflection in effect, certain routers (the route reflectors) pass iBGP information on from one router to the next, which isn't allowed normally. The interesting part in this example is that the route-reflection-client setting is address family specific. So a router may be a route reflector client in IPv4 but not in IPv6, or the other way around. Obviously, such a setup is asking for trouble, so in this case, 172.16.1.5 is a reflector client for both protocols. (And by turning another router into a client, the local router automatically becomes a reflector for that client. The client itself gets no say in the matter.) Exchanging IPv6 routes over an IPv4 BGP TCP session results in routes such as the one in Listing 4-35.

Listing 4-35. *An iBGP Route*

```
bgpd-t# show bgp ipv6 2001:db8:31::/48
BGP routing table entry for 2001:db8:31::/48
Paths: (1 available, best #1, table Default-IP-Routing-Table)
  Not advertised to any peer
  65200
    3ffe:9500:3C:74::10 from 172.16.1.6 (10.0.0.10)
      Origin IGP, metric 0, localpref 100, valid, internal, best
      Last update: Tue Feb 15 00:02:42 2005
```

For some strange reason, the equivalents of the IPv4 show ip bgp ... commands aren't show ipv6 bgp ..., but simply show bgp .... Zebra accepts the command show bgp <prefix> for displaying BGP routing information, but Cisco wants this to be show bgp ipv6 <prefix>, which also works under Zebra. The commands for showing a BGP summary and showing the full BGP table are show bgp summary and show bgp, respectively. The commands show ip bgp neighbors and show bgp neighbors both show all neighbors on Zebra: the IPv4 ones as well as the IPv6 ones.

Anyway, the most interesting part in Listing 4-35 is the line that lists the next hop address (3ffe:9500:3C:74::10), the neighbor address for the TCP session (172.16.1.6) and finally the router identifier for the neighbor (10.0.0.10). Note that as in IPv4, it's necessary to run an internal routing protocol that propagates the next hop addresses throughout the network, or the BGP routers won't be able to forward packets according to iBGP routes. Running OSPFv3 and redistributing connected routes accomplishes this quite nicely. Running OSPFv2 and redistributing connected routes is also useful to allow the routers to find each other's IPv4 addresses so that the iBGP TCP sessions can be established.

■**Note** An address family is only activated for a BGP session when it's configured on the routers on both ends. Use the show ip bgp neighbor ... command to see the capabilities that the local router advertises to its neighbor and that the neighbor advertises to the local router.

Global and Link-Local Next Hop Addresses

Although this isn't apparent when looking at the BGP routing table, multiprotocol BGP actually employs two next hop addresses: a global scope address, which functions just as the IPv4 next hop address, and a link-local next hop address. The reason for this has to do with ICMP redirects, which are used to avoid unnecessary router hops. When a router receives a packet on an interface, and this packet is forwarded out of the same interface, either to its destination or to another router, the source could just as easily have sent this packet directly to the destination or router in question, as it's on the same subnet. The redirect message is used to tell the source about this so that subsequent packets skip the unnecessary hop. Because the IPv6 standards require ICMP messages to point to the link-local address of the next hop router, all routing protocols must exchange link-local addresses. (When the redirect points to the ultimate destination of the packet, it contains the destination address and not a link-local address.) This explains why routes have different next hop addresses in the BGP table than in the IPv6 routing table, as shown in Listing 4-36.

Listing 4-36. *Next Hop Addresses in the BGP and IPv6 Routing Tables*

```
Cisco#show bgp
BGP table version is 3, local router ID is 10.0.0.10
   Network          Next Hop          Metric LocPrf Weight Path
*> 2001:DB8:31::/48 3ffe:9500:3C:74::10
                                          0             0 9000 i
Cisco#show ipv6 route
IPv6 Routing Table - 17 entries
B   2001:DB8:31::/48 [20/0]
     via FE80::20A:95FF:FECD:987A, Ethernet0
```

If desired, the global and/or link-local next hop addresses can be changed in a route map, as shown in Listing 4-37.

Listing 4-37. *Changing Global and Link-Local Next Hop Addresses*

```
!
router bgp 65500
 neighbor 3ffe:9500:3C:74::10 remote-as 65200
 !
 address-family ipv6
 neighbor 3ffe:9500:3C:74::10 route-map setnexthop in
 exit-address-family
!
route-map setnexthop permit 10
 set ipv6 next-hop 2001:DB8:31:2::1 FE80::290:6902:EE02:E43E
!
```

The set ipv6 next-hop line in the route map first sets a global IPv6 address, followed by a link-local address. Although this configuration apparently sets both the global and link-local next hop addresses, it seems that only the global address is affected when the route map is applied to incoming BGP updates, as in the listing. When applying the route map to outbound BGP updates, the link-local address is also changed. Zebra takes a slightly different syntax for this, as shown in Listing 4-38.

Listing 4-38. *Changing Next Hop Addresses Under Zebra*

```
!
route-map setnexthop permit 10
 set ipv6 next-hop local fe80::290:6902:ee02:e43e
 set ipv6 next-hop global 2001:db8:31:2::1
!
```

Interdomain Routing Guidelines

Around the beginning of 2005, the IPv4 global routing table reached a size of 150,000 prefixes, even though there were fewer than 20,000 active ASes. (For IPv6, the numbers were 700 and 500, respectively, at that time.) During the past 15 years, there were several times that router hardware could only barely keep up with the growth of the global routing table. The reason for this state of affairs is manifold, with factors being:

- Lax ISP behavior: not bothering to aggregate several adjacent address blocks into one large one.

- Multihoming: end-user organizations wanting to connect to more than one ISP.

- Traffic engineering: advertising different routes with different properties makes it easier to influence the way traffic flows.

- IPv4 address conservation: Regional Internet Registries are frugal with IPv4 addresses, so people have to come back for more and end up with several nonadjacent small blocks.

The main approach to avoid these problems in IPv6 was to give out very large address blocks to ISPs in order to avoid fragmenting their IPv6 BGP announcements. So while a small

ISP may receive between a /21 and a /19 initially in IPv4, all ISPs get a /32 in IPv6. Even though an end-user gets a /48, no questions asked, in IPv6, a /32 serves some 65,000 customers. A /19 in IPv4 on the other hand, is enough to supply no more than some 8000 customers with just a single IPv4 address. Really large ISPs can even get initial IPv6 blocks that are bigger than a /32.

Unfortunately, there is no easy way to limit the number of prefixes in the global routing table due to multihoming. The IETF is currently working on ways to achieve multihoming benefits without the need to run BGP and inject a prefix into the global routing table, but it's slow going. In the mean time, there are no provisions for multihoming in IPv6. Only ISPs that plan on giving out IPv6 address space to at least 200 customers in two years and operators of critical Internet resources (think root nameservers) can obtain independent IPv6 address blocks. (See Chapters 2 and 11 for more details on obtaining address space.) Everyone else has to obtain addresses from their ISP and renumber when changing ISPs. However, there is considerable pressure to allow provider-independent (PI) address space in IPv6 so that end users can multihome and/or move from ISP to ISP while taking their address space with them.

A practical issue is how to filter. In IPv4, address blocks that are smaller than a /24 are filtered out routinely. So someone who wants to multihome or announce a prefix for some other reason, must at least obtain a /24. This requires fairly extensive documentation of a real-world need for so many addresses, which is a significant hurdle. In IPv6, on the other hand, anyone can get a /48, so if those aren't filtered out, the IPv6 global routing table will most likely become *very* large, much larger than the IPv4 table. A solution to this would be to give out address blocks that are larger than a /48 to people who want to multihome and/or want PI address space. However, then the question becomes: who deserves such a bigger block, and who doesn't?

If you would like to filter out /48s, be careful that several Regional Internet Registries (RIRs) give out /48 blocks to Internet exchanges so the routers of the IX members can interconnect by using independent address space. These prefixes can be filtered out without problems because they're only relevant to networks that connect to those Internet exchanges. However, ARIN, the American Registry for Internet Numbers, also gives out /48 for "critical Internet infrastructure," as explained on http://www.arin.net/reference/micro_allocations.html. These micro allocations currently come from the 2001:500::/30 block. Listing 4-39 implements a prefix length filter that takes micro allocations into consideration.

Listing 4-39. *Sanitizing the IPv6 Global Routing Table*

```
!
router bgp 65500
 neighbor 3ffe:9500:3C:74::10 remote-as 65200
 !
 address-family ipv6
 neighbor 3ffe:9500:3C:74::10 maximum-prefix 2500 80
 neighbor 3ffe:9500:3C:74::10 prefix-list sanitize in
 exit-address-family
!
ipv6 prefix-list sanitize seq 5 permit 2001:500::/30 le 48
ipv6 prefix-list sanitize seq 10 permit 2002::/16
ipv6 prefix-list sanitize seq 15 permit 2000::/3 le 32
ipv6 prefix-list sanitize seq 20 deny ::/0 le 128
!
```

The first line in the prefix list allows prefixes of 48 bits and shorter from the ARIN micro allocation block. The second line allows the 6to4 block. More specific prefixes from this block aren't supposed to leak into the global routing table, because this would import the entire IPv4 table into the IPv6 one. The third line permits prefixes of 32 bits and shorter in the address space currently set aside for global unicast use. In the beginning, ISPs received /35 address blocks, and some of them still announce this block, although those blocks have been upgraded to /32s that encompass the /35s. The filter removes these /35s. Implementations are supposed to treat all other address space, except that which has explicitly been given a different purpose, as global unicast space. However, it's unlikely that address space from outside 2000::/3 is legitimately going to find its way into the IPv6 BGP table any time soon. The last line filters out all prefixes of 128 bits or shorter in the entire IPv6 address space or, in one word: everything. The customary implicit deny at the end of any filter does the same, though.

■Warning New address space is put into use all the time. By the time you read this, the filters in the example may be out of date and filter out legitimate prefixes! Whenever you implement filters like this, you must check on a regular basis, like once a month, whether the filter is still valid. If you are unsure whether you can keep the filter up to date, *please* don't install them, as obtaining previously unused address space and not being able to use it because it's filtered all over the Net causes a lot of grief.

The IANA keeps a list of address space it has allocated to the Regional Internet Registries at `http://www.iana.org/assignments/ipv6-unicast-address-assignments`, and the RIRs keep full records of all allocations and assignments on their FTP servers.

The `maximum-prefix` line instructs the router to disable the BGP session when the number of IPv6 routes learned from the peer reaches 2500. A warning is logged when the number of prefixes increases beyond 80 percent of 2500. Although a maximum prefixes setting doesn't stop bad routing information from coming in, it does stop *too much* routing information from coming in. A sudden increase in the number of routes that a BGP neighbor sends is nearly always due to some problem, such as a neighboring AS leaking routes from an internal routing protocol into BGP.

It's possible to make this filter much stricter, for instance by only allowing the specific /16 blocks that are currently in use. However, there is little additional benefit in doing so, as someone who wants to inject malicious routes can easily do so in (for instance) the 2001::/16 block. Or an attacker could inject 250,000 /48s within 2001:500::/30 into BGP to make the router run out of memory, if there is no `maximum-prefix` setting in effect. A different approach to filtering is to generate filters that allow only known good routes from information in the routing registries. However, the required Routing Protocol Specification Language (RPSL) extensions were a long time in coming, and it's safe to assume that it will take some time before the routing registries are a good reflection of the IPv6 BGP routing that's going on in the real world.

The BGP TCP MD5 option that can be used to authenticate the TCP communication between BGP routers should be available in IPv6 the same way as it's available in IPv4. However, most Zebra routers don't support the option because it operates on the TCP level, which is inaccessible to the routing daemons. Kernel patches may be available, though. Some older IOS versions may also have trouble computing the MD5 hash correctly because the implementation of the option makes assumptions that are incorrect with IPv6.

Avoiding Tunnels

For a long time, running IPv6 meant connecting to the 6bone over a tunnel. As a matter of routine, everyone provided access to everyone else over such tunnels. These days, more and more networks support native IPv6, and the ones that don't generally have their tunneling aligned fairly closely with the IPv4 infrastructure, so as a rule, long distance tunnels between different organizations aren't necessary anymore. However, some of these tunnels remain in operation, and some networks still give away "free transit" by allowing traffic between two remote networks to pass through their network. This is unfortunate, because it's not uncommon for a long distance tunnel to be preferred over several native or short-range tunnel hops by routing protocols. BGP is especially bad in this area, because it mostly looks at the number of AS hops between a source and destination.

In practice, this means that sometimes two ISPs (most end-users don't get to do BGP) have a "shorter" tunneled path between them, as seen by BGP. In Figure 4-5, the native path from ISP1 to ISP4 has two additional hops, while the tunneled path over the remote ISP5 has only one intermediate hop. It's not unheard of for IPv6 packets between two places in Europe to be tunneled to Japan and back in situations like this.

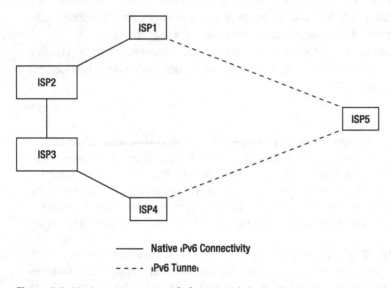

Figure 4-5. *Native versus tunneled connectivity in IPv6*

One way to avoid these problems is simply to not peer (exchange traffic) with these networks. However, if your upstream ISP does peer with them, you may still experience some of the adverse effects. Alternatively, you can use a BGP policy to assign a lower preference to networks that "over-tunnel." This is what Listing 4-40 does.

Listing 4-40. *Lowering the Preference for Tunneled Destinations*

```
!
router bgp 65500
 neighbor 2001:7f8:1::a506:3000:1 remote-as 64900
 neighbor 3ffe:9500:3C:74::10 remote-as 65200
!
 address-family ipv6
 neighbor 2001:7f8:1::a506:3000:1 activate
 neighbor 2001:7f8:1::a506:3000:1 route-map punish-tun in
 neighbor 3ffe:9500:3C:74::10 activate
 neighbor 3ffe:9500:3C:74::10 route-map punish-tun in
 neighbor 3ffe:9500:3C:74::10 route-map prepend2 out
!
ip as-path access-list 66 permit _64512_
ip as-path access-list 66 permit _64999_
!
route-map punish-tun permit 10
 match as-path 66
 set local-preference 66
!
route-map punish-tun permit 20
!
route-map prepend2 permit 10
 set as-path prepend 65500 65500
!
```

The configuration in the example has two neighbors. Both have the IPv6 address family activated, and for both, the route map punish-tun is applied to incoming BGP updates. This route map, listed near the end of the example, first passes all updates through the AS path filter 66, which matches any BGP route with AS 64512 or 64999 in the AS path. These are the AS numbers for networks that do too much tunneling. Then, if there was a match, the set clause of the route map comes into effect, and the local preference for the matching route is set to 66. Because all other routes have an empty local preference value, which equals 100, these routes are now only used if there is no alternative. All BGP updates that didn't match AS path access lists 66 end up at the route-map punish-tun permit 20 line, which doesn't implement any match or set conditions, so the routes that end up there are simply accepted into the BGP table without further changes.

Looking at Figure 4-5, we can imagine that ISP5 would be affected by this route map so that the route from ISP1 to ISP4 over ISP5 will have a local preference of 66, while the route over ISPs 2 and 3 has a default local preference. Because a higher local preference trumps a shorter AS path, packets from ISP1 now flow to ISP4 through ISP2 and ISP3.

ISP4 would have to implement a similar policy for packets to avoid the tunnels on the trip back. Just in case ISP4 doesn't do this, Listing 4-40 also applies the route map prepend2 on outgoing updates toward AS 65200, which is presumably a tunnel-happy AS. The prepend2 route map adds the local AS number 65500 two extra times to the AS path on outgoing updates. This makes paths through AS 65200 artificially longer, making it less likely to "attract" traffic at the expense of native connectivity.

Note BGP uses TCP port 179.

OSPFv3 and BGP for IPv6 on Juniper

So far, the only type of routers (except the one that you build yourself based on UNIX) we've discussed is Cisco. Cisco has a lot of advantages: it makes a lot of fine products, ranging from very small to very big. As a rule, you can learn your way around on a small model and then leverage what you've learned on a larger model. And even though the configuration statements are quaint at times, they're not too hard to follow. All this is very different with Juniper: its smallest models are medium-to-high range, and although its configuration mechanism has a lot going for it, it's hard to understand at first. This made me hesitant to explain IPv6 on Juniper. On the other hand, Juniper implements IPv6 very well, and, more importantly, fast. The Application Specific Integrated Circuit (ASIC) that powers Juniper routers fully supports IPv6, so IPv6 isn't a second-class citizen in Juniper-land.

Note Because of its additional complexity, it's impossible to even scratch the surface of the Juniper configuration syntax. You must be able to configure a Juniper router for IPv4 in order to understand the following listings.

Listing 4-41 shows the first part of a Juniper configuration where interface characteristics are defined.

Listing 4-41. *The "Interfaces" Part of a Juniper Configuration*

```
interfaces {
    ge-0/0/0 {
        vlan-tagging;
        unit 288 {
            vlan-id 288;
            family inet6 {
                address 2001:db8:31:288::/64 {
                    eui-64;
                }
            }
        }
    }
}
```

All this is business as usual, except that there is an "inet6" address family, which accepts an IPv6 address with the eui-64 keyword that indicates that the bottom 64 bits in the address should be copied from a MAC address. Listing 4-42 contains the routing options.

Listing 4-42. *The "Routing-options" Part of a Juniper Configuration*

```
routing-options {
    rib inet6.0 {
        static {
            route 2001:db8:31::/48 {
                discard;
                install;
                readvertise;
            }
            route 2001:db8:31:3000::/52 {
                next-hop 2001:db8:31:3::2;
                install;
            }
        }
    }
    router-id 192.0.2.7;
    autonomous-system 65500;
}
```

The rib inet6.0 on the second line is the standard IPv6 Routing Information Base, so this is where static IPv6 routes normally go. In this case, there is a static route for 2001:db8:31::/48 that discards all packets that it catches (similar to a route to the null0 interface on a Cisco router) and is readvertised into routing protocols. The second static route is for a large chunk of the /48 (a /52) and points to an address to which matching packets should be forwarded. Last but not least, there is a router ID, and the BGP AS number is defined. Listing 4-43 shows the "protocols" part of the configuration.

Listing 4-43. *The "Protocols" Part of a Juniper Configuration*

```
protocols {
    bgp {
        group ibgp {
            type internal;
            local-address 192.0.2.7;
            family inet {
                unicast;
            }
            family inet6 {
                unicast;
            }
            peer-as 65500;
            neighbor 192.0.2.18;
        }
```

```
        group bgp-v6 {
            type external;
            import bgp-v6-in;
            family inet6 {
                unicast;
            }
            export bgp-v6-out;
            neighbor 2001:7f8:1::a506:3000:1 {
                authentication-key "$9$5Fdsikekasi/97dj"; ## SECRET-DATA
                peer-as 64900;
            }
        }
    ospf3 {
        export redist-ospf3;
        area 0.0.0.0 {
            interface lo0.0;
            interface ge-0/2/0.288;
        }
    }
}
```

Under the BGP protocol, there are two groups, with a single neighbor each. The first group holds an iBGP neighbor with an IPv4 address, with both the inet and inet6 address families enabled, so routing information for both IPv4 and IPv6 will be exchanged with this neighbor. The bgp-v6 group holds an external neighbor that we talk to over IPv6. Unlike the iBGP neighbor, routing information to and from this one is filtered by using the bgp-v6-in and bgp-v6-out filters. The authentication-key holds the secret key for BGP TCP MD5 authentication. The router encrypts the key after it's entered for the first time to ward off "over the shoulder attacks," where someone reads the secret key from the screen.

The OSPFv3 configuration is *exactly* the same as an OSPFv2 configuration, save for the extra "3" and that any filters must work on IPv6 prefixes rather than IPv4 ones. Last but not least, Listing 4-44 contains the filters or "policy-options."

Listing 4-44. *The "Policy-options" Part of a Juniper Configuration*

```
policy-options {
    policy-statement import-v6 {
        term 1 {
            from {
                route-filter 2001:16F8::/32 orlonger;
            }
            then accept;
        }
        then reject;
    }
```

```
policy-statement bgp-v6-in {
    term 1 {
        from policy import-v6;
        then reject;
    }
    then {
        local-preference 300;
        accept;
    }
}
policy-statement bgp-v6-out {
    term 1 {
        from {
            route-filter 2001:db8:31::/48 exact;
        }
        then accept;
    }
    then reject;
}
policy-statement redist-ospf3 {
    term connected {
        from protocol direct;
        then accept;
    }
    term static {
        from protocol static;
        then accept;
    }
}
```

The first filter, import-v6, allows the local prefix 2001:db8:31::/48 or longer prefixes within this /48. However, this filter isn't used directly. Rather, it's called by the next one, bgp-v6-in. This filter rejects all packets that match 2001:db8:31::/48 or longer through import-v6 and then goes on to accept all other routes for further processing, assigning them a local preference value of 300 in the process. In this small example, the indirection through import-v6 doesn't make much sense, but in a real-world configuration, it does, because different BGP neighbors or groups are likely to have different filters, and having the same address range (or worse, ranges) in different filters doesn't make for easy configuration management.

The bgp-v6-out filter, on the other hand, isn't set up for future scalability and matches the local prefix directly. Unlike the incoming filter, which rejects our own prefix and any longer prefixes falling inside it, this one matches only the /48 and nothing else in order to avoid leaking more specifics.

The redist-ospf3 filter makes sure that IPv6 connected and static routes show up in OSPFv3.

Site-Local Addresses

In IPv4, it's common to use RFC 1918 private address ranges (10.0.0.0/8, 172.16.0.0/12, and 192.168.0.0/16) for internal communication. The idea was to take private addresses to the next level in IPv6 by introducing the "scope" mechanism. We've already discussed addresses with link-local scope. Because those are only valid on an individual subnet, they can be reused on other subnets without real problems. Site-local addresses are supposed to work in a similar vein: they are only used within an individual "site" so that other sites can reuse the same address range. But can router vendors make that a router that connects to two different sites, manages to keep packets from site A in site A, and packets from site B in site B, even though both sites use the same addresses? This would require hacks such as using different routing tables, depending on the interface a packet was received on. For link-local addresses, this isn't a problem, because packets with those addresses are never forwarded by a router: they flow directly from the source to the destination over the local link; so there is never any real ambiguity. Experience with RFC 1918 addresses has also uncovered other problems, such as packets with private addresses leaking into the global network, where they can't be traced back to the source (to fix the leak) because of their ambiguity. And, when two large organizations that both use private addresses merge, their addresses plans often clash, requiring inconvenient renumbering efforts.

Then there is the problem that the word "site" is ill defined: does it mean the entire network for an organization, possibly spanning multiple locations? The network for the part of an organization in one location? The "inside" network, the DMZ, or both? What happens when direct connectivity between two parts of a "site" breaks so packets have to travel off-site to reach the other part? A narrow interpretation of the word "site" doesn't provide the functionality that users require, while a broad interpretation leads to all kinds of implementation issues.

For all of these reasons, the IETF decided to deprecate the existing site-local specification in RFC 3879. Existing implementations and deployments may continue to use site-local addresses in the address range fec0::/10, but the special behavior associated with site-locals should be removed in future versions of router and host implementations.

Despite problems outlined in this section, site-local addressing has a number of legitimate uses that aren't easily transferred to other types of addresses. Two examples are networks that aren't connected to the Internet at all and networks that have only intermittent connectivity. For instance, an airplane would very likely connect to a network when it's at the terminal so that maintenance personnel can connect to the various on-board systems. When the plane is in the air, it will generally not have connectivity for these types of systems (even though there are some carriers that provide Internet connectivity to passengers during the flight).

To accommodate these needs, the IETF is in the process of defining a new type of site-local addresses: "unique local IPv6 unicast addresses." The idea is that this address type is still local, but it's also globally unique. This means that routers, hosts, and applications can treat them like regular global scope addresses.

Figure 4-6 shows the format of these addresses. The prefix is fc00::/7. The local bit indicates whether the global ID was randomly generated (L = 1) or registered through a registry (L = 0), which may be possible in the future. The 40-bit global ID is large enough to make accidental collisions rate, but they may still happen on occasion. A collision is the situation where two organizations pick the same unique local prefix.

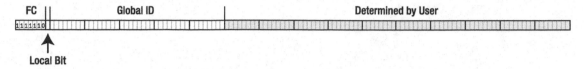

Figure 4-6. *The unique site local IPv6 unicast address format*

In IPv4, it's common practice that all hosts have private addresses that are translated into global addresses at the network border. Due to lack of NAT, this setup is hard to implement in IPv6: the alternative is to use proxies, but these aren't available for all protocols. An alternative is to give all hosts both private/local and public/global addresses. But unless hosts implement advanced source address selection (see Chapter 8), they may try to connect to a global destination address by using a local source address, which won't work. To avoid the reverse, where a host tries to contact a far away server by its local address, it's recommended to keep these addresses out of the DNS (they shouldn't appear in either AAAA or PTR records). Because, obviously, using the addresses means having them in the DNS, this effectively means the IETF is mandating the practice of "two-faced DNS," where a DNS server gives a different reply based on the address of the host performing the query.

CHAPTER 5

■ ■ ■

The DNS

"The author of the Iliad is either Homer or, if not Homer, somebody else of the same name."

—Aldous Huxley

For us humans, it's difficult and not very pleasant to work with IP addresses, especially with IPv6 addresses. Fortunately, the Domain Name System (DNS) allows us to work with much more user-friendly symbolic names most of the time.[1] Because the DNS translates from names to IP addresses for us (and the other way around), the DNS itself needs to be updated to support IPv6. Due to its distributed nature, making the Domain Name System IPv6-aware is much more complex than upgrading a single application. Later in this chapter, we'll look at the Berkeley Internet Name Domain (BIND) DNS server software, but before that, I'll provide a refresher on how the DNS works and the changes that were necessary (and the changes that were not so necessary) for IPv6. Figure 5-1 shows the interaction between different parts of the Domain Name System.

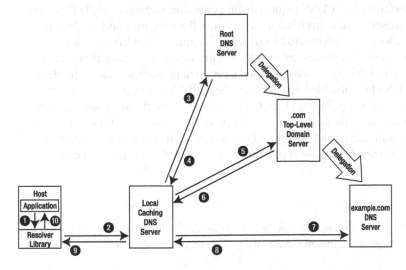

Figure 5-1. *Looking up information in the Domain Name System*

---

1. *DNS and BIND*, by Paul Albitz and Cricket Liu (O'Reilly & Associates), is an excellent guide to the subject. Unfortunately, the fourth edition was published in 2001, so it is outdated on the subject of IPv6 in the DNS.

When an application wants to communicate over the network, it takes the full name of the destination, such as www.example.com (this is often called the "fully qualified domain name," or FQDN),[2] and finds the matching IP address in the DNS. The application does this by calling on the resolver library. This is step 1 in Figure 5-1. The resolver library knows enough about the DNS protocol to be able to send a request for the required information to a "caching" or "recursive" DNS server using the DNS protocol (step 2). If the caching server just started and hasn't had the chance yet to live up to its name by caching the answers to previous requests in its memory, it will have no idea where to find the requested information. So it contacts one of the root DNS servers (step 3). The root servers don't know the address for www.example.com either, but they do have pointers to the DNS servers responsible for all "top-level domains" (TLDs), such as .com, so in step 4, the root server sends back pointers to the .com TLD nameservers. Information received from remote nameservers such as this is kept in the local cache if it was received from a server that's part of the authoritative delegation chain. The caching nameserver proceeds to contact one of the .com TLD servers and repeats the question about the address that goes with www.example.com in step 5. Like the root server, the TLD server doesn't know the answer, but it supplies pointers to the nameservers that are responsible for the example.com domain name in step 6. In step 7, the caching server once again asks for the address information for www.example.com, and this time the answer finally contains the requested information (step 8). The caching server can now send back a response to the resolver library in step 9, which in turn relays the information to the application (step 10). The application now has the information it needs to (for instance) set up a TCP connection to www.example.com.

Representing IPv6 Information in the DNS

Ignoring caching for a moment, every DNS request involves the root nameservers, TLD servers and the destination's nameserver, and often nameservers from the initiator's and/or destination's ISPs. Requiring all those nameservers to be upgraded to support IPv6 in order to be able to look up IPv6 addresses in the DNS would make it almost impossible to deploy IPv6. Fortunately, this isn't necessary. In 1995, RFC 1886 described a very straightforward way to publish IPv6 information in the DNS that provided an easy upgrade path. However, in 2000, a more ambitious way to do the same was published in RFC 2874. This new mechanism was partially implemented, but more detailed analysis and practical experience showed that it was perhaps a bit *too* ambitious, so around 2001, the IETF started moving away from the new method, and in 2003, RFC 1886 was reinstated for the most part but with one small, yet important change (RFC 3596).

Note All implementations of IPv6 reverse DNS lookups from before 2000 and many from before 2003 are outdated and may not work. If they work, they may not continue to do so for much longer.

---

2. Purists always type a period at the end of an FQDN, to indicate that it's an FQDN. This stops the resolver from thinking it needs to stick the local domain name to the end. In the example.com network, www.kame.net may mean www.kame.net.example.com or www.kame.net, but www.kame.net. is always www.kame.net.

RFC 1886: AAAA and ip6.int

In IPv4, addresses are stored in A (address) records, and the reverse mapping is done by creating a special domain name that consists of the values of the individual bytes in the address in reverse order, followed by in-addr.arpa. Looking up such a domain name results in a PTR (pointer) record containing the domain name associated with the address in question. See Listing 5-1.

Listing 5-1. *An IPv4 Address in the DNS*

```
www.example.com.       IN A   192.0.2.17
17.2.0.192.in-addr.arpa. IN PTR www.example.com.
```

As we'll see later in this chapter, these lines don't appear together in the DNS zone files.[3] The names end in a dot to indicate they are absolute addresses (FQDNs), so no additional domain names should be added. RFC 1886 sticks very close to the IPv4 way of doing things, as outlined in RFC 1035. IPv6 addresses are stored in AAAA ("quad A") records. The reverse mapping is done by taking the hexadecimal digits of the IPv6 address (all of them, including zeros that would normally be left out) in reverse order and adding ip6.int, as in Listing 5-2. When RFC was published in the mid-1990s, the .int level domain was the "infrastructure TLD" of choice, probably because at the time, it was the only truly international TLD; .com, .edu, .gov, .mil, .net, and .org were all still considered US-only, and .arpa was a relic from the by-then defunct ARPANET.

Listing 5-2. *An IPv6 Address in the DNS According to RFC 1886*

```
www.example.com. IN AAAA 2001:db8:1bff:c001::390
0.9.3.0.0.0.0.0.0.0.0.0.0.0.0.0.1.0.0.c.f.f.b.1.8.b.d.0.1.0.0.2.ip6.int. IN PTR ➡
www.example.com.
```

RFC 2874: A6, DNAME Bitlabels, and ip6.arpa

> **Note** These mechanisms aren't in use on the Internet at present, so skipping this section is of little consequence.

By the turn of the millennium, basic IPv6 features were well established, so the IETF's attention focused on more subtle issues and on problems that IPv6 *didn't* solve. The biggest problem that IPv6 doesn't solve is routing, as we saw in Chapter 4. One thing would make the routing situation much better: rapid renumbering. If renumbering were trivial, people would be more likely to use address space that can be aggregated by ISPs so the routing tables stay smaller.

---

3. A "zone" is a "the complete database for a particular 'pruned' subtree of the domain space" (RFC 1035). A zone file contains all the DNS records for a domain and any subdomains that aren't delegated to another zone.

The A6 Name-to-Address Mapping

The RFC 2874 approach to renumbering is as follows. Suppose you ask someone for his work phone number, and the answer is "1-512-555-5501." This would enable you to call your friend, as long as nothing changes. Would the answer have been "extension 501 at IBM Research in Austin, Texas," you'd still be able to call (with a little extra effort), even if the actual number didn't work anymore, for instance, because the Austin area code changed. The RFC 1886 AAAA method is similar to simply giving out the requested number. RFC 2874 is more like providing a path through the addressing hierarchy, not unlike giving out a phone number by providing an extension, organization, and city. Listing 5-3 shows what an A6 hierarchy looks like in the DNS.

Listing 5-3. A6 *Records in the DNS*

```
www         IN  A6  64  ::0000:0000:0000:0390  subnet-a
subnet-a    IN  A6  48  0000:0000:0000:c001::  prefix-isp1
subnet-a    IN  A6  48  0000:0000:0000:c001::  prefix-isp2
prefix-isp1 IN  A6  0   2001:0db8:1bff::
prefix-isp2 IN  A6  0   3ffe:9500:003c::
```

Unlike the previous examples, all domain names in Listing 5-3 are relative. Assuming they're in the example.com zone file, the nameserver will add .example.com after each name. Every A6 record provides part of the address and a pointer to where the rest of the address can be found. The first A6 record (the one for www) leaves 64 bits blank to be defined later and continues to provide the IPv6 address ::390 to fill in the 128 − 64 = 64 bits that it does specify. The address bits specified in the A6 record at hand are copied from their respective place in the listed address. The part of the address that isn't specified here must be set to zero in the address provided in the zone file. The name following the IPv6 address-like value in the A6 record points to the place in the DNS hierarchy where the rest of the address can be found; in this case, under the name subnet-a. And indeed, under subnet-a is another A6 record or, rather, two of them. They both set the bits between 48 and 64 to c001 (the rest of the bits is zero) and point to prefix-isp1 and prefix-isp2, respectively, for the rest of the address. Under these names, the remaining bits from 0 to 48 are provided, and a pointer to elsewhere isn't needed, as the address is now complete. Because subnet-a has two pointers for the upper 48 bits, the whole procedure results in two complete addresses: 2001:db8:1bff:c001::390 and 3ffe:9500:3c:c001::390.

With A6 records, updating the DNS when there is a renumbering event is a breeze: rather than having to change all addresses in all domains for a site, only a single A6 record has to be changed. For instance, if the 3ffe:9500:3c::/48 prefix in Listing 5-1 were to be changed to 2007:4580:73::/48, this would only require an update of the prefix-isp2 record, an all A6 records that point to it automatically reflect the new information.

The Bitlabel and DNAME Address-to-Name Mapping

In addition to the A6 method for forward mapping, RFC 2874 also specifies a new way to do the reverse mapping from address to name. It uses two mechanisms that were defined in RFCs 2672 and 2673, respectively: DNAME and bitlabels. The DNAME record is somewhat similar to the CNAME record. But rather than providing an alias for a single name, like CNAME does, DNAME can provide an alias for an entire branch in the DNS tree: a domain or subdomain. Listing 5-4 shows DNAME in action.

Listing 5-4. *The* DNAME *Record*

```
research.example.com            IN DNAME  r-and-d.example.com.
www.plastics.r-and-d.example.com.   IN A      192.0.2.1
www.biotech.r-and-d.example.com.    IN A      192.0.2.2
```

With this DNAME record in effect, all records and subdomains under r-and-d.example.com are also present under research.example.com. So looking up www.biotech.research.example.com has the same result as looking up www.biotech.r-and-d.example.com. To be backward compatible, the nameserver will "synthesize" a CNAME record for the requested information, along with providing the actual DNAME record. However, apparently some older resolver libraries wouldn't handle DNAME records properly.

The idea behind bitlabels (also sometimes called "binary labels") is that the traditional ...4.3.2.1.in-addr.arpa or ...e.f.f.3.ip6.int delegation mechanism is less than perfect because it only allows delegation on 8- or 4-bit boundaries, respectively. So conceptually, a bitlabel is an expression of a very long domain name with individual bits separated by periods. (In the domain name system, the data between two periods is called a "label.") However, within the DNS protocol, a bitlabel is expressed as a single chunk of binary data, regardless of the number of bits it contains, rather than a long list of individual ASCII labels. In the DNS zone files, bitlabels may be specified in either binary, octal, decimal, or hexadecimal, with an explicit value indicating the length in bits. Listing 5-5 shows several bitlabel representations of the same information.

Listing 5-5. *Bitlabels in Zone Files*

```
\[xf0d2b496785a3c1e]            IN PTR www.example.com.
\[b111100001101001010110100100101100111100001011010001110000011110] IN PTR ➡
www.example.com.
\[o7415126445474132170170/64]   IN PTR www.example.com.
\[120.90.60.30].\[240.210.180.150] IN PTR www.example.com.
```

The first bitlabel is in hexadecimal, as denoted by the initial x. The second is in binary (b) and the third is in octal (o). Because one octal digit represents three bits, the 22-character string would normally specify 66 bits. The explicit /64 indicates that only 64 bits should be considered part of the bitlabel. The last line is in dotted-quad decimal notation. Because this notation is limited to 32 bits, we need to concatenate two bitlabels to arrive at the full 64 bits. Note that although *within* each bitlabel the more natural most-significant-to-least-significant notation is used, the domain name system's least-significant-to-most-significant label ordering comes back when concatenating bitlabels. So if 64-bit decimal dotted-quads were allowed, that version of the bitlabel in Listing 5-5 would look like \[240.210.180.150.120.90.60.30]. Together, DNAME and bitlabels allow reverse mapping information to be delegated as in Listing 5-6.

Listing 5-6. *Reverse Mapping with* DNAME *and Bitlabels*

```
\[x20010DB81BFF/48].ip6.arpa.  IN  DNAME  rev.example.com.
\[xC001/16].rev.example.com    IN  DNAME  srvrs.rev.example.com.
\[x0000000000000390/64].srvrs.rev.example.com. IN PTR www.example.com.
www.example.com.         IN  AAAA   2001:db8:1bff:c001::390
```

In real life, the first line would have to be a delegation by an ISP, so it would be in the ISP's zone file. However, the other lines could all be in the same zone file (the one for example.com, for instance), or they can be spread out across several zones for added flexibility and ease of renumbering.

RFC 1886 vs. RFC 2874

When a host that implements RFC 1886 looks up an IPv6 address in the DNS, its resolver library will send out a request for AAAA records. Obviously, the last DNS server in the chain must understand what those are, but the intermediate DNS servers (see Figure 5-1) don't; they just see a resource record type that they don't recognize, but the format is familiar so they know how to process the information. Looking up reverse information in the ip6.int domain is even easier, because to a nameserver, there is nothing special about this domain.

The same is true for processing A6 records: this is all done by the resolver, so again, nameservers in the middle don't have to understand the A6 semantics. However, obtaining an address this way is a fairly involved process, especially if the pointers from one A6 record to the next jump between different servers in different domains, or when the chain of A6 pointers is very long. The fact that this procedure is supposed to be executed by the resolver and not the caching nameserver necessitated a substantial rewrite of the BIND software and the addition of a resolver daemon. The traditional resolver library wasn't really equipped to handle such complex tasks.

Although full support for the DNAME record requires changes to caching nameservers as well as to the nameservers hosting the DNAME information, the synthesis of additional CNAME records makes it possible for unmodified resolvers and caching nameservers to work with DNAME. Things are different for bitlabels, however. DNS queries that contain bitlabels need different processing from queries that only contain traditional ASCII labels, so in addition to the resolver and the nameserver holding the bitlabel information, *all* nameservers in between (the caching nameserver, root, and TLD servers) must understand bitlabels.

RFC 3596: AAAA and ip6.arpa

Not surprisingly, there was considerable debate in the IETF over the relative merits of the RFC 1886 and the RFC 2874 ways of doing things. Part of this discussion condensed in RFCs 3363 and 3364 in 2002. The main arguments in favor of RFC 2874 were flexibility and support for rapid renumbering. The arguments against using A6 records to store IPv6 addresses in the DNS, and bit-labels to perform reverse mapping, were that they add complexity and increase the time needed for looking up the information (if it's spread out over several nameservers). RFC 3364 also notes that A6 records are "optimized for write" even though "reading" DNS information is much more frequent than changing it. It's also hard to imagine a way in which the information in the DNS would remain in sync with the actual addresses used by hosts during a renumbering event.

Eventually, this led to the conclusion that AAAA records would be the best way to store IPv6 addresses in the DNS, and the nibble method the preferred way to do reverse mapping. A nibble is 4 bits, which refers to the ...1.0.0.2.ip6... reverse mapping technique. However, in the mean time, in 2001, the Internet Architecture Board (IAB) had published RFC 3172, stating a preference toward .arpa (now "Address and Routing Parameter Area") as an infrastructure top-level domain, complicating a complete return to RFC 1886 and ip6.int. Subsequently, use of ip6.int was "deprecated" in favor of ip6.arpa in Best Current Practice (BCP) document 49, also known as RFC 3152. All of this culminated in RFC 3596 (2003), which standardizes the use of AAAA records and the nibble method for reverse lookup under ip6.arpa.

The Current Situation

After such turmoil, it's not entirely surprising that implementations were all over the map. Although the A6 record never gained much traction, all the different ways of looking up reverse mapping can still be found "in the wild." A few rather old IPv6 resolver implementations use ip6.int exclusively. This isn't a huge deal, as many people set up both ip6.int and ip6.arpa (nibble method). And if the ip6.int lookup fails, it usually does so with a regular "no such domain" error message, which doesn't lead to additional problems. The IETF seems to want to get rid of ip6.int in a hurry, after which ip6.int-only implementations won't be able to resolve IPv6 addresses into domain names.

A larger group of implementations (including many versions of Red Hat Linux) looks for bit-labels under ip6.arpa first, and then falls back to the nibble method under ip6.int. Because there is no evidence of there ever having been any bitlabel delegations, the first step will always be unsuccessful, even if all the caching nameserver and the ip6.arpa TLD nameservers all understand bitlabel queries. This may not be the case, however, as most of the available DNS server software doesn't support bitlabels. BIND gained support for bitlabels around version 9, but it was removed again in version 9.3.

Then there are some resolver implementations that first look for ip6.arpa using the nibble method, and if they don't find anything, fall back on ip6.int, and finally, there are the implementations that only look for ip6.arpa. A similar spectrum of behavior is present in the DNS utilities dig, host, and nslookup that are part of the BIND distribution. Because these contain their own resolver code, their behavior may or may not match that of the rest of the system.

IPV6 AND THE ROOT SERVERS

For nameservers to resolve information over IPv6, it's necessary that the root nameservers gain IPv6 support. Nameservers find the root DNS server addresses in a local "hints" file, so it would appear that providing the roots with IPv6 connectivity and updating the hints file would do the trick. Unfortunately, there are some complications. Because hints files tend to get out of date, the first thing a nameserver does upon startup is ask one of the nameservers listed in the hints file for the current list of root nameservers. So, for nameservers to be able to communicate with the root nameservers over IPv6, the answer to this initial query must contain IPv6 addresses for at least a subset of all root servers.

In theory, it's fairly trivial to add IPv6 addresses for the root nameservers as "glue" records in the root zone. The problem is that the original DNS specifications only allow for 512 byte DNS messages over UDP. For the current list of 13 root servers, the initial response message is 436 bytes (and that's after "label compression" to avoid repeating the same domain name for different servers), so there is no room to add IPv6 addresses for all root servers without potentially going over the limit. When that happens, some addresses must be dropped from the response, which often means the request must be repeated over TCP. Because many people are unaware that regular DNS queries and not just zone transfers can happen over TCP, this is often filtered in firewalls. RFC 2671 adds support for larger DNS messages through the "EDNS0" mechanism, but a sizeable minority of all nameservers on the Internet don't support EDNS0.

Since mid-2004, TLD registries may have IPv6 addresses included in the root zone as glue records, and some TLDs allow end users to register IPv6 nameserver addresses for their domains. Many of the root nameservers are already reachable over IPv6 (see http://www.root-servers.org/). ICANN and the root server operators are proceeding very cautiously, but addition of IPv6 glue records to the root zone is expected in the not too distant future.

Installing and Configuring BIND

On most UNIX-like systems there is no need to install BIND, as there is generally a BIND 9.x (often 9.2.x) included with the system. (FreeBSD 4.x comes with a recent release of BIND 8.x, but BIND 9 is available in the ports collection.) BIND consists of a number of core programs and supporting utilities. The main program is the named binary. This is the actual nameserver daemon.

■Note Invoke named -v to determine the BIND version installed on the system. You can generally find out the BIND version of a remote nameserver by asking for the TXT record in class "chaos" for the domain name version.bind: host -c chaos -t txt version.bind <nameserver name/address>.

Installing BIND

Different versions of BIND are available from the Internet Systems Consortium (ISC, formerly Internet Software Consortium) at http://www.isc.org/sw/bind/. For full IPv6 support, including IPv6 transport (answering queries received over IPv6), you should choose one of the 9.x versions; 9.2.x for bitlabel and A6 support. However, all the latest releases of currently maintained versions (including 4.9.x) support AAAA records, as do all other major DNS server implementations. A binary distribution of BIND is available for Windows, which runs on Windows NT, 2000, XP, and 2003. This distribution doesn't support IPv6 transport yet. If you want to install BIND on a Windows machine anyway, read the readme1st.txt document carefully. Obviously, the locations of the files discussed below will be different, but otherwise, BIND under Windows is pretty much the same as BIND under a UNIX-like operating system.

Should you wish to install a different version of BIND than the one that came with your Linux or FreeBSD system,[4] just download the source and go through the customary ./configure, make, make install sequence per the instructions in the README file. Execute the configure script with the argument -h to list available options. Getting BIND to compile under MacOS requires advanced UNIX hacking skills: BIND doesn't get along very well with the changes that Apple made to the UNIX/FreeBSD system core.

Starting BIND at Boot Time

Under Red Hat Linux, there is already a startup script for named, but it's not activated by default. This can be done by issuing (as root) the chkconfig named on command to create the necessary symbolic links to the /etc/init.d/named script. Unsurprisingly, chkconfig named off removes the links and stops named from being initiated at system startup. chkconfig --list shows which startup scripts will be executed when changing run levels.

Under FreeBSD, starting named at boot time is done by adding two lines to /etc/rc.conf, as shown in Listing 5-7. Obviously, it helps if the named daemon is indeed located in /usr/sbin/.

---

4. If you're upgrading from a 4.x version of BIND, install an 8.x version first, as the 8.x distribution contains tools to convert 4.x configuration files to the format used by BIND 8.x and later.

Listing 5-7. *Enabling* named *in* /etc/rc.conf *Under FreeBSD*

```
named_program="/usr/sbin/named"
named_enable="YES"
```

Configuring BIND

All of BIND's extensive configuration options are described in the BIND Administrator Reference Manual that comes with the source or binary distribution. BIND isn't hard to run: just typing named starts the daemon. Sending named the HUP signal will make it reload its configuration and zone files. Because named needs access to TCP and UDP port 53, it must be run (at least initially) as root. Sending the HUP signal must be done under the same user as the one named runs under (or as root), which is often inconvenient. An alternate method to control the nameserver is with the remote name daemon control program rndc. rndc connects to named over TCP, so the command can also be used to control remote nameservers, as the name suggests. By default, named listens for incoming connections from rndc on port 953 on the IPv4 and IPv6 localhost addresses only, but this can be changed with the controls configuration command in the named configuration file. rndc expects a configuration file in /etc/rndc.conf, but it's much easier just to execute rndc-confgen -a to create an /etc/rndc.key file, which both rndc and named will then use to authenticate the communication between them.

The nameserver files are often stored in /var/named, but there is no particular reason to adhere to this convention. The named directory and other files must be readable and writable as appropriate for the user that named ends up running under. Because named drops most special root privileges, including the ability to access other user's files, when it runs as root, the files must be accessible to the actual user root itself in this case. The named directory must contain a named.root file, which guides named toward the root servers at startup. This file doesn't change often,[5] and as long as there is still a single correct root server address in it, named will be able to get an up-to-date list of root server addresses from that server. However, if your version is older than January 29, 2004, you may want to download the latest version from ftp://ftp.internic.net/domain/named.root or http://www.iana.org/popular.htm. For an IPv6-only nameserver to be able to reach the root servers, a new named.root needs to be installed when AAAA records for the root servers are added to the root zone.

The location of the named directory and the named.root file must be listed in named's configuration file. Listing 5-8 shows a basic named.conf file.

Listing 5-8. *The* /etc/named.conf *File*

```
options {
  directory "/var/named";
  allow-recursion { 192.0.2.0/24; 2001:db8:1bff::/48; };
  listen-on { 192.0.2.106; }
  listen-on-v6 { any; };
```

---

5. MacOS X Panther comes with a named.root (under the name "named.ca") from 1997, but only two root nameservers have changed addresses between the 1997 and 2004 versions.

```
# forward first;
# forwarders { 192.0.2.53; };
/* C-style comment */
// C++-style comment
};

zone "." {
  type hint;
  file "named.root";
};

zone "0.0.127.IN-ADDR.ARPA" {
  type master;
  file "localhost.rev";
};

zone "example.com" {
  type slave;
  file "example.com";
  masters { 192.0.2.53; };
};

zone "0.0.0.0.f.f.b.1.8.b.d.0.1.0.0.2.ip6.arpa."
  {
    type master;
    file "db.2001:db8:1bff:0";
  };
```

The file starts with an `options` directive, followed by several options between braces. Semicolons terminate statements or items in a list. The first option specifies the directory where named looks for files. The `allow-recursion` option defines for which clients named will perform recursive queries. In this case, it's clients with addresses in prefixes `192.0.2.0/24` and `2001:db8:1bff::/48`. Although there is no direct harm in allowing recursive queries for the whole Internet, and it allows for easier debugging, it can cost extra bandwidth, processing overhead and memory if the rest of the Internet starts using your server en masse. Many of the security problems found in BIND over the years could only be exploited by people for whom the server would do recursive queries. If you want to limit certain things to localhost-only, be aware that the keyword `localhost` only means the IPv4 localhost address in the named.conf file. The IPv6 localhost address must be listed explicitly as `::1`, if desired.

The `listen-on-v6` option directs named to listen for queries on IPv6 TCP and UDP sockets. With BIND 9.2 and earlier, `listen-on-v6` only takes "any" or "none" as arguments. So either the server will listen for incoming queries on all IPv6 addresses, or it won't listen on IPv6 at all. The default is to not listen on IPv6 addresses. As of BIND 9.3, you can have named listen on specific IPv6 addresses.

The next two lines are commented out. In addition to these shell-style comments, named also accepts C and C++ style comments, but it doesn't accept the semicolon as the start of a comment, like in a zone file. The two initial commented-out lines would have instructed the server to forward all its queries to the nameserver on address 192.0.2.53 and only try to resolve the query on its own if the specified server doesn't reply. After the comments, the closing brace ends the options section. Next, there are four zone specifications:

1. The "dot" zone (the root) is a "hints" zone and points to the named.root file.

2. The 0.0.127.in-addr.arpa zone is the reverse zone for the localhost address, and, being a primary zone, authoritative information is present in the localhost.rev file.

3. The example.com zone is a slave zone, and authoritative data is periodically transferred from the nameserver at address 192.0.2.53 and stored in the example.com file.

4. The last zone is a nibble-style ip6.arpa zone for 2001:db8:1bff::/48.

BIND 9.2 supports an allow-v6-synthesis option, which will take A6 records and bitlabel reverse mapping information and turn those into AAAA records and nibble-style ip6.int reverse mapping information. This option was introduced to ease the transition from RFC 1886 to RFC 2874, but now that RFC 2874 has fallen out of grace, the option has been removed again from BIND 9.3. The argument to this option is a list of addresses for which this synthesis is performed. Synthesis is only performed for recursive queries.

BIND 9.3 removes support for bitlabels. Zone files with bitlabel definitions are rejected. Version 9.3 still supports A6 records to some degree; those may be present in zone files and will be included in responses when appropriate. However, unlike BIND 9.2, BIND 9.3 never uses A6 records to find IPv6 address for other servers when following a delegation chain. New in BIND 9.3 is the dual-stack-servers option, which takes one or more names or addresses as its argument. When an IPv4-only named can't resolve a query because it needs IPv6 connectivity, or an IPv6-only named because it needs IPv4-connectivity, it will consult the server listed under dual-stack-servers. This server is supposed to have dual stack IPv4+IPv6 connectivity, so it should be able to perform all possible queries. This option helps BIND deal with a fragmented namespace.

NAMESPACE FRAGMENTATION

If a domain is served by nameservers that only have IPv6 addresses, names under that domain can't be resolved by nameservers that only have IPv4 connectivity. Conversely, IPv6-only nameservers can't resolve names that are only served by IPv4 nameservers. The situation where the domain namespace looks different depending on the IP version used can lead to problems. For instance, suppose a mailserver is only reachable over IPv6, and the nameserver pointing to this mailserver is also only reachable over IPv6. Someone in the IPv4-world will never be able to deliver mail to this server, but worse, they wouldn't even be able to see that the (sub-) domain in question exists in the first place. So, rather than sending back a "message couldn't be delivered" error, the mailserver sends back "domain doesn't exist," which is much more destructive, especially when the lack of connectivity for an IP version is only temporary.

For this reason, it is *highly* recommended that, for the foreseeable future, all DNS zones be served by at least one nameserver (preferably two) with an IPv4 address, even if the zone just contains IPv6-only information.

Choosing an Address for Your Nameserver

Specifying nameservers by name doesn't usually work: if we knew which addresses went with which names, we wouldn't have to consult a nameserver in the first place. So nameserver addresses tend to find their way to lots of different places:

- The address for a caching nameserver will be in lots of /etc/resolv.conf files (or the equivalent on other operating systems).

- The address for primary and secondary DNS servers for a domain will be listed in the TLD zone for that domain.

- The address for a primary DNS server will be in the named.conf of secondary servers.

- Often, the address for secondary DNS servers for local primary zones will be listed as addresses the server will accept zone transfers from.

All of this means that it's a good idea if nameserver addresses are as stable as they can be, and it doesn't hurt if they're easy to remember, either. So using EUI-64-derived IPv6 addresses for nameservers isn't the best idea, as the address will change whenever a network interface card is replaced or the DNS service is moved to another server. So a manually specified address is the best choice. Additionally, it's not a bad idea to put this address in a /64 of its own. This way, it's easy to move the DNS address around the network. It's helpful to use the transfer-source-v6 and notify-source-v6 options to set the source address for outgoing zone transfer requests to the appropriate address.

Adding IPv6 Information to Zone Files

Before you fire up your favorite text editor and start adding AAAA records to all your zone files, you should first consider the implications. When a host's IPv6 address is listed in the DNS, IPv6-capable applications on other IPv6-capable hosts will generally prefer to connect over IPv6 rather than IPv4. When connecting over IPv6 doesn't work, the application may or may not fall back on IPv4. Unfortunately, IPv6 connectivity is still often slower and less reliable than IPv4 connectivity. On the other hand, the only people who'll suffer when IPv6 performance is worse than IPv4 performance are those who enabled IPv6 on their end in the first place, so there is no need to be overly conservative. In most situations, there shouldn't be too many problems advertising an IPv6 address in the DNS, but for certain critical services, it can be better to provide the service over IPv6 under a different name. This is especially true if the applications used to access the service don't automatically fall back on IPv4, or when the time-out when this happens is unacceptable. It never hurts to have the service available under a different name that only has an IPv4 address. For file downloads over HTTP or FTP, it's a good idea to explicitly list IPv4 and IPv6 addresses, so people can choose, as file transfer is one of the applications that is most vulnerable to bandwidth limitations.

When adding AAAA records for popular services to your DNS zone, make sure that you can handle the additional IPv6 traffic. For services that are mostly used over the Internet, the amount of IPv6 traffic relative to IPv4 traffic isn't likely to be a problem. However, if you're upgrading an internal network, it's possible that all the internal hosts that now have IPv6 connectivity connect to the servers that now have an AAAA record over IPv6, effectively moving *all* traffic for the application in question from IPv4 to IPv6 over night. Most routers can handle IPv4 and IPv6 equally well, but some can't. For instance, when Cisco rolled out IPv6 on its large Cisco 12000 routers, IPv6 forwarding was done on the CPU on the linecard. Because those linecards had special IPv4 forwarding hardware on board, the CPUs on these linecards weren't designed to do forwarding at line rate. This meant that a Gigabit Ethernet linecard could handle 1000 Mbps IPv4 traffic, but only some 100 Mbps of IPv6 traffic (or 900 Mbps IPv4 traffic plus 100 Mbps IPv6 traffic). Newer linecards also have IPv6 hardware support so they can handle IPv6 at line rate, but you may still encounter hardware that doesn't handle IPv6 at the same speeds as IPv4. On Cisco routers with "smart" linecards, the linecard that receives a packet is the one that must do the processing required to forward the packet, and the capabilities of the outgoing card are less of an issue. Be sure to do your homework before buying new routers or before making changes to your network that may create a lot of IPv6 traffic.

If the existing servers can't handle IPv6, it may be necessary to set up a different server or cluster of servers to provide an existing service over IPv6. Then, you point one or more A records to the IPv4 server or servers, and one or more AAAA records to the IPv6 server or servers. However, be careful that you use *service* names and not *machine* names when you do this. So if the service name www.example.com points to the machine zeus.example.com, which provides the IPv4 WWW service, you should give the new IPv6 WWW server its own name, and not add an AAAA record to zeus.example.com. That way, you won't end up on poseidon.example.com when you type ssh zeus.example.com because SSH prefers IPv6.

AAAA Records

Listing 5-9 shows a zone file with AAAA records used differently for different services.

Listing 5-9. *A Zone with AAAA Records*

```
;   20041215    IvB created
;   20050209    IvB added AAAA records

$TTL 86400
```

```
@   IN  SOA ns1.example.com. root.example.com. (
                2005020900      ; Serial
                28800           ; Refresh (8 hours)
                7200            ; Retry (2 hours)
                604800          ; Expire (7 days)
                86400 )         ; Minimum (1 day)

            IN  NS      ns1.example.com.
            IN  NS      ns2.beispiel.de.

            IN  MX      100 smtp.example.com.
            IN  MX      200 smtp.ipv4.example.com.

            IN  A       192.0.2.80
            IN  AAAA    2001:db8:31:1:201:2ff:fe29:2640

ns1         IN  A       192.0.2.80
            IN  AAAA    2001:db8:31:53::53
            IN  A6      0 2001:db8:31:53::53

www         IN  A       192.0.2.80
www         IN  AAAA    2001:db8:31:1:201:2ff:fe29:2640
www.ipv4    IN  A       192.0.2.80
www.ipv6    IN  AAAA    2001:db8:31:1:201:2ff:fe29:2640

smtp        IN  A       192.0.2.25
smtp        IN  AAAA    2001:db8:31:1:20a:95ff:fecd:987a
smtp.ipv4   IN  A       192.0.2.25

pop         IN  A       192.0.2.25
popv4v6     IN  A       192.0.2.25
popv4v6     IN  AAAA    2001:db8:31:1:20a:95ff:fecd:987a
```

The file starts with two lines of comments. The $TTL line defines a default time to live value of 86400 seconds (one day), so all records that don't have their TTL set explicitly are cached for 24 hours. The next line starts with an at sign, which means that the record that follows relates to the zone itself rather than a name under that zone. The "start of authority" (SOA) record first lists the name for the primary nameserver for this zone (ns1.example.com) and a contact email address with the at sign replaced by a period (the email address root@example.com). The SOA record continues on the next five lines until the closing parenthesis. The first of those lines contains the serial number, which must be increased whenever a zone file is changed. It's customary to use a YYYYMMDDNN (year, month, day, number) format, where NN is set to zero when the first change on a certain day happens and increased by one on subsequent changes. The other lines define some timers that are best left unchanged.

There is no name in front of the NS records that follow, which means that they apply to the same name as did the previous record, which in this case is the domain itself. The primary nameserver for this domain is listed first, although ordering has no meaning within a zone file. Next are the MX records, which define where the mail for this domain should go to. The value preceding the mailserver names indicates which mailserver is preferred. In this case, smtp.example.com is preferred over smtp.ipv4.example.com because it has a lower preference value. Both names point to the same IPv4 address, but smtp also has an IPv6 address. Should a remote mailserver have trouble with smtp.example.com, it will automatically fall back on smtp.ipv4.example.com. The next two lines supply A and AAAA records for the domain itself. These are useful when someone tries to connect to the domain itself, for instance, with the URL http://example.com/.

The next three lines define the addresses for ns1.example.com. Even though regular applications don't look for A6 records, BIND versions 9.x prior to 9.3 (which are still in wide use) do, so supplying the IPv6 address of the nameserver in this format could speed things up a bit. The AAAA record is more important because it's the official way to publish an IPv6 address.

The www name has both an IPv4 and an IPv6 address and is supplemented by IPv4- and IPv6-only versions (www.ipv4 and www.ipv6, respectively). Having an IPv6-only name is useful for quick IPv6 reachability tests: if the page loads, IPv6 is enabled and it works. If it doesn't, IPv6 either isn't enabled, or there is no connectivity. The addresses for the smtp and smtp.ipv4 names reflect the earlier discussion. Finally, because the POP service is a critical one, and it's difficult for email users to temporarily change the address for their POP server when there is an IPv6 connectivity problem, the name corresponding to this service only has an IPv4 address. However, there is an alternate name popv4v6 with both an IPv4 and an IPv6 address for users who prefer to use IPv6 when available, while maintaining the ability to fall back to IPv4.

Before the new domain can be used, it must be added to the named.conf file as in Listing 5-8. It's a good idea to check the syntax of the zone file and the configuration file before reloading the nameserver, like in Listing 5-10.

Listing 5-10. *Checking a Zone and Configuration Files and Reloading* named

```
# named-checkzone example.com /var/named/example.com
zone example.com/IN: loaded serial 2005020900
OK
# named-checkconf
# rndc reload
```

Reverse Mapping

The reverse mapping zones are by and large the same as regular zones, except that they contain only PTR records, except for the initial SOA and NS records. However, the nibble format is somewhat abrasive. The easiest way to turn IPv6 addresses into nibble format is by using the host command to look up the addresses in question. host will then echo back the nibble format query that it performs, which can then be copied and pasted into the zone file. Listing 5-11 shows the host command and Listing 5-12 the resulting reverse zone file.

Listing 5-11. *The* host *Command*

```
host 2001:db8:31:1:201:2ff:fe29:2640
Host 0.4.6.2.9.2.e.f.f.f.2.0.1.0.2.0.1.0.0.0.1.3.0.0.8.b.d.0.1.0.0.2.ip6.arpa not ➥
found: 3(NXDOMAIN)
```

If the host command tries to perform a bitlabel query, the program came with a BIND version 9.x prior to 9.3. Use host -n instead, and it will do an ip6.int query.

Listing 5-12. *A Reverse Zone*

```
;   20050209   IvB     created

$TTL 86400

@  IN  SOA ns1.example.com. root.example.com. ( 2005020900 28800 7200 604800 ➥
86400 )

            IN  NS      ns1.example.com.
            IN  NS      ns2.beispiel.de.

$ORIGIN 3.5.0.0.1.3.0.0.8.b.d.0.1.0.0.2.ip6.arpa.
; ns1       IN  AAAA    2001:db8:31:53::53
3.5.0.0.0.0.0.0.0.0.0.0.0.0.0.0  IN  PTR     ns1.example.com.

$ORIGIN 1.0.0.0.1.3.0.0.8.b.d.0.1.0.0.2.ip6.arpa.
; www       IN  AAAA    2001:db8:31:1:201:2ff:fe29:2640
0.4.6.2.9.2.e.f.f.f.2.0.1.0.2.0  IN  PTR     www.example.com.

; smtp      IN  AAAA    2001:db8:31:1:20a:95ff:fecd:987a
a.7.8.9.d.c.e.f.f.f.5.9.a.0.2.0  IN  PTR     smtp.example.com.

$ORIGIN 1.3.0.0.8.b.d.0.1.0.0.2.ip6.arpa.
0.0.2.c     IN  NS      ns.research.example.com.
```

The $ORIGIN directive specifies which location in the DNS hierarchy the names that follow are relative to. It's easiest to specify the top 64 address bits in a $ORIGIN line and then specify the remaining 64 bits on each individual line. This makes for one $ORIGIN per subnet and keeps the lines from becoming overly long. It can also be useful to keep the $ORIGIN statements out of the zone file and let all names in the file be relative, so the same zone file can be used for both the ip6.arpa and ip6.int zones.

This file holds the zone for prefix 2001:db8:31::/48, which corresponds to the 1.3.0.0.8.b.d.0.1.0.0.2.ip6.arpa zone. Information for two /64s under this /48 is available in this zone file itself, but 2001:db8:31:c200::/64 is delegated to the nameserver ns.research.example.com in the last line.

■**Note** Remember that there are 32 nibbles in an IPv6 address, so there should be 32 hexadecimal digits separated by dots in a full PTR record, 16 in a /64, and 12 in a /48 $ORIGIN, respectively.

RFC 1886 and 2874 Reverse Mapping Hacks

Some resolver libraries fail in ugly ways because the bitlabel ip6.arpa information that they're looking for doesn't exist. To avoid these problems, you may want to set up fake reverse mapping information for them. This is done in Listings 5-13 (the bitlabel zone) and 5-14 (the relevant part from the named.conf).

Listing 5-13. *Fake RFC 2874 Reverse Mapping*

```
$TTL 86400

@   IN  SOA ns1.example.com. root.example.com. ( 2005020900 28800 7200 604800 ➡
86400 )
                    IN  NS      ns1.example.com.

*.\[x2/3].ip6.arpa. IN  PTR     bit.label.ip6.arpa.

\[x20010db800310001020a95fffecd987a/128].ip6.arpa. IN CNAME a.7.8.9.d.c.e.f.f.f.5. ➡
9.a.0.2.0.1.0.0.0.1.3.0.0.8.b.d.0.1.0.0.2.ip6.arpa.
```

Listing 5-14. *Fake RFC 1886 and 2874 Zones in named.conf*

```
zone "\[x2/3].ip6.arpa." {
  type master;
  file "bitlabel.ip6.arpa";
};

zone "ip6.int." {
  type master;
  file "ip6.int";
};
```

The *.\[x2/3].ip6.arpa. is a wildcard that matches all domains (including bitlabels) under the three-bit bitlabel for 2000::/3, the IPv6 global unicast address space. Using 2000::/3 rather than ::/0 is a bit of a hack, but it avoids conflicts with possible real delegations directly under ip6.arpa, because the ::/0 bitlabel delegation would also have to be directly under ip6.arpa. Because the bitlabel space isn't delegated, there is no risk of this there. The other bit-label at the end of the zone file matches only a single address and redirects the bitlabel version of this address to the nibble version with a CNAME record. This is useful to have the actual reverse mapping information show up for a limited set of addresses (which must all be listed individually). The wildcard record matches all addresses but has the disadvantage that the same reverse mapping information (bit.label.ip6.arpa in this case) is returned for all possible IPv6 addresses, except the ones that have an individual listing.

Listing 5-14 also has a delegation for the ip6.int domain, which can be useful when the real ip6.int zone is taken out of commission. The DNAME record in Listing 5-15 can then be used to redirect ip6.int queries to ip6.arpa. But as long as ip6.int is still active, it's better to do nothing and have the real ip6.int information show up.

Listing 5-15. *Remapping* ip6.int *to* ip6.arpa *Using a* DNAME *Record*

```
$TTL 86400

@   IN  SOA ns1.example.com. root.example.com. ( 2005020900 28800 7200 604800 ➥
86400 )
        IN  NS      ns1.example.com.

@       IN  DNAME   ip6.arpa.
```

Dynamic DNS Updates

RFC 2136 introduced the concept of "dynamic DNS updates." This mechanism allows a client to ask an authoritative server to add information to a zone or delete existing information from the zone. The dynamic update mechanism allows hosts that receive a new address through DHCP or stateless autoconfiguration to update their own DNS records so they remain reachable by their name, despite address changes. However, this capability isn't yet widely implemented in host operating systems, at least not for IPv6.

For obvious reasons, it's not possible for just any client to modify any and all zones. BIND 9.x accepts a zone file configuration option allow-update that lists who may update the zone. The list of authorized users may be in the form of IP address ranges, or it may specify one or more keys that protect the updates. See the BIND documentation for more information. When a zone is set up for dynamic updates, named takes control of the zone file and it's no longer possible to edit the file without first shutting down the named daemon.

CHAPTER 6

■ ■ ■

Applications

"I set up my new computer and turned it on. It now displays C:\> and a small blinking line. What should I do now?"

—Anonymous help desk caller, 1994

Ideally, it shouldn't matter to an application whether it runs over IPv4 or IPv6. Unfortunately, for many applications, it does matter. There are two possible reasons for this. Some of the Application Programmer Interfaces (APIs) that applications use to interact with the network had to be changed to support IPv6. Another group of applications needs to look more closely at IP addresses. For instance, some applications use access restrictions based on the IP address. Other applications, such as peer-to-peer applications, require hosts to refer to either them-selves, their communication partner, or a third party. Often the size of an IPv4 address is hard coded in the communication protocol, so the protocol must be changed and applications must be updated before IPv6 can be used. Despite these difficulties, lots of applications run over IPv6, but in many instances, this isn't readily apparent. Often, an application's IPv6 prowess is only advertised in a throwaway line in the release notes, if at all.

After looking at API issues, I will focus in this chapter on IPv6-enabled applications. It's impossible to discuss them all, or even discuss examples of each type of application, so if a specific application or application type isn't mentioned, this doesn't mean there is no IPv6-enabled version. This is especially true for open source software, because even if the primary developers didn't include IPv6 support, there is often an IPv6 patch available elsewhere. The purpose of this chapter is merely to provide some examples of popular software or protocols that are compatible with IPv6.

API Issues

Modern operating systems and programming languages come with a wealth of APIs and built-in functions and frameworks, so when an application programmer wants her application to communicate over the network, there are often many ways in which she can add this func-tionality. The possibilities range from opening an URL to transmitting a handcrafted packet over a network interface. However, a very large (and heavily used) part of all network-related APIs consists of variations of the BSD socket API that first appeared in the 1983 release of 4.2BSD UNIX.

The socket API doesn't support setting up TCP sessions toward hostnames directly, so applications need to convert an ASCII name to an IP address in binary form. Under UNIX, it turned out to be impossible to change those binary IP address representations so they could contain an IPv6 address without breaking existing programs. For this reason, and because of new features in IPv6, such as the flow label and address scoping, the IETF decided create new socket API calls to support IPv6 rather than modify the existing ones (RFC 3493). Note that the changes are relatively minor: only some initialization and name/address conversions are done differently. The actual reading and writing of information to/from the socket isn't different in IPv6.

IPv4-Mapped IPv6 Addresses

The socket API changes require that in order to support IPv6, small parts of an application must be updated to use the new API calls. For obvious reasons, turning an IPv4-only application into an IPv6-only application isn't all that useful, so RFC 3493 makes it possible for an application that uses the new mechanisms to communicate over IPv4 by using IPv4-mapped IPv6 addresses. An IPv4-mapped address is an IPv6 address that consists of the prefix 0:0:0:0:0:ffff::/96 (or ::ffff:0:0/96) followed by the IPv4 address in question. So the IPv4-mapped address for local-host would be ::ffff:7f00:1. These addresses are often expressed in the more convenient form, ::ffff:127.0.0.1. Even though to the application, an IPv4-mapped address looks like any other IPv6 address, using these addresses results in IPv4 packets on the wire (network), *not* IPv6 packets. IPv6 packets with IPv4-mapped addresses as their source or destination are best filtered out because they could be used to bypass IPv4 filters. In 2002, IPv4-mapped addresses got some bad press when Jun-ichiro itojun Hagino wrote an Internet Draft for the IETF community under the title "IPv4 mapped address considered harmful." The document goes on to explain that IPv4-mapped addresses are dangerous only *on the wire* and not in the API, but the title of the first version didn't capture that nuance. (The title was changed in the next version.)

IPv4-mapped addresses are a good example of how a clear and simple concept can lead to unexpected complications. Daemon applications that listen for incoming connections must tell the system they are interested in incoming TCP sessions or UDP packets on a certain address and a certain port number by "binding" to an address and port. Most daemons specify they are interested in incoming sessions or packets on any address. The trouble starts when an application binds to "any" in IPv6, and also to "any" in IPv4. Because "any" in IPv6 includes IPv4-mapped addresses, the "any" IPv4 binding clashes with the IPv6 one. On some systems, this doesn't lead to problems, but on others, the binding fails. The solution would be to bind to the IPv6 "any" address only, but some systems (such as Windows) never supported IPv4-mapped addresses, and some systems, such as NetBSD, dropped IPv4-mapped address support somewhere along the way or only support them when explicitly enabled (FreeBSD 5 and later). The end result is that whatever an application writer does, there will be trouble on *some* operating system. Some argue that the correct way for a daemon application to support both IPv4 and IPv6 is to request a list of the system's addresses and then bind to each address explicitly rather than to "any" addresses. However, this adds overhead to the system and the application because there are now more sockets that need attention periodically, and, worse, the list of addresses may change over time, requiring additional complexity.

The inconsistent handling of IPv4-mapped IPv6 addresses across different operating systems is probably the reason why BIND 9.2 only supports listening to the IPv6 "any" address: on most systems, the specific bindings for individual IPv4 addresses preempt the IPv6 "any" binding so there aren't any problems. RFC 3493 solves this problem by introducing the IPV6_V6ONLY socket option. By setting this option, an application indicates that it doesn't want to use IPv4-mapped addresses so that IPv4 and IPv6 bindings no longer clash. As the option is implemented in operating systems, applications can start to expect consistent behavior when using IPv4 and IPv6 bindings side by side. The IPV6_V6ONLY option was implemented in the Linux kernel in version 2.4.21 and in FreeBSD in version 4.4. You can enable or disable IPv4-mapped addresses under FreeBSD with a

```
ipv6_ipv4mapping="YES"
```

line in the /etc/rc.conf file. The default is for IPv4-mapped addresses to be disabled, which is the opposite of the 4.x behavior. In both versions, it's possible to toggle the availability of IPv4-mapped addresses with the net.inet6.ip6.v6only sysctl. 0 means disabled, 1 means enabled. It's best to stick to the default unless you really need a different setting, in order to avoid confusing applications that take their cue regarding IPv4-mapped address availability from the OS version at compile time rather than the current state of the kernel at runtime.

Handling Multiple Addresses

Even when IPv4-mapped addresses are supported, it isn't always enough to replace the traditional socket API calls with the ones that support IPv6 to make an application completely IPv6-compatible. Some protocols embed IP addresses inside the protocol. For instance, peer-to-peer applications need to tell one peer about another, and they nearly always use IP(v4) addresses for this. These protocols must be changed to support IPv6, as do the applications that implement them. The tragedy here is that applications that don't need any changes, except using the new API, are exactly those that work well with Network Address Translation (NAT) in the first place, and one of the big advantages of IPv6 is that it eliminates the need for NAT. So this lands us in the position where most of the applications that support IPv6 are the ones that need it the least. A good example is the Web.

Because an IPv6 system with a single IPv6 address more often than not also has an IPv4 address, it's a very good idea for IPv6 applications to cycle through all the addresses that they find in the DNS when looking up the name for a remote system. This way, when the first (IPv6) address doesn't work, the application still gets to connect to a subsequent (IPv4) address. Although it's possible for a single host to have more than one address in IPv4, most IPv4 applications don't try the extra addresses when connecting to the first one fails, so this functionality must be added when IPv6-enabling an application.

Higher-level APIs can generally be modified to support IPv6 without breaking existing applications. For instance, the Java java.net package has an InetAddress class, which always represented an IPv4 address. When Sun added IPv6 support in the J2SDK/JRE 1.4 release, the InetAddress class was summarily changed to encompass both IPv4 and IPv6 addresses, making all Java applications IPv6-capable in the process. That is, as long as both the Java Runtime Environment and the system support IPv6. This is a mixed blessing, because in addition to allowing a large number of Java programs to work over IPv6 without changes, it may also break some applications that make assumptions about the IP address length.

Old School: FTP, Telnet, and SSH

FTP and Telnet are the oldest applications found on the Internet. They even date back to before the introduction of IPv4 in the early 1980s. It's only fitting that these applications are the first to gain IPv6 support. Linux, FreeBSD, MacOS, and Windows all have command line `ftp` and `telnet` programs, and they all support IPv6. Except for the Windows incarnation, they all try all addresses for a host, so they should fall back to IPv4 if IPv6 connectivity is broken.

The `telnet` and `ftp` programs aren't the workhorses they used to be. The Telnet protocol has been largely replaced by SSH because SSH supports encryption. Even though a lot of downloading happens over HTTP these days, the FTP protocol is still going strong, but users prefer more user-friendly graphical FTP clients. However, the original `telnet` and `ftp` are great for debugging. With `telnet`, it's possible to connect to arbitrary TCP services to see if the service in question is running, and `ftp` is very useful for measuring available bandwidth, because it displays an accurate kilobyte per second value after transferring a file. Under FreeBSD and MacOS, `ftp` accepts HTTP and FTP URLs as arguments, which is great for downloading files from within a script.

The FTP server daemons on FreeBSD and MacOS both support IPv6. The Telnet daemon does as well, but it's disabled on both systems. Under Red Hat Linux, there is no FTP or Telnet daemon installed by default.

The SSH client and server programs that come with Linux, FreeBSD, and MacOS all support IPv6. Like most IPv6-enabled applications, the `ssh` program prefers IPv6 addresses over IPv4 ones if there is IPv6 connectivity. On all three systems, `ssh` will fall back on additional (IPv4 or IPv6) addresses when it can't connect to the first address. VanDyke Software has a commercial SecureCRT SSH (and more) client for Windows that supports IPv6 in version 5. SecureCRT 5 can be downloaded for a free 30-day trial from http://www.vandyke.com/. There is also Putty, a free multi-OS SSH client that is popular under Windows and supports IPv6. Putty is available at http://www.chiark.greenend.org.uk/~sgtatham/putty/.

The FTP and SSH services are disabled by default under MacOS. They can be enabled in the System Preferences under Sharing, on the Services tab, as shown in Figure 6-1. The SSH service is called "Remote Login" in the System Preferences.

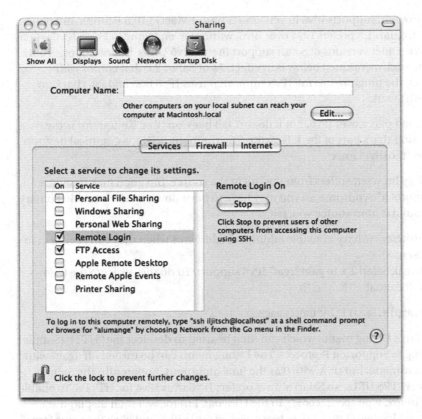

Figure 6-1. *Enabling the FTP and SSH services under MacOS*

Browsing the Web

Web browsing is a very good example of an application that doesn't really need IPv6 support, because the HTTP protocol isn't bothered by network address translation. On the other hand, the Web is the most visible part of the Internet experience, so it's a good place the gain some real-world IPv6 exposure. And good luck finding a dancing turtle anywhere else than on the IPv6-version of the `http://www.kame.net/` website! The IPv6 status of the leading browsers is as follows:

Internet Explorer supports IPv6 under Windows. It doesn't support the [`2001:db8:31:1::2`] literal IPv6 address format in URLs (RFC 2732). Internet Explorer for the Mac doesn't support IPv6.

Netscape has a few IPv6-enabled versions (Linux), but they're not always easy to find.

Mozilla, on the other hand, has more extensive IPv6 support, but it's still common to find IPv4-only binaries, especially for the Mac.

Firefox, the newest member of the Netscape/Mozilla family, supports IPv6 in all distributions, although it's disabled by default on the Mac (see Figure 6-2).

Safari, Apple's browser, supports IPv6 in version 1.3 under MacOS 10.3 Panther, but you wouldn't know it: Safari 1.3 prefers IPv4 over IPv6, without even falling back on IPv6 when IPv4 doesn't work. Older versions of Safari support literal IPv6 URLs, but newer ones only do this when the trick mentioned below is in effect. As of Safari 2.0 that comes with MacOS 10.4 Tiger, the program has full IPv6 support: it tries IPv6 first and falls back on IPv4 if IPv6 doesn't work.

Konqueror will load pages over IPv6, but it doesn't fall back on IPv4. Konqueror is the browser application that's part of the K Desktop Environment (KDE), a graphical desktop environment for (mostly) Linux.

Lynx, the text-only browser, suffers from the "it's in the source, but good luck finding a binary that supports it" syndrome, so you may have to hunt down an IPv6-enabled binary distribution or build it from source yourself.

As a rule, Web browsers will try available additional addresses when they can't connect to the first address chosen.

It's possible to tweak Safari 1.x to gain "real" IPv6 support. To do this, execute the following command in the Terminal:

```
defaults write com.apple.Safari IncludeDebugMenu 1
```

This enables Safari's Debug menu, which can then be used to deselect the "HTTP (Simple Loader)" under Debug ➤ Supported Protocols. The Debug menu can be turned off again with the same Terminal command, but now with 0 as the final argument. Apparently, the Simple Loader isn't used for HTTPS URLs, so Safari always prefers IPv6 over IPv4 for HTTPS. To enable IPv6 in the MacOS Firefox, type about:config in the URL bar. Firefox will then display a staggering number of variables. Scroll down to network.dns.disableIPv6 and click the value "true" on the same line, so it changes to "false," as in Figure 6-2.

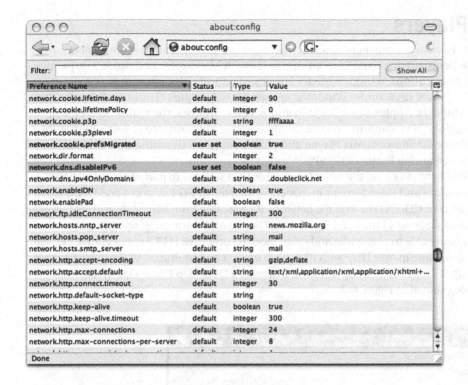

Figure 6-2. *Enabling IPv6 in Firefox under MacOS*

Mail Clients

Unlike its cousin Internet Explorer, Microsoft Outlook Express doesn't support IPv6. Many of the UNIX/Linux mail clients, such as Thunderbird under Linux, are fully IPv6-enabled. Like Firefox, Thunderbird supports IPv6 under Windows, too, but not on the Mac. But unlike Firefox, there doesn't seem to be a way to enable IPv6 when it's disabled or disable it when it's enabled. However, Apple's Mail application has IPv6 on board and prefers the new protocol over IPv4.[1] But despite the fact that Mail will happily work over IPv6, it won't function when the system doesn't have an IPv4 nameserver configured. Actual IPv4 connectivity to the mail server or the rest of the world isn't required, but without an IPv4 DNS address, Mail won't connect to the mail server. If you want to run Apple Mail in an IPv6-only network, add 127.0.0.1 as an additional DNS server in your network settings, and Mail will work without trouble.

---

1. You may run into problems sending email over IPv6 with Mail 2.0, the version that comes with MacOS 10.4 Tiger. The easiest way to work around this is to configure Mail with an SMTP hostname that only has an A record in the DNS.

Media Players

After the inconsistencies between Web and mail behavior under Windows and MacOS, the trend of there being no discernable trend continues with Microsoft's and Apple's respective media player applications. Windows Media Player will happily play content that it downloads with HTTP over IPv6, under Windows, at least. So will Apple's iTunes, both under MacOS and Windows. Apple's other flagship audio/video product, the QuickTime Player, also recently gained IPv6 support in some configurations. I was unable to test whether the QuickTime Player, Windows Media Player, and iTunes support streaming over IPv6 with the Real-Time Streaming Protocol (RTSP).

Video LAN Client (VLC), on the other hand, takes IPv6 support to a whole new level. VLC plays nearly all audio and video formats in existence, such as MPEG 1, 2, and 4 and DIVX, either directly from a file or CD/DVD or over the network. It's available from `http://www.videolan.org/` for Windows, MacOS, many Linux dialects, the BSD family, and some other operating systems. In addition to being able to play audio and video received over IPv6 HTTP connections, VLC can play streams that come in over UDP with IPv6, both unicast and multicast. VLC can also stream content over IPv6. This is done by opening (for instance) a DVD with File ➤ Open Disc. This opens the dialog shown in Figure 6-3.

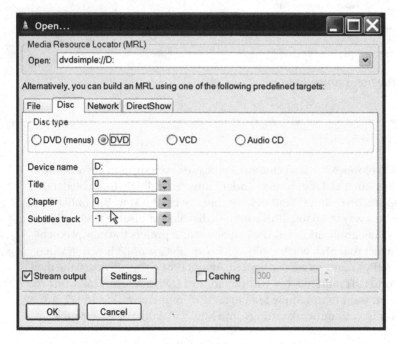

Figure 6-3. *Opening a DVD in VLC (Windows)*

It's best to disable DVD menus for streaming by selecting DVD rather than DVD (menus). After selecting the Stream output checkbox, you can click the Settings button to enter the Stream output dialog in Figure 6-4, where you get to select (among others) the streaming protocol and the encapsulation method. Select UDP and provide an IPv6 destination address. This can be the unicast address of the host receiving the stream, or it can be a multicast address, such as `ff15::1`, so that multiple hosts can receive the same stream. The IPv6 address must be between brackets. (See Chapter 2 for information on the different multicast address types.)

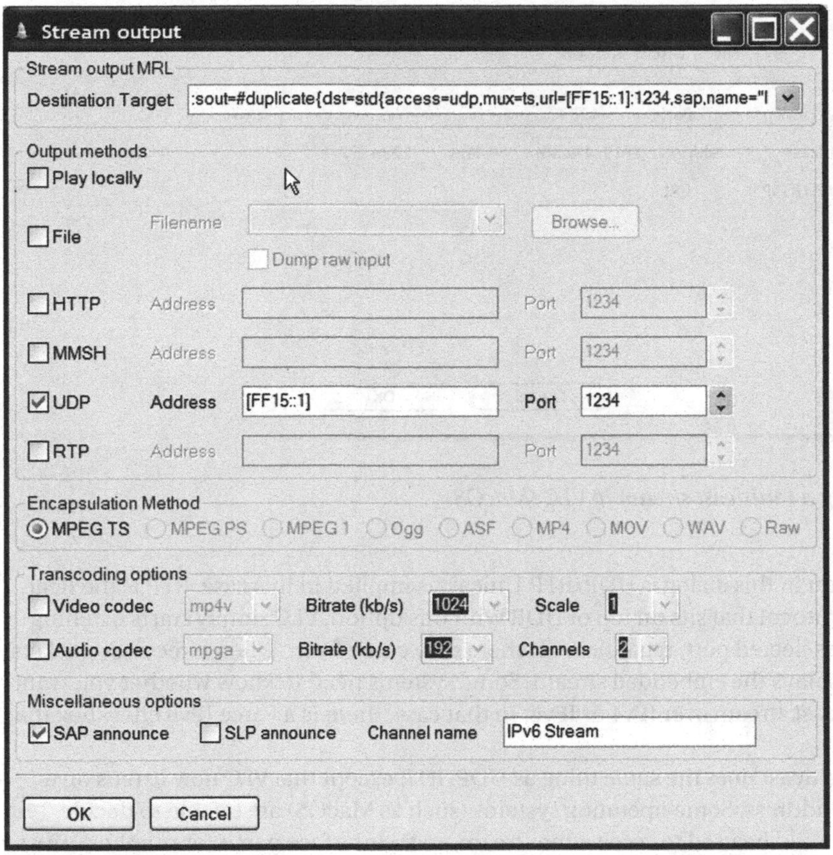

Figure 6-4. *Enabling multicast streaming output in VLC (Windows)*

Selecting SAP announce and filling in a channel name makes VLC send out an announcement about the stream, which some clients can detect and present to the user in lieu of manually selecting the multicast address for a stream. However, manually entering a multicast address is more reliable. Do this by selecting File ➤ Open Network in VLC. This opens the dialog shown in Figure 6-5.

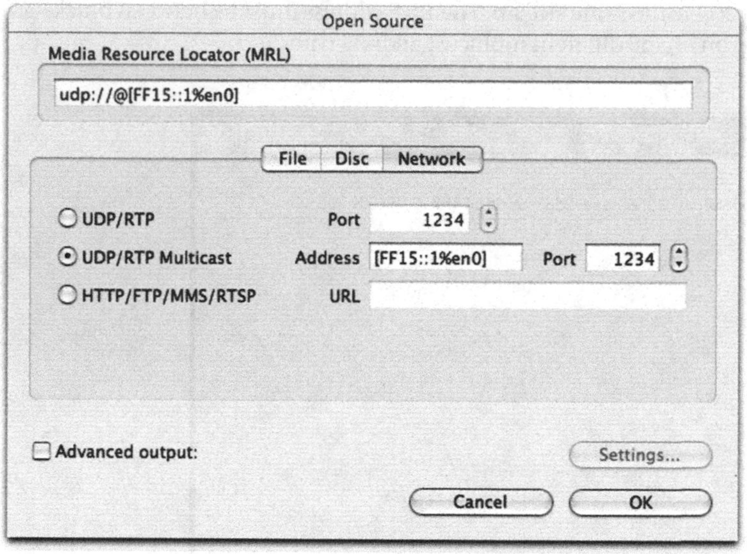

Figure 6-5. *Opening a multicast stream in VLC (MacOS)*

The first option in this dialog is UDP/RTP. Unicast is implied in this case. RTP is the Real-Time Transport Protocol that sits on top of UDP. With this option, VLC simply starts listening for packets on the selected port, regardless of where they come from. When it receives packets, it decodes and displays the embedded stream. Some systems need to know whether you want to receive the unicast stream over IPv4 or IPv6. In that case, there is a Force IPv6 checkbox that selects IPv6.

UDP/RTP multicast does the same thing as UDP/RTP, except that VLC now listens on a specific multicast address. Some operating systems (such as MacOS) are unable to decide which interface should be used to receive the stream, so an interface name (or number) must be tacked onto the address, preceded by a percent sign. In this case, it's %en0 for the built-in Ethernet interface on a MacOS system. Under Windows, adding an interface generally isn't necessary, but if it is, it's in the form of an interface index number. Use the netsh interface ipv6 show interface command to determine the index number. Don't forget to enter the same port number that's used to source the stream, if this is different from VLC's default port 1234. The HTTP/FTP/MMS/RTSP option retrieves a stream or file referenced with an URL from a server.

■**Note** IEEE 802.11, 11b, and 11g wireless networks aren't suitable for transporting audio and especially video streams over multicast because of limitations on how 802.11 and its successors handle multicasts. See the section about IPv6 over Wi-Fi in Chapter 8 for more information.

The Apache 2 Web Server

Apache, the most popular Web server software, gained IPv6 support in version 2. Although Apache 2 was released in 2002, version 1.3 is still in wide use. For instance, MacOS X Panther still comes with Apache 1.3, although MacOS X Server has Apache 2 on board. Red Hat 9, on the other hand, comes with Apache 2. Use httpd -v to determine the Apache version installed. (You may have to hunt down the location of the httpd; the Apache binaries are usually installed under an Apache directory rather than one of the usual directories for binaries.) On most systems, it's pretty straightforward to install Apache 2 from the source (http://www.apache.org/) with the usual ./configure, make, make install sequence.[2] However, be careful when upgrading from 1.3 to 2, as the interface to external modules such as PHP has changed, making it necessary to install new versions of all modules in use. A binary distribution for Windows is also available on the Apache Web site. As always, Apache is a complex piece of software, and the information here alone isn't enough to be able to set it up, so consult additional documentation. Hint: when running Apache out of the box, point a browser to the newly installed server to read the documentation. The documentation is, of course, also available on the Apache Web site.

■Note It's not a problem to run Apache versions 1.3 and 2 concurrently, as long as they're installed in different places and they bind to different IP addresses and/or ports. For instance, Apache 1.3 can handle IPv4 while Apache 2 handles IPv6.

Listening

On most systems, Apache takes advantage of IPv4-mapped addresses so that IPv4 and IPv6 sessions can be handled on a single socket. The exact behavior of Apache's address binding is determined in the configuration file with the Listen directive. The Listen keyword takes either an IP address with a port number or just a port number as an argument. IPv6 addresses must be between brackets. You can specify more than one address or port for Apache to listen on by issuing additional Listen lines. In most cases, one or two Listen lines, like in Listing 6-1 , are sufficient.

Listing 6-1. *The* Listen *Statement in the Apache Configuration*

```
# Standard HTTP port:
Listen 80
# HTTPS HTTP over SSL port:
Listen 443
```

The Apache documentation claims that IPv4-mapped addresses are automatically disabled by the configure script on FreeBSD, OpenBSD, and NetBSD to comply with system policy. This is probably true as of FreeBSD 5.0, because on FreeBSD 4.9, IPv4-mapped addresses are still used.

---

2. Apache 2.0.54 won't compile under MacOS X Panther because the configure script somehow concludes that it can use the poll() function, which MacOS doesn't have. Hacking the source to use Apache's own poll() replacement is left as an exercise for the reader. Tiger doesn't have this problem.

You can force the use of IPv4-mapped addresses with the `--disable-v4-mapped` or `--enable-v4-mapped` arguments to `configure`. When IPv4-mapped addresses are disabled, the address-less `Listen` directive in Listing 6-1 results in an IPv6-only Web server. To overcome this problem, Apache must be configured to listen for IPv4 and IPv6 sessions on separate sockets. This is what Listing 6-2 does.

Listing 6-2. *Making Apache Listen on Separate IPv4 and IPv6 Sockets*

```
Listen 0.0.0.0:80
Listen [::]:80
Listen 0.0.0.0:443
Listen [::]:443
```

Be sure to check whether Apache actually starts correctly with separate `Listen` directives for IPv4 and IPv6, because if inadvertently IPv4-mapped addresses aren't disabled, the IPv4 and IPv6 bindings may clash on some systems (such as Linux with kernel 2.4.20 or earlier). When this happens, Apache can't bind to the IPv4 and IPv6 sockets as configured, and it will refuse to start. It is, of course, also possible to specify the actual IPv4 and IPv6 addresses of the server, rather than the wildcard addresses for IPv4 and IPv6. However, this is inconvenient when these addresses change. The difference between configuring Apache per Listing 6-1 or 6-2 is readily visible with the FreeBSD and MacOS `netstat` command, as shown in Listing 6-3.

Listing 6-3. *Showing Listening Sockets*

```
> netstat -a
Active Internet connections (including servers)
Proto Recv-Q Send-Q Local Address   Foreign Address  (state)
tcp46    0      0    *.https         *.*              LISTEN
tcp46    0      0    *.http          *.*              LISTEN
tcp6     0      0    *.pop3          *.*              LISTEN
tcp4     0      0    *.pop3          *.*              LISTEN
```

In this example, the HTTP and HTTPS services are bound to the `tcp46` protocol or, in other words, TCP over both IPv4 and IPv6. The POP3 service, on the other hand, is bound to an IPv4 socket and an IPv6 socket separately.

Virtual Hosting

It turns out that hosting Web content is addictive: once you start with a single Web site, you soon find yourself wanting to host more. Much to the dismay of hardware vendors around the world, Apache (and other Web server software) will happily run multiple virtual Web servers on a single physical machine. In the early days of the Web, this was done by adding additional IP addresses to the server and serving up different content based on the IP address clients connected to. However, this IP-based virtual hosting uses up a lot of addresses and requires a lot of configuration work. As of HTTP 1.1, it became possible for the client (browser) to tell the server which domain name it tried to connect to, so it became possible to run different virtual hosts on a single IP address. This capability was also added to Web browsers that otherwise use HTTP 1.0, so today, all browser applications support name-based virtual hosts. Listing 6-4 shows a simple name-based virtual host configuration for Apache 2. Note that this is only a small part of a working Apache `httpd.conf` file. Consult the example `httpd.conf` and the Apache documentation for more details. If you only want to run a single Web site at this point in time, it's not necessary to configure a virtual host, but it isn't any harder, and it makes adding additional servers later easier.

Listing 6-4. *Name-Based Virtual Hosts with Apache*

```
NameVirtualHost *

<VirtualHost *>
ServerName www.example.com
ServerAlias www.ipv4.example.com www.ipv6.example.com
DocumentRoot /usr/local/www/data/
</VirtualHost>

<VirtualHost *>
ServerName www.beispiel.de
ServerAlias *.beispiel.de *.beispiel.au
DocumentRoot /usr/local/www/data/beispiel/
</VirtualHost>
```

The `NameVirtualHost *` line tells Apache that we'll be using name-based virtual hosts on all addresses that Apache is configured to `Listen` to. When mixing real IP-based virtual hosts with name-based virtual hosts, this command is used to separate the addresses used for IP-based virtual hosts from the ones used for name-based virtual hosts. The virtual host configuration for `www.example.com` follows after this. The asterisk in the `<VirtualHost *>` line works in conjunction with the one in the `NameVirtualHost` command to match any address. It's also possible to list one or more IP addresses or domain names (that will be resolved into IP addresses when reading the configuration) here, separated by spaces. Everything between `<VirtualHost *>` and `</VirtualHost>` only applies to the virtual host in question. The `ServerName` is matched against the domain name supplied by the Web client. So if the browser tells the server that it's trying to contact `www.example.com`, the settings for the virtual host with `ServerName` `www.example.com` will be used. The names following `ServerAlias` are additional domain names that are equivalent to the name listed in `ServerName`. In this case, a client asking for `www.ipv4.example.com` or `www.ipv6.example.com` will see the same content as one asking for `www.example.com`. Of course, this works only if the DNS records also point to the same address. The second virtual host has wildcard records in `ServerAlias` that match all domain names ending in `beispiel.de` and `beispiel.au`. The `DocumentRoot` points to the directory that is the root directory for the virtual server.

Because IP addresses aren't exactly scarce in IPv6, you may decide to go with IP-based virtual hosts. In this case, it's probably still a good idea to configure the virtual hosts as name-based, because this keeps the Apache configuration file free of IP addresses. In theory, a client can then connect to an address that belongs to one domain and issue a request for another domain. In practice, this won't happen unless there is a reason for people to go out of their way to make their system do this. An additional reason to avoid configuring IP-based virtual hosts as such is to keep Apache from having to perform DNS lookups when it parses its configuration. Failure to complete these lookups can keep Apache from starting or make virtual hosts unavailable.

> ■**Tip** You can check the virtual host configuration in the httpd.conf file with httpd -S. This reports errors and provides some information on the configured virtual hosts, but this information isn't very complete.

There is one case where name-based virtual hosts can't be used: with SSL/HTTPS. The SSL protocol needs to know the hostname a client is connecting to for its security negotiations before the HTTP protocol becomes active. Because the SSL configuration needs a lot of settings, it's impractical to provide an example. Have a look at the sample httpd.conf and ssl.conf file that come with Apache. Skip over the SSL documentation at your peril.

> ■**Note** If you use scripts on your Web server, those scripts may now receive an IPv6 address from Apache in the variable REMOTE_ADDRESS.

The Sendmail Mail Transfer Agent

Ten years of experience as a sendmail user has taught me that trying to understand the sendmail configuration process in terms of system administration leads to madness. As black magic, however, it makes a lot of sense. So I'm not in the best position to tell others how to do this. I wouldn't recommend installing sendmail on a system that doesn't come with it, unless you *really* know what you're doing. Still, I got the sendmail that came with FreeBSD 4.9 to use IPv6, so I can at least share how that's done. In FreeBSD 5.4, sendmail is configured to use IPv6 by default. Listing 6-5 shows the relevant lines in a .mc file. Under FreeBSD, that would be the /etc/mail/<host.name.tld>.mc file.

Listing 6-5. sendmail *IPv6-relevant .mc Configuration*

```
DAEMON_OPTIONS(`Name=MTA-IPv4, Family=inet')
DAEMON_OPTIONS(`Name=MTA-IPv6, Family=inet6')
define(`confBIND_OPTS', `WorkAroundBrokenAAAA')
```

The third line makes sendmail work around DNS servers that respond incorrectly to AAAA queries. After adding the IPv6 lines to the .mc file, you should use the m4 utility to create a .cf sendmail configuration file. FreeBSD has a Makefile in /etc/mail that will do this when you type make in that directory.

Under Red Hat ES Linux, this mostly works the same way, except that the .mc file may be named sendmail.mc, and you need the sendmail-cf package to generate the .cf file from the .mc file. However, Linux suffers from IPv4-mapped problems, so you should only enable the IPv6 MTA, which will also accept connections over IPv4. If you enable both IPv4 and IPv6, sendmail will complain about a "wedged" socket in /var/log/maillog and quit.

If you are brave enough to edit the .cf file by hand, you can add lines like the ones in Listing 6-6 to the appropriate .cf file to make sendmail IPv6-aware.

Listing 6-6. `sendmail` *IPv6-relevant* `.cf` *Configuration*

```
# SMTP daemon options
O DaemonPortOptions=Name=MTA-IPv4, Family=inet
O DaemonPortOptions=Name=MTA-IPv6, Family=inet6

# name resolver options
O ResolverOptions=WorkAroundBrokenAAAA
```

After editing the configuration file, you must restart `sendmail`. FreeBSD will do this for you with a `make restart`, but a good old-fashioned `killall -HUP sendmail` works, too. Note that within the context of SMTP (and thus `sendmail` configuration files, including the access file), literal IPv6 addresses are represented as `IPv6:address`, such as `IPv6:2001:db8:31:1::2` (RFC 2821). This means that the localhost address becomes `IPv6:::1`. However, `sendmail` versions older than 8.12 use the `[2001:db8:31:1::2]` format.

■**Note** See the `sendmail` installation instructions on how to compile a binary with IPv6 support, if the `sendmail` that came with your system is IPv4-only.

The UW POP and IMAP Servers

With an IPv6-enabled email client and an IPv6-enabled MTA, the only missing piece of the puzzle is a way of getting messages from the server to the client over IPv6. Two protocols accomplish this: POP3 and IMAP. IMAP is superior to POP in almost every way, so if you have the choice, install IMAP on your server. Better yet, install both POP3 and IMAP.[3] The University of Washington has POP3 and IMAP (with the obsolete POP2 protocol thrown in for good measure) server implementations to go along with their Pine email client. Even though the unpatched Pine distributed by UW doesn't support IPv6, the UW POP3 and IMAP servers do. The software is available from `http://www.washington.edu/imap/`. Although the distribution is called "imap," it contains both the POP and IMAP daemons. Installation is a bit different than usual; see the instructions. You need to edit the Makefile and change "IP=4" to "IP=6" to enable IPv6 support. If you have trouble building the software, this is generally because the OpenSSL headers or library can't be found. Building without SSL is tempting, because this will generally work without problems. However, this isn't a very good idea because then the POP3 and IMAP protocols aren't encrypted, so email will flow over the network in the clear. It's possible to protect passwords without SSL by using more advanced authentication protocols, but this isn't really worth the trouble: hunt down the right include and library paths, and build SSL-capable versions of the daemons.

The UW POP3 and IMAP daemons start from the `inetd`. Listing 6-7 shows the relevant lines from a FreeBSD `/etc/inetd.conf` file.

---

3. There is an aspect of personal preference and a lot depends on the capabilities of the client, but I recommend giving IMAP a try if you haven't done so before.

Listing 6-7. *Enabling POP3 and IMAP in* /etc/inetd.conf

```
pop3    stream  tcp     nowait  root  /usr/local/libexec/ipop3d  ipop3d
pop3    stream  tcp6    nowait  root  /usr/local/libexec/ipop3d  ipop3d
imap4   stream  tcp     nowait  root  /usr/local/libexec/imapd   imapd
imaps   stream  tcp46   nowait  root  /usr/local/libexec/imapd   imapd
```

Don't forget to issue a killall -HUP inetd or similar after editing the inetd.conf. The (non-SSL) POP3 service is provided on two different sockets for IPv4 and IPv6, but the configuration is otherwise the same. The non-SSL IMAP service (imap4, port 143) is only available over IPv4, but the SSL-protected version (imaps, port 993) is accessible over both IPv4 and IPv6 through a single socket. This only works if the system supports IPv4-mapped addresses. Note that neither the ipop3d nor the imapd requires a configuration file.

CHAPTER 7

■ ■ ■

The Transition

flag day: n.

A software change that is neither forward- nor backward-compatible, and which is costly to make and costly to reverse.

The Online Hacker Jargon File, version 4.4.7

Although IPv6 is by no means a simple protocol in and of itself (this will become very clear in Chapter 8), most of the complexities related to running IPv6 stem from the transition from IPv4 to IPv6, and the coexistence of the two protocols. From the start, the IETF realized that it would be impossible for the entire Internet to switch from IPv4 to IPv6 on a predetermined "flag day." This realization led to the development of several transition mechanisms (see RFC 2893), which can roughly be grouped into three categories:

1. Dual stack (also called "dual layer" or "Dual Stack Transition Mechanism," DSTM)

2. Tunnels

3. Translation and proxying

So far, we've implicitly assumed that IPv6 capability would be an *addition* to existing IPv4 capability. Obviously, at some point, IPv4 will have to be turned off, as running dual stack indefinitely doesn't solve any problems. Rather, it makes everything (slightly) harder, as it's still necessary to do everything that must be done to support IPv4 as before and add IPv6 on top of that. On the other hand, it's very attractive to run dual stack, as this only *adds* new capabilities without taking existing ones away. A dual stack host can talk to anyone: other dual stack hosts, IPv4-only hosts, and IPv6-only hosts.

Tunneling is a very powerful transition mechanism, as it allows existing IPv4 infrastructure to be leveraged for IPv6 communication. Tunnels can be removed one at a time as native IPv6 connectivity becomes available, so the use of tunnels as a transition mechanism doesn't add transition difficulties.

Translation between IPv4 and IPv6 is the most controversial of the transition mechanisms, as translation between IP versions has many of the same limitations of the dreaded Network Address Translation now common in IPv4 that IPv6 is supposed to get rid of in the first place. On the other hand, without any form of translation, there are only two options: upgrade *all* IPv4 hosts to dual stack before the first host can start running IPv6-only, or live with a fragmented Internet where IPv4-only hosts can't talk to IPv6-only hosts during the transition. Proxying is less controversial but not as generally applicable as translation because the application must explicitly support the use of a proxy.

Planning the Transition

The first question that requires an answer when contemplating IPv4-to-IPv6 transition plans is: should we bother at all? Isn't IPv6 going to be a huge failure?

Well, Nils Bohr said it:

"Prediction is very difficult, especially if it's about the future."

With that caveat out of the way, I see no way in which we could still be running IPv4 30 years from now similar to the way we do today. On the other hand, I don't see how we can switch to IPv6 in three months. On a warm and sunny August day, it's very likely that the next day will also be warm and sunny. And the day after that. But it's unlikely that it's still warm and sunny by January. *Something* will have change between three months and 30 years from now.

IPv4 Address Depletion and the HD Ratio

Everyone knows that a tube can only hold a finite amount of toothpaste. So, considering the amount of toothpaste used every day, it should be easy to figure out when the tube will be empty. In practice, the tube is never really "empty"—it just gets harder and harder to get at the remaining toothpaste hiding in the corners of the tube. At some point, it's just easier to throw away the tube and open a new one. Address space is exactly like that: at some point, the effort required to manage the increasingly used-up address space becomes too great, so it's easier to expand it. In RFC 3194, Alain Durand and Christian Huitema came up with a number that expresses address utilization in a way that makes it possible to draw conclusions on past experience. This number is the "HD ratio," which is calculated as

$$HD = \frac{\log(\text{addresses used})}{\log(\text{total addresses})}$$

So if an organization has an old class B network with 65,536 addresses in it, and 4096 of those addresses are in use, the HD ratio would be log(4096) / log(65536) = 12 / 16 = 0.75 or 75%. In this example, the base for the logarithm is two, but any base can be used because it's the ratio between the logarithms that's important, not the absolute value. After looking at various address types such as French and North American phone numbers and a worldwide DECnet network, Durand and Huitema concluded that an HD ratio of 80% or lower corresponds to a comfortable level, and at 87% or higher, the address space becomes so hard to manage that the address length is expanded, or techniques to reduce address use are deployed.

The reason it's impossible to attain an HD ratio of close to 100% is that address space is lost whenever there is an administrative delegation boundary. For instance, when there are lots of unused phone numbers in area code 401, that really doesn't help against a shortage in area code 213. Or when there are two /24 IPv4 subnets and both have only 150 addresses in them, that's 300 addresses used and 200 that remain unused but that can't be used elsewhere.

Note Out of the 256 /8 blocks, 32 are class D (224–239, multicast) and class E (240–255, reserved) and three others are also unusable: 0, 10, and 127. Of the 221 usable /8s, 72 were unused as of March 2005. See http://www.iana.org/assignments/ipv4-address-space for the most recent information.

According to the ISC Domain Survey at http://www.isc.org/ds/, 317 million IPv4 hosts had a domain name in January 2005.

For the IPv4 address space with 317 million out of 3.7 billion addresses used, the HD ratio is 88.9%. But 1.2 billion addresses still have the shrink-wrap on them in the IANA warehouses. The HD ratio for the 2.5 billion addresses that are delegated to the Regional Internet Registries (or sometimes directly to users) would be 90.5%. Assuming we can reach a similar HD ratio for the remaining 1.2 billion addresses, there is enough room to number 163 million more hosts, for a total of 480 million IPv4 hosts.

Obviously, the HD ratio replaces information about actual delegation boundary losses with a rule of thumb, so this isn't a hard limit, but it does show that the IPv4 address space is more limited than it would seem at first glance.

IPv6 vs. Network Address Translation

I suppose it's possible to ignore IPv6 and solve address scarcity problems by large-scale adoption of NAT. NAT is already in wide use today, and it works very well for client/server applications, such as the Web and email, where the client is behind a NAT device. But NAT doesn't work so well for peer-to-peer applications such as Voice over IP and client/server applications, where more than one server is behind the NAT device, and it severely restricts possible new applications, such as home automation or ubiquitous computing. To make NAT really useful as an address conservation technique, it would have to allow multiple servers/peers to share a single IP address. Because obviously two different server or peer-to-peer applications on the same IP address can't share a single port number, this means the end of the "well-known port" concept. In essence, the TCP or UDP port number would become part of the address. The changes required to make this work are probably similar in scale to the ones needed to make IPv6 work. However, a lot of the work required to get IPv6 off the ground has already been done, so I don't think we'll see NAT as a permanent replacement for IPv6. Still, with NAT in place, it's going to take a little more time to burn up the remaining unused IPv4 address space.

Making a Plan

With the HD ratio and NAT limitations in mind, we can reasonably assume that adoption of IPv6 at some point in the future may not be inevitable but is certainly likely. This answers the "if" question, bringing us to the "when" and "how" questions. The way I see it, there are four major phases in the move from IPv4 to IPv6:

1. **Gaining some basic IPv6 experience**. This phase entails turning on IPv6 on a small number of systems, seeing what happens, and doing some tests. All that's required here is an IPv6 tunnel and some hardware that isn't used for anything important. At this point, it's entirely possible to jettison IPv6 and keep running just IPv4.

2. **Adding limited IPv6 support**. At this point, it's possible to do certain things over IPv6, but other things may still require IPv4 connectivity. There are some risks here, as IPv6 is used on production systems for production traffic, but going back to IPv4 is still possible (with some loss of face as the worst consequence).

3. **Promoting IPv6 to a full equivalent of IPv4**. This means retiring IPv4-only hardware and software or using transition techniques to make IPv4-only services available over IPv6 (and/or the other way around). It's hard turn back to IPv4 after reaching this point because users may now depend on the IPv6 capability.

4. **Turning off IPv4**. Turning off IPv4 completely won't be possible for a long time, but running IPv6-only in parts of a network may happen relatively soon, especially with the aid of transition techniques so that IPv4-only services elsewhere can still be used.

At this point, I recommend for everyone to enter phase one and get familiar with IPv6. For some people moving into phase two will be easy and painless, but for others, there may be obstacles: hardware or tools that don't support IPv6 (even if the application software does), lack of a multihoming[1] solution, and so on. However, if customers are asking for IPv6, you may not have much of a choice. If a service provider wants to make its services available over IPv6, this means that the software used to provide the service must be IPv6-capable. It also means that the service provider's ISP needs to provide IPv6 connectivity, and, if the software vendor takes testing seriously, the software vendor's ISP must do so as well. This can lead to a low-key snowball effect.

If you decide to wait with phase two at this point, revisit the issue periodically. This is especially important when planning the acquisition of new hardware or software. Buying products that aren't IPv6-ready and can't be upgraded to IPv6 could be a big problem if IPv6 suddenly takes off. For instance, if you're an ISP, you should be very careful with investing in high-speed hardware (ASIC) forwarding-based routers that can only support IPv6 in software. Usually, new network services don't take off overnight. However, IPv6 has the potential to be different as users move traffic flows from IPv4 to IPv6. If two organizations exchange lots of big files by using FTP, all this traffic *can* move from IPv4 to IPv6 overnight. That would be a bad morning indeed for a router linecard that can do gigabit at linespeed for IPv4 but only 10% of linespeed at IPv6.

For most organizations, going to phase three is probably not a good idea yet. However, for software vendors, it could make sense to remove any IPv4 dependencies, effectively moving them to phase three. Organizations that mostly communicate internally may want to move to phase three and even phase four because removing IPv4 from parts of the network makes for easier network design.

A good way to plan for the transition to IPv6 would be to create a plan that lands you in phase three after three years, with deliverables or milestones for important steps. See Listing 7-1.

---

1. The ability to connect to two or more ISPs at the same time; see Chapter 4.

Listing 7-1. *An IPv6 Deployment Plan for an ISP*

```
Phase Month Milestone
1     1     Get IPv6 tunnel
            Enable IPv6 on spare Windows XP office PC and test FreeBSD server
      3     Set up OSPFv3 routing in the lab

2     6     Obtain IPv6 allocation from Regional Internet Registry
            Set up IPv6 BGP session with transit ISP A
            Enable IPv6 on NOC workstations and NS2 nameserver
      9     Register NS2 IPv6 address with TLD registries
            Set up IPv6 BGP session with transit ISP B
            Set up IPv6 BGP sessions with internet exchange peers
            IPv6 training for NOC personnel
      12    Set up experimental tunnel server for customers
      15    Upgrade all routers to IPv6, install OSPFv3 and IPv6 over iBGP
      18    Enable IPv6 on proxy server, make proxy software IPv6-aware

3     21    Add support for native IPv6 to DSL infrastructure
      24    Add IPv6 support to provisioning system
      27    Evaluate possibilities for IPv6 load balancing on WWW cluster
      30    Enable IPv6 on all servers
            Make SMTP, POP, and IMAP servers IPv6-aware
      33    Implement IPv6 WWW cluster load balancing
            IPv6 training for support personnel
```

Then, put the plan in the back of a filing cabinet and take it out once or twice a year and determine if it's necessary to implement the next milestone. So if IPv6 gains popularity quickly, you'll just execute the plan as intended, and you're at full IPv6 support fairly soon. On the other hand, if IPv6 uptake is slow, you'll end up waiting relatively long between the successive steps, so the time and money required to implement the plan are limited. If it turns out there is no reason to proceed with IPv6 at all, the only thing you've done is waste a few hours drawing up a plan. So whatever happens, your bases are covered.

Obviously, there are circumstances when it makes sense to go about IPv6 adoption very differently. For instance, in some cases, it may be useful to start with an IPv6-only network and use transition mechanisms to use IPv4, rather than the other way around. An interesting aspect here is that tunneling individual IPv4 addresses to systems that need them over IPv6 makes it possible to utilize 100% of the available IPv4 addresses, while a traditional IPv4 network always wastes some part of its addresses due to the limited flexibility of subnet sizes and so on.

Turning Off IPv4?

It seems premature to talk about running IPv6-only hosts or even an IPv6-only network at this point, but disabling IPv4 on a test system once in a while is extremely useful to flush out hidden assumptions about the availability of IPv4 in the system or applications. I've tried it a few times, generally with limited success. Many operating systems assume the presence of IPv4. Windows is especially bad in this area, as it doesn't support looking up domain names over

IPv6 transport. MacOS is more advanced: the graphical user interface even allows IPv4 to be turned off, but it soon turns out that applications such as Mail, which are otherwise IPv6-aware, won't function without an IPv4 address present.[2] In my opinion, ignoring the future need to run IPv6-only with the argument that we're not there yet leads to problems such as the IETF failing to come up with a good way to find DNS resolvers that are reachable over IPv6 after almost a decade of IPv6 standardization work.

Application Transition Scenarios

When considering the implementation of transition mechanisms such as translation and proxying, it's important to keep in mind the different communication models used by different applications. For instance, email clients only communicate with a specific server, and the servers communicate among each other, as depicted in Figure 7-1. Let's call this the "email model."

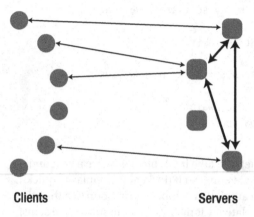

Clients   **Servers**

Figure 7-1. *The email communication model*

In the email model, it's very easy for clients to migrate from IPv4 to IPv6; as long as the specific server the client uses is dual stack, there won't be any problems. However, because any server potentially needs to communicate with any other server, the last server must become dual stack before the first server can move to IPv6-only.

The communication model for the Web is very different. As a rule, Web servers don't communicate with each other; all communication is between clients and servers. Unlike email, a client doesn't communicate with a specific server, but with any server. See Figure 7-2 for the "Web model."

---

2. You can trick Mail into working on an IPv6-only Mac by adding an extra (fake) IPv4 nameserver address in the network settings. 127.0.0.1 is a good choice.

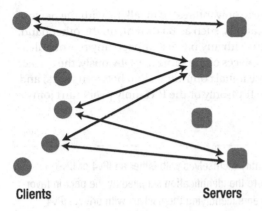

Figure 7-2. *The Web communication model*

In the Web model, all servers that are part of the World Wide Web must be dual stack before the first clients can move to IPv6-only. Of course, a dual stack client can still communicate over IPv6 with a dual stack server, and private networks can move to IPv6-only without waiting for the Web at large to do the same.

A third model is the peer-to-peer model. There are many peer-to-peer applications, and they don't all communicate in the same way. But in most cases, there are servers of some kind that communicate with other servers. Clients communicate with the servers but *also* with other clients, hence the peer-to-peer moniker for this group of applications. Figure 7-3 shows a general peer-to-peer communication model.

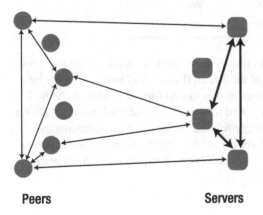

Figure 7-3. *Peer-to-peer commununciation*

Even though different peer-to-peer applications use a similar communication model, there is a very important difference between different types of peer-to-peer applications. One type, which includes Voice over IP (VoIP), requires a given peer to communicate with a *specific* other peer. When making calls over the Internet, we're only interested in talking with the person we called, no substitutions. With file sharing applications, such as BitTorrent, on the other hand, there is no requirement to be able to communicate with any particular peer: any reasonable subset of all available peers will do, as they all have pieces of the same file. Obviously, the tracker (BitTorrent jargon for the server that coordinates the initial communication between peers) and a number of peers must be dual stack, or either the IPv4-only or the IPv6-only peers can't join the "swarm" successfully.

Note The BitTorrent specification allows peers to identify themselves with either an IPv4 or IPv6 address or a hostname. However, trackers generally ignore the identification supplied by the peer in favor of the remote address they see to avoid problems with peers identifying themselves with private IPv4 addresses. And of course, just like so many other applications, most BitTorrent clients don't know how to work with IPv6 even though the protocol supports it.

With the two different peer-to-peer communication models, the total number of application communication models comes to four, as listed in Table 7-1.

Table 7-1. *Communication Models*

Model	Client-to-Client	Client-to-Server	Server-to-Server
Email model	no	one-to-one	yes
Web model	no	one-to-many	no
VoIP model	specific peer	one-to-one	yes
BitTorrent model	any peer	one-to-one	no

By now, it should be clear that the transition to IPv6 is the easiest for applications that conform to the email or BitTorrent models. In the email model, an IPv6-only client only has to be able to communicate with a single (dual stack) server, and in the BitTorrent model, an IPv6-only peer can communicate with a dual stack server and IPv6-only or dual stack peers. The Web and VoIP models are hampered by a chicken-and-egg problem: there aren't any advantages to upgrading until everyone has upgraded. This is where translation and proxy mechanisms come in: they "upgrade" Web and VoIP model applications to email model applications. In essence, the translator or proxy becomes the dual stack server.

Proxying

Although many more applications lend themselves to being proxied, proxies are mostly used for HTTP and FTP. For most other applications or protocols, the availability of proxy support in the application and IPv6-aware proxy software is such that proxying is either impossible or not worth the trouble. The most popular Web and FTP proxy is Squid, but unfortunately, Squid doesn't have built-in IPv6 support (although there is ongoing work and there are third-party patches). A good alternative is Apache, which we already installed in the previous chapter.

A very nice feature of a dual stack HTTP/HTTPS/FTP proxy is that it both allows IPv6-only clients to connect to the IPv4 Web and also IPv4-only clients to connect to IPv6-only sites.

Apache as a Proxy

To be able to proxy, it's necessary to compile Apache 2 with support for several additional modules. Listing 7-2, when executed in Apache's source directory, builds Apache with SSL support and several proxy options. The SSL support isn't required for proxying, though.

Listing 7-2. *Building Apache with Proxy Support*

```
make clean
./configure --enable-so --enable-ssl --enable-mods-shared="proxy proxy_http proxy_➥
ftp proxy_connect auth_digest"
make
make install
```

The make clean line removes files left over from a previous build. Note that this particular ./configure line enables shared object support. The different (shared) modules respectively allow proxying in general: the HTTP, FTP, and HTTPS proxies and digest authentication. If your existing Apache didn't include SSL support, you should probably leave out the --enable-ssl options. If Apache is already running, stop it with apachectl stop before issuing make install and start the newly built Apache with apachectl start. Listing 7-3 shows the lines that must be added to the Apache configuration file to enable proxying.

Listing 7-3. *Configuring Apache to Be a Proxy*

```
LoadModule    proxy_module           modules/mod_proxy.so
LoadModule    proxy_http_module      modules/mod_proxy_http.so
LoadModule    proxy_ftp_module       modules/mod_proxy_ftp.so
LoadModule    proxy_connect_module   modules/mod_proxy_connect.so
LoadModule    auth_digest_module     modules/mod_auth_digest.so

ProxyRequests On

<Proxy *>
  Order allow,deny
  Allow from 2001:db8::/32 192.0.2.0/24 example.com
</Proxy>
```

The ProxyRequests On line enables proxying, but before that can happen, the necessary shared objects must be loaded. Also, it's a very bad idea to run a proxy without any kind of access control. Spammers just love "open" proxies because those allow them to spill their sewage all over the Net with impunity because the proxy hides their address. For the same reason, anti-spam groups hate open proxies, so they hunt them down and put them in blacklists. Many people use these blacklists to block incoming mail from hosts that run an open proxy, so you really don't want your server to end up on such a list.

When I set up Apache 2 for the first time, I wanted to run it side by side with Apache 1.3 to see if everything worked as it should. So I configured Apache 2 to listen on IPv6 and also on

IPv4 on port 8080, which is a traditional proxy port. Within minutes, the "proxy" was discovered. To avoid unnecessary prodding by both sides in the spam war, it's easier to run the proxy on port 80 along with any regular Web sites that Apache serves. It also saves one or two lines of configuration. On the other hand, there is something to be said for running a completely separate Apache instance for proxying. This way, you can take the proxy offline without disturbing regular Web service.

Anyway, the <Proxy *> line tells Apache that the configuration statements that follow (until </Proxy>) are about proxy requests. The asterisk means that we're talking about *all* proxy requests. The Order allow,deny line looks rather strange to the untrained eye. Its purpose is to indicate that we're explicitly going to allow certain things and that everything else should be denied. With order deny,allow, on the other hand, the reverse would happen: everything that wasn't explicitly denied would be allowed. The Allow line tells Apache that proxy requests from listed IPv6 and IPv4 address ranges and all hosts within the domain example.com are allowed.

Another way to set up proxy access restrictions is to limit access to the proxy based on a login and a password rather than on address ranges or domain names. This makes it much easier for "road warriors" to connect to the Internet wherever they happen to find themselves and still use the proxy. Unfortunately, it doesn't seem to be possible to allow unauthenticated users in certain address ranges or domains while forcing users outside those trusted parts of the network to authenticate themselves with a password. The Apache module needed to perform user authentication was already loaded in Listing 7-3, and Listing 7-4 provides the finishing touches, which should replace the <Proxy *> to </Proxy> lines in Listing 7-3.

Listing 7-4. *Limiting Proxy Access with a Login and Password*

```
<Proxy *>
  order allow,deny
  allow from all
  authname proxy
  authdigestfile /etc/proxypasswd.digest
  authtype digest
  require valid-user
</Proxy>
```

This configuration allows access to the proxy from everywhere (allow from all) but also requires a valid user. It is, of course, also possible to require one or more named users instead. Apache reads user information from the file that authdigestfile points to. Users can be added to such a file with Apache's htdigest utility. Listing 7-5 uses htdigest to create a user/password combination.

Listing 7-5. *Creating Users for Digest Authentication*

```
# /usr/local/apache2/bin/htdigest /etc/proxypasswd.digest proxy iljitsch
Adding user iljitsch in realm proxy
New password:
Re-type new password:
```

Listings 7-4 (the authname line) and 7-5 both use a "realm" called proxy. Realms can be used to keep authentication for different Web sites or parts of Web sites served by the same Apache apart. Many browsers display the realm when prompting the user for a login and a password. Apache supports several authentication methods. The simplest is "basic," which doesn't encrypt the password, so it's very insecure. The newer variation of the "digest" method implemented in the mod_auth_digest module (as opposed to the older mod_digest module) uses fairly strong security, but *only* for the password: the HTTP requests and their results pass over the network in clear text. However, Apache also supports HTTPS proxying, where the data is of course fully encrypted, even as it passes through the innards of the proxy. HTTPS requests are proxied differently from regular HTTP requests. When the client wants to do an HTTPS request through a proxy, it first connects to the proxy, asks the proxy to connect to the destination server, and then sets up a secure sockets layer (SSL) connection directly with the destination server. The proxy only copies the encrypted data to and from the client and doesn't get to see the unencrypted request or response data.

Caution Although the digest user/password file stores MD5 hashes of the passwords rather than the clear-text passwords that go in the htaccess files used for "basic" authentication, it's still a good idea to keep the file outside the view of prying eyes. *Never* put password files in the HTTP document tree.

Last but not least, Apache supports FTP proxying. However, because the proxy requests are done over HTTP and the HTTP and FTP protocols are very different, there are many limitations to using FTP through a proxy. That said, it generally works well for the type of FTP requests that browsers make.

Note When testing digest authentication, I had problems with Internet Explorer 6 and Safari 1.2.4. Requests for URLs with a question mark in them (such as Web searches) weren't understood by the proxy. With address- or domain-based rather than password-based access control, these URLs would load just fine. Firefox didn't have any problems with digest authentication.

Caching

Although bandwidth is cheap and plentiful these days, it makes sense to have the proxy cache the HTML pages and files that flow through it. Apache 2 does provide caching functionality, but at the time of this writing, most of the caching options were still marked as "experimental," and with good reason: caching of remote Web resources on disk didn't work to any useful degree.

Tip There is much more to proxying with Apache. Read its documentation for more options.

Using a Proxy

In Internet Explorer under Windows, you can enable a proxy by choosing Tools ➤ Internet Options ➤ Connections ➤ LAN Settings, selecting the Use a Proxy Server for Your LAN checkbox, and filling in the proxy particulars, as shown in Figure 7-4.

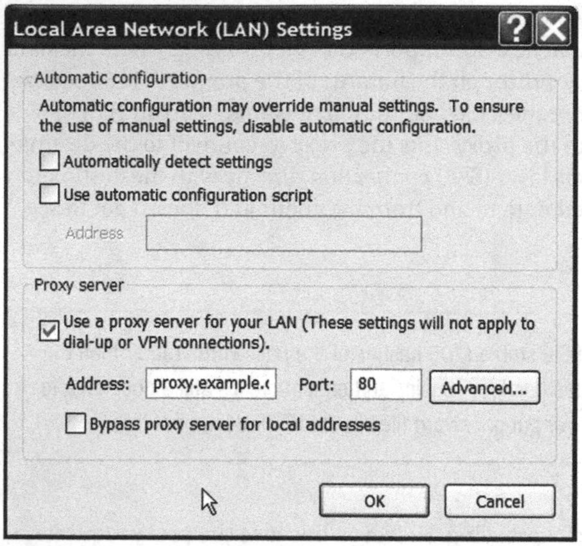

Figure 7-4. *Setting up a proxy in Internet Explorer*

In Firefox, use Tools ➤ Options ➤ Connection Settings, as shown in Figure 7-5.

MacOS takes a slightly different approach: proxies are configured as part of the network settings. This means that you can have different proxy settings for different "network locations." To change the proxy settings, open System Preferences and select Network and optionally choose a location. After that, you have to select a network interface under "Show." The proxy settings will be used only if you're connected to the Internet through the interface for which the proxy is configured. Set up proxies under the "Proxies" tab, as shown in Figure 7-6.

Setting up the proxy password in System Preferences often doesn't work all that well, but that shouldn't be a problem, as the system will ask for the proxy login and password when accessing the proxy for the first time.

■**Tip** Firefox under MacOS doesn't use the system proxy settings, so you should set up a proxy for Firefox the same way as for other operating systems.

■**Note** None of these systems accepts an IPv6 address in the proxy configuration, but they will use IPv6 to connect to the proxy if the proxy's name has an AAAA record.

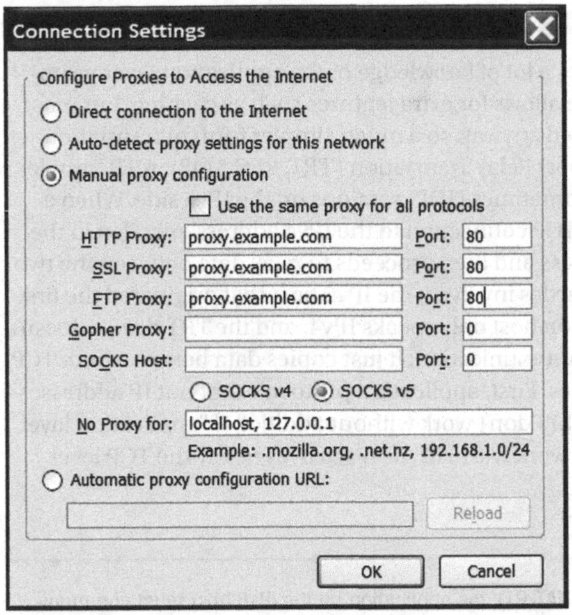

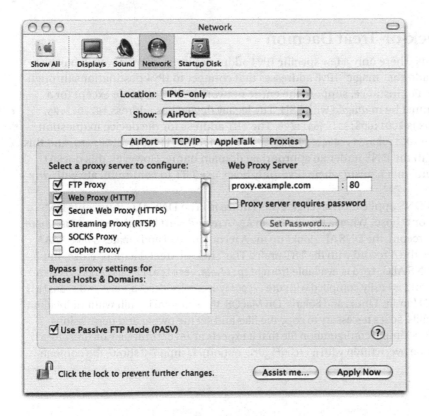

Figure 7-5. *Setting up a proxy in Firefox*

Figure 7-6. *Setting up a proxy under MacOS*

Transport Protocol Translation

A disadvantage of proxying is that it requires a lot of knowledge of the application layer protocols such as HTTP and FTP. This knowledge allows for extra features such as caching, but most
of the time, these extra features aren't needed anyway, so a much simpler form of translation
between IPv6 and IPv4 can be used: Transport Relay Translation (TRT, RFC 3142). A TRT implementation listens for incoming TCP (and sometimes UDP) sessions on the IPv6 side. When a
session comes in, the TRT device sets up a TCP connection to the IPv4 address encoded in the
bottom 32 bits of the IPv6 destination address and then proceeds to relay data between the two
TCP sessions. This works very well for all parties involved: the IPv6 host that originated the first
session only speaks IPv6, the IPv4 destination host only speaks IPv4, and the TRT device doesn't
have to know about the particulars of the communication; it just copies data between both TCP
sessions. There are only two slight downsides. First, application protocols that put IP addresses
in the data stream (such as FTP, SIP, and RTSP) don't work without additional "application layer
gateway" (ALG) glue. Second, IPsec doesn't work with TRT, as IPsec lives below the TCP level
and is therefore not translated or forwarded.

Note Don't forget that in order to use TRT (or NAT-PT), the application on the IPv6 host must communicate over IPv6. If the application tries to communicate over IPv4 instead, TRT or NAT-PT won't be of any use.

DNS ALG: Trick-or-Treat Daemon

In small installations where only a few specific IPv4 addresses must be made available over
IPv6, it's easiest to add the "magic" IPv6 addresses that connect to IPv4 destinations through
TRT to a DNS zone. For instance, suppose the entire network is IPv6-capable except for a
legacy device that must be managed with SSH. The legacy device has address 192.0.2.25,
and the magic prefix is 2001:db8:31:6464::/96. The TRT address for the device in question
would then become 2001:db8:31:6464::192.0.2.25 or 2001:db8:31:6464::c000:219, and this
address can be put in the DNS under an appropriate domain name. However, this doesn't
work well as a general mechanism where IPv6-only hosts use TRT to communicate with *any*
IPv4-only host.

This is where a DNS application layer gateway comes in. The DNS ALG intercepts DNS
lookups by the IPv6-only hosts. When a request for an AAAA record can't be satisfied because there
simply isn't an AAAA record, the DNS ALG looks up the A record instead and creates a fake AAAA
record by combining the A record with the TRT prefix. The "trick-or-treat daemon" (totd) implements such a TRT DNS ALG. totd is available from http://www.vermicelli.pasta.cs.uit.no/
ipv6/software.html and is easily compiled with the ./configure, make depend, make, make install
sequence on the BSD family, Linux, and Solaris. On MacOS, the software is built without incident,
but the installation fails, so it's necessary to copy the files and set the owner and permissions
manually. totd needs a simple configuration file that it expects at /etc/totd.conf or /usr/local/
etc/totd.conf (may be overwritten with a ./configure option). Listing 7-6 shows the contents
of this file.

Listing 7-6. *The* `totd.conf` *File*

```
forwarder 2001:db8:31::53
prefix 2001:db8:31:6464::
```

The `forwarder` line points toward a resolving DNS server, and the `prefix` line supplies the TRT magic prefix.

■Caution It's important to keep `totd` well isolated from the normal DNS service to avoid the fake AAAA records from polluting the DNS namespace. A good way to do this when the DNS ALG is only required on a limited number of systems is to run `totd` locally on each system.

Faith on FreeBSD

Probably the first implementation of TRT is `faith` in the KAME IPv6 stack, which is the basis of the IPv6 implementation in FreeBSD and other members of the BSD family. The `faith` TRT consists of two parts: a `faith` network interface, and the `faithd` daemon. FreeBSD normally has a `faith0` interface, and new `faith` interfaces can be created with `ifconfig faith create`. For the interface to do any useful work, it's necessary to enable it by using a `sysctl` setting, and the TRT prefix must be routed to the interface. This is accomplished in Listing 7-7.

Listing 7-7. *Enabling the* `faith` *Interface*

```
# sysctl -w net.inet6.ip6.keepfaith=1
# ifconfig faith0 inet6 2001:db8:31:6464::127.0.0.1/96
```

Because FreeBSD lacks a more direct way to route a prefix toward an interface, it's easiest to configure an address in the TRT prefix on the `faith` interface. The `localhost` address is a good choice, as it's unlikely that this will get in the way of anything. The next step is running the `faithd` daemon. Before starting the daemon, it's important to set up access restrictions to keep the rest of the IPv6 Internet from using your relay. This is done in the `/etc/faithd.conf` file, as shown in Listing 7-8.

Listing 7-8. *Restricting Access to* `faithd`

```
2001:db8:31::/48 permit 0.0.0.0/0
```

This line instructs `faithd` to allow relaying from any address in `2001:db8:31::/48` toward any IPv4 address. See the `faithd` man page for more details. The easiest way to run `faithd` is to start it with the port number that will be relayed as an argument. (The daemon can also be run from `inetd`, but this is more complex.) Each TCP port that must be relayed requires a separate instance of `faithd`, and it's *not* possible to relay a port with TRT if there is service running locally on that port. As a result, `faithd` has only limited usability as a general-purpose transition mechanism.

pTRTd on Linux

Because the Linux IPv6 stack doesn't have any KAME ancestry, it doesn't have `faith`. However, for Linux, there is the Portable Transport Relay Translator Daemon (pTRTd),[3] which is even better. pTRTd supports UDP, doesn't clash with local services, and a single daemon handles all ports. pTRTd is available at `http://www.litech.org/ptrtd/` and is installed using the customary `./configure`, `make`, `make install` sequence. pTRTd depends the `ip` package (see Chapter 3) and the `tuntap` network driver. Both are included in the Red Hat 9 distribution.

If started without arguments, the `ptrtd` daemon will use site local `fec0:0:0:ffff::/96` prefix as the magic TRT prefix. Because pTRTd doesn't include any access restrictions, it would be a good idea to have the TRT prefix in site local space. Unfortunately, this doesn't work: the system keeps complaining that it "cannot assign" addresses. Specifying a prefix in global unicast space with (for instance) `ptrtd -p 2001:db8:31:6464::` works much better. To make sure that others won't abuse the relay, it's important to set up firewall rules or a router access list to limit access to the relay. See Chapter 9 for this.

Caution I was unable to use pTRTd to connect from other IPv6 hosts to the IPv4 Internet on Red Hat ES4 Linux, even though the Red Hat machine itself was capable of going through pTRTd. But because this host must be dual stack anyway, that doesn't do much good.

Network Address Translation–
Protocol Translation

An even more general mechanism than transport layer translation is Stateless IP/ICMP Translation (SIIT) as specified in RFC 2765. As the name indicates, SIIT doesn't require an implementation to keep around information about what kind of communication is going on. However, it does need to know which IPv4 address is to be translated to which IPv6 address and vice versa. This means that SIIT on its own is useful in a very limited number of situations, so it's generally used as the "PT" part in NAT-PT: Network Address Translation–Protocol Translation. NAT-PT adds IPv4 NAT behavior on top of SIIT so that an IPv6 host can simply connect to a synthetic IPv6 address generated by a DNS ALG. The NAT part will then keep track of which address and port number combinations go together so the PT or SIIT part can do the actual translation. Because NAT-PT works at the IP layer, it's at least theoretically possible to keep IPsec ESP intact when translating. Other than that, it provides pretty much the same service as TRT.

---

3. Contrary to popular belief, pTRTd doesn't stand for "Pretty Tasty Routing Toad Demon."

There are no NAT-PT implementations for Linux, FreeBSD, MacOS, or Windows, except ones that are too experimental to be useful. Apparently, Cisco has a good NAT-PT implementation, but, unfortunately, this feature is only available in a small number of software images for a small number of hardware platforms, so I haven't been able to test this myself.

Tip To my surprise, TRT/NAT-PT turned out a lot less useful than I thought it would be, because there are very few applications that support IPv6, but for which it's not possible to run an IPv6 server or proxy yourself. So even though in theory, a pTRTd/NAT-PT setup allows for much broader connectivity to the IPv6 world, in practice, having a dual stack proxy and mail server provide much the same benefits.

CHAPTER 8

■ ■ ■

IPv6 Internals

"What of, let us say, his inner organs?"

*"In the overworld, such parts are considered unnecessary and even somewhat vulgar.
In short, there are no inner parts."*

Cugel's Saga, Jack Vance

This chapter will look at IPv6 internals. A lot of this is pretty dry stuff: options, headers, more options, lifetimes. But along the line, you'll learn more about some of IPv6's idiosyncrasies, which is very helpful in troubleshooting the protocol (see more in Chapter 10). In some cases, such as with renumbering and multicast group membership management issues, it's necessary to learn a good deal of background information before it's possible to understand the issue well. For this reason, several subjects that aren't strictly internal to IPv6 are somewhat "buried" in this chapter.

Differences Between IPv4 and IPv6

All knowledge about IPv6 begins with studying the IPv6 header format and the ways in which it is different from the IPv4 header format. Even though at the time the IPv6 specifications were written, 64-bit CPUs were few and far between, the IPv6 designers elected to optimize the IPv6 header for 64-bit processing. For this reason, I've drawn the IPv6 header "64-bit wide" in Figure 8-1, which is a little different from the way it's usually depicted. Because 64-bit CPUs can read 64-bit wide memory words at a time, it's helpful that fields that are 64 bits (or a multiple of 64 bits) wide start at an even 64-bit boundary. Because every 64-bit boundary is also a 32-bit boundary, this doesn't get in the way of 32-bit CPUs. The IPv4 header is presented in the usual form that highlights its 32-bit background.

IPv4 Header

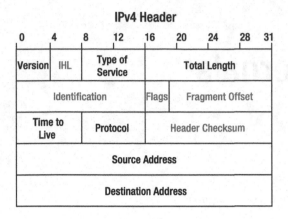

IPv6 Header

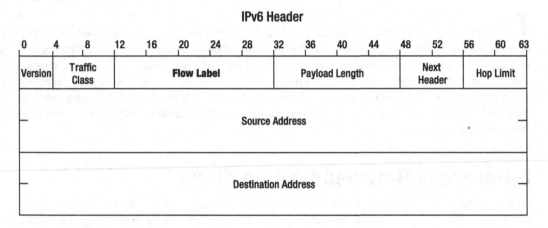

Figure 8-1. *The IPv4 and IPv6 headers*

The fields in the IPv4 header that aren't present in the IPv6 header have gray text; the field that's present in IPv6 but not in IPv4 is shown in bold. The changes from IPv4 to IPv6 are

Version now always contains **6** rather than **4**.

The **Internet Header Length** (IHL) field that indicates the length of the IPv4 header is no longer needed because the IPv6 header is always 40 bytes long.

Type of Service is now **Traffic Class**. The original semantics of the IPv4 Type of Service field have been superseded by the diffserv semantics per RFC 2474. However, in IPv4, both interpretations of the field are in use (although most routers aren't able or configured to look at the field anyway). The IPv6 RFCs don't mandate a specific way to use the Traffic Class field, but generally the RFC 2474 diffserv interpretation is assumed.

The **Flow Label** is new in IPv6. The idea is that packets belonging to the same stream, session, or flow share a common flow label value, making the session easily recognizable without having to look "deep" into the packet. Recognizing a stream or session is often useful in Quality of Service mechanisms. Although few implementations actually look at the flow label, most systems do set different flow labels for packets belonging to different TCP sessions. A zero value in this field means that setting a flow label per session isn't supported or desired.

The **Total Length** is the length of the IPv4 packet including the header, but in IPv6, the **Payload Length** doesn't include the 40-byte IPv6 header. This saves the host or router receiving a packet from having to check whether the packet is large enough to hold the IP header in the first place, making for a small efficiency gain.

The **Identification**, **Flags**, and **Fragment Offset** fields are used when IPv4 packets must be fragmented. Fragmentation in IPv6 works very differently (explained later this chapter), so these fields are relegated to a header of their own.

Time to Live is now called **Hop Limit**. This field is initialized with a suitable value at a packet's origin and decremented by each router along the way. When field reaches zero, the packet is destroyed. This way, packets can't circle the network forever when there are loops. Per RFC 791, the IPv4 Time to Live field should be decremented by the number of seconds that a packet is buffered in a router, but this turned out to be too hard to implement, so each router lowers the contents of the field by one, regardless of buffering time. The new name is a better description of what actually happens.

The **Protocol** field in IPv4 is replaced by **Next Header** in IPv6. In both cases, the field indicates the type of header that follows the IPv4 or IPv6 header. In most cases, this would be 6 for TCP or 17 for UDP. Because the IPv6 header has a fixed length, any options such as source routing or fragmentation must be implemented as additional headers that sit between the IPv6 header and the higher-layer protocol such as TCP, forming a "protocol chain."

The IPv4 **Header Checksum** was removed in IPv6.

The **Source Address** and **Destination Address** serve the same function in IPv6 as in IPv4, except that they are now four times as long at 128 bits.

Note Despite the name, the Payload Length field includes the length of any additional headers, not just the length of the user data. The maximum value for this field is 65,535, so with the 40-byte IPv6 header, this makes for a maximum IPv6 packet size of 65,575 bytes. However, RFC 2675 specifies a way to create even larger IPv6 packets.

All IPv6 hosts and routers are required to support a maximum packet size of at least 1280 bytes. For lower-layer protocols that can't support a Maximum Transfer Unit (MTU) of 1280 bytes, the relevant "IPv6 over . . ." standard must have a mechanism to break up and reassemble IPv6 packets so that the minimum of 1280 bytes can be accommodated. In IPv4, the official minimum size is 68 bytes, which isn't workable.

THE IPV4, TCP, AND UDP CHECKSUM

The checksum algorithm for the IPv4 header, TCP, and UDP is "the 16-bit one's complement of the one's complement sum of all 16-bit words in the header" (RFCs 791 (IP), 792 (ICMP), 793 (TCP), and 768 (UDP), respectively). One's complement math is slightly different from normal math. When adding the decimal values 32768 and 49152, the result is 81920. In hexadecimal, that would be 0x8000 + 0xC000 = 0x14000, or 0x4000 with a carry bit when using 16 bits. In one's complement additions, the carry bit is added to the result, making the 16-bit one's complement addition of 0x8000 and 0xC000 equal to 0x4001.

As usual with checksums and CRCs, the value is computed at the source and transmitted along with the data. The destination performs the same computation and compares the value found in the packet with the new result. If they're the same, presumably the packet didn't change in transit.

An interesting property of one's complement math is that the values 0x0000 and 0xFFFF are equivalent: adding 0x0000 to a value has the same result as adding 0xFFFF to that value. For instance: 0x6201 + 0x0000 = 0x6201 (obviously). 0x6201 + 0xFFFF would normally be 0x16200, but with the special treatment for the carry bit, this also becomes 0x6201. This means that the value 0x0000 can be inserted in the UDP checksum field to indicate that a checksum wasn't computed.

The TCP, UDP, and ICMPv6 checksums are computed over a "pseudo header" and the TCP, UDP, or ICMPv6 header, and user data respectively. The pseudo header consists of the source and destination addresses, the upper-layer packet length, and the protocol number. Including this information in the checksum calculation makes sure that TCP, UDP, or ICMPv6 don't process packets that were delivered incorrectly, for instance, because of a bit error in the IP header.

Checksums

In IPv4, the IP header is protected by a header checksum, and higher-layer protocols generally also have a checksum. The checksum algorithm for the IPv4 header, ICMP, ICMPv6, TCP, and UDP is the same (see sidebar), except that in IPv4, UDP packets may forego checksumming and simply set the checksum field to zero. In IPv6, this is no longer allowed: UDP packets must have a valid checksum.

IPv6 no longer has a header checksum to protect the IP header. This means that when a packet header is corrupted by transmission errors, the packet will very likely be delivered incorrectly. However, higher-layer protocols should be able to detect these problems so they're not fatal. Also, lower layers almost always employ a CRC to detect errors. A Cyclic Redundancy Check (CRC) is similar to a checksum but uses a more complex calculation than a simple one's complement addition so it has much better error detection properties. Ethernet, for instance, uses a 32-bit CRC that is automatically computed by the Ethernet hardware.

Extension Headers

To allow special processing along the way, IPv4 allows the IP header to be extended with one or more options. These options are rarely used today, both because they don't really solve common problems but also because packets with options can't be processed in the "fast path," and many routers and firewalls block some or all options. Not unlike the checkout counters at a grocery store, many routers have several "paths" that packets may follow: a fast one, implemented in hardware or highly optimized software, that supports only the most common operations ("no checks"), and one or more slower paths that use more advanced but slower software code that supports less common operations such as looking at IP options. However, many modern routers only have a "fast path," so using additional features doesn't lead to a performance penalty.

Because the header is fixed length in IPv6, options can't be tagged onto the IP header as in IPv4. Instead, they're put in a header of their own that sits between the IPv6 header and the TCP or UDP (or other higher level protocol) header. The most common extension headers are

Hop-by-Hop Options: See the section that follows.

Routing: Similar to the Source Route option in IPv4.

Fragment: Used for fragmentation; see later in this chapter.

Authentication: Authenticates the user data and most header fields.

Encapsulating Security Payload (ESP): Encrypts and/or authenticates user data.

Destination Options: See the section that follows.

The Hop-by-Hop Options and Destination Options headers are container headers: they have room for multiple suboptions. The Hop-by-Hop Options are processed by all routers along the way. All other options are normally ignored by routers and processed only by the destination. Obviously firewalls, or routers configured to perform filtering, may also look at these options. The Hop-by-Hop Options, Routing, Fragment, and Destination Options extension headers are defined in RFC 2460. The Authentication and ESP extension headers are part of IPsec, which you'll learn about in Chapter 9.

■Note There is no standard extension header format. This means that when a host encounters a header that it doesn't recognize in the protocol chain, the only thing it can do is discard the packet. Worse, firewalls and routers configured to filter IPv6 have the same problem: as soon as they encounter an unknown extension header, they must decide to allow or disallow the packet, even though another header deeper inside the packet would possibly trigger the opposite behavior. In other words, an IPv6 packet with a TCP payload that would normally be allowed through could be blocked if there is an unknown extension header between the IPv6 and TCP headers.

ICMPv6

The IPv6 version of the Internet Control Message Protocol (ICMP) serves mostly the same purposes as its IPv4 counterpart, but there are some changes.[1] In IPv4, when a router or the destination host can't process the packet properly, it sends back an ICMP error message along with the original IP header and the first eight bytes of the higher-layer header. For UDP and TCP, this is enough for the source of the original host to see which TCP session or UDP association generated the offending packet. Because IPv6 supports an arbitrary number of

---

1. The IPv4 ICMP is standardized in RFC 792 and IPv6 ICMP in RFC 2463.

extension headers between the IPv6 header and the higher-layer header, ICMPv6 returns as much of the original packet as will fit in the minimum MTU size of 1280 bytes. In addition to error messages, which are recognizable by an ICMP type of 127 or lower, there are also informational messages, with a type of 128 or higher. Because informational messages aren't the result of an error, they don't include an original packet or part thereof. The most common ICMPv6 message types are

1: Destination unreachable. The destination IP address, protocol, or port number is unreachable, or communication is "administratively prohibited."

2: Packet too big. The packet is too large to be transmitted to the next hop.

3: Time exceeded. The Hop Count field reached zero.

4: Parameter problem. This message is sent when a router or host encounters an invalid value in a header field or an unknown extension header or option.

128: Echo request. These are the packets sent by the ping6 utility.

129: Echo reply. These are the ping replies.

130: Multicast listener query. Routers use this query to ask hosts for their multicast group memberships.

131: Multicast listener report. Hosts use this message to report their multicast group memberships.

132: Multicast listener done. Hosts use this message to report that it leaves a multicast group.

133: Router solicitation. Hosts send this message to trigger a router advertisement.

134: Router advertisement. Routers send this message to allow hosts to perform stateless autoconfiguration.

135: Neighbor solicitation. Routers and hosts use this message to ask for a neighbor's MAC address.

136: Neighbor advertisement. Routers and hosts send this message in reply to a neighbor solicitation.

137: Redirect message. Routers use these messages to tell hosts to use a different next hop address for a certain destination.

ICMP and ICMPv6 messages also include a "code" that indicates the exact nature of the ICMP message within a certain type. As with ICMP, ICMPv6 calculates a checksum over the control message, but unlike with ICMP, the ICMPv6 checksum calculation also includes a pseudo header. Another departure from IPv4 is the fact that hosts and routers are required to limit the number of ICMPv6 messages they send. So if a router receives 100 packets per second toward an unreachable destination, it's not supposed to send back ICMPv6 packets at the same rate of 100 per second.

The ICMPv6 redirect message works slightly different from the ICMP redirect message in IPv4. Like its IPv4 counterpart, the ICMPv6 redirect can be used by a router to inform a host that it should use a different router to reach the destination in question. But routers can also use the IPv6 Redirect to tell a host that the destination is reachable on the local subnet. So two hosts that have addresses in different prefixes can communicate directly after receiving redirects from a router.

■**Tip** See `http://www.iana.org/numbers.html` for ICMPv6 type and code numbers and other protocol numbers.

Neighbor Discovery

When a system wants to send an IPv6 packet to another system connected to the same subnet or link, it needs to know what MAC address (or "link address" in the new IPv6 terminology) it should address the packet to, unless the interface in question is a point-to-point interface. Neighbor discovery allows systems to discover each other's MAC addresses, similar to ARP on Ethernet with IPv4.

Each IPv6 system joins the "solicited node" multicast group that corresponds to each of its addresses. Because the solicited node group address consists of the prefix `ff02:0:0:0:0:1:ff00::/104` followed by the bottom 24 bits of the address in question, addresses in different prefixes based on the same interface identifier (including the link-local address) all map to the same solicited node address.

Whenever a system needs to find out the link address for another system residing on the same link, it sends a neighbor solicitation to the solicited node address that the IPv6 address of the remote system maps to. For good measure, the source host includes its own MAC address in the neighbor solicitation, so the neighbor knows where to send the reply.

Because multiple IPv6 addresses can map to the same single solicited node address, a system receiving a neighbor solicitation message will first check whether the request is indeed for one of its addresses. If so, the system sends back a neighbor advertisement with its link address in it. At the same time, the system stores the IPv6/MAC address combination from the request in its neighbor discovery mapping table, also called "neighbor cache."

You can list and manipulate the system's list of IPv6 neighbors with the ndp command under FreeBSD and MacOS and show the neighbor list with `show ipv6 neighbors` under Cisco IOS. See Chapter 10 for more information about using the ndp command.

■**Note** RFC 2461 requires IPv6 implementations to buffer at least one packet per neighbor while waiting for neighbor discovery to complete. With IPv4, when a neighbor's MAC address isn't in the ARP table, many implementations send out an ARP and then throw away the packet that triggered the ARP request.

Neighbor Unreachability Detection

RFC 2461 also specifies a procedure for neighbor unreachability detection. IPv6 hosts and routers actively track whether their neighbors are reachable. They do this by periodically sending neighbor discovery messages directly to the neighbor. If the neighbor answers, it's reachable; if it doesn't, there must be some kind of problem, and the system will discard the neighbor's MAC address and try a regular multicast neighbor discovery procedure. This allows IPv6 systems to detect dead neighbors and neighbors that change their MAC address. But it's most useful to detect dead *routers*. On a subnet with more than one router, a host can simply install a default route toward another router when the router that is has been using becomes unreachable.

Windows XP, Linux, MacOS, and FreeBSD all take the situation where a router loses its IPv6 address and no longer runs IPv6 in stride and switch over to another router without incident. However, turning off the active router has much more severe effects: at the very least, ongoing downloads stall for a while, and in some cases, the session breaks. I have no explanation for this difference in behavior.

Stateless Address Autoconfiguration

Hosts and routers always configure link-local addresses on every interface on which IPv6 is enabled. The link-local address is nearly always derived from the interface's MAC address, but to guarantee uniqueness, it's necessary to perform Duplicate Address Detection (DAD), as discussed later this chapter.

Once a host has a link-local address, it can proceed to obtain one or more global IPv6 addresses by using RFC 2462 stateless address autoconfiguration. As discussed in Chapter 2, IPv6 routers send out router advertisement (RA) packets (ICMPv6 type 134) periodically and in response to router solicitations. The information in RAs includes:

- An 8-bit "cur hop limit" field that tells hosts what value to use in the Hop Limit field of outgoing IPv6 packets.

- The "managed address configuration" (M) flag. This flag isn't terribly well defined, but the basic idea is that when it's set, hosts use a stateful mechanism (presumably, DHCPv6) to configure their addresses, and when the flag isn't set, they use stateless address autoconfiguration.

- The "other stateful configuration" (O) flag. This flag is similar to the M flag but indicates that the host should use a stateful mechanism to discover for nonaddress configuration.

- A 16-bit "router lifetime" value in seconds. This value tells hosts how long the default route that was created as the result of this RA should remain valid.

- The 32-bit "reachable time" value in milliseconds. This value indicates how long a neighbor should be considered reachable after receiving a "reachability confirmation," which is generally a neighbor advertisement but could be any packet.

- The 32-bit "retrans timer" value in milliseconds. The retrans timer tells hosts how long they should wait before retransmitting neighbor solicitation messages when there is no answer.

When fields that determine a value are set to zero, this means the value isn't specified in the RA, so hosts must come up with that value through other means. In addition to the preceding, router advertisements may also contain one or more options, such as:

- "Source link-layer address," the router's MAC address.

- MTU, the maximum packet size that should be used on this subnet.

- Prefix information, which specifies the prefixes used on the subnet and their properties.

Tip On some interface types, Cisco routers use the MTU option in their router advertisements to inform hosts of the MTU the router itself uses, even if it's the 1500 byte Ethernet default. Use `show ipv6 interface ...` to list the MTU used with IPv6 for an interface and `mtu ...` in the interface context to set the MTU for all protocols or `ipv6 mtu ...` to set the IPv6 MTU for an interface.

The "prefix information" option, in turn, has its own list of attributes. (Are you getting a headache yet?)

- The address prefix itself and its length. For stateless address autoconfiguration to work, the prefix must be 64 bits long.[2]

- The "on-link" flag. This flag tells hosts that the prefix is "on-link," so systems with addresses within this prefix are reachable on the subnet in question without help from a router.

- The "autonomous address configuration" flag. This flag tells hosts that they can create an address for themselves by combining this prefix with an interface identifier.

- A 32-bit "valid lifetime" in seconds. This value indicates how long the prefix should be considered on-link and how long autoconfigured addresses using the prefix may be used.

- A 32-bit "preferred lifetime" in seconds. This flag tells hosts how long autoconfigured addresses using this prefix are preferred.

Duplicate Address Detection

To avoid the situation where two IPv6 systems use the same address, systems perform Duplicate Address Detection for (nearly) all new IPv6 addresses before they're used. DAD is done for global unicast addresses—and not just those created using stateless address autoconfiguration, but also for link-local addresses. For obvious reasons, there is no DAD for anycast addresses, as the whole point of anycast is that multiple systems have the same address. It's also permitted to skip DAD for addresses that have an (EUI-64-based) interface identifier that was already tested

---

2. RFC 2462 requires only that the length of the address prefix as advertised by routers and the length of the interface identifier combined is 128 bits, but RFC 3513 mandates 64-bit interface identifiers in EUI-64 format for all IPv6 address space except in the ::/3 prefix.

for uniqueness. So if a host just uses stateless address autoconfiguration with an EUI-64 interface identifier, it only needs to perform DAD for the link-local address.

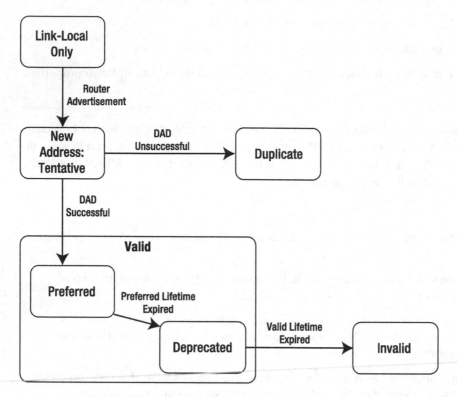

Figure 8-2. *The life cycle of an IPv6 address*

As depicted in Figure 8-2, a host starts with only a link-local address. DAD is also done for the link-local address, but this isn't shown in the figure. When a host receives a router advertisement that contains one or more prefixes with the autonomous address configuration flag set, the host creates addresses with interface identifiers derived from the EUI-64 and possibly also a randomly generated one, if the host uses RFC 3041 address privacy. (See Chapter 2.) The host marks the resulting addresses as "tentative" and proceeds to execute the Duplicate Address Detection procedure. It does this by joining the solicited node multicast group for the address in question and sending out one or more neighbor solicitation messages for the address. (If the number of DAD retries is configured to be zero, no DAD is performed.) Then, one of the following situations will occur:

- The host receives a neighbor advertisement from another host that is holding the address.

- The host receives a neighbor solicitation message from another host that is performing DAD. (It can tell because the source address is set to the unspecified address and the MAC address is different from its own.)

- There is no answer. (Except maybe that the host hears its own neighbor solicitation.)

The first two cases indicate a conflict, and the addresses are marked "duplicate." When this occurs, the address remains unused. Only when there is no answer is the address used. If there is a conflict, the system is supposed to log the error and wait for manual intervention.

Address Lifetime

After successfully maneuvering past the DAD hurdle, addresses configured through stateless address autoconfiguration can be used until the "preferred lifetime" from the router advertisement message expires. In most cases, this won't happen because new RAs refresh the timers. But if there are no more RAs, eventually, the preferred lifetime will elapse and the address becomes "deprecated." New sessions shouldn't use deprecated addresses but prefer "preferred" (non-deprecated) addresses, if available. However, existing sessions will continue to use the deprecated address. Eventually, the "valid lifetime" will also run out, and the deprecated address is removed from the interface. This will break any sessions that are still using the address.

■**Note** Many UNIX-like operating systems will continue to send packets containing a source address that has been removed from the system as long as there are sessions that use this address. This has the advantage that if an address disappears and comes back quickly (for instance, when a wireless link goes down for a moment because of bad reception), the sessions are still alive.

Renumbering

Having different preferred and valid timers for the router advertisement itself and also for any prefixes contained in it makes it possible to do two things: renumber easily and shoot yourself in the foot. It's even possible to do both at the same time. With stateless autoconfiguration, renumbering couldn't be easier: simply give the router an address in the new prefix and set the preferred lifetime for the old prefix to zero, as in Listing 8-1.

Listing 8-1. *Installing a New Prefix and Deprecating an Old One*

```
!
interface Ethernet0
 ipv6 address 2001:db8:4500:17c::/64 eui-64
 ipv6 address 2001:db8:31:2::/64 eui-64
 ipv6 nd prefix 2001:db8:31:2::/64 infinite 0
!
```

In this example, a Cisco router is configured with an address in prefix 2001:db8:4500:17c::/64. This would be the new prefix, which is automatically added to the list of prefixes in router advertisements with the autonomous address configuration flag set. The following line specifies the old prefix (2001:db8:31:2::/64), and the line after that sets up an infinite valid lifetime (the 32-bit field set to all ones or 0xffffffff) but a preferred lifetime of zero. This makes hosts create one or more new addresses and deprecate any existing ones in the old prefix as soon as they receive the resulting router advertisement. After that, all new communication should start using the new address immediately. Existing TCP sessions and UDP associations will continue to use the same address as before. After some time, all communication that started before the change should have stopped so that the old addresses can be removed safely. This process is started with Listing 8-2.

Listing 8-2. *Setting the Valid Lifetime to Two Hours in Router Advertisements*

```
!
interface Ethernet0
 ipv6 nd prefix 2001:db8:31:2::/64 7200 0
!
```

This sets the preferred lifetime to zero and the valid lifetime to 7200 seconds. As a precaution against attackers, hosts are not supposed to trust a valid lifetime of less than 7200. Older versions of Linux (such as Red Hat 9 with its 2.4 kernel) don't bother with this check, though. Make sure that the hosts have received at least one RA after setting the valid lifetime to 7200, and then set both the lifetimes to zero and remove the autonomous address configuration flag for the prefix:

```
ipv6 nd prefix 2001:db8:31:2::/64 0 0 no-autoconfig
```

Two hours later, all hosts should have removed the addresses in this prefix so you can remove the prefix from the router, as in Listing 8-3.

Listing 8-3. *Removing a Prefix from a Router*

```
!
interface Ethernet0
 no ipv6 address 2001:db8:31:2::/64 eui-64
 no ipv6 nd prefix 2001:db8:31:2::/64
!
```

You can monitor address lifetimes with `netsh interface ipv6 show address` under Windows, `ip -6 addr show` under Linux, and with `ifconfig -L` under BSD/MacOS. It's too bad that the hard part in renumbering isn't the actual address renumbering of hosts, but rather hunting down addresses in all kinds of configuration files, filters, and of course the DNS and then changing the addresses in all those places in such a way that everything keeps working, or at least the interruptions are as short-lived as possible.

■**Caution** When you renumber because you're switching from one ISP to another, it's unavoidable that at some point, packets with source addresses in address space from ISP A end up at ISP B, or the other way around. If ISP B employs anti-spoofing or ingress filtering, it won't allow these packets through, so you'll suffer reduced connectivity.

You can ask one ISP to remove the filters temporarily and then send out all your outgoing traffic over that ISP (or one that didn't filter in the first place). However, don't expect too much cooperation from your ISP unless you're a non-tiny customer.

Address Prefix and Router Lifetime Mismatch

Earlier, I mentioned the potential for shooting yourself in the foot because router advertisements and the prefixes they contain have independent lifetimes. This allows for four permutations:

- The RA lifetime is valid, and the prefix lifetime is valid: IPv6 works.

- The RA lifetime is invalid, and the prefix lifetime is invalid: IPv6 is disabled.

- The RA lifetime is valid, but the prefix lifetime is invalid: The system has an IPv6 default route but no global IPv6 address.

- The RA lifetime is invalid, but the prefix lifetime is valid: The system has a global IPv6 address but no IPv6 default route.

When a host has no global addresses but does have an IPv6 default route (case 3), it can't reach the rest of the IPv6 Internet. Unfortunately, FreeBSD and MacOS hosts don't know that: they try anyway, with long delays as a result. Only after trying all the remote destination's IPv6 addresses and timing out, the system falls back on IPv4 (for applications that try more than one address). Linux, on the other hand, doesn't install or ignores the IPv6 default route when there are no global IPv6 addresses present, so the timeout is immediate.

Windows XP does install the default route but magically manages to avoid lengthy timeouts anyway. On the other hand, Windows XP suffers timeouts when it has an IPv6 address but no default route (case 4). This is because Windows implements the on-link assumption: it will first do neighbor discovery on the local subnet for any IPv6 addresses. Only after neighbor discovery times out will Windows falls back on IPv4. FreeBSD and MacOS, however, don't implement the on-link assumption, so they immediately notice that the IPv6 destination address is unreachable and fall back on IPv4, if an IPv4 address is available and the application cycles through all addresses. With Linux, the default route doesn't seem to expire even though the timers eventually reach zero and lower. But addresses do expire and are removed when the lifetime for the associated prefix has timed out.

Address Selection

Choice is good, but it comes with problems of its own, as anyone who has ever ordered a cup of coffee at Starbucks can attest to. The explicit support for multiple addresses in IPv6 requires the system or applications to choose which address to use for a given communication session. The coexistence of IPv4 and IPv6 in the same host makes this issue even more pressing. RFC 3484 provides guidelines in this area. It lists no fewer than 10 rules for choosing a destination address and eight rules for selecting a source address. Most of these rules are fairly obvious, such as preferring a non-deprecated address over a deprecated one and not using a link-local source address to communicate with a destination that has a global address. It gets more interesting with the "policy table." On systems that support this mechanism, such as Windows XP and FreeBSD 5.4, the administrator can instruct the system to prefer certain address ranges over others. Listing 8-4 displays the default policy table under FreeBSD. Coincidently, this is the suggested policy table in RFC 3484.

Listing 8-4. *Displaying the FreeBSD Address Policy Table with* ip6addrctl

```
# ip6addrctl show
Prefix                    Prec Label    Use
::1/128                    50    0       0
::/0                       40    1     8892
2002::/16                  30    2       0
::/96                      20    3       0
::ffff:0.0.0.0/96          10    4       0
```

The policy table honors the longest match first rule, so overlapping prefixes are possible, but having the same prefix in the table more than once isn't allowed. The precedence value for each prefix determines the relative merit of addresses falling in that prefix. A higher value means more preferred. The label value makes it possible to select the right source address (the one with the same label) for a given destination address. It works like this. Suppose that a destination has two addresses in the DNS: 2001::db8:31:2::1 (a regular address) and 2002:dfe0:e1e2:2::1 (a 6to4 address). The regular address falls within the prefix ::/0, so it gets assigned a precedence value of 40. The 6to4 address also falls within ::/0 and within 2002::/16. The latter has a longer prefix, so it's more specific, and the 6to4 address inherits a precedence value of 30. If there are no complications such as deprecated addresses, the system will select the regular address to reach this destination. Next order of business is to select an accompanying source address. The destination address has a label of 1, so if the system has any addresses that also have label 1 (i.e., regular non-6to4 addresses), it will select one of those. Additionally, when there are multiple addresses with the same precedence or label, the system will select the destination address that has the most bits in common with a local address and use a source address that has the most bits in common with the destination address. So if the local system has addresses 2600:9700:c0::1 and 3ffe:9700:c0::1, it will try to reach the destination 2001::db8:31:2::1 from the 2600:9700:c0::1 source address. These two addresses have their first five bits in common, while 2001::db8:31:2::1 and 3ffe:9700:c0::1 have only the first three bits in common.

You can remove entries from the policy table with ip6addrctl delete <prefix> and create new entries with ip6addrctl add <prefix> <precedence> <label>. For instance, ip6addrctl add 3ffe::/16 35 5 adds a policy table entry for the 6bone address space that has a lower precedence. This way, the system will only try to contact remote systems over a 6bone address if there are no addresses out of the RIR or production range, in anticipation of the dismantling of the 6bone. Without the policy rule, the system would give 6bone and RIR addresses equal priority and use them in turn for different sessions.

You can also use the IPv6 address policy table to determine whether the system prefers IPv6 over IPv4 or the other way around. For instance, ip6addrctl add ::ffff:83.0.0.0/104 60 4 adds a rule that prioritizes the IPv4 address range 83.0.0.0/8 over everything else (precedence 60). The label is the same as that for the existing IPv4 range (::ffff:0.0.0.0/96, in IPv6 mapped notation), so the system will select an IPv4 source address, even if it falls outside 83.0.0.0/8.

Listing 8-5 shows the default address policy table under Windows XP and the effect of adding a policy entry.

Listing 8-5. *The Address Policy Table Under Windows XP*

```
C:\>netsh
netsh>interface ipv6
netsh interface ipv6>show prefixpolicy
Querying active state...

Precedence  Label  Prefix
----------  -----  -------------------------------
         5      5  3ffe:831f::/32
        10      4  ::ffff:0:0/96
        20      3  ::/96
        30      2  2002::/16
        40      1  ::/0
        50      0  ::1/128

netsh interface ipv6>set prefixpolicy ::ffff:83.0.0.0/104 60 4
Ok.

netsh interface ipv6>show prefixpolicy
Querying active state...

Precedence  Label  Prefix
----------  -----  -------------------------------
        60      4  ::ffff:83.0.0.0/104
```

The first entry is for an experimental Teredo prefix, which is given a precedence that's even lower than that of IPv4. For some reason, adding a policy table entry makes Windows forget the default entries. You can remove entries with delete prefixpolicy <prefix>, but the default entries don't come back. As with other netsh commands, the prefix policy commands take a store=active or store=persistent option. The default is persistent, allowing the policy entries to survive a reboot.

■**Note** RFC 3484 mandates that regular public addresses are preferred over RFC 3041 temporary addresses by default in order to avoid problems with the temporary addresses timing out or lack of a proper reversed DNS mapping. According to the RFC, applications should specifically request the use of temporary addresses if this is appropriate for the communication.

■**Caution** Don't be too enthusiastic with adding policy table entries, because a policy makes the system consistently choose the same address. If this address doesn't work, sessions will consistently fail unless the application tries all available addresses in turn.

Path MTU Discovery and Fragmentation

Because routers can't fragment IPv6 packets, PMTUD[3] is mandatory in all cases where links with MTUs larger than 1280 bytes are used for IPv6. This means it's imperative that routers generate ICMPv6 packet too big messages and that these messages make it back to the source of the offending packet. Filtering out these ICMPv6 messages, like the Windows XP Service Pack 2 firewall does with its own packet too big messages when it's configured to be an IPv6 router, makes it impossible to communicate reliably.

■**Note** If you absolutely, positively *have* to filter ICMPv6 packet too big messages, you *must* use an MTU equal to the IPv6 mandatory minimum of 1280 bytes across your network so there is no need for PMTUD.

Upon reception of a packet too big message, TCP will reduce its packet size to accommodate the smaller MTU on the path in question. However, protocols that run over UDP often can't arbitrarily reduce their packet size. In IPv4, UDP packets are generally sent without the don't fragment bit set, so routers will fragment them if necessary.[4] In IPv6, this is not possible; if the packet is too large, the source host has to fragment it. The source host does this by first splitting the packet into unfragmentable and fragmentable parts. The IPv6 header and any headers that must be processed by routers along the way make up the unfragmentable part; the payload data and any headers that only have to be processed on the destination host are the fragmentable part. The fragmentable part is then split into as many parts as required to fit in the path MTU, and each part is transmitted as a packet containing the unfragmentable part, a fragment header and one of the fragments of the fragmentable part.

The fragment header is 8 bytes in size, and except for a next header field and two reserved fields, it contains the same fragment offset, more fragments, and identification fields as the IPv4 header. The identification field is now 32 bits long and is used to indicate which fragments belong to the same original packet. All fragments except the last one have the more fragments bit set and are multiples of 8 bytes.

After receiving the first fragment (which isn't necessarily the first fragment of the original packet), a host waits up to 60 seconds for all other fragments to come in and, if they do, reassembles the original packet by combining all the fragments with the same source and destination addresses and identification field into a single packet. If one or more fragments are lost, the packet can't be reassembled, so the entire packet is lost.

■**Note** IPv6 fragmentation has the same problem as IPv4 fragmentation: the TCP or UDP port numbers are available only in the first fragment. This makes it hard for firewalls and the like to filter fragmented packets. Common solutions are to reassemble the packet prior to filtering or to discard all fragments.

---

3. See the sidebar about path MTU discovery in Chapter 4.
4. Some systems set the DF bit on IPv4 UDP packets, too, which invariably leads to problems when the packet is too big for a link MTU along the way.

DHCPv6

DHCPv6 (RFC 3315) is the IPv6 version of the Dynamic Host Configuration Protocol (DHCP). Because IPv6 has stateless address autoconfiguration, DHCP occupies a very different part of the landscape in IPv6, compared to IPv4. Although the details are different in the by-now-expected places (address length, use of multicasts, some streamlining), the DHCPv6 protocol itself is quite similar to the IPv4 version of DHCP. The more important differences are the way in which the protocol is used. DHCPv6 has three purposes:

- Address configuration: Giving out addresses to individual hosts.

- Non-address configuration: Giving out other configuration information, such as DNS resolver addresses and domain search lists.

- Prefix delegation: Giving out entire prefixes to routers (RFC 3633).

A DHCPv6 client interested in an address and/or other configuration information sends out a solicit message indicating its needs to the link-local scope multicast address ff02::1:2, port 547. (Server-to-client messages are addressed to port 546.) DHCPv6 servers that receive the solicit message either directly or forwarded by a relay and are able to accommodate the request respond with an advertise message. The client considers the offers in the various advertise messages and directs a request message to the server of its choice. The server then replies with a reply message, confirming the address and/or configuration information. Alternatively, if the client only wants to receive configuration information and no addresses or prefixes, it can send a request-information message, and the server immediately sends back a reply message, so only half the messages are exchanged and the whole process completes much faster. The client may also us the "rapid commit" option to indicate that it wants to use the expedited procedure for address or prefix assignment if it's pretty sure that it will take up the offer from the first DHCPv6 server that responds. As expected, IPv6 addresses assigned with DHCPv6 come with a preferred and a valid lifetime. Sometime before this timer expires, the client sends a renew message, asking the server if it can continue to use the address. When it has no more use for the address, the client sends a release message. There are some other messages for less common situations.

To allow servers to recognize clients, each device that implements DHCPv6 has DHCP Unique Identifier (DUID). In IPv4, DHCP clients use a MAC address or user-supplied string as a Client Identifier. In DHCPv6 this is always the DUID. Devices may create their DUID in various ways, as long as the DUID is unique and not subject to change, if at all possible. Cisco routers create their DUID based on the lowest MAC address in the system. Because even modular Cisco routers have stable MAC addresses, this works well. For hosts with removable Ethernet interfaces, the DUID should be created based on a MAC address and the DUID creation date. After all, an Ethernet card can reside in only one host at a time. The resulting DUID should be stored for further use, even after the Ethernet card in question is removed from the system.

DHCPv6 supports an authentication mechanism that allows clients and servers to interact in a secure way, so third parties can't inject false DHCP messages or modify legitimate ones. However, this mechanism must be pre-configured manually on all servers and clients, partially negating the advantages of DHCP over manual configuration.

KAME DHCP6

The KAME Project has a DHCPv6 implementation available on the KAME FTP site
ftp.kame.net in the directory /pub/kame/misc under the name kame-dhcp6 followed by a version number. Due to the differences between the KAME and the Linux IPv6 implementations, the DHCP6 client, server, and relay daemons won't compile under Linux. I also ran into trouble compiling them under MacOS, but FreeBSD worked just fine. The implementation is still largely experimental and doesn't support DHCPv6 address assignment. The dhcp6s server daemon requires a configuration along the lines of Listing 8-6.

Listing 8-6. *A KAME* dhcp6s.conf *File*

```
option domain-name-servers 2001:db8:31:2::53;
option domain-name "example.com";

host router
  {
    duid 00:03:00:01:00:04:27:FE:24:9F;
    prefix 2001:db8:4700::/48 86400 259200;
  };
```

All systems that ask for DNS servers and/or a domain name search list will receive the information in the first two lines. The system with a matching DUID (regardless of whether its name is "router") will also receive the prefix 2001:db8:4700::/48, with a preferred lifetime of one day and a valid lifetime of three days. (Opposite order from other examples!) See the dhcp6s.conf man page for more options. The dhcp6s daemon takes an interface as its argument, and optionally some flags or an alternative location for the configuration file with the -s option. The daemon can be controlled (or rather, *must* be controlled—there is no reasonable other way to do it) with the dhcp6sctl program, but the configuration required for that isn't part of Listing 8-6. Listing 8-7 shows a configuration for the dhcp6c client daemon.

Listing 8-7. *A KAME* dhcp6c.conf *File*

```
interface xl0
  {
    information-only;
    script "/etc/dhcp6clientscript.sh";
  };
```

The dhcp6c daemon sets various environment variables (see the man page) and then calls the indicated script. Listing 8-8 is a very simple version of such a script.

Listing 8-8. *DHCPv6 Client Script*

```
#!/bin/sh
echo >/etc/resolv.conf domain $new_domain_name
echo >>/etc/resolv.conf nameserver $new_domain_name_servers
```

It would be a bad idea to use this script in practice, because if the DHCPv6 server doesn't provide an option, the environment variable remains empty, resulting in a broken resolv.conf file. Also, there may be more than one nameserver, but the resolv.conf wants to see those on separate lines. The $new_domain_name variable contains the list of domains to be searched, not just the domain for this host.

Linux DHCPv6

The DHCPv6 project found on SourceForge (http://dhcpv6.sourceforge.net/) is based on the KAME DHCPv6 implementation. It's not a straight Linux port: it also adds address assignment. Despite the claim on the project Web site that it supports all POSIX systems, the source won't compile under FreeBSD or MacOS. In my tests, this implementation didn't work very well. For instance, the dhcp6c was unable to successfully create a DUID. Also, there doesn't appear to be a way to put the information learned through DHCPv6 to good use, as the script configuration command isn't implemented.

Cisco IOS DHCPv6

Recent versions of Cisco's IOS have very good DHCPv6 support. A Cisco router can act as either a DHCPv6 client, a relay, a server, or a combination. Making a router a relay is the simplest option, as shown in Listing 8-9. 2001:db8:31:2::547 is the address of the DHCPv6 server.

Listing 8-9. *A Cisco Router as a DHCPv6 Relay*

```
!
interface Ethernet0
 ipv6 dhcp relay destination 2001:db8:31:2::547
!
```

Having a router relay DHCPv6 messages makes it possible to have a central DHCP server rather than having to run one on each subnet. Cisco's DHCPv6 implementation doesn't support address assignment, but it does support informing clients of non-address configuration information and prefix delegation, as you can see in Listing 8-10.

Listing 8-10. *A Cisco Router as a DHCPv6 Server*

```
!
ipv6 dhcp pool dhcpv6-pool
 prefix-delegation 2001:DB8:AA5E::/48 00030001000427FEAA5E lifetime 7200 900
 prefix-delegation 2001:DB8:246E::/48 00030001000427FE246E
 dns-server 2001:db8:31:2::53
 domain-name example.com
!
interface Ethernet0
 ipv6 dhcp server dhcpv6-pool
!
```

The DHCPv6 "pools" work differently from IPv4. In IPv4, they may be associated with a subnet or with a specific client. In IPv6, a pool is associated with an interface. In the example, the pool "dhcpv6-pool" is associated with the Ethernet0 interface. Other interfaces may share the same pool or have a different one. When a DHCPv6 request comes in on the Ethernet0 interface, the subsequent reply will contain information from the dhcpv6-pool pool. In the example, all clients receive the DNS and domain information, but only the two clients with the listed DUIDs receive a prefix. The first prefix has a valid lifetime of 7200 seconds and a preferred lifetime of 900 seconds; the second one uses the default lifetimes.

So far so good. But things only really start cooking with a Cisco router as a DHCP prefix delegation *client*, as in Listing 8-11.

Listing 8-11. *A Cisco Router as a DHCPv6 Prefix Delegation Client*

```
!
interface Ethernet1
 ipv6 address autoconfig
 ipv6 dhcp client pd dhcpv6prefix
!
interface Ethernet2
 ipv6 address dhcpv6prefix 0:0:0:A0::/64 eui-64
!
```

In this example, interface Ethernet1 is configured to obtain an IPv6 address by acting as a Stateless Autoconfiguration client. This isn't really pertinent to prefix delegation, as DHCPv6 can be executed on interfaces that don't have a global address. But if the router doesn't have a global address, this leads to strange traceroutes.

Anyway, in the next line, the interface becomes a DHCPv6 client and is configured to ask for a prefix. The resulting prefix is conceptually stored in the variable "dhcpv6prefix," which is then used to configure the IPv6 address for interface Ethernet2. The prefix obtained from the DHCP server is combined with the partial prefix 0:0:0:a0::/64 and the EUI-64 to form a full address. The prefix delegated by the DHCP server is 2001:db8:6:7000::/56. This makes the /64 for this interface:

```
2001:0db8:0006:70xx
xxxx:xxxx:xxxx:xxa0
------------------- +
2001:0db8:0006:70a0
```

The resulting prefix is advertised in router advertisements as usual for prefixes configured on an interface, while the preferred and valid lifetimes are inherited from the ones provided by the DHCP server in the prefix advertisement. The router will renew the lease before the preferred lifetime runs out. If the renewal succeeds, all addresses derived from the prefix remain available. If the renewal doesn't succeed, for instance, because the DHCPv6 server delegates a new prefix as a result of a network renumbering, there won't be any more RAs for the old prefix. Addresses in this prefix then go to "deprecated" and disappear after the valid lifetime expires. In the meantime, the router now advertises the new prefix, so the renumbering should be completely painless.

Obviously, a /64 directly connected route is added to the routing table (and propagated in any IPv6 routing protocols that redistribute connected routes), but the same is true for the entire delegated prefix, as the router installs a route toward the Null0 interface for that prefix.

■**Tip** Use the show ipv6 dhcp interface ... command to list delegated prefixes and their properties, show ipv6 dhcp to learn the router's DUID, and clear ipv6 dhcp client ... to restart the DHCP client.

IPv6 Over...

Even a protocol as advanced as IPv6 can't do everything on its own. Like IPv4 and other network-layer protocols, IPv6 needs the assistance of lower layer protocols to get packets from one system to the next. Protocols at these lower layers are all about turning electromagnetic signals into bits (the OSI physical layer) and a stream of bits into a coherent frame (the OSI datalink layer). "Frame" is the datalink layer term for what becomes a "packet" at the network layer. Because lower layer protocols can have very different characteristics, typically, they need their own standard for carrying IPv6 packets. This is standardized in various "IPv6 over ..." RFCs.

IPv6 over Ethernet

Ethernet has a long history, and all aspects of the protocol except one have changed somewhere along the way: the cables are now Unshielded Twisted Pair (UTP) or fiber rather than coaxial cable; the speed can now also be 100, 1000, or 10,000 megabits per second in addition to the original 10 Mbps; we now use switches rather than a single shared cable or hubs; and so on. The only thing that has stayed the same is the frame format, as shown in Figure 8-3.

Destination 48 bits	Source 48 bits	Type 16 bits	User Data 46 - 1500 bytes	FCS 32 bits

Figure 8-3. *The Ethernet II frame format*

Putting an IP packet in an Ethernet frame is extremely straightforward: the IPv4 or IPv6 packet simply occupies the "user data" portion of the frame, and the Type field is set to 0x800 (IPv4), 0x806 (IPv4 ARP), or 0x86dd (IPv6) (RFCs 894, 826, and 2464, respectively). Because the user data has a minimum length of 46 bytes, it's possible that the IP(v4) packet doesn't occupy the entire Ethernet frame and there are some extra bytes to fill up the minimum length. Because the IP header carries its own length field, this doesn't lead to problems. If you've ever spent a lot of time learning about networks, you may be familiar with IEEE 802.3, SAP, SNAP, and the like. These are further developments of the Ethernet II standard. However, they are completely irrelevant to IPv4 and IPv6, as IP is always encapsulated in Ethernet II frames, as shown in Figure 8-3. This is sometimes called "ARPA encapsulation."

Multicast

Ethernet has very simple but powerful support for multicast. When bit 7 in the MAC address is set to 1, the MAC address is a group address. Modern Ethernet cards can be programmed to listen for several group addresses. Packets addressed to those are sent over to the software driver for further processing, the same way that frames addressed to the card's MAC address are. Obviously, there are some limitations to the filtering the Ethernet hardware can do, so drivers must also be prepared to filter, but under normal circumstances, all multicasts that the host or router isn't interested in are ignored at the hardware level. To use this hardware capability, it's necessary to map IP multicast addresses to Ethernet multicast addresses. In IPv4, this happens by taking the bottom 24 bits of the IP multicast address and appending them to the IETF's IEEE OUI, 00:00:5E, or rather the IETF OUI with the group bit set, 01:00:5E.[5] Apparently, the IEEE has a policy against giving out blocks of OUIs, so it wasn't possible to obtain a block of 16 OUIs so the entire 28-bit IPv4 multicast address space (224.0.0.0/4) could be mapped to Ethernet group addresses one-to-one. The cost of $1000 per OUI may also have been an issue. In any event, four different IPv4 multicast addresses map to the same Ethernet group address, which may lead to some additional processing of unwanted multicasts, but otherwise, there is no harm in this.

With IPv6, the IETF adopted another strategy. Rather than use a globally unique OUI, the Ethernet multicast groups for IPv6 are MAC addresses with the unique/local bit set to "local." IPv6 multicasts map to Ethernet MAC addresses with the top 16 bits set to 33:33 and the bottom 32 bits copied from the bottom 32 bits of the IPv6 multicast address. Under FreeBSD and MacOS, the netstat -ia command shows the different multicast addresses present on an interface. See Listing 8-12.

Listing 8-12. *Listing Multicast Addresses on FreeBSD or MacOS*

```
> netstat -ia
Name   Mtu Network     Address              Ipkts Ierrs   Opkts Oerrs  Coll
xl0    1500 <Link#1>    00:01:02:29:26:40   681428     0  169451     0     0
                        33:33:5b:81:52:75
                        33:33:00:00:00:01
                        33:33:ff:29:26:40
                        01:00:5e:00:00:01
xl0    1500 192.0.2.65/24  sequoia           154437     -  164922     -     -
                        ALL-SYSTEMS.MCAST.NET
xl0    1500 fe80:1::201 fe80:1::201:2ff:f     1359     -    2389     -     -
                        ff02:1::2:5b81:5275(refs: 1)
                        ff02:1::1          (refs: 1)
                        ff02:1::1:ff29:2640(refs: 1)
xl0    1500 2001:db8:31 2001:db8:31:2:201:2  33034     -    2866     -     -
                        ff02:1::2:5b81:5275(refs: 1)
                        ff02:1::1          (refs: 1)
                        ff02:1::1:ff29:2640(refs: 1)
```

The Ethernet card in Listing 8-10 listens for five MAC addresses:

- 00:01:02:29:26:40 is the card's burned-in MAC address.

- 33:33:5b:81:52:75 maps to ff02::2:5b81:5275, which is the ICMPv6 node information group address for this host's domain name. This group address allows other systems on the subnet to find the local system based on its name. ICMPv6 node information is not an RFC (yet), but it's implemented in KAME-derived IPv6 stacks. See Chapter 9 for more information.

- 33:33:00:00:00:01 is always present, as it maps to the all-hosts address ff02::1.

---

5. Multicast for IPv4 was introduced in RFC 1112 in 1989.

- 33:33:ff:29:26:40 maps to the solicited node address (ff02::1:ff29:2640) for both the global and link-local addresses (2001:db8:31:2:201:2ff:fe29:2640 and fe80::201:2ff:fe29:2640).

- Last but not least, 01:00:5e:00:00:01 maps to the IPv4 all-hosts address 224.0.0.1 (or ALL-SYSTEMS.MCAST.NET in the example).

The fe80:1::201:2ff:f and 2001:db8:31:2:201:2 addresses are truncated. You may also notice that all the listed IPv6 multicast addresses and link-local addresses have an extra "1" occupying bits 17 through 32 in the address, for instance, turning the all-node group address ff02::1 into ff02:1::1. This is where the system encodes the interface number in the address in order to disambiguate multicast and link-local addresses that may be present on more than one interface.

Under Linux, you can inspect IP multicast addresses, but not Ethernet multicast addresses, with netstat -gn. The -n flag is necessary to suppress strange address-to-name mappings.

Group Membership Management

Multicast on an old-fashioned shared medium Ethernet is simple: all Ethernet cards see all packets anyway, so all that's needed is to ignore the uninteresting ones. Things get more complex when the multicasts have to traverse one or more routers or switches. In the case of multicast routing, the routers need to know which multicast groups are active on which subnet. They also need a whole battery of multicast routing mechanisms, but fortunately, that's beyond the scope of this book.

In IPv4, multicast-aware routers periodically send out Internet Group Management Protocol (IGMP) queries. Hosts respond to these queries by telling the router which multicast groups they're currently listening to. The protocol also provides join and leave messages. An interesting aspect of IGMP is that although switches aren't party to IGMP, the more intelligent ones implement "IGMP snooping." In other words, they listen in on IGMP exchanges and enable or disable multicast forwarding on a per-address basis for each port. This way, IP multicast traffic is only forwarded to ports connecting to systems interested in those multicasts. Less sophisticated switches simply treat all multicasts as broadcasts and forward them to all ports. IPv6 Multicast Listener Discovery (MLD, RFC 2710) is very similar to IGMPv2. The differences are that MLD has room for IPv6 addresses and it is part of ICMPv6, rather than having its own protocol number.

■Caution Some switches, especially multilayer switches that are also IPv4 routers, implement IGMP snooping in an IPv6-incompatible way: they only allow Ethernet multicasts through after successfully snooping a corresponding IGMPv2 message. Consequently, the Ethernet multicast addresses used by IPv6 are always blocked. Because this blocks all IPv6 discovery functions, you need to disable IGMP in these cases to be able to use IPv6. You can diagnose this situation with tcpdump (see Chapter 10); the host won't receive any router advertisements and/or neighbor solicitations.

IPv6 over Wi-Fi

Wi-Fi or IEEE 802.11 is a wireless LAN technology. It operates in the unlicensed 2.4 GHz band.[6] This has the advantage that IEEE 802.11 doesn't require any licenses, but the downside is that there are several other users in this frequency band, such as microwave ovens, cordless phones, and Bluetooth short-range computer-to-peripheral or mobile phone-to-peripheral communication. To survive in such a hostile environment, the IEEE 802.11 standard spreads its signal over a very large part of the 2.4 GHz band. So wide, in fact, that of the 11 channels that are available in the U.S., only channels 1, 6, and 11 can be used without much overlap. The wideband signal contains a lot of redundancy, so it can withstand a lot of interference from other signals.

■**Note** Some channel overlap can be tolerated. In practice, having three or even two empty channels in between two active channels is enough. In most of Europe, channels 1–13 are available, and using 1, 5, 9, and 13 works very well. 1, 4, 8, 11 (in the U.S.) or 1, 4, 7, 10, 13 (in Europe) also often work well, if the base stations aren't too close together.

IEEE 802.11 communication can happen in one of two modes: with the independent BSS (Basic Service Set) or the infrastructure BSS. Unsurprisingly, this terminology never gained mainstream acceptance. Independent BSS (which is what IBSS stands for, if you encounter it) is better known as ad-hoc or peer-to-peer, because there is no access point in this mode. Infrastructure BSS doesn't really have a common use name, as it's the default mode that uses one or more access points. In IBSS mode, frames travel directly from the source node to the destination node, while in infrastructure BSS, all frames must go through an access point. The former is somewhat more efficient when the communication is directly between wireless nodes. The latter has the advantage that each node only has to be able to reach an access point to be able to communicate with all other nodes and the wired network that access points generally connect to. In peer-to-peer mode, it's possible for three nodes, A, B, and C, to be positioned such that A and C can both communicate with B but not with each other.

Because 802.11 hides its internal workings from higher layers, there is no separate "IPv6 over IEEE 802.11" RFC: to IPv6, IEEE 802.11 looks like ordinary Ethernet. However, there are some practical differences, especially with regard to multicast. Transmission over the air has a relatively high error rate, so all unicast IEEE 802.11 frames are acknowledged and, if necessary, retransmitted at the datalink layer. However, there is no reasonable way for the receivers to acknowledge the receipt of multicasts or broadcasts. This means that the access point transmits multicasts at a "safe" speed and hopes for the best. Transmitting the multicasts at low speeds is necessary to accommodate old 802.11 implementations that are limited to 2 Mbps. It also increases the chances of the multicast packet making it to all recipients. However, this means that often, less than a megabit per second worth of multicasts can saturate the entire wireless channel. And there is still a significant chance that multicasts are lost. In theory, this

---

6. Except for IEEE 802.11a, which operates in the 5GHz band.

means that IPv6 over IEEE 802.11 is less reliable than IPv4, because IPv6 relies on multicasts so heavily. However, in practice, wireless LANs that are usable with IPv4 are also usable with IPv6.

IPv6 over IEEE 1394

IEEE 1394 (or Firewire, as Apple calls it) is a very interesting link technology. Roughly speaking, it shares aspects of USB and Ethernet. Like USB, it can be used to connect various peripherals to a computer. But unlike USB, it can also be used to connect several computers together. Physically, IEEE 1394 shows up as either a small four-lead connector, a somewhat larger six-lead connector, or a nine-lead connector. The four- and six-lead connectors support 100, 200, and 400 Mbps speeds (IEEE 1394a), and the nine-lead connector also supports 800 Mbps (IEEE 1394b). In each case, a cable has two twisted pairs that carry the data in opposite directions. The six-lead version adds two power leads so that small devices may be powered over the Firewire bus, and the nine-lead version adds additional ground signals. Devices with different connectors can be interconnected using special cables or adapters. The limits of the least-capable connector apply in these cases. Firewire cables have a maximum length of 4.5 meters (just under 15 feet). IEEE 1394 supports three communication modes:

- Asynchronous block writes
- Asynchronous stream packets[7]
- Isochronous stream packets

Block writes are transactions where one node on the IEEE 1394 bus writes data to another node, and the receiving node sends back an acknowledgement if everything went well. Stream packets are similar to IP's "unreliable datagram" service and aren't acknowledged. Asynchronous communication can happen at any time when the bus isn't occupied, but isochronous communication allows for bandwidth allocation, so it's very suitable for real-time audio and video applications. RFCs 2734 and 3146 specify the use of either asynchronous block writes or isochronous stream packets for unicast IP communication and asynchronous stream packets for broadcasts and multicasts.

Tip Although Firewire adapters contain an EUI-64 in lieu of a 48-bit MAC address, packets on the IEEE 1394 bus aren't delivered based on the destination's EUI-64 but rather based on a temporary six-bit node identifier. This may lead to unexpected EUI-64s (such as `ff:ff:ff:ff:ff:ff:ff:ff` or `00:00:00:00:00:00:00:00`) in the output of tools such as `tcpdump`. When a cable is plugged in or removed, the Firewire bus goes through a bus reset cycle, and node identifiers are reassigned.

---

7. Although this is the datalink layer, so the word "frame" would be appropriate, "packet" is generally used here.

Maximum packet sizes in IEEE 1394 aren't fixed like they are in Ethernet. The maximum packet size depends on the speed of the communication. For 100 Mbps nodes, the maximum packet size is 512 bytes, and with each doubling of the link speed, the packet size also doubles. So at 400 Mbps, packets may be 2048 bytes and at 800 Mbps, 4096 bytes. Because 512 isn't a usable packet size for IPv4 and IPv6 requires a minimum MTU of 1280 bytes, the IPv4 and IPv6 over IEEE 1394 RFCs specify a fragmentation and reassembly procedure. A host implementing IP over IEEE 1394 will break up a single IP packet into several IEEE 1394 packets when necessary, and the receiving IP over IEEE 1394 node will reassemble the fragments before handing over the packet to the IPv4 or IPv6 layer. So to the IP layer, the MTU always looks reasonably large, even though the physical MTU may be reduced when operating at 100 or 200 Mbps. RFCs 2734 and 3146 specify a default MTU of 1500, but Apple implements an MTU that is only slightly smaller than the hardware's maximum 2048 or 4096 bytes. However, despite this MTU mismatch when Firewire 400 and Firewire 800 Macs are connected, the Firewire 400 Macs are capable of receiving packets of more than 4000 bytes successfully over the Firewire link. Because this almost certainly requires link-layer fragmentation, performance may be less than optimal.

Currently, IP over IEEE 1394 in general and IPv6 over IEEE 1394 in particular aren't very well supported. It works well on Macs. Under Windows XP, networking over IEEE 1394 is often possible (and XP will even bridge IP between Ethernet and IEEE 1394, with full spanning tree no less), but support for it isn't all that reliable. For instance, I remember doing IP over IEEE 1394 on Windows XP before installing any Service Pack, but with Service Pack 2 installed, the IEEE 1394 adapter doesn't show up as a network interface. Linux and FreeBSD are even worse: they don't support the proper way of encapsulating IP in IEEE 1394 but rather allow sending of Ethernet frames over Firewire as a quick (and unreliable) hack.

Caution The IEEE 1394 design allows one device on the bus to access another device's memory, without any help from software drivers. So, in the absence of specific information about the vulnerability of a certain host and/or operating system, make sure you connect only to trusted devices through Firewire.

IPv6 over PPP

The Point-to-Point Protocol (PPP) is a very versatile protocol that is used on all kinds of point-to-point links. Once PPP is underway, it's extremely simple: basically, it only provides a type field to keep different protocols (such as IPv4 and IPv6) apart. It also recognizes the beginning and end of frames and implements a CRC, if the hardware doesn't already perform these functions. Because by definition, only two systems are connected to a point-to-point subnet, there is no need for link-layer addresses or address resolution. But PPP contains its share of nifty tricks that come into play *before* packets start to flow. Before anything else happens, the Link Control Protocol (LCP) negotiates the Maximum Receive Unit (MRU, a close relative of the MTU), authentication parameters (if any), and some other details. When LCP is done, the Network Control Protocols (NCPs) for the different network layer protocols may start their negotiations. IPCP, the IP Control Protocol, typically negotiates the IP address for one side of the link, along with DNS server addresses.

Not so for the IPv6 Control Protocol (IPV6CP). RFC 2023, which governs IPv6 over PPP, only specifies the negotiation of a unique 32-bit token that can be used as an interface identifier. Presumably, IPv6 systems that do not have an IPv6 address will use Stateless Autoconfiguration to obtain an IPv6 address on the interface. However, this doesn't always work very well in practice. Listing 8-13 shows the command line for starting a PPP session on a MacOS system. FreeBSD and Linux use the same PPP implementation, but they use different tty devices.

Listing 8-13. *Starting a PPP Session*

```
sudo /usr/sbin/pppd /dev/tty.USA19H3b1P1.1 38400 noauth local passive persist ➥
silent ipv6 ::2005
```

The arguments are

/dev/tty.USA19H3b1P1.1: The device name for the serial interface. Under Linux, PC COM ports 1–4 are numbered ttyS0–ttyS3.

38400: The serial interface speed.

noauth: Don't ask the peer to authenticate itself (this is why we need to be root to execute pppd).

local: Don't use modem control lines (i.e., the connection is through a null modem).

passive: Wait for the other side to initiate the LCP session.

persist: Try to reopen the PPP session after a failure.

silent: Wait with sending LCP packets until the other end becomes active.

ipv6 ::2005: Use 0x00002005 as the identifier for the local end and an empty identifier for the remote end.

By using this syntax, the PPP device will enable IPv6 and create a link-local address. However, even though the Cisco router on the other end sends router advertisements, the interface never configures a global IPv6 address. If you want to run IPv6 over a PPP link, you should probably use a script to set up IPv6 addresses manually, or maybe use DHCPv6 prefix delegation.

## CHAPTER 9

Security

"The only real security that a man will have in this world is a reserve of knowledge, experience, and ability."

Henry Ford

Many people like to think (or say) that IPv6 is more secure than IPv4. But that's too simple. It's like saying an egg is round. While it's hard to deny that eggs exhibit a lot of roundness, they don't exactly conform to the $x^2 + y^2 + z^2 = r^2$ formula that describes a perfect sphere. Similarly, many security aspects of IPv6 improve on those of IPv4, but IPv6 also has attributes that defy comparison to IPv4. More importantly, talking about "security" as if it's some kind of condiment that can be added in accordance with one's taste makes me profoundly uncomfortable. To me, security is a state of mind. It means knowing what can go wrong, taking reasonable measures to avoid those situations from occurring, and preparing for when they do anyway. This goes against human nature, which drives us to conserve mental energy, guess a likely or desired outcome for any given action, and ignore other possible outcomes. Unfortunately, the people out to take our data or money don't mind spending a little more brain power, and Murphy's Law tells us that what can go wrong invariably will.

Anyway, this chapter will explain the differences between IPv6 and IPv4 with regard to security (the good and the bad), as well as explain how standard security devices such as packet filters apply to IPv6. No discussion of IPv6 security is complete without a treatment of IPsec. IPsec is a very interesting technology that has unsurpassed security properties, but it has yet to live up to its potential.

Differences from IPv4

Many of the changes between IPv4 and IPv6 have security implications. This is especially true for the much wider use of ICMP, the larger address space and link-local addresses.

Leveraging the Hop Limit

In IPv4, it's necessary to filter out ICMP redirect messages on links to the rest of the Internet, as attackers may try to confuse hosts by sending falsified redirect messages. In IPv6, this problem could have been much worse, as in IPv6, the use of ICMP was greatly expanded. However, the writers of RFC 1970 in 1996 and its replacement RFC 2461 in 1998 came up with a clever trick to reject ICMPv6 messages sent by remote attackers. neighbor discovery and all other ICMPv6 types that are only used on a single subnet have their Hop Limit set to 255 by the originating system. This allows the receiving system to determine if a packet was sent by a system on the same subnet or by a remote system. If the sender and receiver share a subnet, the packet can't have traversed any routers, so the Hop Limit should still be 255 at the receiver. A remote attacker can craft a packet with all other fields set to whatever best serves her fraudulent purposes, but she can't make the packet have a Hop Limit of 255 at the destination. If the attacker sends a packet with a Hop Limit of 255, the receiver will see a lower value, as routers along the way will have decremented the field. Setting an initial Hop Limit lower than 255 obviously won't do any good either, and a higher Hop Limit is impossible because 255 is the highest value that fits inside the 8-bit field.

Unfortunately, despite the fact that this trick was first documented in the mid-1990s, many other protocols that use link-local communication, such as RIPng, OSPFv3, and DHCPv6, don't implement it. In 2004, the mechanism was introduced into BGP under the name "Generalized TTL Security Mechanism" (GTSM) in RFC 3682. Because both sides need to implement and (manually) enable GTSM, it's not very widespread yet.

Note I don't know whether IPv6 implementations indeed reject packets with an incorrect Hop Limit, but they all set the outgoing Hop Limit to 255 as required by RFC 2461.

The Larger Address Space

The Net has seen many worms (sometimes called "viruses") the past years, but the "SQL Slammer" or "Sapphire" worm in January 2003 was something special: because the entire worm was contained in a single UDP packet, the spread rate of this worm was unprecedented. Because UDP doesn't require a handshake or feedback from the other side, infected hosts could just send out packets containing the worm to random destinations at maximum speed. This allowed SQL Slammer to double the number of infected systems every 8.5 seconds, infecting 90% of all vulnerable hosts connected to the Internet in 10 minutes. This makes it the first and so far only "Warhol worm."[1] In IPv6, the address space is 2^{96} times bigger, so finding a vulnerable system would take 2^{96} times as long. So in IPv6, the number of infected hosts would presumably double every $2^{96} \times 8.5$ seconds, or every 2500 billion *billion* years. I think we can agree that people who haven't patched their systems by then have only themselves to blame.

In other words: IPv6's huge address space makes it impossible for attackers to find victims by randomly scanning for vulnerable systems. However, a determined and patient attacker may still be able to find systems with targeted scanning. Scanning a /64 subnet still takes too much time, but only scanning IPv6 addresses derived from an Ethernet MAC address from a specific vendor "just" takes some 17 million packets. A DSL connection can move that number of packets in a matter of hours, so a scan like this isn't completely unfeasible.

On-link Dangers

The fact that IPv6 always has link-local addresses is great if you want routers to communicate even though they don't share a subnet prefix or if you want to create an ad-hoc network with no

---

1. After Andy Warhol's famous quote: "In the future, everyone will be famous for 15 minutes."

connectivity to the Internet. But it's not so great when a system gains IPv6 connectivity (even just on the local link) without you realizing it. Now that more and more flavors of Linux, BSD, and other UNIX or UNIX-like operating systems gain IPv6-support in the kernel, it's becoming fairly common for these systems to have link-local connectivity without the owner realizing it. To add insult to injury, existing IP packet filters or software firewalls generally filter only IPv4 and don't get in the way of IPv6 packets. Most systems don't rely on these types of filters to avoid unwanted connections, but it's something to keep in mind.

While scanning an entire subnet one address at a time isn't really an option, there are other ways to find IPv6 systems connected to the local subnet. An obvious one is the "broadcast ping" to the all-hosts multicast address, as shown in Listing 9-1.

Listing 9-1. *Finding IPv6 Systems on the Local Subnet with a Multicast Ping*

```
# ping6 -I eth0 -c 2 ff02::1
PING ff02::1(ff02::1) from fe80::201:2ff:fe29:23b6 eth0: 56 data bytes
64 bytes from ::1: icmp_seq=1 ttl=64 time=0.078 ms
64 bytes from fe80::20a:95ff:fecd:987a: icmp_seq=1 ttl=64 time=0.366 ms (DUP!)
64 bytes from fe80::204:27ff:fefe:249f: icmp_seq=1 ttl=64 time=2.07 ms (DUP!)
64 bytes from fe80::20a:95ff:fef5:246e: icmp_seq=1 ttl=64 time=82.7 ms (DUP!)
64 bytes from ::1: icmp_seq=2 ttl=64 time=0.076 ms

--- ff02::1 ping statistics ---
2 packets transmitted, 2 received, +3 duplicates, 0% packet loss, time 1006ms
rtt min/avg/max/mdev = 0.076/17.066/82.734/32.842 ms
```

You don't need to be root for this, but under Red Hat Linux, regular users don't have /usr/sbin/ where ping6 resides in their path. The -I flag supplies the outgoing interface. KAME-derived implementations (the BSD family and MacOS) also accept the ff02::1%interface syntax. The -c 2 tells ping6 that it should send out two echo request messages. Sending just one won't do any good, as ping6 then stops after receiving the first reply. In this case, that's the reply from the host itself, which shows up as the reply from ::1.

Node Information Queries

The KAME IPv6 stack also supports the ICMPv6 "node information query" mechanism to provide even more information to inquiring minds armed with the KAME ping6 command. The most interesting ones are as follows:

-a ag asks for a list of the target's global unicast addresses.

-a al asks for a list of the target's link-local addresses.

-w asks for the target's hostname.

-N tries to find a system with the listed name on the local subnet.

See the ping6 man page for more information. Some useful combinations of options are

ping6 -c 2 -I xl0 -w ff02::1 for a list of hostnames for all KAME IPv6 systems connected to interface xl0.

ping6 -c 2 -I xl0 -a ag ff02::1 for a list of global IPv6 addresses for each KAME-compatible IPv6 system connected to interface xl0.

ping6 -c 2 -I xl0 -N -a ag server for a list of global addresses for each KAME-compatible IPv6 system named "server" (domain suffixes are ignored) connected to interface xl0 (the probe packets are addressed to a special multicast address that maps to the name we're looking for, similar to the solicited node address).

ping6 -c 1 -a ag www.kame.net for the list of global addresses for the KAME-compatible IPv6 system "www.kame.net".

ping6 -c 1 -w 2001:db8:31:5::2 for the hostname configured on the KAME-compatible IPv6 system at address 2001:db8:31:5::2.

The last two also work over the Internet rather than just on the local subnet. There is also a -a ac option that asks for the target's IPv4-compatible and IPv4-mapped IPv6 addresses. These addresses are very interesting as they contain the target's IPv4 address, but as far as I can tell, this option doesn't work.

Tip It looks like node information queries are only implemented in KAME-derived IPv6 stacks as found on FreeBSD, other members of the BSD family and MacOS, and, curiously, Apple Wi-Fi base stations, which use link-local IPv6 connectivity so they can be configured more easily.

Filters

In a perfect world, there would be no need for filters: it's usually better to make the decisions whether to allow a certain type of IP traffic at the application level. Different applications have different access control needs, and the mechanisms that applications use to support those needs are, or at least can be, quite sophisticated. When I connect to my bank, I know it's their server I'm talking to because of the X.509 certificate that my browser checked before it displayed a little lock in the corner of its window. Or when I connect to the mail server, the server knows it's me because I provide my login and the password that only I know. Compared to that, filtering on IP addresses and protocol numbers is rather primitive. Worse, the usefulness of this type of filtering is greatly reduced by the fact that IP addresses tend to change from time to time, and application writers and users sometimes actively work around filters by using nonstandard or even dynamic port numbers. Also, many fields in the IP packet can easily be "spoofed" by an attacker.

Nevertheless, IP filters are often useful or necessary.

Caution Before we start filtering, a word of warning: it's very easy to set up a filter in a way that breaks network connectivity in such a way that you're unable to connect to the host in question and repair the damage. So don't experiment with filters on important systems, and preferably only experiment when you have physical access to the machine or you have another way to recover from mistakes.

■**Caution** Filtering out packets can do damage in non-obvious ways. Make sure you're familiar with issues such as Path MTU discovery and fragmentation as well as ICMPv6 in general and neighbor discovery in particular before attempting to implement filters in a production environment. Chapter 8 can be helpful here.

TCP Wrappers

The TCP wrapper functionality is a good example of something that was added to the stereotypical UNIX environment at one point and that has remained there while the world around it changed. I doubt that many people will use TCP wrappers with IPv6, but sometimes it's good to consider our humble beginnings. The idea is that daemons started by inetd, or any other daemon that is linked against the right support library, gain some extra logging and access control capabilities. Originally, there was an /etc/hosts.allow file with hosts that are allowed access to services and an /etc/hosts.deny file with, you guessed it, hosts that were denied access to services. Later, both types of clauses were moved to the hosts.allow file. Listing 9-2 shows a simple hosts.allow file.

Listing 9-2. *A* hosts.allow *File*

```
# wrap inetd daytime service
daytime : .example.com : deny
daytime : 10.53.64.0/255.255.192.0, [2001:db8:31:2::53] : allow
# The rest of the daemons are protected.
ALL : ALL \
        : severity auth.info \
        : twist /bin/echo "You are not welcome to use %d from %h."
```

In this example, all connections from hosts in the domain example.com toward the "daytime" service are rejected without further ado. Although the TCP wrappers don't fall for the most obvious DNS tricks, checking the DNS only provides a very limited level of security. Hosts in 10.53.64.0/18 and the host with address 2001:db8:31:2::53 are allowed to use the daytime service. The hosts.allow file works on a "first match" basis, so when host venus.example.com has address 10.53.65.1, it's rejected based on its domain name, and the address match on the next line doesn't come into play. Different versions of the TCP wrapper support slightly different hosts.allow clauses, but the ones I was able to test didn't support prefix notation for IPv4 address ranges or any kind of wildcard matching for IPv6. The final clause logs any attempts to use any services (that are active and use TCP wrappers) and sends back an error message. Depending on the protocol, this message may or may not be displayed to the user.

On Red Hat 9 Linux, the TCP wrappers worked unreliably. Under FreeBSD, they worked well, with the caveat that when a daemon receives an incoming connection and the TCP wrappers reject the connection, the daemon sees a strange termination of the incoming request. For the MySQL daemon, this was enough to crash. This can be solved either by using a packet filter as discussed below or binding the service to the localhost address so connection attempts from the outside world aren't possible. In MacOS 10.4, the xinetd daemon doesn't support TCP wrappers, but other daemons may still be compiled with TCP wrapper support. This is the case for the built-in sshd, for example.

■**Tip** See the man pages for `tcpd`, `hosts_access(5)`, and `hosts_options` for more information. However, these manual pages are often out of date, with no clear way to determine what version of the actual software is installed on the system.

Stateful Filtering to Replace NAT

When several hosts share a single public IPv4 address, this makes it hard for the Network Address Translation box that implements this sharing to determine what to do with incoming TCP session establishment requests. By default, these requests will be rejected, thereby shielding the hosts behind the NAT device from potentially harmful and potentially useful incoming traffic alike. The situation is similar for UDP: only when the incoming UDP packet is a reply to an earlier outgoing request does the NAT device know how to translate the packet.

In IPv6, the assumption is that there is no NAT, so there is no automatic protection against uninvited incoming traffic either. For TCP, this is easily fixed by filtering out packets that contain a TCP header with the SYN bit set and the ACK bit cleared. This makes it impossible to establish TCP sessions from the outside to the inside, while all other TCP packets, such as session establishment acknowledgements for sessions initiated from the inside or packets belonging to already established sessions, can pass through.

For UDP, it gets more complicated, as there is no way to determine whether a UDP packet is an incoming request or the reply to an earlier outgoing request by just looking at the packet. So to block uninvited UDP traffic, it's necessary to implement a *stateful* filter that keeps track of outgoing UDP packets so it can determine whether incoming packets were invited or not. A stateful filter can also reject TCP packets that would slip past a normal filter that only looks at the TCP flags. (However, the receiving host would reject those packets anyway because they don't belong to valid TCP sessions.) Last but not least, stateful filtering often gets the job done with a smaller number of filter rules.

However, stateful filtering also has a few downsides. To successfully determine whether a packet belongs to an existing session, the stateful filter needs to keep a lot of information (or state) around. Smart stateful filtering implementations know how to search through this information very efficiently, but it still takes memory and CPU resources to manage all the state information. Also, a stateful filter can only do its work when it can observe the packet flow in both directions.[2] When the filter is located on the filtered host itself, that isn't much of a problem (although even there it's not impossible that a packet goes out on interface A and the reply comes in through interface B), but it can be when the filter is implemented in an external system that functions as a firewall. If there is only one such a firewall, then obviously all packets will flow through it in both directions. The trouble starts when there is more than one firewall, so that for some traffic, one firewall gets to see the outgoing packets for a given session and another the incoming packets.

Of the IP filters discussed here, `ipf`, PF and Cisco IOS can do stateful filtering in IPv6.

---

2. I once had occasion to test a stateful filter in the core network of a medium-sized ISP. Of the 250,000 packets per second that traversed the Gigabit Ethernet cable, 10,000 initiated new sessions. Even though the filtering itself happened in hardware, the CPU of the device couldn't program the filter hardware with new session state fast enough to keep up.

Linux ip6tables

The 2.2 Linux kernel did its IP packet filtering with ipchains. As of kernel 2.4, the preferred method for this is iptables. The name for the actual filter is the "Netfilter subsystem," but I find these names impossible to remember, so it's easier to talk about the executable that provides the user interface. Red Hat Linux comes with iptables (the IPv4 version) but not with ip6tables (the IPv6 version). Listing 9-3 shows how to download and install ip6tables, along with a newer version of iptables that the ip6tables RPM needs. The output of the commands is left out.

Listing 9-3. *Downloading and Installing* ip6tables

```
# service iptables stop
# chkconfig iptables off
# wget http://download.fedoralegacy.org/redhat/9/updates/i386/➥
iptables-ipv6-1.2.8-8.90.1.legacy.i386.rpm
# wget http://download.fedoralegacy.org/redhat/9/updates/i386/➥
iptables-1.2.8-8.90.1.legacy.i386.rpm
# rpm --upgrade iptables-1.2.8-8.90.1.legacy.i386.rpm
# rpm --install iptables-ipv6-1.2.8-8.90.1.legacy.i386.rpm
# service ip6tables start
# chkconfig --level 345 ip6tables on
```

The Red Hat and ip6tables documentation is adamant that ipchains, iptables, and ip6tables are mutually exclusive, so the first two lines stop the running iptables and stop it from being loaded at startup in the future. The next two lines download the RPM files, and the two lines after that upgrade the existing iptables and install ip6tables, respectively. The two remaining lines start ip6tables and make it start at boot time. Because iptables only handles IPv4 and ip6tables only handles IPv6, it's enormously inconvenient to be unable to run both. So I started iptables again when ip6tables was running, with no immediate bad effects. Your mileage may vary.

According to the documentation, Red Hat Enterprise Linux has ip6tables on board, but it doesn't. I haven't been able to check this, but it seems the way to install ip6tables on such a system is to determine the version of iptables that's installed (simply type iptables at the prompt, and it will print its version number) and then find an RPM for the corresponding version of ip6tables and install it as in Listing 9-3.

iptables gets its name from the different "tables" that in turn each contain one or more "chains" with filter rules. The table we're interested in is the default one named "filter," which by default contains three chains: input, output, and forward. The input chain contains the rules that apply to packets that come in destined for local consumption. The output chain contains the rules that apply to locally generated packets as they leave the system. The rules in the forward chain operate on packets that are forwarded when the system acts as a router. The filter rules in a chain are evaluated one by one, and as soon as a packet matches a rule, the indicated action is taken, regardless of any following rules. Listing 9-4 implements a filter that blocks several types of traffic.

Listing 9-4. *Filtering with* ip6tables

```
# ip6tables -A OUTPUT -p tcp --dport 25 -j DROP
# ip6tables -A INPUT -s 2001:db8::/32 -j DROP
# ip6tables -A INPUT -p icmpv6 --icmpv6-type echo-request -d ff02::1 -j DROP
# ip6tables -I INPUT -p tcp --syn -j DROP
# ip6tables -D OUTPUT -p tcp --dport 25 -j DROP
```

The -A flag appends filter rules at the end of a chain, while -I inserts them at the beginning and -D deletes existing rules. (It's also possible to use line numbers for explicit ordering.) The -p tcp in the first rule matches TCP packets, but --dport 25 limits this to packets with destination port number 25 (SMTP). The -j flag specifies the action to be taken. DROP means the packet is discarded unceremoniously, without returning an ICMP message. The documentation also mentions REJECT (along with some other options), which does send back an ICMP unreachable, but ironically, my attempts to add filter rules with a REJECT action were rejected.

The second rule uses -s 2001:db8::/32 to match all packets that have a source address inside the IPv6 documentation prefix. Unlike the first rule, this one is applied to incoming packets. The third rule is a bit more complex: it matches the ICMPv6 protocol and then only the packets that are ICMPv6 type "echo request." But the rule goes on to specify the all node multicast address as the destination with -d ff02::1. With this rule in effect, the system won't respond to pings sent to the all node multicast address anymore, as these packets are filtered out before they can be processed. The fourth rule matches all TCP session establishment packets. ip6tables allows specifying each individual TCP flag, but in this case, using the --syn option that matches session establishment packets is easier. This line effectively provides the same filtering NAT does, for TCP at least. Blocking outgoing SMTP traffic makes it hard to send mail, so the final line removes the first one again, by virtue of the -D in place of the -A or -I option. Use ip6tables -F to flush all filter rules rather than having to delete them one by one. Without further arguments, ip6tables -F flushes all chains, but you can also supply the chain name to flush.

These rules work under the assumption that the default policy for any unmatched packets is to allow them through. Alternatively, you can make filter rules that accept allowed traffic (with the ACCEPT rather than the DROP action), and then reject everything else. You can change the default policy for a table with (for instance) ip6tables -P INPUT DROP or ip6tables -P FORWARD ACCEPT. ip6tables -L lists the chains and their default policies. See the ip6tables man page for more information on how to use ip6tables. You can also find more information about Netfilter in general at http://www.netfilter.org/.

MacOS and FreeBSD ip6fw

The IPFirewall, or ipfw in IPv4 and ip6fw in IPv6, has been around for a long time in FreeBSD. These days, many FreeBSD users prefer ipf instead, which we'll discuss later. MacOS doesn't come with ipf, but ip6fw is enabled by default, so on the Mac, using ip6fw is the logical choice. Under FreeBSD, you can enable ip6fw by adding the following lines to /etc/rc.conf:

```
ipv6_firewall_enable="YES"
ipv6_firewall_script="/etc/rc.firewall6"
ipv6_firewall_type="open"
```

The purpose of the first line is obvious. The second line points to the system-supplied script that sets up the IPv6 filter rules and the last line passes the argument "open" to this script. Have a look at the script in /etc/rc.firewall6 for the options other than "open," which allows all packets, or "closed," which filters out all packets. But if you want to use one of these other options, you need to customize the script. The following rule is always present:

```
65535 deny all from any to any
```

So if you want to allow anything (or everything), you must install one or more rules with a lower number. This makes it a very bad idea to have just the line ipv6_firewall_enable="YES" in the /etc/rc.d without a script to set up filter rules. You can change the default behavior to allowing all packets by compiling the kernel with a special option as described in the ipfirewall man page. On the Mac, however, things work slightly differently, and the default action is to allow all packets.

■Note The MacOS ip6fw man page is the same as the FreeBSD one, even though the default behavior of the filter is the opposite under MacOS. Apparently, man pages for BSD utilities that are incorporated in MacOS aren't updated, even if the utilities themselves are.

Unlike the Linux Netfilter/ip6tables, ip6fw has only a single system-wide filter list. However, it's possible to apply individual filter rules to just input or output packets. Listing 9-5 does the same with ip6fw as Listing 9-4 did with ip6tables.

Listing 9-5. *Filtering with* ip6fw

```
% sudo ip6fw -q add unreach admin tcp from any to any 25 out
% sudo ip6fw -q add deny ipv6 from 2001:db8::/32 to any
% sudo ip6fw -q add deny ipv6-icmp from any to ff02::1 in icmptype 128
% sudo ip6fw -q add deny tcp from any to any setup in
% sudo ip6fw list
00100 unreach admin tcp from any to any 25 out
00200 deny ipv6 from 2001:db8::/32 to any
00300 deny ipv6-icmp from any to ff02::1 in icmptype 128
00400 deny tcp from any to any in setup
65535 allow ipv6 from any to any
% sudo ip6fw delete 100
```

The ip6fw commands themselves are the same on FreeBSD and MacOS, but because the root isn't enabled by default on MacOS, it's necessary to use the sudo tool to execute privileged commands. The first line installs a filter rule that blocks outgoing TCP port 25 packets. When such a packet hits the filter, an ICMPv6 type "unreachable" code "administratively blocked" message is sent back so the application promptly returns an error. The next line blocks all IPv6 packets from the documentation range, regardless of their destination and whether the packets are incoming or outgoing. There are no ICMPv6 unreachables or TCP resets for filters with a deny action. The third line blocks all incoming ICMPv6 echo request packets (type 128, see

Chapter 8) with the all-node multicast address as their destination. The fifth line blocks all incoming TCP session establishment packets.

The next order of business is to delete the filter rule that blocks port 25. All ip6fw filter rules have a line number. Because we didn't supply a line number, the rules were numbered automatically, and the only way to delete a rule is by using its number. So we need to display the list of rules with ip6fw list. A nice property of ip6fw is that the output from the list subcommand follows the rules for the add subcommand, making for easy copying and pasting. The -q flag suppresses interactive input and output. When adding lines without providing the -q flag, ip6fw returns "00000" after each rule. Apparently, the idea is to echo back the line number for the new rule, but this effort isn't entirely successful.

If the default policy (rule 65535) is to reject all packets, you may need to install a line like the following:

```
ip6fw add 65534 allow ipv6 from any to any
```

However, with this line in effect, ip6fw is no longer able to automatically number lines, as 65534 is the highest possible number for user-defined rules; 1 is the lowest. There can be more than one rule with a given number. In that case, evaluating or removing them happens in the order in which they were installed. See the ip6fw man page for more options.

IPFilter

The IPFilter is an IP filter that's available for several UNIX and UNIX-like systems. It's included in FreeBSD, and the examples below are for FreeBSD, but if the documentation is to be believed, IPFilter also works with Linux as of the 2.4 kernel (some kernel hackery required). Under FreeBSD 5.x, IPFilter works out of the box after enabling it in /etc/rc.conf, but under FreeBSD 4.x, you need to compile a custom kernel to be able to use IPFilter. In theory, it's also available as a loadable kernel module, but that doesn't work (see FreeBSD bug 53966). See the chapter "Configuring the FreeBSD Kernel" in the FreeBSD handbook at http://www.freebsd.org/. You need to add following line in the kernel configuration file:

```
options IPFILTER
```

You can enable IPFilter on FreeBSD by adding the following lines to the /etc/rc.conf file:

```
ipfilter_enable="YES"
ipfilter_program="/sbin/ipf"
ipfilter_rules="/etc/ipf.rules"
ipv6_ipfilter_rules="/etc/ipf6.rules"
```

By default, ipf is compiled to allow all packets, but wouldn't you hate to find out that your installation uses the opposite default? This would be especially bad because, unlike other filters, IPF works both on IPv4 and IPv6. So if you lock yourself out of your machine, you *really* lock yourself out of your machine. The /etc/ipf.rules file mentioned above contains the ipf filter rules for IPv4, while /etc/ipf6.rules contains the rules for IPv6. These files aren't present by default, so you need to create them and put in some default rules. For instance:

```
# allow everything
pass in all
pass out all
```

Even though `ipf` uses the same programs to manipulate IPv4 and IPv6 rules, those rules are kept in separate tables: it's not possible to have a single rule that acts on both IPv4 and IPv6 packets. In addition to the IPv4/IPv6 split, `ipf` has separate rule sets for input and output. This makes for the following permutations:

IPv4 input rules, which can be listed with `ipfstat -i`

IPv4 output rules, which can be listed with `ipfstat -o`

IPv6 input rules, which can be listed with `ipfstat -6 -i`

IPv6 output rules, which can be listed with `ipfstat -6 -o`

■**Note** The filtering logic in `ipf` is the exact opposite of that of the other filters discussed so far: rather than stopping when the first matching filter rule is found, `ipf` continues to evaluate rules all the way to the end of the list, and only then does it apply the action specified in the *last* matching rule.

Listing 9-6 implements filter rules similar to those in Listings 9-4 and 9-5.

Listing 9-6. `ipf` *Filter Rules*

```
pass in all
pass out all
block out proto tcp from any to any port = 25
block in from 2001:db8::/32 to any
block in proto ipv6-icmp from any to ff02::1 icmp-type 128
block return-rst in proto tcp from any to any flags S
```

The first two filter rules set up a default action. The next rule filters out any outgoing TCP packets with destination port 25. The rules after that filter out incoming packets with source addresses in the IPv6 documentation prefix, filter incoming `ping6` packets to the all-hosts address, and, last but not least, block all incoming TCP packets with the SYN bit set. This last rule also sends back TCP resets. FreeBSD 5.4 did generate the reset packets, but FreeBSD 4.9 didn't. FreeBSD 4.9 also didn't allow using `icmp6` instead of `ipv6-icmp`.

You can add the rules in Listing 9-6 to `/etc/ipf6.rules` to have them loaded on startup. There doesn't seem to be a way to add/remove rules on the fly without loading them from a file. Use the command `ipf -6 -Fa -f ipf6.rules` to do that. The -6 flag indicates that we're talking about IPv6, -Fa tells `ipf` it should flush all existing rules both for input and output, and the -f argument makes it read new rules from a file. See the man page for more options. Editing a file with filter rules and then reloading the rules from the file isn't entirely without danger: if parsing the file fails halfway through, only part of the rules are loaded, and you may lock yourself out of your machine. However, the "apply the last matching rule" philosophy is helpful here: if the first rules allow all packets until subsequent rules block certain types of traffic, missing rules result in a less restrictive filter set rather than a more restrictive one.

You can keep `ipf` from evaluating additional rules with the `quick` keyword after the in or out in a rule. So `pass out all quick` means that all outgoing packets are allowed through, regardless of what additional rules you may specify. `ipf` can also perform stateful filtering; see Listing 9-7.

Listing 9-7. *Stateful Filtering with* ipf

```
pass in all
pass out all
pass out proto tcp/udp from any to any keep state
block return-rst in proto tcp from any to any
block in proto udp from any to any
```

The third rule permits outgoing TCP and UDP packets and keeps their state to allow return traffic. This happens automatically. The fourth line blocks all remaining TCP packets and sends back a reset, and the final line blocks all unsolicited UDP packets. The appropriate action would be to send back an ICMPv6 unreachable message with code administratively prohibited, but ipf doesn't have much documentation, so I was unable to determine the correct syntax.

FreeBSD Packet Filter

In version 5.3, FreeBSD gained a port of the OpenBSD Packet Filter (PF). PF is a lot like ipf, but it has some more advanced functions and, more importantly, extensive documentation, which you'll find at http://www.openbsd.org/faq/pf/. You can also download the documentation in PDF format from this page, but be warned that the text is often exceptionally tiny. Another interesting difference between PF and the other filters is that in PF IPv4 and IPv6 are fully integrated: a single rule can apply to both protocols. Listing 9-8 is the PF version of our by now familiar filter.

Listing 9-8. *PF Filter Rules*

```
pass all
unroutable="{ 2001:db8::/32 192.0.2.0/24 }"
block in from $unroutable to any
block out proto tcp from any to any port = 25
block in proto icmp6 from any to ff02::1 icmp6-type echoreq
block return-rst in proto tcp from any to any flags S/SA
```

As you can see, PF rules look very similar to ipf rules. However, there are some important differences. PF allows rules that apply both to incoming and outgoing packets, so a single pass all accomplishes the same thing as pass in all and pass out all. PF also adds support for macros, like the one in the second line. The contents of the macro must be between quotes and can be an address, protocol, port, and so on. In this case, it's a list, another new feature. A list is a set of addresses, protocols, or ports between braces, optionally separated by commas. The list in the second line of Listing 9-8 contains the IPv6 and IPv4 documentation prefixes. The third line blocks all packets that have a source address in either of the documentation prefixes by referencing the macro.

The fourth line filters out traffic toward port 25. Because there are no addresses or an explicit inet or inet6 after the out keyword, this rule applies to both IPv4 and IPv6. The second to last rule filters out incoming ICMPv6 echo requests. The icmp6-type keyword isn't documented, but the documentation mentioned earlier does have a link to a list of ICMPv6 types that contains the names PF requires; it doesn't accept numerical values like ipf does. The final rule blocks incoming TCP packets that out of the S and A flags only have the S flag set. PF won't accept the rule without this "mask" (the SA flags in the example).

You can load the filter rules from a file (called `pf.rules` in this case) with the command `pfctl -f pf.rules`. There is no need to flush the rule set first; this is done automatically when loading new rules. If there is an error in one of the rules, none of the rules is loaded and the old ones remain in effect. You can manually flush the rules with `pfctl -F rules`. You can display the current list of rules with `pfctl -s rules`, as in Listing 9-9.

Listing 9-9. *Displaying PF Filter Rules*

```
# pfctl -s rules
No ALTQ support in kernel
ALTQ related functions disabled
pass all
block drop in inet6 from 2001:db8::/32 to any
block drop in inet from 192.0.2.0/24 to any
block drop out proto tcp from any to any port = smtp
block drop in inet6 proto ipv6-icmp from any to ff02::1 icmp6-type echoreq
block return-rst in proto tcp all flags S/SA
```

Don't worry if `pfctl` complains about ALTQ. This is a bandwidth management mechanism that PF supports, but PF will also work without ALTQ present. It's interesting to see that the list from Listing 9-8 is expanded to two different filter rules. This always happens with lists and is not the result of mixing IPv4 and IPv6. PF also supports "tables," which are similar to lists but don't get expanded in this way. Instead, the contents of a table is stored in a special data structure in memory that can be searched very efficiently. So if you have a large list of IP prefixes that you want to block or allow through, it's best to store them in a table. Obviously, tables only work for addresses, and there are some other limitations as well. PF also noticed that our anti-ping rule is IPv6-specific, so it added the keyword `inet6`. Rules without `inet` or `inet6` apply to both IPv4 and IPv6. Listing 9-10 is a stateful PF filter.

Listing 9-10. *Stateful Filtering with PF*

```
scrub in all
pass all
pass out proto { tcp, udp } from any to any keep state
block return in proto { tcp, udp } from any to any
```

The command `scrub in all` tells PF to remove inconsistencies from incoming packets, reassembles fragmented packets, and blocks packets with invalid TCP flag combinations. The rest of the filter is very simple: the second line sets up the familiar default policy that allows ICMP and unknown protocols through the filter. The third line directs PF to keep state information for all outgoing TCP and UDP packets. In the absence of any TCP flags, this applies to `all` outgoing TCP packets, not just outgoing TCP session establishment packets. The last line then blocks all incoming TCP and UDP packets that weren't already allowed through by virtue of the state created by the third line. The `return` keyword makes PF send back a TCP reset for incoming TCP packets and an ICMP port unreachable for incoming UDP packets that were blocked. Use `pfctl -s state` to display the state table and `pfctl -F state` to clear it.

■**Caution** PF often errs on the side of security, so make sure your filter isn't more restrictive than you intend, especially when using more advanced options such as scrubbing.

PF AND NAT

According to the documentation, PF can also perform Network Address Translation. That's not very unusual, but without saying it in so many words, the documentation suggests that NAT also works with IPv6. *That* would be very unusual. One of the reasons to move to IPv6 would be to get back to the situation where any two arbitrary hosts can communicate with each other without NATs that get in the way. And what's the advantage of IPv6+NAT over IPv4+NAT, anyway? NAT doesn't solve the long-term address shortage in IPv4 completely, but it certainly takes the sting out of the problem. At the same time, the benefits of IPv6+NAT aren't quite as compelling as those of IPv6 without NAT. Also, because currently the expectation is that NAT won't be deployed to a significant degree in IPv6, vendors aren't likely to include NAT traversal mechanisms in their IPv6 products like they do with IPv4 products.

It turns out that PF does indeed support NAT with IPv6. If you want to see for yourself, set up a PF-capable host with "internal" and "external" interfaces, enable router advertisements on the internal interface, and turn on IPv6 forwarding. (This is all explained in Chapter 3 and Chapter 4.) Then, feed PF filter/translation rules like the following:

```
nat on gif0 from 2001:db8:6::/64 to any -> 2001:db8:6:172::2
pass all
```

The gif0 argument is the external interface, which has the address 2001:db8:6:172::2. The 2001:db8:6::/64 prefix is the prefix for the internal network. That's it. To the outside world, any communication from the hosts in 2001:db8:6::/64 will now seem to come from 2001:db8:6:172::2. For simple client/server interactions, such as the HTTP protocol, this works well, but any protocols that embed addresses in their communication will fail. The prime example of such a protocol is FTP. When requesting a file from an FTP server, the client tells the server which address and port it should connect to to transmit the file. With the client behind NAT the address supplied by the client won't be reachable. With IPv6, this leads to the following error:

```
230 Login successful.
Remote system type is UNIX.
Using binary mode to transfer files.
ftp> ls
500 Illegal EPRT command.
500 Unknown command.
425 Use PORT or PASV first.
```

The offending EPRT command is the IPv6 version of the original FTP PORT command. The interesting thing is that with many IPv4 NATs, the exact same FTP behavior does work. The reason for this is simple: NAT vendors include workarounds for many protocols to make them work through the NAT. In this case, the internal address as supplied by the client in the FTP PORT is changed to the external address of the NAT. In the case of FTP, all of this is mostly moot because the protocol was extended with a "passive" mode that doesn't require the client to pass its address to the server. However, other protocols such as RTSP, SIP, and peer-to-peer applications aren't as easy to fix.

Windows netsh firewall

The Windows netsh utility that we put to good use in earlier chapters can do more than just manipulate IPv6 settings. As of Windows XP Service Pack 2, netsh also contains a "firewall" context. This is probably a matter of opinion, but I didn't find the netsh firewall context very useful as a general-purpose packet filter, although it has some options to facilitate this type of filtering. However, the Windows XP firewall has a very useful feature that lacks in the filters discussed so far: it allows filtering based on the program that receives the packets, rather than on just the information found in the packet itself and information like the input/output interface.

The Windows XP firewall is enabled by default as of Service Pack 2 and acts as a stateful filter that allows return traffic for all outgoing packets. The firewall blocks some ICMPv6 types but not others. For instance, pinging a host directly works, but Windows XP Service Pack 2 hosts don't reply to pings to the all node multicast address, unless you disable the firewall completely with set opmode mode=disable. This happens despite the presence of a multicastbroadcastresponse setting, which is enabled by default. Windows *really* doesn't like it when the firewall is disabled, though, and immediately pops up a warning. Most IPv6 traceroutes toward the Windows system don't work with the firewall enabled either, as the traceroute program generally uses UDP packets to unoccupied ports to solicit ICMPv6 "port unreachable" messages. As the stateful firewall doesn't expect these UDP packets, they are dropped and there is no ICMPv6 message. However, Windows uses ICMP echo request messages in its traceroutes, which are allowed through by the Windows XP firewall.

Caution The firewall blocks outgoing ICMPv6 "packet too big" messages, which becomes problematic when the system is configured to be an IPv6 router. See Chapter 4.

Type netsh firewall to enter the firewall context and then type ? or a command followed by ? to learn more about netsh firewall commands.

Cisco IPv6 Access Lists

Cisco routers use "access lists" to filter packets. Over the years, Cisco has slowly changed the way access lists work. Originally, IOS only supported numbered access lists, with different number ranges for different protocols or access list types. For instance, access list numbers from 1 to 99 were for "standard" IPv4 access lists that only support filtering on source address, while numbers 100 to 199 were for "extended" access lists that can also look at destination addresses, protocols, and protocol-specific information such as port numbers. In IOS 11.2, Cisco introduced a new syntax for "named access lists." IPv6 access lists are very similar to IPv4 named access lists, except that there is no longer a difference between standard and extended access lists: all IPv6 access lists are extended access lists.[3] Note that there can't be an IPv4 and an IPv6 access list with the same name.

3. In older IOS versions, IPv6 access lists could only look at source and destination IPv6 addresses.

Applying Access Lists to Interfaces

When filtering traffic that is forwarded by the router, access lists are applied to individual interfaces, either for input or output (or both). Listing 9-11 shows incoming and outgoing access lists that implement filters similar to the ones in Listings 9-4, 9-5, 9-6, and 9-8.

Listing 9-11. *Filtering by Using IPv6 Access Lists on a Cisco Router*

```
!
interface Ethernet1
 ipv6 traffic-filter in-ipv6-acl in
 ipv6 traffic-filter out-ipv6-acl out
!
ipv6 access-list in-ipv6-acl
 deny ipv6 2001:DB8::/32 any
 deny icmp any host FF02::1 echo-request
 permit tcp any any established
 deny tcp any any
 permit ipv6 any any
!
ipv6 access-list out-ipv6-acl
 deny tcp any any eq smtp
 permit ipv6 any any
!
```

The first line in `in-ipv6-acl` filters out all IPv6 packets from the documentation prefix, regardless of their destination. The `ipv6` keyword seems superfluous, as this is an IPv6 access list, but it indicates that the filter rule matches *all* IPv6 packets, regardless of whether the payload is TCP, UDP, ICMPv6, or something else. The next line rejects ICMP messages (the "v6" part is implied) toward the all node multicast address that are echo requests. The line after that allows all TCP packets that are part of established sessions and then all other TCP packets are rejected. Finally, all packets that didn't match any of the preceding filter rules are permitted through.

Rather than denying all remaining TCP packets that aren't part of an established session, it's possible to allow UDP and ICMPv6 and have the unwanted TCP packets filtered out by the implicit deny clause at the end of the access list. However, this would also reject all non-TCP/UDP/ICMPv6 packets. This could be desirable in very security conscious environments, but such a "deny unknown protocols" policy has the downside that it makes it harder to deploy new protocols. Also see the discussion on filter limitations later this chapter.

In the `ip6tables` and `ip6fw` examples we removed the outgoing SMTP filter again at the end of the listing. Listing 9-12 does this for a Cisco router with the access lists from Listing 9-11 installed.

Listing 9-12. *Removing an Access List Line*

```
Router#show running-config | begin ipv6 access-list out-ipv6-acl
ipv6 access-list out-ipv6-acl
 deny tcp any any eq smtp
 permit ipv6 any any
!
Router#conf t
Enter configuration commands, one per line.  End with CNTL/Z.
Router(config)#ipv6 access-list out-ipv6-acl
Router(config-ipv6-acl)#no deny tcp any any eq 25
Router(config-ipv6-acl)#^Z
Router#show running-config | begin ipv6 access-list out-ipv6-acl
ipv6 access-list out-ipv6-acl
 sequence 20 permit ipv6 any any
!
```

When listing the access list as it appears in the configuration before removing the SMTP line, the access list lines don't have numbers, but afterward, the remaining line does. The router automatically adds sequence numbers to all filter rules as they are entered, as you can see with the show ipv6 access-list command. This makes it possible to insert lines in the middle of an access list later by supplying the desired sequence number manually. For instance, adding the SMTP filter again without a sequence number would place this filter rule at the end of the access list, but with deny tcp any any eq 25 sequence 10, it's placed before the permit ipv6 any any line like before.

Stateful Filtering with Reflexive Access Lists

Although the filters in Listing 9-12 manage to keep out a lot of unwanted traffic, we can do better by doing stateful filtering on routers where this is appropriate, such as the ones acting as Customer Premises Equipment (CPE). Cisco IOS has a mechanism called "reflexive access lists" for this, as shown in Listing 9-13.

Listing 9-13. *Stateful Filtering with a Reflexive Access List*

```
!
no ipv6 access-list out-ipv6-acl
no ipv6 access-list in-ipv6-acl
!
ipv6 access-list out-ipv6-acl
 permit tcp any any eq 22 reflect state-acl timeout 7500
 permit ipv6 any any reflect state-acl
!
ipv6 access-list in-ipv6-acl
 evaluate state-acl
 deny tcp any any log-input
 deny udp any any log-input
!
```

First order of business is to remove the existing `out-ipv6-acl` and `in-ipv6-acl` access lists. Both access lists are still referenced under the Ethernet1 interface (see Listing 9-12), but because they no longer exist, all traffic is allowed through. However, as soon as the first line for `out-ipv6-acl` is entered, this is no longer true: the access list exists once again, and all TCP traffic toward port 22 (SSH) is allowed through. But because the next line hasn't been entered yet, all non-SSH packets are caught by the ever-present implicit deny.[4] This is, of course, fixed by adding the second line, which allows all packets through. Both lines pass the packets through the reflexive access list "state-acl" in order to set up filtering state. The first line sets up a timeout of 7500 seconds for SSH sessions. The second line doesn't mention a timeout, so the default one of 300 seconds applies. 7500 seconds (two hours and five minutes) is a good value for SSH sessions that may go idle for long periods, as many systems send out a TCP keepalive once every two hours on idle TCP sessions. TCP session state is also removed when the session terminates, but UDP and ICMP echo lines must time out because there is no way for the filter to know when such a "session" terminates. Use `show ipv6 access-list state-acl` to monitor the reflexive access list.

The `in-ipv6-acl` access list passes traffic through the reflexive access list set up in the outgoing filter and reject all other TCP and UDP traffic while logging it. The reflexive access list itself is created on-demand by the router, so it doesn't show up in the configuration. The filter rules in the reflexive access list are all `permit` rules that match specific address and TCP/UDP port combinations or addresses/ICMP echo reply combinations. The `evaluate` clause passes all traffic through the reflexive access list. All packets that are permitted there are allowed through, but packets that aren't permitted by the reflexive access lists aren't denied, but rather handed back to the calling access list (`in-ipv6-acl`) for further processing.

Caution It's important to allow ICMPv6 neighbor solicitation and neighbor advertisement packets through access lists, or communication over IPv6 won't be possible on the interface the access list is applied to. For this reason, as of Cisco IOS 12.0(23)S, IPv6 access lists include implicit `permit icmp any any nd-na` and `permit icmp any any nd-ns` rules preceding the customary implicit deny at the end of the access list. If you want to supply your own `deny ipv6 any any` or `deny icmp any any` rule for logging purposes, you also need to add your own permit rules for neighbor discovery.

As mentioned before, the reflexive access list allows incoming TCP and UDP packets that match earlier outgoing packets, as well as ICMPv6 echo replies that match earlier outgoing ICMPv6 echo requests. However, reflexive access lists aren't smart enough to allow incoming ICMPv6 "port unreachable" and "time exceeded" messages belonging to outgoing traceroute probes, so `traceroute6` doesn't work. You can fix this by adding the lines `permit icmp any any port-unreachable sequence 12` and `permit icmp any any time-exceeded sequence 14` to the `in-ipv6-acl` access list. Because these ICMP messages are dealt with by the IPv6 stack (rather than applications) on the receiving host, allowing them shouldn't pose any security risks. Also, ICMPv6 error messages aren't supposed to generate ICMP messages in return, so they can't be used to trick hosts to send back a message for scanning purposes.

---

4. This is not the most efficient way to manage access lists on a Cisco router, but it's important to be familiar with this type of access list behavior. It's the same for most, if not all, types of IOS access lists.

When implementing reflexive access lists, beware that IPv6 traffic generated on the router itself doesn't go through any outgoing access lists: it's always allowed. So with Listing 9-13 in place, trying to `telnet`, `ping`, or `traceroute` from the router command line won't work: because the outgoing packets aren't seen by `out-ipv6-acl`, no filter lines are added to the reflexive access list, so `in-ipv6-acl` will reject the return traffic. If this poses a problem, you can either permit the specific protocols that are desired toward the IPv6 addresses of the router in the incoming access list(s) or opt for nonreflexive stateless filters such as those in Listing 9-11.

Filtering Services on the Router

An ISP would generally want to allow Telnet traffic to flow through its network. Even though Telnet isn't as widely used as it once was, many places around the Net still use the protocol, so filtering it out wholesale would be an unpopular move. On the other hand, an ISP would probably want to limit Telnet access to its routers to trusted addresses only[5] to discourage password guessing and to avoid problems with vulnerabilities in the Cisco remote access implementation, which have occurred several times in the past. One way to do this would be to filter out packets on port 23 (the Telnet port) in access lists on all interfaces, but this is very tedious. IOS has a better way to accomplish the same result: it's possible to apply an access list to most protocols or services running *on* the router, without affecting traffic flowing *through* the router. Listing 9-14 implements a filter for remote access to the command line with Telnet.

Listing 9-14. *Filtering IPv6 Telnet Access to a Cisco Router*

```
!
ipv6 access-list manage-ipv6
 permit ipv6 2001:db8:31::/48 any
!
line vty 0 4
 ipv6 access-class manage-ipv6 in
 transport input telnet
!
```

The access list `manage-ipv6` only has a single filter rule that matches all IPv6 packets with a source address in the prefix `2001:db8:31::/48` and any destination address. This access list is then applied to virtual TTYs 0 to 4 with the `ipv6 access-class manage-ipv6 in` command. VTYs 0 to 4 are available on all Cisco routers for incoming sessions with protocols like Telnet and rlogin, but some routers allow more VTYs. In this case, incoming sessions are only allowed over the Telnet protocol, and the access list makes sure that only sessions from hosts with addresses in `2001:db8:31::/48` are accepted.

■**Caution** Protocols that can be enabled without access restrictions or are enabled without access restrictions by default, such as Telnet, need *both* IPv4 and IPv6 filters. For instance, with Listing 9-14 in place, the router will still accept Telnet sessions from all IPv4 addresses.

---

5. It's better to use SSH rather than Telnet, because unlike Telnet, SSH encrypts the login session. However, not all Cisco IOS images and platforms support SSH. It can also be useful to have Telnet access as a backup in case SSH isn't available, for instance, when hopping from one router to the next.

Unicast Reverse Path Forwarding

In BCP 38/RFC 2827, the IETF recommends that ISPs only accept packets from their customers with source addresses that were actually assigned to those customers. This makes it impossible to send out abusive IP packets with falsified source addresses. Forcing attackers to use their real IP address makes it easier to filter out the packets in question and trace back the source. Implementing such filters is generally a good idea whenever downstream hosts are not under your control or have a higher than average risk of being compromised. However, maintaining access lists on all such router interfaces is a lot of work. This is where Cisco's unicast Reverse Path Forwarding (uRPF) feature comes in handy.

The original Reverse Path Forwarding check is a mechanism to make sure that only a single copy of a multicast packet is forwarded by a router. Figure 9-1 shows a network with six routers. Let's assume the routers in this network forward multicast packets and that these multicasts enter the network at Router 1. Router 1 replicates the packet and sends copies to Routers 2 and 3. Router 2 in turn sends copies to Routers 4 and 5. So far so good. But Router 3 sends copies of the packet to Routers 5 and 6, which means that Router 5 gets two copies of each packet. Depending on the topology of the network, Router 5 can tell Router 3 that it doesn't want to receive packets addressed to the relevant group address, but if Routers 5 and 6 are connected to the same interface on Router 3, Router 3 can't selectively send the packet to Router 6 but not to Router 5. This is where the RPF check comes in: for every multicast packet that Router 5 receives, it looks at the combination of the incoming interface and the source address of the multicast packet. If the router would use this same interface to send outgoing packets toward the address in the multicast packet's source address field, the packet is allowed through. If the router would use another interface to reach the source address in question, the packet is filtered out.

In Figure 9-1, Router 5 has a default route toward Router 2, so any multicast packets coming in from Router 3 fail the RPF check, and they're filtered.

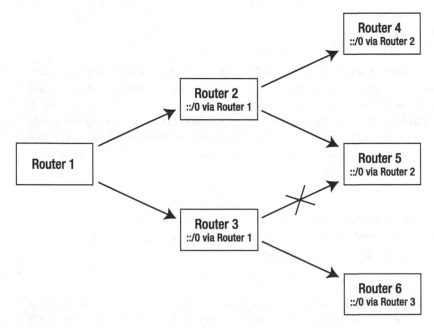

Figure 9-1. *The Reverse Path Forwarding check*

Unicast RPF uses the same mechanism to check unicast packets: on an interface with uRPF enabled, only packets with source addresses that are reachable over that interface are accepted. In essence, uRPF uses the routing table as a filter. This has two important advantages: there's no need to maintain filters manually, and filtering is more efficient because the routing table can be searched with very efficient algorithms while access list lines are evaluated one at a time from top to bottom until there is a match.

There are two different commands that enable uRPF. The simple syntax is `ipv6 verify unicast reverse-path` in interface configuration mode, optionally followed by an IPv6 access list name. Packets permitted by the access list (if supplied) are allowed through, even if the RPF check fails. Some IOS versions contain a more powerful uRPF implementation, which is enabled for an interface with `ipv6 verify unicast source reachable-via`, followed by one or more parameters. If the first parameter is `rx`, the RPF check is performed as described previously. Alternatively, it's possible to specify `any`, in which case the RPF check ignores the output interface that it finds in the routing table and checks only whether the source address is reachable via any interface. This "loose" uRPF form makes it possible to apply the mechanism to links toward upstream ISPs or peering links with other ISPs. The strict form can't be used here without additional measures because it can't handle destinations being reachable over more than one interface. The loose RPF check isn't as useful as the strict one, as it only rejects packets with source addresses that aren't in the routing table. However, the IPv6 address space is very big and sparsely populated, so this will still get rid of most packets with randomly generated source addresses. Additional arguments are `allow-default`, which makes the RPF check consider the default route, and `allow-self-ping`, which is self-explanatory, and of course, an override access list, to allow packets that would otherwise have been rejected by the RPF check. In the simple version, `allow-default` and `allow-self-ping` are implied.

According to the Cisco documentation, the unicast RPF mechanism doesn't use the regular IPv6 routing table, but rather the highly optimized IPv6 Cisco Express Forwarding (CEF) table. So, for uRPF to work, IPv6 CEF must be enabled. However, in my tests on low-end Cisco routers, uRPF also seemed to work correctly without CEF configured. See Chapter 4 on how to enable CEF.

■**Caution** Be *very* careful with uRPF on router interfaces other than ones connecting to hosts or customers with a single connection. Any other interface is likely to receive legitimate packets for which the interface isn't the best or only connection, and uRPF will block this traffic.

Filter Limitations

There are two important limitations to any filter that works on a per-packet basis with IPv6. The first one is that, like in IPv4, when a packet is fragmented, the TCP or UDP port numbers are present only in the first fragment. When blocking packets based on port number, this isn't much of an issue: the fragment with the port number in it will be blocked, even though all other fragments are allowed through. (This depends on the configured action for the fragment header or the filter's default action, of course.) Without the initial fragment that holds the TCP or UDP header, it's not possible to reassemble the original packet, so in essence, the packet is blocked. However, if you want to allow TCP or UDP traffic based on port numbers, you also need to allow all fragments, because they could be part of an allowed TCP or UDP packet. Under normal circumstances, you shouldn't see fragmented TCP packets in IPv6: because fragmentation is done at the source, sending a smaller TCP packet is just as easy. Other protocols may still be fragmented when applications or upper layer protocols use packets that are too big for the (path) MTU. To avoid unpleasant interactions between fragmentation and filtering, some firewalls and filters (optionally) reassemble the packet before passing it through the filter engine.

The other problem is that of unknown extension headers. Most extension headers conform to the de-facto "standard" that the first byte contains a next header value and the second byte the contains the length of the header. Unfortunately, the IETF never managed to make this a requirement, so when a filter encounters a header it doesn't recognize, it can't skip past this header, because it can't be sure how large the unknown header is. This means that anything following the problematic header (such as a regular TCP or UDP payload) is invisible to the filter. So unless packets with any next header or this specific unknown next header type are allowed through, the filter will reject the packets based on the unknown header rather than allowing it based on the ultimate payload.

IPsec

IPsec is a collection of mechanisms to protect IP traffic from eavesdropping, modification in transit, and more. The "sec" part, which should be written in lower case, stands for "security," but using "IP security" easily leads to confusion with the IPv4 Security Option, which is something very different: the old Internet Protocol Security Option carries information about the security level of the payload data in an IP option. This makes it possible to ensure that classified data doesn't leak into a non-classified part of the network.

IPsec Headers, Modes, and Algorithms

There are two IPsec headers: the Authentication Header (AH), which (surprise) provides authentication, and the Encapsulating Security Payload (ESP) header, which provides either authentication or encryption, or both. The difference between AH and authentication-only ESP is that AH also protects most fields in the IP header, while ESP can only protect the headers and data following the ESP header. Both AH and ESP are applied in one of two modes: transport mode or tunnel mode. In transport mode, the AH or ESP header sits between the IP header and transport protocol headers. In tunnel mode, the AH or ESP header precedes the original IP header, and a new IP header is put in front of the AH or ESP header. IPsec transport mode makes it possible to implement IPsec in a "security gateway" rather than in the source or destination host itself. A common setup is one where two such security gateways implement a Virtual Private Network (VPN) on top of the Internet. When a host in one location wants to communicate with a host in the other location, the VPN gateway in the first location adds an ESP header (AH isn't used much) along with a new IP header with a source address belonging to the gateway itself and a destination address belonging to the remote gateway. Upon reception of the ESP packet, the remote gateway strips off the outer header, processes the ESP header by checking the authentication and decrypting the packet, and forwards the packet, which is now back to its original form, to the destination host. Alternatively, in transport mode, the source and destination hosts do the IPsec processing themselves. Some people consider transport mode more secure because (with ESP encryption) the original source and destination addresses are hidden, but this isn't necessarily a huge security boon: when tunnel mode is used between two hosts rather than a host and a security gateway or two security gateways, an attacker knows the addresses of the two communicating hosts anyway. The only difference is that the attacker may not realize this. The downside of tunnel mode implemented in security gateways is that the packet is carried in clear text over part of the network. This part is supposed to be trusted, but that mostly means that it's an attractive target for attackers. There may also be MTU issues, because if a host sends a 1280 byte packet, after encapsulation by the security gateway, the packet will be larger, requiring path MTU discovering, even though the host limited its packets to 1280 bytes.

So far, we have eight permutations of different IPsec options:

- AH, both transport mode and tunnel mode.

- ESP with authentication, both transport mode and tunnel mode.

- ESP with encryption, both transport mode and tunnel mode.

- ESP with authentication and encryption, both transport mode and tunnel mode.

But the header and mode permutations are just the beginning. Both authentication and encryption can be provided by a host of different algorithms. Popular authentication algorithms are HMAC-MD5-96, a 96-bit Hash-based Message Authentication Code (HMAC) based on the MD5 one-way hash function, and HMAC-SHA-1-96 based on the SHA-1 one-way hash function. Encryption algorithm choices include DES (no longer considered safe), 3DES, and AES. Both the HMAC authentication and the encryption algorithms require secret keys, which should change regularly for optimum security. Last but not least, it's also necessary to decide which packets are eligible for IPsec treatment and which aren't.

HMAC AUTHENTICATION

When communicating over a network, it's very helpful to be certain that a packet was indeed sent by the apparent sender and that the packet wasn't changed in transit. HMAC authentication accomplishes both tasks with cryptographic hash functions such as MD5 and SHA-1. These hash functions generate a relatively short hash (128 bits for MD5, 160 bits for SHA-1) for source data of any length, and the tiniest change in the source data results in a different hash. The hash function is designed so that it's as good as impossible to create a piece of data that generates a given hash. This makes it possible to compare the hash over a received message, file, or packet with the known hash for that message, file, or packet. If the hashes match, it's a safe bet that the data is identical to the original.

A Hash-based Message Authentication Code is created by computing a cryptographic hash function over both the packet data (and IP header fields that aren't supposed to change in transit in the case of AH) and a secret key that is only known by the sender and receiver. The resulting HMAC is then placed in the AH or ESP header and transmitted along with the packet data. The receiver repeats the hash computation and checks whether the result matches the HMAC in the received packet. Only when both HMACs are identical is the packet accepted for further processing.

Continues

An impostor can't successfully create a fake packet, because he doesn't have the secret key. If the impostor uses a different key, the resulting HMAC won't match the one the receiver computes, and the packet is rejected. Similarly, if a "man-in-the-middle" intercepts the packet and changes its content, the HMAC that the receiver computes over the changed packet won't match the one in the packet. The chance of successfully generating a packet with a "good" HMAC without knowing the secret key is estimated at two to the power of half the hash length in bits. So with a 96-bit HMAC, that would be one in 2^{48} or about one in 281 trillion. Unlike with other applications of cryptographic hash functions, the impostor can't see whether he has a working packet/HMAC combination himself, so HMACs provide a very high level of security. At least, as long as the hash functions aren't vulnerable to "collision attacks." MD5 seems to be walking on its last legs in this regard; it is not (yet) possible to create fake MD5 hashes, but vulnerabilities have been found in various parts of the MD5 algorithm.

Exchanging Keys and Security Associations

The preceding is *a lot* of information to put in a set of configuration files. But the real clincher is that *all these settings must be the same on both the sending and the receiving side for IPsec to work*. The Internet Key Exchange (IKE) protocol makes it possible to negotiate most of these settings between two hosts that implement IPsec. IKE itself is stitched together from several parts, including the Internet Security Association and Key Management Protocol (ISAKMP) and parts of the Oakley Key Determination Protocol. IKE works in two phases. During phase 1, IKE checks the identity of the correspondent and negotiates a secure channel so that further IKE communication can be encrypted. Then during phase 2, the protocol negotiates Security Associations (SAs) that are used to protect packets from other applications.

The actual IPsec encryption and authentication is generally implemented in the kernel with the aid of two databases: the Security Policy Database (SPD) and the Security Association Database (SAD). The SPD is a lot like an IP filter: packets are matched based on source and destination addresses or prefixes, protocol, and port numbers. Matching packets are either allowed through, blocked, or piped through AH or ESP in transport mode or tunnel mode. When packets match an AH/ESP entry in the SPD, the SAD is consulted to determine the exact authentication and encryption parameters. If there are no SAD entries, the IKE daemon is triggered, which then negotiates a Security Association with its counterpart on the remote system. See Figure 9-2 for an overview of how these different mechanisms interact.

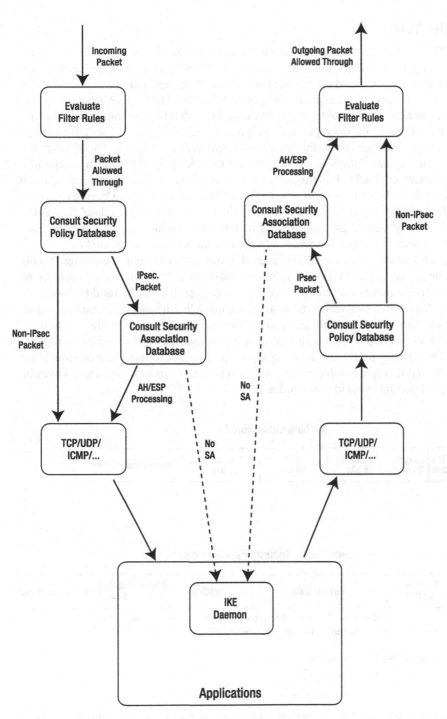

Figure 9-2. *IPsec processing overview*

IPsec on the Wire

When IPsec AH or ESP packets flow through the network, they carry one of the headers shown in Figure 9-3. The AH header is simply inserted between the IP header and the higher-level (TCP or UDP) header along with the user data. For the ESP header, things get a bit more complex: the higher-level header and user data are put in the "payload data" field of the ESP header. If there is ESP encryption, this field is encrypted, along with the padding that fills out the payload data to an even block as required by the encryption algorithm, along with the padding length and next header fields. "Next header" isn't really the appropriate term in this case, as the "next" header (the contents of the payload data field) *precedes* the next header field. When both encryption and authentication are enabled in ESP, the packet is first encrypted, and only then is the authentication data computed. This allows the receiver to reject fake packets without having to (try to) decrypt them first. If ESP authentication wasn't enabled, the "authentication data" field isn't present. Note that encryption without authentication is insecure because an attacker can modify the encrypted packet in dangerous ways even without knowing the encryption key.

The Security Parameters Index (SPI) field is used by the receiver to map incoming packets to the right Security Association in the SA database, similar to the function of the port numbers in TCP and UDP. The sequence number field contains a counter that can be used to thwart "replay attacks." This is an attack where the attacker records a legitimate packet exchange and then later sends out another copy of those packets. The first packet for any SA always has a sequence number of one, and the sequence number is increased by one for every new packet. If the receiver wants replay protection, it simply rejects packets with a sequence number lower than the last packet it received and higher than the next packet it expects, with a small margin to account for packets that come in out of order.

Authentication Header

Nxt Hdr 8 bits	Length 8 bits	Reserved 16 bits	SPI 32 bits	Sequence 32 bits	Authentication Data

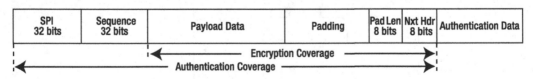

Encapsulating Security Payload Header

SPI 32 bits	Sequence 32 bits	Payload Data	Padding	Pad Len 8 bits	Nxt Hdr 8 bits	Authentication Data

Encryption Coverage

Authentication Coverage

Figure 9-3. *The AH and ESP header formats*

Note Security Associations and SPIs only work in one direction. So if an exchange is protected in both directions, there are always at least two SAs with accompanying SPIs involved. A Security Association is uniquely identified by the SPI, the security protocol (AH or ESP), and the destination address, so it's possible to use the same SPI for different SAs toward different destination hosts.

IKE uses UDP port 500. ESP uses protocol number (next header) 50, AH 51. Don't forget to allow these protocols in any IP filters that are present on hosts running IPsec!

The KAME IPsec Implementation

Even more so than with other subjects discussed in the book, IPsec provides *many* ways to shoot yourself in the foot if you don't know what you're doing. The examples below are merely intended to show that it's actually possible to run IPsec on BSD/Linux in practice, something that is hard to believe at first because of the complexity of the protocols and the many, many ways in which the racoon IKE daemon can fail when things aren't set up just right.

IPsec has been part of the KAME effort from the beginning. MacOS comes with KAME IPsec built in, and for FreeBSD, it's only a kernel compile away. See the FreeBSD manual as mentioned earlier this chapter and add the following lines to your kernel configuration:

```
options IPSEC
options IPSEC_ESP
```

You can install the KAME setkey and racoon utilities from security/racoon (not racoon2) in the ports collection. The easiest way to do this is to type /stand/sysinstall as root, select Configure then Packages, choose an FTP server, and find racoon in the security section. The program will guide you through the rest of the installation procedure.

The Linux 2.6 kernel also has a KAME-like IPsec implementation on board.[6] Unless you have Red Hat ES Linux or another distribution that comes with setkey and racoon, you'll have to download IPsec-Tools that contains Linux versions of the racoon and setkey utilities, available at http://ipsec-tools.sourceforge.net/.

To use IPsec, you need to have three things in place:

- A properly configured IKE daemon.

- A way to authenticate the remote end.

- One or more entries in the Security Policy Database.

The racoon daemon comes with an example configuration file, which is long and confusing. It's generally found in /etc/racoon/racoon.conf or /usr/local/etc/racoon/racoon.conf, depending on your system. Listing 9-15 is the minimum you need to get everything to work.

Listing 9-15. *A Simple* racoon.conf *File*

```
path include "/etc/racoon";
path pre_shared_key "/etc/racoon/psk.txt";

listen { }
```

---

6. There is also a "FreeS/WAN" Linux IPsec implementation, but it's no longer maintained and it doesn't support IPv6. However, at least one of the forks does.

```
remote anonymous
  {
    exchange_mode aggressive,main;
    my_identifier fqdn "host1.example.com";
    proposal
      {
        encryption_algorithm 3des;
        hash_algorithm sha1;
        authentication_method pre_shared_key;
        dh_group 2;
      }
  }

sainfo anonymous
  {
    encryption_algorithm aes, 3des;
    authentication_algorithm hmac_sha1;
    compression_algorithm deflate;
  }
```

The first line tells racoon where it can find its files. The second line points to the file that contains "pre-shared keys." Make the necessary changes if the directory where the racoon config files are isn't /etc/racoon/ on your system. The listen { } directive tells racoon to listen for incoming sessions on all addresses. This is all the global configuration that you need; the default settings are fine for everything else. However, you do need remote and sainfo specifications. When you communicate with several destinations by using IPsec, you'll probably need to have remote and sainfo entries for each of these destinations, or at least most of them. This is rather tricky, so carefully study the racoon.conf man page. But the anonymous settings work well as long as all settings (except the pre-shared keys) are the same for all destinations.

The exchange_mode specifies that we'll try to be aggressive and cut down on the number of round trips if possible and fall back to the regular way of doing things otherwise. The local identifier is specified to be the fully qualified domain name host1.example.com. Listing encryption and hash algorithms under proposal is mandatory, as is an authentication method, which we already decided should be pre-shared key. The dh_group setting specifies the group used for the Diffie-Hellman exponentiations. Not knowing what that means doesn't buy you a free pass: you need to specify a group. All these settings relate to phase 1 of the IKE negotiations. Finally, the sainfo settings determine the encryption and authentication algorithms, along with the compression algorithm to be used prior to encryption, that apply to the SAs established in IKE phase 2. You can simply type racoon (as root) to start the daemon, or racoon -F to make it stick to the TTY and show debugging output. Listing 9-16 is a sample psk.txt file. There doesn't seem to be any way to make racoon reload its configuration; you need to stop and start the daemon for this.

Listing 9-16. *A Pre-Shared Key*

```
host2.example.com          NoMoreSecretS
```

Make sure that the file containing the pre-shared key is only readable and writable by root. In this example, the identifier is a FQDN, but you can also use an IP address or user@FQDN as the identifier. The FQDN in the psk.txt file is the one for the remote end. At that end, there must be an entry for our identifier with *the same* pre-shared secret. The pre-shared key is never used to actually encrypt or authenticate anything but only to authenticate the other side in the IKE phase 1. Last but not least, you need to create Security Policy Database entries. This is best done by creating a file like the one in Listing 9-17.

Listing 9-17. *SPD Entries*

```
spdflush;

spdadd 2001:db8:31::/48[any]
       2001:db8:2:5::2[80]
       tcp -P out ipsec esp/transport//require;

spdadd 2001:db8:2:5::2[80]
       2001:db8:31::/48[any]
       tcp -P in ipsec esp/transport//require;
```

The first line in the file flushes all existing entries in the Security Policy Database. After that, two new entries are specified. Newlines ignored as commands are terminated by a semicolon. The first line of the first entry matches all packets with a source address in 2001:db8:31::/48 with any source port, but the second line narrows this down to packets with host 2001:db8:2:5::2 as their destination, with the destination port being 80. This would be appropriate if the local system has an address in 2001:db8:31::/48. The final line of the first entry specifies the TCP protocol. Any packets that match all this and are on their way out get IPsec treatment with ESP transport mode. The following entry matches packets belonging to the same TCP session toward host 2001:db8:2:5::2 on port 80, but in the incoming direction.

Caution Make sure that you don't specify an SPD policy that matches ICMPv6 packets on the local subnet, because if these packets are blocked for some reason (IKE negotiations fail or haven't completed yet) neighbor discovery no longer works. This is even a problem if you only match global addresses, as these are used for Neighbor Unreachability Detection (Chapter 8).

You can load these policies in the SPD with setkey -f spd.txt or similar. You need to be root to do this. You can monitor the Security Policy Database with setkey -DP and the Security Association Database with setkey -D. However, racoon doesn't negotiate SAs with the other side until there is traffic that matches an entry in the SPD. After this, SAs are inserted in the SAD and stay there until they time out. You can change SPD entries without having to restart racoon.

If you want to test between two hosts, you can simply use the same files on both ends, with just the identifiers swapped in the racoon.conf and psk.txt files and "in" and "out" swapped in the SPD entries on the second system.

IPsec Advantages and Limitations

So far, IPsec hasn't been deployed as a general-purpose, end-to-end encryption and authentication mechanism the same way SSL has. That's too bad, because IPsec has considerable security advantages over SSL: SSL runs on top of TCP, so disrupting the TCP session is enough to disrupt the SSL communication happening over the TCP session in question as well. Breaking TCP sessions is entirely trivial for an attacker who can observe the TCP traffic and is often doable with some effort for long-lived TCP sessions even without the ability to observe traffic. Fortunately, disrupting an SSL session just blocks the communication: it doesn't allow an attacker to inject falsified data successfully or decrypt encrypted information.

IPsec, on the other hand, is able to reject disruptive packets before TCP, UDP, or any other higher-layer protocol looks at them. It's also not just limited to TCP or transport protocols that are similar to TCP. An attacker who can't observe traffic can't even make the receiving host waste time executing authentication algorithms because the falsified packets are rejected based on the SPI and replay counter. This is an important advantage over the BGP TCP MD5 protection mechanism, which is vulnerable to "crypto DoS," where an attacker injects fake packets that fail the authentication test for the purpose of consuming CPU resources on the victim system. However, an important downside of IPsec is that it needs to carry encryption and authentication housekeeping information in each individual packet, which adds a significant amount of overhead. It's also generally more efficient to authenticate or encrypt/decrypt a large amount of data in one go (like with SSL when transferring big blocks of data) rather than doing the same for a number of individual packets carrying the same amount of data.

One of the reasons that IPsec never gained much traction other than for VPNs is probably that it operates at a very low level. For instance, an application that wants to use SSL can be redistributed with its own SSL code, without any impact to other applications. Having applications supply their own IPsec isn't realistically possible because IPsec operates deep inside the system.

Unfortunately, even on a system that has IPsec support in the kernel, it's very hard or even impossible to create IPsec policies based on anything other than IP addresses. In other words, to be able to communicate over IPsec, you need to know the IP addresses of your correspondents in advance. For applications like VPNs, this isn't much of a problem, but for a general-purpose SSL replacement, it's unworkable. However, there is an API that applications can use to enable IPsec for their communication, so there are still possibilities. In the meantime, it's hard to avoid the conclusion that mandatory IPsec support in IPv6 so far hasn't helped IPv6 security in the real world.

Note Many IPsec RFCs are found in the RFC 2401 to RFC 2412 range, and RFC 2401 is an overview of how the underlying protocols make up IPsec.

CHAPTER 10

■■■

Troubleshooting

"If there are two or more ways to do something, and one of those ways can result in a catastrophe, then someone will do it."

Edward A. Murphy, Jr.

Over the years, I've had occasion to speak about IPv6 to very different audiences. At one point, I was talking about the protocol in front of a group of people who weren't all that technical. I started the talk by showing them two screenshots of a Web browser: "On the left, you see a Web page over IPv4. On the right, you see the same page over IPv6." Naturally, the images were exactly the same, making my point that for average users, nothing changes with the advent of IPv6. In every day use, it's great that users can't tell the difference between IPv4 and IPv6: both just work.[1] For troubleshooting, it's not so great: it's important to know whether an application that works is using IPv4 or IPv6 and which of the two protocols, and in what order, an application is trying when it doesn't work.

The first part of this chapter explains tcpdump, a popular tool for inspecting packets flowing over the network. tcpdump will tell you which IP version you're using without fail. Armed thusly, we can look at different kinds of problems that can keep IPv6 from working as it should.

tcpdump

tcpdump intercepts packets flowing in and out of a network interface and displays their content, decoding many protocols in the process. Linux, FreeBSD, and MacOS have it installed out of the box, but you can find the most recent version on http://www.tcpdump.org/. Use tcpdump -H to find out which version you have. There is also a Windows port under the name "WinDump," which is available at http://www.winpcap.org/windump/ (with pointers to the accompanying WinPcap library). However, the Windows version isn't as stable as the UNIX version. There is also ethereal (http://www.ethereal.com/), which is often even more powerful than tcpdump. However, ethereal is mostly a graphical application, so it isn't as widely available as tcpdump.

In addition to the tcpdump application that provides the user interface, two other mechanisms are involved in intercepting and displaying packets: the Packet Capture library (pcap library or libpcap) and the Berkeley Packet Filter (BPF). To the system, the BPF looks like a device. When an application opens a BPF device, it supplies a network interface along with

---

1. Arguably, this is a bit of a problem for IPv6 marketing: people aren't interested in overhauling their network just so they can conduct their business as usual.

a filter program, and the application then gets to receive copies of the packets flowing through the specified network interface that match the filter. For efficiency reasons, the filter is implemented as a program in assembly code running on a virtual CPU. Applications can also *write* packets to a BPF device. These packets are then transmitted over the selected network interface. Not all programmers are comfortable working directly with devices under UNIX, and having to write assembly code to specify filters isn't exactly everyone's cup of tea either. The pcap library provides a higher-level interface to the BPF functionality in the form of a standard C library. Most notably, the pcap library takes filter expressions in plain text and generates filter programs from them. The tcpdump program relegates the actual filtering to the pcap library and mainly concerns itself with decoding and displaying the received packets.

Note To use tcpdump and similar tools, you need a certain level of knowledge about the intercepted protocols.

---

tcpdumping ICMPv6

Even if you don't expect to do much tcpdumping, you may want to use tcpdump from time to time to monitor certain ICMPv6 functions, such as router advertisements and neighbor discovery. In Listing 10-1, tcpdump intercepts a router advertisement message.

Listing 10-1. *Intercepting a Router Advertisement Message*

```
# tcpdump
tcpdump: listening on eth0
13:33:33.436664 fe80::204:27ff:fefe:249f > ff02::1: icmp6: router advertisement➡
[class 0xe0]

1 packets received by filter
0 packets dropped by kernel
```

Listing 10-1 is on a Red Hat Linux system, where tcpdump is run as root, as regular users don't get to open BPF devices on almost all systems. tcpdump automatically selects the desired interface: eth0. You can display the list of possible interfaces with -D (useful under Windows, which uses hard-to-guess interface names) and select one with the -i flag:

```
tcpdump -i eth1
```

Each tcpdump line starts with a timestamp, which is formatted as hours, minutes, and seconds (no surprises there), followed by fractions of seconds all the way down to microsecond precision. Note that the BPF device adds this timestamp, so this information is not entirely trustworthy: there could have been a delay between the moment the packet was received by the hardware and the moment BPF processed it. Also, intercepting the same packet twice (for instance, by running two instances of tcpdump) will generally result in non-identical timestamps.

Next up are the source and destination addresses. The source address is the link-local address of the router sending out the router advertisement, and the destination is the all-node multicast address. tcpdump concludes that the packet is an ICMPv6 packet containing a router advertisement. The line ends with the contents of the Traffic Class field, as it contains a non-default value. Apparently, Cisco decided to honor RFC 791 (even though that RFC is specifically about IPv4) and use the Type of Service value indicating "internetwork control" for router advertisements.

The meaning of the "packets received by filter" and "packets dropped by kernel" values differ from system to system, but in most cases, the former is the number of packets that the pcap library read from the BPF device, while the latter is the number of packets that the BPF device couldn't deliver to the pcap library because the buffer was already full when a new packet came in. This happens when the application (tcpdump) doesn't process the packets fast enough to keep up with network traffic. By default, tcpdump doesn't decode the contents of router advertisements, but Listing 10-2 uses the -v flag to enable this.

Listing 10-2. *Decoding a Router Advertisement Message*

```
# tcpdump -v -s 0
tcpdump: listening on eth0
13:52:05.259531 fe80::204:27ff:fefe:249f > ff02::1: icmp6: router advertisement( ➥
chlim=64, pref=medium, router_ltime=1800, reachable_time=0, retrans_time=0)(src ➥
lladdr: 00:04:27:fe:24:9f)(mtu: mtu=1500)(prefix info: LA valid_ltime=2592000,pr ➥
eferred_ltime=604800,prefix=2001:db8:31:53:/64) [class 0xe0] (len 64, hlim 255)
```

The -v option triggers more verbose output, and -s 0 tells tcpdump to capture the entire packet, rather than the first 68 or 96 bytes, which is the default. The additional information that's now decoded contains the current Hop Limit (64), the router lifetime (1800), the reachable and retransmission times (0 for undefined), the MAC or link-layer address for the router, and the MTU (1500 bytes). tcpdump also tells us pref=medium, but this information seems to be made up by the program, as there is no "pref" field in router advertisements. Last but not least, there is a prefix option with the prefix 2001:db:31:53::/64, which has the L (on-link) and A (autonomous address configuration) bits set and contains valid and preferred lifetimes of 30 and 7 days, respectively. The Traffic Class is as before, and tcpdump now also displays the contents of the Payload Length (64) and Hop Limit (255) fields in the IPv6 header.

Listing 10-3 shows a neighbor discovery interaction between two hosts.

Listing 10-3. *Decoding a Neighbor Discovery Exchange*

```
# tcpdump -v -s 0 -e
tcpdump: listening on eth0
15:02:27.471601 0:a:95:f5:24:6e 33:33:ff:29:23:b6 ip6 86: host3.example.com > ➥
ff02::1:ff29:23b6: icmp6: neighbor sol: who has host5.example.com(src lladdr: ➥
00:0a:95:f5:24:6e) (len 32, hlim 255)
15:02:27.471708 0:1:2:29:23:b6 0:a:95:f5:24:6e ip6 86: host5.example.com > host3 ➥
.example.com: icmp6: neighbor adv: tgt is host5.example.com(SO)(tgt lladdr: 00:0 ➥
1:02:29:23:b6) (len 32, hlim 255)
```

The -e flag tells tcpdump to show link-layer information. In this example, that's the source MAC address, the destination MAC address, and the ethertype and the size of the packet as reported by the interface logic. The Ethernet Frame Check Sequence at the end of the packet isn't displayed.

The first packet is from host3 toward host5's solicited node address (notice the Ethernet multicast MAC address) and inquires about host5's link-layer address. host3 lists its own link-layer address so host5 knows where to send the reply. The second packet is the unicast reply from host5 to host3, with the solicited and override flags set. This indicates that this is a reply to an earlier request and the link-layer address in the packet should overwrite a cached one.

■Note When router advertisements or multicast neighbor solicitations don't seem to come through, either in one direction or both directions, this usually indicates an IGMP snooping issue. In those cases, it usually helps to turn off IGMP snooping. See Chapter 8.

---

tcpdumping UDP

Listings 10-4 to 10-7 show the output for different invocations of tcpdump when capturing a DNS request and reply over UDP.

Listing 10-4. *Standard* tcpdump *Output*

```
# tcpdump
tcpdump: listening on eth0
13:12:33.935061 host5.example.com.32782 > ns.example.com.domain:  15025+ AAAA? ➡
ns.example.com. (32)
13:12:33.948362 host5.example.com.domain > host5.example.com.32782:  15025* 1/2/2 ➡
(148)
```

After the timestamp, the next items in the output line are the source address and port, followed by the destination address and port. By default, tcpdump looks up addresses in the DNS (possibly incurring a noticeable delay in the process) and port numbers in the /etc/services file. In this example, the source port wasn't a known service, which is normal for source ports. However, many systems choose their source port numbers from ranges that include registered ports, which can be confusing when tcpdump displays the name of a completely unrelated protocol in the source port field. You can suppress address and port lookups with the -n flag.

For DNS packets such as this one, tcpdump displays the query identifier, the query type, and the name for which information is requested. The last value on the line is the length of the DNS packet, excluding the length of the IP and UDP headers. More information may be present when the queries are non-standard. For replies, the program also displays the query identifier and the packet length, and, between those, the number of answer records, the number of name server records, and the number of additional records separated by slashes. If tcpdump captured enough of the packet, the contents of the answer are also displayed. The plus and the asterisk in the listing signify that the client requested recursion and that the answer was authoritative, respectively. Listing 10-5 displays more information.

Listing 10-5. *More Verbose* tcpdump *Output and Capturing Full Packets*

```
# tcpdump -v -s 0
13:06:07.693110 host5.example.com.32775 > ns.example.com.domain: [udp sum ok]  ➥
65043+ AAAA? ns.example.com. (32) (len 40, hlim 64)
13:06:07.710238 ns.example.com.domain > host5.example.com.32775: [udp sum ok]  ➥
65043* 1/2/2 ns.example.com. AAAA 2001:db8:31:53::53 (148) (len 156, hlim 60)
```

With the extra verbosity and the entire packet available, tcpdump double checks the UDP checksum and tells the user whether the checksum in the packet was correct. With the full DNS reply available, the answer section of the reply is now also displayed. Listing 10-6 uses an even higher verbosity setting.

Listing 10-6. *Even More Verbose* tcpdump *Output When Capturing Full Packets*

```
# tcpdump -vv -s 0
tcpdump: listening on eth0
13:07:17.811560 host5.example.com.32778 > ns.example.com.domain: [udp sum ok]  ➥
45697+ AAAA? ns.example.com. (32) (len 40, hlim 64)
13:07:17.827372 ns.example.com.domain > host5.example.com.32778: [udp sum ok]  ➥
45697* q: AAAA? ns.example.com. 1/2/2 ns.example.com. AAAA 2001:db8:31:53::53 ns:  ➥
example.com. NS ns.example.com., example.com. NS ns2.beispiel.de. ar:  ➥
ns.example.com. A 192.0.2.80, ns.example.com. A6 0 2001:db8:31:53::53  ➥
(148) (len 156, hlim 60)
```

In addition to the answer section, tcpdump now also displays ns: followed by the name server section and ar: with the additional information section. If the output is delayed, this is probably due to reverse DNS lookups of some of the addresses in the DNS packet. Again, use -n to disable this. Using -vvv doesn't provide extra information over -vv for DNS requests. However, if you really want to know every possible detail, use -X to obtain a hexdump of the packet, like in Listing 10-7.

Listing 10-7. *Displaying Packet Contents in a Hexdump with* tcpdump

```
# tcpdump -X -s 0
11:24:03.310136 host5.example.com.64875 > ns.example.com.domain:  29533+ AAAA?  ➥
ns.example.com. (32)
        0x0000:  6000 0000 0028 1140 2001 0db8 0002 0000  `....(.@........
        0x0010:  020a 95ff fef5 246e 2001 0db8 0031 0053  ......$n.....1.S
        0x0020:  0000 0000 0000 0053 fd6b 0035 0028 938e  .......S.k.5.(..
        0x0030:  735d 0100 0001 0000 0000 0000 026e 7307  s]...........ns.
        0x0040:  6578 616d 706c 6503 636f 6d00 001c 0001  example.com.....
11:24:03.327441 ns.example.com.domain > host5.example.com.64875:  29533* 1/2/2  ➥
AAAA 2001:db8:31:53::53 (148)
        0x0000:  6000 0000 009c 113f 2001 0db8 0031 0053  `......?.....1.S
        0x0010:  0000 0000 0000 0053 2001 0db8 0002 0000  .......S........
        0x0020:  020a 95ff fef5 246e 0035 fd6b 009c 7f6e  ......$n.5.k...n
        0x0030:  735d 8580 0001 0001 0002 0002 026e 7307  s]...........ns.
```

```
0x0040:    6578 616d 706c 6503 636f 6d00 001c 0001    example.com.....
0x0050:    c00c 001c 0001 0001 5180 0010 2001 0db8    ........Q.......
0x0060:    0031 0053 0000 0000 0000 0053 c00f 0002    .1.S.......S....
0x0070:    0001 0001 5180 0002 c00c c00f 0002 0001    ....Q...........
0x0080:    0001 5180 0011 036e 7332 0862 6569 7370    ..Q....ns2.beisp
0x0090:    6965 6c02 6465 00c0 0c00 0100 0100 0151    iel.de.........Q
0x00a0:    8000 04c0 0002 50c0 0c00 2600 0100 0151    ......P...&....Q
0x00b0:    8000 1100 2001 0db8 0031 0053 0000 0000    .........1.S....
0x00c0:    0000 0053                                   ...S
```

It's easy to recognize the IPv6 header in the beginning of the two packets because of the initial "6" in the dump. Apparently, no special quality of service handling is requested, and the Flow Label is set to zero, as the remaining 28 bits of the first 32 bits (two groups of four hexadecimal digits) of the header are all zero. The next 16 bits (one group) contain the payload length and the following group the Next Header field, which is 17 (0x11 in hexadecimal) for UDP, along with the Hop Limit. The addresses that follow are easy to recognize in the hexdump. In the second packet, it's remarkable that even though the DNS reply packet contains the actual reply for the query, two name server records and two additional records, there are only two recognizable domain names present. This happens because of "label compression" in the DNS protocol. The -X option can be combined with other output options when desired.

tcpdumping TCP

The output of tcpdump gets a bit harder to decipher when capturing TCP, simply because TCP is a much more complex protocol than UDP or ICMPv6. Listing 10-8 shows the same DNS request as Listings 10-4 to 10-7 but now over TCP, with no flags in effect to change tcpdump's output.

Listing 10-8. tcpdump *of a DNS Request/Reply over TCP*

```
% sudo tcpdump
tcpdump: WARNING: en0: no IPv4 address assigned
tcpdump: verbose output suppressed, use -v or -vv for full protocol decode
listening on en0, link-type EN10MB (Ethernet), capture size 96 bytes
14:32:35.468540 host3.example.com.58231 > ns.example.com.domain: S 2265400865: ➡
2265400865(0) win 65535 <mss 1440,nop,wscale 0,nop,nop,timestamp 631301731 0>
14:32:35.484974 ns.example.com.domain > host3.example.com.58231: S 3739752857: ➡
3739752857(0) ack 2265400866 win 57344 <mss 1220> [flowlabel 0x6c66e]
14:32:35.485197 host3.example.com.58231 > ns.example.com.domain: . ack 1 win 65535
14:32:35.485722 host3.example.com.58231 > ns.example.com.domain: P 1:35(34) ack 1 ➡
win 65535 45278+[|domain]
14:32:35.503456 ns.example.com.domain > host3.example.com.58231: P 1:151(150) ack ➡
35 win 58560 45278*[|domain] [flowlabel 0x6c6bd]
14:32:35.507729 host3.example.com.58231 > ns.example.com.domain: F 35:35(0) ack ➡
151 win 65535
```

In this example, tcpdump runs under MacOS (so we need sudo) on a currently IPv6-only interface. The program warns us that the interface doesn't have an IPv4 address, but this is of no consequence to its operation. Because tcpdump contains its own protocol decode logic, you can even use it to monitor IPv6 packets on a system that doesn't have any IPv6 support on board. We are also told that the "link-type" is 10 Mbps Ethernet, but don't be fooled: the speed is irrelevant, as all flavors of Ethernet use the same link-layer header format. So EN10MB is displayed for Ethernet of any speed.

The first captured packet is a SYN packet from the client to the server that sets up a new TCP session. The packet contains no fewer than four different TCP options. The first one is the Maximum Segment Size (MSS) option, which has a value of 1440 bytes, counting just the TCP payload and assuming a 20 byte TCP header. Together with the 40 byte IPv6 header, this makes for a total of 1440 + 20 + 40 = 1500 bytes, which is the MTU for the outgoing interface. The MSS option allows TCP to discover a smaller MTU on the remote end very efficiently, although Path MTU Discovery is still necessary to find reduced MTUs in the middle of a path. The NOP ("no operation") options are necessary to fill out the option space in the TCP header to an even 32 bits. The window scale (wscale) and timestamp options are part of the RFC 1323 TCP extensions for high performance.

The 2265400865:2265400865(0) part represents the sequence number of the first byte in this packet and the first sequence number in the next packet or segment. The (0) means there are zero data bytes in this TCP segment. This is tcpdump's roundabout way of telling us the initial sequence number chosen by the client. The server does the same on the next line, and also acknowledges the client's first sequence number. In subsequent packets, the sequence number is displayed as a value relative to the initial sequence number. Both initial packets have an S following the destination host/port specification, indicating that the SYN bit is set. Other common flags are P for PUSH and F for FIN. TCP packets with no special flags set get a period in this place. The server uses a flow label for this session, but the client doesn't, and tcpdump doesn't display the 0x0 flow label value in that case. The third packet is the acknowledgment back from the client to the server, completing the session setup.

Shortly after establishing the session, the client sends the first actual data packet: the DNS query, which is 34 bytes long. The snaplen (the amount of data that tcpdump copies from each packet that matches its filter) is 96 bytes, but 14 of those are used by the Ethernet header, 40 by the IPv6 header, and 20 by the TCP header. So only the first 22 bytes of the DNS query are available for tcpdump to decode. The [|domain] message indicates that further decoding was impossible somewhere during the processing of the DNS protocol. The same happens for the reply, which is even longer at 150 bytes. The reply acknowledges the segment that contained the request by indicating that the next expected byte in the session is number 35 (relative to the initial sequence number). After the client sends its FIN packet in order to tear down the session, there are some additional FIN and ACK packets, but you get the picture. For some reason, tearing down TCP sessions often involves a lot of misunderstanding between the two ends in the communication.

TCP HIGH PERFORMANCE EXTENSIONS

On a 100 Mbps Ethernet, it's possible to transmit a full size packet every 6.7 microseconds. With the maximum TCP window size of 65,535 bytes, the sender must stop sending data after 43 packets (288 microseconds) and wait for the receiver to acknowledge the first packet before sending the 44th one. However, on a transatlantic link, it takes some 80 milliseconds for the first acknowledgment packet to return because of speed of light delays. So for 79.712 milliseconds out of 80, the sender is just waiting for an acknowledgment without sending any data, severely limiting TCP performance. The maximum bandwidth that TCP can use is one window size per round trip, or some 800 kilobytes per second in this example.

Because even the IETF can't change the speed of light and the Earth isn't getting smaller any time soon, RFC 1323 allows bigger windows to increase performance over high-delay, high-bandwidth links. Rather than change the window size field in the TCP header from 16 to 32 bits, RFC 1323 introduces a "window scale" option. The window scale is a multiplier factor that is applied to the window size field in the TCP header. So if the TCP header has a window size of 65,535, and the window scale option at the beginning of the TCP session was 16, the actual window is 1,048,560 bytes, or about a megabyte. This is enough to saturate a 100 Mbps connection with an 80 ms roundtrip time. Both sides must have a window scale option in their initial TCP packets to enable this feature. A window scale option of zero means that the sending system supports the option if the other end desires to use it but won't be using it itself for outgoing packets during this session.

The timestamp option allows for much better roundtrip time estimates, which is necessary to achieve high performance. When both sides support the option, each inserts a timestamp of its own along with the last-seen timestamp from the other side in every packet, which adds 12 bytes of overhead to every TCP packet. The average packet size on the Internet is around 500 bytes, so having 12 bytes extra overhead in every packet reduces bandwidth efficiency by 2%. This extra overhead is a small price to pay if it means being able to use the full available bandwidth, but unfortunately, the timestamp option is used in *every* packet, regardless of whether the window scale option is really activated (i.e., there is an actual window scale of two or higher), the application requests it, or traffic patterns warrant it. In addition to having RFC 1323 support, It's also necessary for both ends that either the system or the application to set large enough send and receive windows to enable high performance. The send and receive buffers limit the maximum TCP windows.

However, the system generally uses a "one size fits all" default, and very few applications set their own buffer sizes. So most of the time, RFC 1323 support just wastes 12 bytes per TCP packet. You can disable both the window scale option and the timestamp option on FreeBSD and MacOS systems by setting the `sysctl` variable `net.inet.tcp.rfc1323` to zero. Linux uses two `sysctl` variables for this: `net.ipv4.tcp_window_scaling` and `net.ipv4.tcp_timestamps`. Setting them to zero to turns off the behavior, both for IPv4 and IPv6.

Some stateful filters perform checks on the TCP sequence numbers but don't support the RFC 1323 extensions. Obviously, this leads to problems when a window scale option of 2 or higher is in effect. For instance, IPF suffers from this problem. See Chapter 9 for more information about IPF.

Promiscuity

By default, tcpdump will try to put the interface into "promiscuous mode," so that it pulls *all* packets off the wire, rather than just the ones addressed at its own MAC address, along with the usual broadcasts and multicasts of interest. Promiscuous mode, of course, only applies to interfaces that use MAC addresses, such as Ethernet. With the proliferation of Ethernet switches, this mode isn't as useful as it once was: when the tcpdumping host is connected to a switch, the only extra packets it sees are multicasts that the switch didn't filter out (simple switches treat multicasts as broadcasts) and "unknown unicast" traffic. These are packets for which the switch doesn't know on which port the MAC address in question lives. So the only thing the switch can do is "flood" these packets to all ports. In most cases, inspecting packets to and from the host running tcpdump is good enough, so being connected to a switch isn't a problem. Still, it's not a bad idea to keep an old hub around just in case you ever want to look at packets to and from a system that you can't run tcpdump on, such as a router. When you connect the host running tcpdump and the system that is the source or destination of interesting packets to a hub, you'll be able to see all the traffic to and from that system. More advanced switches generally have some kind of "port monitoring" capability that allows you to receive copies of all packets passing through a certain switch port. The -p option tells tcpdump that it shouldn't try to put the interface in promiscuous mode. However, the interface may be in promiscuous mode for another reason (such as another tcpdump without the -p flag having the interface open), so you may see all packets anyway; filter when necessary.

Filters

So far, we've run tcpdump without providing a filter, so it displayed all packets that passed the interface in question. In most cases, this is not what you want, if only because the information overload makes it harder to decipher the program's output for relevant packets. The pcap library and, by extension, the tcpdump program don't use a fixed filtering syntax. Simple filters just look at addresses or fields such as port numbers, possibly accompanied by a protocol identifier. More complex filters are created by stringing together smaller filter fragments with AND and OR clauses and parentheses. Examples of simple filters are as follows:

ip looks for IPv4 packets.

ip6 looks for IPv6 packets.

host 192.0.2.53 looks for packets with IPv4 address 192.0.2.53. This includes IPv4 packets to and from this address and also ARP packets for this address.

host 2001:db8:31:53::53 matches any packet to or from this IPv6 address.

host ns.example.com looks up the domain name ns.example.com and matches all the IP addresses that the DNS returns (both IPv4 and IPv6).

ip6 host ns.example.com looks up the domain name ns.example.com and matches all the IPv6 addresses that the DNS returns.

net 2002::/16 matches any packet to or from prefix 2002::/16 (6to4 address space).[2]

src net fe80::/16 matches packets with a link-local source address.

dst ff02::1 matches packets addressed to the all-hosts multicast address.

port 53 matches all TCP and UDP packets with port number 53 (DNS).

---

2. If the "net" keyword doesn't seem to work as expected for IPv6, you may have an older version of tcpdump or pcap with a bug in the net filter code.

dst port 80 matches all TCP and UDP packets with a destination port 80.

tcp matches TCP packets.

udp matches UDP packets.

icmp6 matches ICMPv6 packets.

ether host 0:3:93:e0:ea:2 looks for packets with the specified MAC address.

ether proto 0x86dd matches packets with ethertype 0x86dd (IPv6). The ethertype may also be supplied in decimal.

ip6 proto 58 matches IPv6 packets with a Next Header value of 58 (ICMPv6). You can also use protocol names present in /etc/protocols, but they must be escaped with a back-slash if they're also tcpdump filter keywords.

ip6 protochain ipv6-icmp matches ICMPv6 packets with possible intermediate headers between the IPv6 and ICMPv6 headers. ("ipv6-icmp" is the name for ICMPv6 in /etc/protocols.)

"protochain \tcp" looks for IPv4 or IPv6 packets with a TCP payload, possibly at the end of a protocol chain. The backslash escapes the TCP keyword, so the entry named "tcp" in the file /etc/protocols provides the required protocol number. Without the slash, tcpdump generates a parse error. The quotation marks are necessary to keep the shell from interpreting the backslash.

When specifying IP payload protocols such as TCP, UDP, and ICMPv6, the respective keywords only make tcpdump check for the specified protocol in the IPv4 Protocol field or the IPv6 Next Header field. So the filter "tcp" won't match an IPv6 packet with an IPsec AH header followed by the TCP header. For this, use the "protochain" keyword. However, following the protocol chain is hard work for BPF, so this may be slower than other filters.

You can create more complex filters by combining multiple clauses with "and," "or," and "not." Don't forget to use parentheses when necessary, and use quotes to keep the shell from interpreting the parentheses in this case. And if this doesn't address your filtering needs, have a look at the tcpdump man page for information on creating more sophisticated filters.

IPV4 CHECKSUM AND LENGTH STRANGENESS

A good number of Ethernet network interface cards supports "checksum offloading" with IPv4. Some cards can just do the IP header checksum calculations, others can also handle the TCP and UDP checksum. For incoming packets, this is of little consequence for tcpdump, but for outgoing packets, you may encounter various "bad checksum" messages. This happens because (obviously) the BPF device copies packets before the interface card computes the checksum.

Because of Ethernet's 64 byte minimum packet size, when using the -e option, you may see packets that have the minimum link layer length of 60 bytes, while the actual payload is (much) smaller. (The 4-byte Frame Check Sequence is counted in the Ethernet specifications but not by tcpdump.) With IPv6, this can't happen for normal packets as the Ethernet header (14 bytes), the IPv6 header (40 bytes) and the TCP (20 bytes), and UDP (8 bytes) or ICMPv6 (8 bytes) headers add up to at least 62 bytes.

IPv6 Connectivity

As we saw in Chapter 8, strange things can happen when a host has an IPv6 address but not a default route, or an IPv6 default route but no global unicast address. You can tell whether a system has an IPv6 default route by listing the entire IPv6 routing table with netstat -r -A inet6 under Linux or netstat -r -f inet6 under FreeBSD or MacOS. (Add a -n flag to speed up the output by suppressing DNS lookups.) If the output contains a ::/0 route, the system was configured with a default route in some way, most likely by router advertisements. Use netsh interface ipv6 show route under Windows.

Address Availability and DAD Failures

If there is a default route, the next order of business is checking for available IPv6 addresses. Listing 10-9 shows the netsh output on a Windows XP system. This will list all available IPv6 addresses on the system. However, in this particular case, there is an address conflict: another system on the subnet uses the same address as the Windows machine tried to configure for itself.

Listing 10-9. *Listing Addresses Under Windows, Uncovering a DAD Failure*

```
netsh interface ipv6>show address
Querying active state...

Interface 5: Local Area Connection 3

Addr Type  DAD State   Valid Life   Pref. Life   Address
---------  ----------  -----------  ------------ ----------------------------
Temporary  Preferred    6d23h59m39s   23h56m52s  2001:db8:31:2:ff8f:41ae:c9f6:a97
Public     Duplicate   29d23h59m58s  6d23h59m58s 2001:db8:31:2:201:2ff:fe29:23b6
Link       Preferred      infinite     infinite  fe80::201:2ff:fe29:23b6
```

Listing 10-10 shows lines from the syslog and the output of the ifconfig command under MacOS when a DAD failure occurs. The FreeBSD output is virtually the same.

Listing 10-10. *Syslog and* ifconfig *Output Under MacOS/FreeBSD After a DAD Failure*

```
% tail /var/log/system.log
May  4 17:16:40 localhost kernel: en1: DAD detected duplicate IPv6 address 2001 ⇒
:0db8:0031:0002:0204:27ff:fefe:249f: NS in/out=0/1, NA in=1
May  4 17:16:40 localhost kernel: en1: DAD complete for 2001:0db8:0031:0002:0204 ⇒
:27ff:fefe:249f - duplicate found
May  4 17:16:40 localhost kernel: en1: manual intervention required
% ifconfig en1
en1: flags=8863<UP,BROADCAST,SMART,RUNNING,SIMPLEX,MULTICAST> mtu 1500
        inet6 2001:db8:31:2:201:2ff:fe29:23b6 prefixlen 64 duplicated
        inet6 fe80::230:65ff:fe24:f106 prefixlen 64 scopeid 0x5
        ether 00:30:65:24:f1:06
        media: autoselect status: active
        supported media: autoselect
```

On a Cisco router, the failure is logged to the logbuffer and may be observed with the show
ipv6 interface ... command, as in Listing 10-11.

Listing 10-11. *DAD Failure on a Cisco Router*

```
3wOd: %IPV6-4-DUPLICATE: Duplicate address 2001:DB8:31:2:204:27FF:FEFE:249F on ➥
Ethernet0
Cisco#show ipv6 interface ethernet 0
Ethernet0 is up, line protocol is up
  IPv6 is enabled, link-local address is FE80::204:27FF:FEFE:249F
  Global unicast address(es):
    2001:DB8:31:2:204:27FF:FEFE:249F, subnet is 2001:DB8:31:2::/64 [EUI/DUP]
    3FFE:FFFF:310:3:204:27FF:FEFE:249F, subnet is 3FFE:FFFF:310:3::/64 [EUI]
  Joined group address(es):
    FF02::1
    FF02::2
    FF02::9
    FF02::1:FFFE:249F
  MTU is 1500 bytes
  ICMP error messages limited to one every 100 milliseconds
  ICMP redirects are enabled
  ND DAD is enabled, number of DAD attempts: 1
  ND reachable time is 30000 milliseconds
  ND advertised reachable time is 0 milliseconds
  ND advertised retransmit interval is 0 milliseconds
  ND router advertisements are sent every 200 seconds
  ND router advertisements live for 7200 seconds
  Hosts use stateless autoconfig for addresses.
```

In this case, the Cisco router has two global unicast addresses, and only one suffers from
an address collision, despite the fact that both use the same interface identifier. So the first
address is rendered unusable, but the second remains viable. The same thing happened under
Windows, where the EUI-64 derived address was a duplicate but the temporary RFC 3041
address is still usable.

Note DAD failures for one or more of a router's global unicast addresses generally don't cause too much
trouble. But if DAD fails for a router's link-local address, the whole interface is rendered unusable for IPv6.

When the system has an IPv6 default route but no IPv6 global unicast addresses, you may
see somewhat strange DNS-related behavior under MacOS and Linux. Both of them won't try
to connect to IPv6 addresses if the local system doesn't have a global IPv6 address and report
"no address associated with nodename" (MacOS) or "cannot assign requested address" (Linux)
when trying to force IPv6, such as with traceroute6. Windows does mostly the same thing. For
instance, a tracert to a destination that has an IPv6 address will normally use the IPv6 address,
but if the local system doesn't have a global IPv6 address, tracert will use the IPv4 address for

the traceroute instead. `tracert6`, on the other hand, will use IPv6 regardless of the availability of a global IPv6 address on the local system, which means it uses a link-local address in the source address field of outgoing traceroute probes, which works for the first hop but not for subsequent hops. FreeBSD ignores any lack of global IPv6 addresses and tries to connect over IPv6 when there is an IPv6 default route.

Even though, apparently, under Windows, Linux, and MacOS, the system returns IPv4 addresses to applications that do a name lookup when there are no global IPv6 addresses, `host`, `dig`, and `nslookup` will still show IPv6 addresses, as those tools bypass the system's resolver library and query the DNS server directly.

ndp

On KAME-derived IPv6 stacks, you can use the `ndp` utility to display information learned through neighbor discovery, including router advertisements and the subsequent autoconfiguration on BSD and MacOS systems. `ndp -a` displays a list of neighbors along with their link-layer addresses, similar to `arp -a` with IPv4. See Listing 10-12.

Listing 10-12. *Displaying the Neighbor Cache on FreeBSD or MacOS with* ndp

```
% ndp -an
Neighbor                         Linklayer Address  Netif Expire    St Flgs Prbs
::1                              (incomplete)        loO  permanent R
2001:1af8:6::20a:95ff:fef5:246e 0:a:95:f5:24:6e     en1  permanent R
fe80::1%loO                     (incomplete)        loO  permanent R
fe80::204:27ff:fefe:249f%en1    0:4:27:fe:24:9f     en1  23h57m56s S  R
fe80::20a:95ff:fef5:246e%en1    0:a:95:f5:24:6e     en1  permanent R
```

As always, the `-n` flag suppresses address-to-name lookups. Using this flag is pretty much required when using `ndp` on MacOS, as the system will otherwise list its own name whenever a name lookup was unsuccessful. Apparently, this is the result of a bug. Listing 10-13 uses `ndp` to list interface-specific information.

Listing 10-13. *Listing Information for an Interface with* ndp

```
% ndp -i xlo
linkmtu=1500, curhlim=64, basereachable=30s0ms, reachable=40s, retrans=1s0ms
Flags: nud accept_rtadv
```

This form of the `ndp` command is the only way to reliably determine the IPv6 MTU for an interface on KAME IPv6 stacks. For unknown reasons, FreeBSD always reports that router advertisements are accepted (see the listing) while MacOS always reports that they aren't, both regardless of the real situation. Have a look at the `ndp` man page for more esoteric options, such as the ones for adding and removing neighbor entries.

traceroute6

If the system has both an IPv6 default route and a usable global unicast address, you can do a `traceroute6` (`tracert6` under Windows, and `tracert` also supports IPv6) to determine whether there is actually any IPv6 connectivity. A traceroute to `2002::` is often a good choice if you're not sure whether the DNS is working correctly. Because this is a 6to4 address for IPv4 address 0.0.0.0, the trace won't complete, but it will stall at the nearest 6to4 gateway. If you see at least a couple of working hops in the traceroute6 output, the local router and the next one are working. You can, of course, also do a traceroute toward a valid IPv6 host, but for this, you either need to know the host's IPv6 address or the DNS must be working.

When there is valid IPv6 connectivity and you experience application delays or things just don't work, it's important to determine whether the application is trying to use IPv6 and, if it is, whether it falls back on IPv4 if IPv6 doesn't work. When the application is connected over TCP, the easiest way to find out whether it's using IPv4 or IPv6 is with netstat. On all systems, netstat -n will list active TCP connections and display the local and remote ends as addresses, so it's easy to tell the IP version for the session. See Listing 10-14.

Listing 10-14. *Determining a Session's IP Version with* netstat

```
% netstat -n | more
Active Internet connections
Proto Recv-Q Send-Q  Local Address           Foreign Address        (state)
tcp6      0      0    2001:db8:31::20a.55858  3ffe:ffff:2310:2.993   ESTABLISHED
tcp4      0      0    192.0.2.6.55672         192.0.2.225.22         ESTABLISHED
tcp6      0      0    2001:db8:31::20a.52731  2001:db8:2:5::2.80     CLOSE_WAIT
udp6      0      0    *.5353                  *.*
udp4      0      0    *.5353                  *.*
```

Piping the output through more makes sure the information doesn't scroll off the screen immediately. The first session is a TCP connection over IPv6 toward a Secure IMAP server (port 993). The second line is an IPv4 SSH session (port 22), and the last TCP connection, which has already been closed, was an HTTP session. The two last lines indicate that the system is listening for incoming UDP packets on port 5353[3] for both IPv6 and IPv4 on separate sockets.

Alternatively, you can tcpdump with a filter that matches either the application's port number or the remote address and see whether the packets that flow over the interface are IPv4 or IPv6. (Again, use -n to suppress DNS lookups in order to see the addresses.)

traceroute and ping on a Cisco Router

On IPv6-capable IOS systems, both traceroute and ping will use IPv6 when possible. If you want to force the IPv6 version, use ip or ipv6 as the first argument following ping or traceroute, before the destination address or hostname. You can perform a ping or traceroute with many more options by typing traceroute or ping without any arguments. The router will then ask you for values for different options. Note that you can't provide a source address for ping, but you can for traceroute. This is often useful because the router may have a point-to-point link with an ISP using addresses from a very different range than what the rest of the site uses. The router will often select such a point-to-point address by default, which makes it impossible to compare the traceroute or ping results with those of regular hosts within the site. By making the

---

3. The Multicast DNS service that is used by the IETF's Zeroconf protocol, implemented by Apple under the names Rendezvous and later Bonjour.

router use a source address from the site's own address range, the traceroute results should be the same as those obtained by a regular host behind the router.

Forcing the IP Version

Unfortunately, IPv6 is still more fragile than IPv4. It's not unheard of for a host that has an IPv6 address in the DNS to have no actual IPv6 connectivity, so trying to contact it over IPv6 results in an annoying timeout. And it's not uncommon for downloads to go slower over IPv6 than IPv4. The reverse may also occur. Some of these problems are tolerable in the name of progress, but at some point, things should just work. In those cases, it's necessary to force the use of IPv4. In other cases, it may be necessary to force the use of IPv6 because an application won't use the protocol when left to its own devices. There are four ways to force the use of a specific IP version:

- Use application mechanisms. As we discussed in Chapter 6, Firefox allows the user to enable and disable IPv6 support. Many command line utilities, such as ssh and many versions of telnet and ftp, take a -4 or -6 argument, with easy-to-guess results.

- Select an IPv4-only or IPv6-only DNS name. When you have control over the DNS, it's always good to have IPv4- and IPv6-only aliases for important dual-stack domain names. Simply selecting the DNS name that links to the right IP version in the application will then do the trick.

- Use a literal address. Unfortunately, there are still applications that support IPv6 but can't handle literal IPv6 addresses, such as Internet Explorer. However, when the application must use a literal address, there can't be any doubt as to which IP version it uses, and there is no dependency on the DNS or possible DNS caching in the operating system or the application.

- Under FreeBSD 5 or Windows, modify the address policy table to give the desired protocol a higher preference or the undesired protocol a lower preference, for the destination in question, as discussed in Chapter 8.

Path MTU Discovery and Fragmentation

In IPv4, Path MTU Discovery causes lots of problems for people who use links in their networks with an MTU smaller than 1500 bytes. This happens when people use PMTUD (pretty much everyone has PMTUD enabled because having it enabled is the default setting in all major TCP/IP stacks), but somehow the packet too big messages that inform the source that it should use smaller packets don't make it back to the sending IP stack. In IPv6, this hasn't been as large a problem, probably because the proliferation of tunnels clearly illuminates the problem when it occurs, so it's usually fixed, and also because IPv6 has a reasonable minimum packet size of 1280 bytes that people can use if they don't want to run PMTUD.

However, IPv6 isn't immune to this problem: when people filter ICMPv6 packet too big messages, like Windows does by default when it's configured as an IPv6 router, path MTU discovery can't work and packets larger than 1280 bytes won't make it through to the other side. This results in the typical behavior that TCP sessions establish without problems, as the initial packets are smaller than 1280 bytes, but as soon as the actual data transfer starts, the session hangs and nothing happens. Pings don't show any problems, as those also use small packets by default. (And the DF generally isn't set in IPv4 pings.) You can diagnose the problem by doing a ping6 with packets larger than 1280 bytes. If the ping works, the problem lies somewhere else, but if the ping doesn't work after several attempts, you have a PMTUD black hole on your hands.

However, what happens when you execute an oversized ping6 is a little strange. The fact that it's impossible to let routers fragment oversized packets has the strange side effect that, in IPv6, Path MTU Discovery also works for UDP and even ICMPv6. First, let's look at a normal ping in Listing 10-15.

Listing 10-15. *Route Cloning Under Linux*

```
# ping6 -c 1 www.kame.net
PING www.kame.net(orange.kame.net) 56 data bytes
64 bytes from orange.kame.net: icmp_seq=1 ttl=47 time=345 ms

--- www.kame.net ping statistics ---
1 packets transmitted, 1 received, 0% packet loss, time 0ms
rtt min/avg/max/mdev = 345.453/345.453/345.453/0.000 ms
# ip -6 route get 2001:200:0:8002:203:47ff:fea5:3085
2001:200:0:8002:203:47ff:fea5:3085 via fe80::204:27ff:fefe:249f dev eth0  proto ➡
kernel  src 2001:db8:31:2:201:2ff:fe29:23b6 metric 1024 expires 59sec mtu 1500 ➡
advmss 1440
```

After a single packet ping6 to www.kame.net, the ip -6 route get ... command shows a "cloned" route toward www.kame.net's address with an MTU of 1500 bytes. Listing 10-16 repeats the ping with a packet size of 1300 bytes. Actually, the IPv6 packet is 1348 bytes: the specified 1300 bytes, 8 bytes ICMPv6 header, and 40 bytes IPv6 header. Naturally, I chose this destination because I have to reach it through a tunnel with a 1280 byte MTU.

Listing 10-16. *Fragmentation Under Linux*

```
# ping6 -c 1 -s 1300 www.kame.net
PING www.kame.net(orange.kame.net) 1300 data bytes
From 2001:288:3b0::55 icmp_seq=1 Packet too big: mtu=1280

--- www.kame.net ping statistics ---
1 packets transmitted, 0 received, +1 errors, 100% packet loss, time 0ms

# ip -6 route get 2001:200:0:8002:203:47ff:fea5:3085
2001:200:0:8002:203:47ff:fea5:3085 via fe80::204:27ff:fefe:249f dev eth0  src ➡
2001:db8:31:2:201:2ff:fe29:23b6  metric 0
    cache  expires 587sec mtu 1280 advmss 1440
```

The ping6 output indicates that the ping packet encountered a link with a 1280 byte MTU. Because the original packet didn't make it to its destination and, subsequently, there was no reply, ping6 reports 100% packet loss. The cloned route now lists the 1280 byte path MTU, along with a longer expire time, apparently because of the non-standard MTU. If we send another 1300-byte ping, it will be fragmented at the source, so it seems logical that this ping should receive a reply. But it doesn't. The reason is simple: the reply to our 1300 byte ping is also larger than 1280 bytes, so the return packet will also trigger PMTUD for the other direction. However, the third 1300 byte ping packet is answered. The ping6 syntax under FreeBSD or MacOS is the same as the Linux ping6 syntax in Listings 10-15 and 10-16, but looking up a (cloned) route is done with route get -inet ... on KAME-derived IPv6 implementations.

CHAPTER 11

■ ■ ■

Providing Transit Services

Moving IPv6 packets through the network isn't that different from moving IPv4 packets, and for most services that run on top of IP, such as the World Wide Web and mail, the difference is minor as well. So providing IPv6 transit services to customers isn't radically different from doing the same with IPv4. However, there are a few exceptions. The most important difference is the way in which customers get their addresses, both because IPv6 has stateless autoconfiguration but mostly lacks DHCP and because the address space is so much larger, making for very different address policies.

Getting Address Space

The first order of business if you plan to provide IPv6 access to customers is getting IPv6 address space yourself. As I'm writing this in the summer of 2005, the prerequisites for getting a provider aggregatable (PA) IPv6 address block are pretty much the ones outlined in Chapter 2: being a Local Internet Registry, not being an "end site," and intending to assign 200 /48 prefixes to others connected to your network in the next years. However, this policy is under pressure, and some RIRs have already changed it to some degree. As of this writing, the policies are as follows:

- In the APNIC and RIPE regions, you must plan to make 200 assignments in the next two years.

- In the ARIN region, either you need to be an existing ISP or you must plan to make 200 assignments in the next *five* years.

- In the AfriNIC and LACNIC regions, you must show a detailed plan to provide IPv6 connectivity in the region and for making assignments, and you must plan to announce the allocation as a single aggregated block in BGP within a year.

Ironically, the regions with the strictest policies have the largest number of PA block allocations: RIPE has more than 500, APNIC 250, ARIN around 150, LACNIC some 35, and AfriNIC a handful.

If you're a very large wholesale IP carrier and only provide transit services to ISPs with their own IPv6 address space, strictly speaking, you don't need address space of your own. In practice, you'll probably have some customers who don't have their own address space, and even if that's not the case, you need address space for your own network. The 200-customer rule is problematic here: you may not be in the position to assign address space to 200 customers within two years.

It's a bad idea to misrepresent the truth toward an RIR when requesting resources such as address space, but there are no rules against optimism. You won't get into trouble if you base your expectation to reach 200 /48 assignments within two years on optimistic (but reasonable) predictions toward a growth in customers and a speedy adoption of IPv6 that never materialize.

■Tip Don't forget to request delegation of the DNS reverse mapped zones for your new address block.

Provisioning Customers

While the IPv6 Provider Aggregatable address block allocation policies are quite strict, the policy for assigning address space to customers is the exact opposite. The IETF isn't in the policy business; the RIRs are free to decide on address allocation and assignment policies per their respective policy development processes, which are based on community consensus. However, in RFC 3177, the IAB and the IESG write:

> This document provides recommendations to the addressing registries (APNIC, ARIN and RIPE-NCC) on policies for assigning IPv6 address blocks to end sites. In particular, it recommends the assignment of /48 in the general case, /64 when it is known that one and only one subnet is needed and /128 when it is absolutely known that one and only one device is connecting.

You can find the various RIR policies on their Web sites. So far, the RIRs have all followed the RFC 3177 recommendations. So not only can you give customers a single address, a /64 subnet, or a /48 block as you feel appropriate and/or as is desired by the customer, but you don't even have to bother with red tape such as request forms and whois registration. The only thing you need to do is keep records about which address block was used for what, which your Regional Internet Registry may want to look at at some point. Only when a customer needs more than a /48 do you need to check back with the RIR.

Single Address Customers

Although it's possible that some customers may never need more than a single address, this is probably rare; and if it happens, it's hard to predict that this customer *really* won't need any additional addresses in the future. So it's probably not worth it to allow for this specifically in your provisioning plans.

Single Subnet Customers

In these days of ubiquitous Ethernet switching, relatively few people need more than a single subnet. Customers who don't require a block of IPv6 address space that they break into subnets themselves are best served by stateless autoconfiguration, but in some cases, manual configuration is more appropriate.

Stateless Autoconfiguration

Stateless autoconfiguration works especially well when each customer has his own physical or virtual subnet. This is common both in many server hosting environments, where systems from a single customer are put in a per-customer VLAN, and in most DSL and some cable setups, where there is a per-customer ATM PVC. Just configure your router interface with a /64 for the customer and enable router advertisements. The customer systems will automatically configure themselves with addresses within the /64 and use your router(s) without the need for any configuration at the customer side.

You can also use stateless autoconfiguration in much the same way if you have customers sharing a link or subnet. In server hosting environments, it's common to have shared VLANs with systems from several customers on them. Enabling autoconfiguration on such a subnet works very well but has the disadvantage that it's very hard to determine which IPv6 address belongs to which customer, especially when customers use RFC 3041 temporary addresses. This means there is no accountability and no possibility of billing based on IP-level traffic metering. And customers who didn't ask for IPv6 connectivity but found IPv6 and stateless autoconfiguration enabled without realizing it may be quite surprised about their system's unexpected behavior.

Note Cisco's DSL concentrators support a feature called routed bridge encapsulation (RBE) that allows the customer premises equipment (CPE) to be in bridge mode while the concentrator does mostly regular IPv4 routing. Apparently, RBE is supported for IPv6 as well, but I haven't been able to test this. Look up the `atm route-bridged` command in the Cisco documentation to learn more. Alternatively, you can set up a routed PVC for IPv6 customers as explained later this chapter.

Manual Configuration

Because DHCPv6 for address configuration is as good as nonexistent, the only alternative for stateless autoconfiguration on shared subnets is manual configuration. In theory, you can do manual *address* configuration and still have customer systems find IPv6 routers by virtue of router advertisements, but this is too dangerous: when a customer has a BSD system that accepts RAs but doesn't have a (manually configured) IPv6 address, the host will still try to connect to remote hosts over IPv6 without success, incurring lengthy timeouts.

On the other hand, if you don't have existing customers or only have customers who are interested in IPv6 on the subnet where you're going to provide IPv6 connectivity, you may want to use RAs without actual stateless autoconfiguration, as in Listing 11-1.

Listing 11-1. *Router Advertisements Without Stateless Address Autoconfiguration*

```
!
interface Ethernet0
 ipv6 address 2001:DB8:31:3::/64 eui-64
 ipv6 enable
 ipv6 nd prefix 2001:DB8:31:3::/64 no-autoconfig
!
```

The `ipv6 address` ... line configures an IPv6 address for the interface. The lower 64 bits are derived from the interface's MAC address. This has the advantage that there can be more than one router on the subnet without having to worry about which router got which address. The `ipv6 enable` line enables the sending of router advertisements, even though this often also happens without specifically enabling it. The line after that disables stateless autoconfiguration for this prefix. If you have several prefixes configured on the interface, you need to disable autoconfiguration for all of them.

Note Don't forget to redistribute connected routes into your internal IPv6 routing protocol so that the other routers in your network know how to reach the customer addresses.

If you choose not to use router advertisements to inject a default route into customer's systems, it's best to use the "1" address in a subnet for your router. For instance, in the `2001:db8:31:3::/64` subnet, your router would have address `2001:db8:31:3::1`, which is the address customers point their IPv6 default route to. There are basically three ways to assign addresses on a shared subnet to customers:

- Use individual addresses within a shared /64 prefix.

- Use ranges of addresses within a shared /64 prefix.

- Use a /64 prefix per customer.

The first option isn't all that attractive because, after some time, you'll have a long list of address-to-customer mappings, even if you have only a small number of customers with several systems each. The second option doesn't have this downside. For instance, if you give a /112 range of addresses to every customer, they get to determine the last four digits in the IPv6 address themselves, and you only need map one address range to each customer. Notice the distinction between a /112 address *range* within a /64 subnet as opposed to a /112 *prefix*. Because the range falls within a larger subnet prefix, a customer with address range `2001:db8:31:3::e01:0` to `2001:db8:31:3::e01:ffff` (which equals a /112) can have an address `2001:db8:31:3::e01:53/64` with a default route pointing to `2001:db8:31:3::1`. If the customer were to use the address `2001:db8:31:3::e01:53/112` instead, the default gateway would have to be within that same /112,[1] so you'd need a different default gateway address for each customer.

As you can see, the prefix size mechanics can get a bit complicated, and having a range of addresses in a shared prefix has another disadvantage: it's not really possible to move a customer from a shared subnet to a dedicated subnet without the customer having to renumber. So in most cases, having a dedicated /64 per customer, even though the subnet is shared, is the best choice. This allows for customers to be moved from one subnet to another without renumbering, it's easier to explain, and it also allows easy switching between manual configuration and stateless autoconfiguration. In this setup, the top 64 bits already identify the

---

1. Don't forget that bit 70 in the IPv6 address (bit 6 in the interface identifier) should be zero to indicate a non-universal interface identifier. So an address like `2001:db8:31:3:e01::53` would be ill-advised because of the "e" in the address that makes this bit one.

customer so that EUI-64 derived addresses may be used without trouble. The only downside of having a /64 for each customer is that an interface that connects to a lot of customers on a shared subnet will end up with a large number of IPv6 addresses/prefixes.

Customers must configure their addresses and, if applicable, a default route using the same commands that we used for manually configured tunnels in Chapter 3. Apart from configuring the "1" address within each prefix used by one or more customers on the subnet in question and possibly suppressing stateless autoconfiguration, there is no special configuration at your end.

Tip If you have more than one IPv6 router on a subnet where customers use a static default route, you may be able to use an anycast address for the default router address. However, as of this writing, Cisco and Juniper routers don't support anycasting, and I haven't been able to test how this works on non-Cisco equipment. In theory, the load should be split over the routers sharing the anycast address, and when one router goes down, the traffic should shift to another. How well this works in practice is impossible to say without experimentation.

PROTOCOL VLANS

All but the cheapest Ethernet switches support Virtual LANs (VLANs) these days. The usual way to create VLANs is to group switch ports together. However, some switches also support the notion of "protocol VLANs." Protocol VLANs let you have different VLANs for different protocols on the same switch port. So an IPv4 packet on a certain port would go into one VLAN, and an IPv6 packet on the same port into another VLAN. The switch recognizes the different protocols by their ethertype.

Having different VLANs for IPv4 and IPv6 traffic toward a customer can be very useful, because it allows a customer who has a dedicated VLAN for IPv4 to be part of a shared VLAN for IPv6, or the other way around. So if you have customers in a shared VLAN for IPv4 with no easy way to move them to a dedicated VLAN because their IPv4 addresses are intermingled with those of other customers, you can still have a dedicated VLAN for IPv6 for that customer. This makes using stateless autoconfiguration to provision customers less bothersome.

Consult your switch documentation for details.

Multi-Subnet Customers

If a customer wants more than a single subnet, current wisdom is to give them a /48. Recently, the discussion about whether giving out /48s to everyone who needs more than a single /64 subnet was refueled because even though the IPv6 address space is very large, the necessary levels of hierarchy in large service provider networks *may* land us uncomfortably close to its limits in the long term. So at some point in the future, the RFC 3177 recommendation to give a /48 to customers who need more than one subnet may be revisited. In the meantime, there is no harm in giving out /48s now as the IPv6 address space use the next few years is completely inconsequential compared to even the most conservative estimates for several decades from now. There is, however, an important advantage to standardizing on the /48 boundary: this makes it much easier for customers to renumber when they switch ISPs. Of course, making it easy for customers to move to the competition doesn't have a very high priority for most businesses, but it works in the other direction, too: the standard prefix size makes it easy for customers to move from a competitor to you.

Note If a customer wants or needs more than a /48, they have to fill in a request form that you must present to the RIR for evaluation.

Because it's infeasible to keep track of up to 65,536 subnets for each customer, you'll want customers with a /48 to have their own IPv6 router. You can then route their /48 to their router or routers in one of three ways:

- With manual configuration

- With DHCPv6

- With a routing protocol

Manual Configuration

If a customer's IPv6 router is configured with a static IPv6 address and a static route toward your router as outlined earlier this chapter, you only have to set up a static route for the customer's /48 toward his router. The most straightforward way to do this is to use a separate /64 between your router and the customers router and use the "1" address for your router and the "2" address in that /64 for the customer's. It gets even easier to remember when you select a number that identifies the customer and then put this number in a fixed place in both the /64 you use between your router and the customer's and the customer's /48. So if your prefix is 2001:db8::/32, customer 100 would have 2001:db8:2:100::/64 for the router-to-router communication (with 2001:db8:2:100::1 for your router and 2001:db8:2:100::2 for his) and 2001:db8:100::/48 for his own use. Customer a4ff would then have 2001:db8:2:a4ff::/64 and 2001:db8:a4ff::/48. See Listing 11-2.

Listing 11-2. *Manual Configuration for Two Multi-Subnet Customers*

```
!
interface Ethernet1
 description Customer 100
 ipv6 address 2001:DB8:2:100::1/64
 ipv6 nd suppress-ra
!
interface Ethernet2
 description Customer A4FF
 ipv6 address 2001:DB8:2:A4FF::1/64
 ipv6 nd suppress-ra
```

```
!
ipv6 route 2001:DB8:100::/48 2001:DB8:2:100::2
ipv6 route 2001:DB8:A4FF::/48 2001:DB8:2:A4FF::2
!
```

Each of the two interfaces connecting the customers (which can be subinterfaces or VLAN interfaces) just has an IPv6 address, and router advertisements are suppressed with the ipv6 nd suppress-ra command in order to avoid problems with accidental stateless autoconfiguration, although problems aren't likely in this case, so suppressing RAs is probably not necessary. The /48s are routed to the customer's routers in the last two lines.

Note You need to redistribute static routes into your IPv6 IGP to make the /48s reachable from other routers.

DHCPv6 Prefix Delegation

In theory, IPv6 prefix delegation is a very attractive way to hand out IPv6 prefixes to customers, because it works completely automatically and allows for easy renumbering. However, in practice, this is hard to do. Not only is there a lack of (reliable) DHCPv6 implementations, but having prefixes assigned to customers automatically is only useful if *everything* happens automatically. This includes all configurations at the customer's end and also the DNS. See Chapter 8 for DHCPv6 examples.

Using a Routing Protocol Toward the Customer

In some cases, it can be beneficial to have dynamic routing between you and the customer. This is typically the case when the customer has two separate connections, two separate routers, or both. When the links between you and the customer are susceptible to going down, such as good old-fashioned T1, T3, or fractional T3 lines, or dark fiber, it's very helpful to be able to automatically reroute all traffic away from the broken link to the working one. For in-house links, it's not all that likely that any given link will be down for a significant amount of time, so having a routing protocol in place usually isn't worth the trouble. However, even for connections within the same building, it can be a good idea to have two routers at your end and/or two routers at the customer end to minimize the impact of router failures.

Two routing protocols are appropriate here: BGP and RIPng. BGP has the advantage that it's created for the specific purpose of interconnecting different networks, so the required filtering is easy to accomplish. You can simply configure the customer with BGP as you would any other (IPv4 or IPv6) BGP customer (see later this chapter), except that this customer uses a private AS number in the 64,512 to 65,534 range, and you don't announce the customer BGP route to anyone else.

In cases where BGP isn't the logical choice, for instance, because the router doesn't support it or you or the customer isn't comfortable with the protocol, RIPng is a reasonable alternative. RIP is nice and simple so it won't burn up too many CPU cycles when something goes wrong, and the required filtering can be done without trouble. Listing 11-3 shows the service provider configuration for this.

Listing 11-3. *Multi-Subnet Customer Provisioning with RIPng, ISP Side*

```
!
interface Ethernet1
 ipv6 address 2001:DB8:2:100::/64 eui-64
 ipv6 nd suppress-ra
 ipv6 rip cust100 enable
 ipv6 rip cust100 default-information only
!
ipv6 router rip cust100
  distribute-list prefix-list cust100-in in
!
ipv6 prefix-list cust100-in seq 5 permit 2001:DB8:100::/48
!
```

As before, the first order of business is to set up a subnet prefix for communicating with the customer. (This will probably also work with just link-local addresses, though.) As there are no static routes that need the Ethernet1 address as a next hop address, we can use EUI-64 based addresses without problems. After this, router advertisements are again suppressed. Next, we enable a RIPng instance for this specific customer and configure it to limit outgoing routing updates on this interface to just a default route. After leaving the interface context, in the ipv6 router rip context for this RIPng process, we set up a filter that limits incoming updates to just the customer's /48 and nothing else, with the aid from the cust100-in prefix list. Listing 11-4 is the corresponding customer-side configuration.

Listing 11-4. *Multi-Subnet Customer Provisioning with RIPng, Customer Side*

```
!
interface Ethernet0
 ipv6 address 2001:DB8:2:100::/64 eui-64
 ipv6 nd suppress-ra
 ipv6 rip customer enable
 ipv6 rip customer summary-address 2001:DB8:100::/48
!
ipv6 route 2001:DB8:100::/48 Null0
!
ipv6 router rip customer
 redistribute static
!
```

On the customer side, the configuration is quite similar, except that here, outgoing updates aren't limited to a default route, but rather to the customer's /48. The summary-address line filters out the individual /64s (or other more specific prefixes) that fall within the /48 and only allows the /48 prefix to be propagated. For the /48 to be inserted into RIP, it's necessary to have a matching route in the routing table, hence the route toward the Null0 interface. The static route must also be redistributed into the RIPng process, which happens in the last two lines of the listing. As you can see, there is no requirement that the RIPng process names on both ends match.

Multihomed Customers

In IPv4, you may have customers who are connected to another ISP in addition to being your customer. So when one ISP (or the connection to that ISP) fails, they simply reroute their communication sessions over the other. By announcing the same address block to both ISPs over BGP, the rerouting is completely transparent to applications. However, in IPv6, it's not possible for end users to get their own provider independent (PI) address space, like they can in IPv4. So customers who want to multihome with BGP and don't qualify for their own PA address block[2] can only do so if they take a /48 from one of their ISPs and announce those addresses over BGP to both ISPs. Because many ASes filter out /48s, this provides a lower level of redundancy than an independent PI or PA address block would. But as long as the primary ISP (the one that provides the address space) accepts the /48 in question from the secondary ISP, the end user will still be reachable if there is a local problem at or toward the primary ISP. As most problems that impact connectivity for end users are local ones, such as a broken circuit or a power failure at the ISP, this way of multihoming is still useful. Listing 11-5 is the BGP configuration that supports this.

Listing 11-5. *Configuration to Have a Semi-Multihomed Customer*

```
!
router bgp 40000
 no synchronization
 neighbor 2001:DB8:2:100::2 remote-as 50000
 neighbor 3FFE:9500:3C:74::10 remote-as 45000
 !
 address-family ipv6
 neighbor 2001:DB8:2:100::2 activate
 neighbor 2001:DB8:2:100::2 prefix-list cust-100-bgp-in in
 neighbor 2001:DB8:2:100::2 filter-list 12 in
 neighbor 3FFE:9500:3C:74::10 activate
 neighbor 3FFE:9500:3C:74::10 prefix-list import in
 neighbor 3FFE:9500:3C:74::10 prefix-list export out
 neighbor 3FFE:9500:3C:74::10 filter-list 2 out
 network 2001:DB8::/32
 exit-address-family
!
ip as-path access-list 2 permit ^$
ip as-path access-list 2 permit ^50000$
ip as-path access-list 12 permit ^50000$
!
ipv6 prefix-list import seq 5 permit 2001:DB8:100::/48
ipv6 prefix-list import seq 10 deny 2001:DB8::/32 le 128
ipv6 prefix-list import seq 15 permit ::/0 le 48
```

2. Apart from regular end-user organizations that don't qualify for an IPv6 address block of their own and ISPs that do, you may also encounter organizations that provide "critical infrastructure." Those can get a micro-allocation from ARIN (see Chapter 4), but they get regular /32 prefixes from the RIPE NCC.

```
!
ipv6 prefix-list export seq 5 permit 2001:DB8::/32
ipv6 prefix-list export seq 10 permit 2001:DB8:100::/48
!
ipv6 prefix-list cust-100-bgp-in seq 5 permit 2001:DB8:100::/48
!
```

Under the router bgp directive that initiates the BGP part of the configuration (and provides the local AS number), there is a reminder to always configure no synchronization and two BGP neighbors: the first one (AS 50000) is the customer, the second one (AS 45000) is our own upstream ISP. The rest of the settings for these neighbors are configured in the address-family ipv6 segment. We use two filters for the customer: AS path filter 12 and prefix filter "cust-100-bgp-in." These filters are listed below the BGP configuration. The AS path filter is very simple: it only allows the AS number of the customer.[3] The prefix filter allows the customer's /48 and nothing else.

The configuration toward the ISP is very similar, except that there is now also an "export" filter that controls which prefixes are allowed out. These prefixes are the local PA block 2001:db8::/32 (see the network statement) and also the customer's prefix 2001:db8:100::/48. Although the latter falls within the former, it's not allowed by the first line because the match isn't exact. The "import" filter is very important: this rejects incoming routing updates that have our own addresses in it. If not rejected, such updates could potentially be used by attackers elsewhere to intercept traffic or block services. The first line in this filter allows the customer's prefix. Without this, it wouldn't be possible to reach the customer through her secondary ISP if our direct link to her goes down. The second line rejects our own block, including any prefixes that are smaller, all the way up to a /128. Last but not least, we allow all prefixes up to a /48. See Chapter 4 for more BGP filtering considerations and an example of the customer-end BGP configuration.

■Caution There is one thing your customers should be aware of before they decide to multihome by using a /48 prefix from one of their ISPs: because many networks filter out the /48s, in places where the /48 is present, it's often through a path that's longer than necessary. Because of the longest match first rule, packets will flow toward the /48, so they may incur detours. If possible, do some experimenting to determine whether this is the case and how bad it is before committing to this solution.

Hybrid Autoconfig/Manual Configuration

For customers on a dedicated subnet, you can easily create a standard hybrid configuration that allows the customer to use either a single /64 with stateless autoconfiguration or a subnet /48 with manual configuration by setting up an IPv6 router themselves. Listing 11-6 combines a configuration very much like Listing 11-2 with stateless autoconfiguration.

---

3. You'll probably want to use a more sophisticated filter that also allows for AS path prepending in a real setup, such as ^(50000_)+$, which allows an AS path consisting of one or more times AS number 50000 and nothing else.

Listing 11-6. *Hybrid Stateless Autoconfiguration and Manual Routing of a* /48

```
!
interface ATM0.100
 description Customer 100
 ipv6 address 2001:DB8:2:100::1/64
!
ipv6 route 2001:DB8:100::/48 2001:DB8:2:100::2
!
```

If you look closely, you'll see that the only substantial change from Listing 11-2 is the removal of the suppress-ra command. Also notice that the interface is an ATM subinterface; apart from the usual settings that are also necessary to set up an ATM PVC for IPv4 routing, the configuration in Listing 11-6 is all that's required to support IPv6 over DSL and other ATM-based infrastructures.

THE SIZE OF IPV6 POINT-TO-POINT SUBNETS

Although larger end-user networks may also run into this issue, it mainly comes up in ISP networks: what is the correct subnet size for IPv6 point-to-point links? There is no consensus on the right answer just yet, even though an entire RFC is devoted to this subject (RFC 3627). But there are some tradeoffs you should be aware of.

First of all, it's a perfectly valid choice to have no global IPv6 address on an interface at all. Link-local addresses will simply pick up the slack, and everything should work just fine. When a global address is required for sending back ICMP messages, the router will borrow a global address from another interface. On a Cisco router, you can use the ipv6 unnumbered ... syntax to force which interface the address will be borrowed from.

On the other hand, having a dedicated global address for an interface is useful for debugging: you can ping it to see if the interface is up, and you can add a descriptive DNS name that will show up in traceroutes. The smallest possible subnet size for a point-to-point link that must accommodate two routers (or a router and a host, for that matter) is a /127, which allows for two addresses. Unlike IPv4, IPv6 doesn't have a subnet broadcast address, so the address with all ones in the host part is a usable address. However, the same isn't true for the address with all zeros in the host part: this is the subnet all routers anycast address. If you configure a /127 on a point-to-point link with a router that doesn't implement the all routers anycast address (such as Cisco and Juniper) holding the higher of the two addresses, there won't be any problems, regardless of whether the other router implements the all routers anycast address. However, if a router that does implement the anycast address holds the higher address, this router won't be able to send packets to the router with the lower address. But even if everything works today, you may run into nasty surprises when a software upgrade adds support for the all routers anycast address. So stay away from /127 subnets in IPv6.

The next possibility is a /126. With two bits to number hosts and one address lost because of the all routers anycast address, a /126 allows for three hosts, so it will accommodate a point-to-point link just fine. However, there is a complication: RFC 2526 specifies that the highest 128 addresses (with the universal/local bit set to "local," if applicable) in a subnet are reserved anycast addresses, so the minimum subnet size must be a /120. It's not clear what is supposed to happen when a longer prefix is configured, and in practice, a /126 works fine. But it's not entirely inconceivable that at some point, some routers will not handle subnet prefixes shorter than /120.

Continues

A /120 allows for 2^{56} subnets within a single /64, which is probably more than you need. A /112 still allows for 2^{48} subnets within a /64 and has the slight advantage that the entire last hexadecimal number in the IPv6 address belongs to the same subnet.

Alternatively, you can just use a /64 for point-to-point links and use EUI-64 addressing. This has the advantage that you don't have to keep track of which router holds which address. However, this only works well if you don't have to point any static routes to the other router's address, because EUI-64 addresses are hard to type in correctly and change when you replace the hardware.

IPv6 Dial-Up

If you want to provide IPv6 connectivity over dial-up, you have a challenge on your hands, because there is no easy way to assign addresses over dial-up links. On the customer side, it's possible to get around this by assigning addresses statically, so the customer's equipment always has the same address. However, for regular dial-up service, you don't know which modem or ISDN line the customer is going to connect to, so there is no obvious way to set up routing toward the customer's address or address range. In the future, this should get easier as more support for RFC 3162 IPv6 RADIUS extensions becomes available. RADIUS is the main protocol that allows dial-up concentrators to get authentication and configuration information from a central server when a customer connects.

Alternatively, when both your equipment and the customer's support DHCPv6 prefix delegation, you can configure the dial-up concentrator to supply the customer with a prefix when she connects. Another option is to exchange routing information with RIP. Router advertisements aren't really compatible with the standard way of configuring dial-up by using a template interface configuration that is cloned when a call comes in.

None of these alternatives make much sense in mass deployment, so your best bet is probably to wait until you can use RADIUS or to give IPv6 dial-up customers a static IPv4 address and configure a tunnel with this static address as the endpoint.

DNS and Customer Service

Most ISPs host domains for at least some of their customers and usually make a nice profit in the process. As we saw in Chapter 5, IPv6 requires some changes to the DNS. For most domains, the changes are inconsequential: a few AAAA records for servers that are reachable over IPv6. However, even something as small as this can be quite problematic: if your DNS management software doesn't support AAAA records, you need to either upgrade the software or find a different way to inject these records in the domains where they're needed, such as delegating a subdomain to a different DNS server that can handle the AAAA records. Still, if the tools you use to manage the DNS *do* support IPv6, you're not entirely out of the woods: the people who work with the system need to know enough about IPv6 to be able to enter and change the records. This isn't a huge amount of IPv6 knowledge, but without it, expect frustrated staff and customers.

Then there is the reverse DNS. In large IPv4 installations, such as cable, DSL, or dial-up networks, it's common practice to pre-populate the DNS with both forward and reverse mapping information, so every IP address has working DNS name. In IPv6, this is no longer possible because of the large address space. There are several ways to deal with this:

- Ignore the issue and forego reverse mapping. Obviously, this isn't an ideal solution, but life is possible without reverse DNS mappings.[4]

- Use dynamic DNS updates. Although there is some client support for dynamic DNS updates in current operating systems, this doesn't yet include updating the IPv6 reverse DNS. Also, opening the relevant zones for client updates may not be what you want.

- Generate the reverse mapping from the AAAA records. This can work well if you host all the "forward" zones for domains used in your network and if there is a good system in place to update the AAAA records themselves.

- Manually maintain the reverse zones. Not much fun, but as long as you only have a few IPv6 systems, this can be easier than setting up complex systems to do it.

- Delegate the reverse zones to customers. This is common for customers with their own prefix. The prefix doesn't have to be a /48 for this; you can delegate on any 4-bit boundary. Some tunnel brokers even allow customers to enter two nameservers when signing up for the tunnel and the delegation is then done automatically.

Running a Private 6to4 Gateway

Although 6to4 tunneling has many downsides, it's a great invention because it allows many people to connect to the IPv6 Internet very quickly, often in minutes. None of this would be possible without the generous contribution of time, effort, and bandwidth from the people who run public 6to4 gateways. Don't worry, I'm not going to tell you that you'll earn lots of karma points by running one of those. Instead, I'm going to tell you to look out for number one and optimize your own connectivity to and from 6to4 addresses by running a *private* 6to4 gateway. The fact that this serves the public good by lowering the load on public 6to4 gateways is just an added bonus.

When you're first starting with IPv6, you may already have customers who use IPv6. However, because you weren't providing IPv6 services before, they must be using either a manually configured tunnel toward a remote tunnel broker or 6to4. By running a private 6to4-to-IPv6 gateway, you'll probably increase performance for these customers, because their packets toward regular IPv6 addresses no longer have to flow through a remote 6to4 gateway. Listing 11-7 implements a gateway in the 6to4-to-IPv6 on a Cisco router.

Listing 11-7. *A Cisco 6to4-to-IPv6 Gateway Configuration*

```
!
interface Loopback2002
 ip address 192.88.99.1 255.255.255.255
!
interface Tunnel2002
 ipv6 enable
 ipv6 mtu 1280
 tunnel source 192.88.99.1
 tunnel mode ipv6ip 6to4
!
```

---

4. As a rule, RFC 3041 temporary addresses don't have reverse mappings anyway.

Even though the 6to4 hosts address packets to the anycast gateway address `2002:c058:6301::`, there is no need to configure this address on the gateway; before the gateway sees the packets, they are already encapsulated in an IPv4 packet addressed to `192.88.99.1`. This is the address that must be configured as a local address on the gateway and also as the tunnel source on the tunnel interface. In the listing, this address configured on a loopback interface. (Don't forget that Cisco routers support multiple loopback interfaces.) Without the 6to4 anycast address present and configured as the tunnel source, the router won't recognize the 6to4 packets toward the 6to4 anycast gateway address. To able to act as a 6to4 gateway in this direction, the router must participate in the IPv4 routing protocol and have at least a default route for IPv6, and the `192.88.99.1` address must be redistributed into the IPv4 interior routing protocol in order to attract 6to4 packets.

It may seem more natural to also configure the `2002::/16` prefix, but this can have an unpleasant side effect. As the router then considers the entire `2002::/16` range "directly connected," it will try to send packets to those destinations by using 6to4 tunneling. However, these tunneled packets will have `192.88.99.1` as their source address, per the `tunnel source` directive. In many cases, this will work just fine, but it's also possible that packets with those source addresses are filtered out, either by your own IPv4 anti-spoofing filters or by your upstream's ingress filters. After all, `192.88.99.1` isn't an address registered to you.

Not having an IPv6 address on the 6to4 interface does have one odd side effect: whenever the router must return ICMP messages, the router must select a valid global scope IPv6 address from another interface as the source address for the ICMP packet. This means that when a 6to4 user does a `traceroute`, the first hop in the `traceroute` shows a regular IPv6 address for the router rather than a 6to4 address.

■ **Tip** Make sure that you can provide production quality service for your 6to4 gateway: a non-working gateway is *much* worse than no gateway, because it cuts your customers off from working gateways elsewhere, especially if you run a public gateway by advertising `192.88.99.0/24` and/or `2002::/16` to other ISPs.

Although a private gateway in the 6to4-to-IPv6 direction is nice to have and can increase performance for 6to4 users on your network, it doesn't have a lot of long-term potential: as soon as you start rolling out native (or tunneled) IPv6 services, 6to4 use on your network will decline, and the gateway won't have much to do. However, at this point, when regular IPv6 traffic increases, it becomes beneficial to run a private gateway in the IPv6-to-6to4 direction, as shown in Listing 11-8.

Listing 11-8. *A Private 6to4 Gateway in the IPv6-to-6to4 Direction*

```
!
interface Tunnel2002
 ipv6 address 2002:DFE0:E1E2::/16
 ipv6 mtu 1280
 tunnel source 223.224.225.226
 tunnel mode ipv6ip 6to4
 !
```

In this listing, the tunnel does have an IPv6 address, which mostly serves to make the 2002::/16 address block "directly connected" through the tunnel interface, so the router will use 6to4 to reach 6to4 destinations. The tunnel source address (from which the IPv6 was derived) is one of the router's regular IPv4 addresses configured on another interface, so outgoing packets have a normal source address, and anti-spoofing filters won't kick in. Don't forget to redistribute the connected 2002::/16 route into your IPv6 IGP.

Unfortunately, it's not possible to have more than a single 6to4 tunnel interface on a Cisco router. So if you want to have a 6to4 gateway in both directions, either you need to use two ·separate routers or you'll have to use the 192.88.99.1 address and make sure that outgoing packets with this address as their source address aren't filtered.

Setting up a 6to4 gateway in the IPv6-to-6to4 direction under FreeBSD or Linux is very simple: just use the listings from Chapter 3, but leave out the default route to the 6to4 gateway address, and make sure that the 2002::/16 prefix is routed to the Linux or FreeBSD system in question. You can run a private 6to4 gateway in the 6to4-to-IPv6 by setting up the 192.88.99.1 anycast gateway address as an alias on one of the system's interfaces and propagating this address in the internal IPv4 routing protocol.

If you want to run a public gateway, you should probably contact one or more existing 6to4 gateway operators first. Look up 192.88.99.0/24 in the RIPE whois database to find contact information.

APPENDIX A

■ ■ ■

The IETF and RFCs

Most people know that technical standards for the Internet are written down in RFCs and that the IETF produces RFCs. Of course, there is much more to it than that. The RFC series originally started in 1969 as a series of "request for comments" documents: someone would write a short text and request comments from others, much the same way we do now with email mailing lists. Later, the RFC series became a mechanism to publish a variety of documents.

An Internet Standard doesn't come into existence overnight. Like all RFCs, standards documents start their life as "Internet drafts." These drafts are published by the IETF for a period of six months and then deleted. This forces draft authors to resubmit updated drafts twice a year to escape oblivion. Most drafts are related to IETF working groups and as such are subject to working group and Internet Engineering Steering Group (IESG) review. It's also possible to have the RFC Editor publish an informational or experimental RFC without going through the IETF/IESG, but when the RFC Editor suspects that the work may overlap with IETF work, she or he asks the IESG to review the draft before publication as an RFC.

Although IETF working groups can also publish informational or experimental RFCs, their work usually enters the "standards track." Standards track protocol RFCs are initially published as "proposed standard." A proposed standard usually doesn't have any implementations or operational experience (there are exceptions to this rule), but it should be a complete specification. Then, after two independent implementations have been shown to interoperate, a protocol may move to "draft standard" status. Finally, a widely implemented protocol that is successful in wide deployment may become an "Internet standard." The specification then receives an STD number, but it keeps its RFC number. In most cases, exposure to the real world requires some protocol revisions. Existing RFCs are never updated, so revisions always require the publication of a new RFC. Depending on the nature and size of the changes, the IESG may keep a protocol at its current maturity level, move it back, or allow it to advance.

However, only a fraction of all RFCs are standards documents. The others specify older versions of current standards, specify an experimental protocol, contain "historic" information, provide guidelines that are considered "best current practice," or just "provide information for the Internet community." The status of an RFC can be any of the following:

Informational: The RFC just provides information and doesn't specify a standard.

Experimental: The RFC specifies an experimental protocol that isn't recommended in production environments.

Proposed standard: The protocol is standards track but has no operational experience yet.

Draft standard: There is limited operational experience with the protocol.

Standard: The RFC specifies a mature protocol.

Obsolete: The RFC doesn't specify the most recent version of the protocol (this doesn't say anything about the status of the *protocol*).

Historic: The RFC is no longer in use, but it is of historical value.

The best current practice (BCP) status seems to be independent of the document or protocol status. For instance, RFC 3152 is a BCP, but it's also made obsolete by RFC 3596.

Over the years, there has been a deflation (in the monetary sense) of the standards track levels, to the degree that it's almost impossible to gain "Internet standard" status for complex protocols. For instance, protocols such as HTTP and BGP, which can hardly be called immature, are stuck at the "draft standard" level.

The RFC Editor keeps an RFC index that reflects the current status of all RFCs. (The following list of RFCs was taken from this index.) There is also a document that contains all standards and BCPs. The documents are available at ftp://ftp.isi.edu/in-notes/rfc-index.txt and http://www.rfc-editor.org/rfcxx00.html, respectively. Especially the former is rather large. The RFCs themselves are available from http://www.rfc-editor.org/ and many other places. If you know the number, http://www.ietf.org/rfc.html is a quick way to obtain the RFC.

The RFCs mentioned in this book are as follows:

0768 User Datagram Protocol. J. Postel. Aug-28-1980. (Format: TXT=5896 bytes) (Also STD0006) (Status: STANDARD)

0791 Internet Protocol. J. Postel. Sep-01-1981. (Format: TXT=97,779 bytes) (Obsoletes RFC0760) (Updated by RFC1349) (Also STD0005) (Status: STANDARD)

0792 Internet Control Message Protocol. J. Postel. Sep-01-1981. (Format: TXT=30,404 bytes) (Obsoletes RFC0777) (Updated by RFC0950) (Also STD0005) (Status: STANDARD)

0793 Transmission Control Protocol. J. Postel. Sep-01-1981. (Format: TXT=172,710 bytes) (Updated by RFC3168) (Also STD0007) (Status: STANDARD)

0826 Ethernet Address Resolution Protocol: Or Converting Network Protocol Addresses to 48-Bit Ethernet Address for Transmission on Ethernet Hardware. D.C. Plummer. Nov-01-1982. (Format: TXT=22,026 bytes) (Also STD0037) (Status: STANDARD)

0894 Standard for the Transmission of IP Datagrams over Ethernet Networks. C. Hornig. Apr-01-1984. (Format: TXT=5697 bytes) (Also STD0041) (Status: STANDARD)

1035 Domain Names—Implementation and Specification. P.V. Mockapetris. Nov-01-1987. (Format: TXT=125,626 bytes) (Obsoletes RFC0973, RFC0882, RFC0883) (Updated by RFC1101, RFC1183, RFC1348, RFC1876, RFC1982, RFC1995, RFC1996, RFC2065, RFC2136, RFC2181, RFC2137, RFC2308, RFC2535, RFC2845, RFC3425, RFC3658, RFC4033, RFC4034, RFC4035) (Also STD0013) (Status: STANDARD)

1112 Host Extensions for IP Multicasting. S.E. Deering. Aug-01-1989. (Format: TXT=39,904 bytes) (Obsoletes RFC0988, RFC1054) (Updated by RFC2236) (Also STD0005) (Status: STANDARD)

1323 TCP Extensions for High Performance. V. Jacobson, R. Braden, D. Borman. May 1992. (Format: TXT=84,558 bytes) (Obsoletes RFC1072, RFC1185) (Status: PROPOSED STANDARD)

1886 DNS Extensions to Support IP Version 6. S. Thomson, C. Huitema. December 1995. (Format: TXT=6424 bytes) (Obsoleted by RFC3596) (Updated by RFC2874, RFC3152) (Status: PROPOSED STANDARD)

1918 Address Allocation for Private Internets. Y. Rekhter, B. Moskowitz, D. Karrenberg, G. J. de Groot, E. Lear. February 1996. (Format: TXT=22,270 bytes) (Obsoletes RFC1627, RFC1597) (Also BCP0005) (Status: BEST CURRENT PRACTICE)

1970 Neighbor Discovery for IP Version 6 (IPv6). T. Narten, E. Nordmark, W. Simpson. August 1996. (Format: TXT=197,632 bytes) (Obsoleted by RFC2461) (Status: PROPOSED STANDARD)

2023 IP Version 6 over PPP. D. Haskin, E. Allen. October 1996. (Format: TXT=20,275 bytes) (Obsoleted by RFC2472) (Status: PROPOSED STANDARD)

2136 Dynamic Updates in the Domain Name System (DNS UPDATE). P. Vixie, Ed., S. Thomson, Y. Rekhter, J. Bound. April 1997. (Format: TXT=56,354 bytes) (Updates RFC1035) (Updated by RFC3007, RFC4033, RFC4034, RFC4035) (Status: PROPOSED STANDARD)

2401 Security Architecture for the Internet Protocol. S. Kent, R. Atkinson. November 1998. (Format: TXT=168,162 bytes) (Obsoletes RFC1825) (Updated by RFC3168) (Status: PROPOSED STANDARD)

2402 IP Authentication Header. S. Kent, R. Atkinson. November 1998. (Format: TXT=52,831 bytes) (Obsoletes RFC1826) (Status: PROPOSED STANDARD)

2406 IP Encapsulating Security Payload (ESP). S. Kent, R. Atkinson. November 1998. (Format: TXT=54,202 bytes) (Obsoletes RFC1827) (Status: PROPOSED STANDARD)

2407 The Internet IP Security Domain of Interpretation for ISAKMP. D. Piper. November 1998. (Format: TXT=67,878 bytes) (Status: PROPOSED STANDARD)

2408 Internet Security Association and Key Management Protocol (ISAKMP). D. Maughan, M. Schertler, M. Schneider, J. Turner. November 1998. (Format: TXT=209,175 bytes) (Status: PROPOSED STANDARD)

2409 The Internet Key Exchange (IKE). D. Harkins, D. Carrel. November 1998. (Format: TXT=94,949 bytes) (Updated by RFC4109) (Status: PROPOSED STANDARD)

2411 IP Security Document Roadmap. R. Thayer, N. Doraswamy, R. Glenn. November 1998. (Format: TXT=22,983 bytes) (Status: INFORMATIONAL)

2412 The OAKLEY Key Determination Protocol. H. Orman. November 1998. (Format: TXT=118,649 bytes) (Status: INFORMATIONAL)

2460 Internet Protocol, Version 6 (IPv6) Specification. S. Deering, R. Hinden. December 1998. (Format: TXT=85,490 bytes) (Obsoletes RFC1883) (Status: DRAFT STANDARD)

2461 Neighbor Discovery for IP Version 6 (IPv6). T. Narten, E. Nordmark, W. Simpson. December 1998. (Format: TXT=222,516 bytes) (Obsoletes RFC1970) (Status: DRAFT STANDARD)

2462 IPv6 Stateless Address Autoconfiguration. S. Thomson, T. Narten. December 1998. (Format: TXT=61,210 bytes) (Obsoletes RFC1971) (Status: DRAFT STANDARD)

2463 Internet Control Message Protocol (ICMPv6) for the Internet Protocol Version 6 (IPv6) Specification. A. Conta, S. Deering. December 1998. (Format: TXT=34,190 bytes) (Obsoletes RFC1885) (Status: DRAFT STANDARD)

2464 Transmission of IPv6 Packets over Ethernet Networks. M. Crawford. December 1998. (Format: TXT=12,725 bytes) (Obsoletes RFC1972) (Status: PROPOSED STANDARD)

2474 Definition of the Differentiated Services Field (DS Field) in the IPv4 and IPv6 Headers. K. Nichols, S. Blake, F. Baker, D. Black. December 1998. (Format: TXT=50,576 bytes) (Obsoletes RFC1455, RFC1349) (Updated by RFC3168, RFC3260) (Status: PROPOSED STANDARD)

2526 Reserved IPv6 Subnet Anycast Addresses. D. Johnson, S. Deering. March 1999. (Format: TXT=14,555 bytes) (Status: PROPOSED STANDARD)

2529 Transmission of IPv6 over IPv4 Domains Without Explicit Tunnels. B. Carpenter, C. Jung. March 1999. (Format: TXT=21,049 bytes) (Status: PROPOSED STANDARD)

2671 Extension Mechanisms for DNS (EDNS0). P. Vixie. August 1999. (Format: TXT=15,257 bytes) (Status: PROPOSED STANDARD)

2672 Non-Terminal DNS Name Redirection. M. Crawford. August 1999. (Format: TXT=18,321 bytes) (Status: PROPOSED STANDARD)

2673 Binary Labels in the Domain Name System. M. Crawford. August 1999. (Format: TXT=12,379 bytes) (Updated by RFC3363, RFC3364) (Status: EXPERIMENTAL)

2675 IPv6 Jumbograms. D. Borman, S. Deering, R. Hinden. August 1999. (Format: TXT=17,320 bytes) (Obsoletes RFC2147) (Status: PROPOSED STANDARD)

2710 Multicast Listener Discovery (MLD) for IPv6. S. Deering, W. Fenner, B. Haberman. October 1999. (Format: TXT=46,838 bytes) (Updated by RFC3590, RFC3810) (Status: PROPOSED STANDARD)

2732 Format for Literal IPv6 Addresses in URLs. R. Hinden, B. Carpenter, L. Masinter. December 1999. (Format: TXT=7984 bytes) (Obsoleted by RFC3986) (Updates RFC2396) (Status: PROPOSED STANDARD)

2734 IPv4 over IEEE 1394. P. Johansson. December 1999. (Format: TXT=69,314 bytes) (Status: PROPOSED STANDARD)

2765 Stateless IP/ICMP Translation Algorithm (SIIT). E. Nordmark. February 2000. (Format: TXT=59,465 bytes) (Status: PROPOSED STANDARD)

2821 Simple Mail Transfer Protocol. J. Klensin, Ed.. April 2001. (Format: TXT=192,504 bytes) (Obsoletes RFC0821, RFC0974, RFC1869) (Status: PROPOSED STANDARD)

2827 Network Ingress Filtering: Defeating Denial of Service Attacks Which Employ IP Source Address Spoofing. P. Ferguson, D. Senie. May 2000. (Format: TXT=21,258 bytes) (Obsoletes RFC2267) (Updated by RFC3704) (Also BCP0038) (Status: BEST CURRENT PRACTICE)

2858 Multiprotocol Extensions for BGP-4. T. Bates, Y. Rekhter, R. Chandra, D. Katz. June 2000. (Format: TXT=23,305 bytes) (Obsoletes RFC2283) (Status: PROPOSED STANDARD)

2874 DNS Extensions to Support IPv6 Address Aggregation and Renumbering. M. Crawford, C. Huitema. July 2000. (Format: TXT=44,204 bytes) (Updates RFC1886) (Updated by RFC3152, RFC3226, RFC3363, RFC3364) (Status: EXPERIMENTAL)

2893 Transition Mechanisms for IPv6 Hosts and Routers. R. Gilligan, E. Nordmark. August 2000. (Format: TXT=62,731 bytes) (Obsoletes RFC1933) (Status: PROPOSED STANDARD)

3041 Privacy Extensions for Stateless Address Autoconfiguration in IPv6. T. Narten, R. Draves. January 2001. (Format: TXT=44,446 bytes) (Status: PROPOSED STANDARD)

3056 Connection of IPv6 Domains via IPv4 Clouds. B. Carpenter, K. Moore. February 2001. (Format: TXT=54,902 bytes) (Status: PROPOSED STANDARD)

3068 An Anycast Prefix for 6to4 Relay Routers. C. Huitema. June 2001. (Format: TXT=20,120 bytes) (Status: PROPOSED STANDARD)

3142 An IPv6-to-IPv4 Transport Relay Translator. J. Hagino, K. Yamamoto. June 2001. (Format: TXT=20,864 bytes) (Status: INFORMATIONAL)

3146 Transmission of IPv6 Packets over IEEE 1394 Networks. K. Fujisawa, A. Onoe. October 2001. (Format: TXT=16,569 bytes) (Status: PROPOSED STANDARD)

3152 Delegation of IP6.ARPA. R. Bush. August 2001. (Format: TXT=5727 bytes) (Obsoleted by RFC3596) (Updates RFC2874, RFC2772, RFC2766, RFC2553, RFC1886) (Also BCP0049) (Status: BEST CURRENT PRACTICE)

3162 RADIUS and IPv6. B. Aboba, G. Zorn, D. Mitton. August 2001. (Format: TXT=20,492 bytes) (Status: PROPOSED STANDARD)

3172 Management Guidelines & Operational Requirements for the Address and Routing Parameter Area Domain ("arpa"). G. Huston, Ed.. September 2001. (Format: TXT=18,097 bytes) (Also BCP0052) (Status: BEST CURRENT PRACTICE)

3177 IAB/IESG Recommendations on IPv6 Address Allocations to Sites. IAB, IESG. September 2001. (Format: TXT=23,178 bytes) (Status: INFORMATIONAL)

3194 The H-Density Ratio for Address Assignment Efficiency: An Update on the H ratio. A. Durand, C. Huitema. November 2001. (Format: TXT=14,539 bytes) (Updates RFC1715) (Status: INFORMATIONAL)

3315 Dynamic Host Configuration Protocol for IPv6 (DHCPv6). R. Droms, Ed., J. Bound, B. Volz, T. Lemon, C. Perkins, M. Carney. July 2003. (Format: TXT=231,402 bytes) (Status: PROPOSED STANDARD)

3363 Representing Internet Protocol Version 6 (IPv6) Addresses in the Domain Name System (DNS). R. Bush, A. Durand, B. Fink, O. Gudmundsson, T. Hain. August 2002. (Format: TXT=11,055 bytes) (Updates RFC2673, RFC2874) (Status: INFORMATIONAL)

3364 Tradeoffs in Domain Name System (DNS) Support for Internet Protocol Version 6 (IPv6). R. Austein. August 2002. (Format: TXT=26,544 bytes) (Updates RFC2673, RFC2874) (Status: INFORMATIONAL)

3484 Default Address Selection for Internet Protocol Version 6 (IPv6). R. Draves. February 2003. (Format: TXT=55,076 bytes) (Status: PROPOSED STANDARD)

3493 Basic Socket Interface Extensions for IPv6. R. Gilligan, S. Thomson, J. Bound, J. McCann, W. Stevens. February 2003. (Format: TXT=82,570 bytes) (Obsoletes RFC2553) (Status: INFORMATIONAL)

3513 Internet Protocol Version 6 (IPv6) Addressing Architecture. R. Hinden, S. Deering. April 2003. (Format: TXT=53,920 bytes) (Obsoletes RFC2373) (Status: PROPOSED STANDARD)

3587 IPv6 Global Unicast Address Format. R. Hinden, S. Deering, E. Nordmark. August 2003. (Format: TXT=8783 bytes) (Obsoletes RFC2374) (Status: INFORMATIONAL)

3596 DNS Extensions to Support IP Version 6. S. Thomson, C. Huitema, V. Ksinant, M. Souissi. October 2003. (Format: TXT=14,093 bytes) (Obsoletes RFC3152, RFC1886) (Status: DRAFT STANDARD)

3627 Use of /127 Prefix Length Between Routers Considered Harmful. P. Savola. September 2003. (Format: TXT=12,436 bytes) (Status: INFORMATIONAL)

3633 IPv6 Prefix Options for Dynamic Host Configuration Protocol (DHCP) Version 6. O. Troan, R. Droms. December 2003. (Format: TXT=45,308 bytes) (Status: PROPOSED STANDARD)

3682 The Generalized TTL Security Mechanism (GTSM). V. Gill, J. Heasley, D. Meyer. February 2004. (Format: TXT=23,321 bytes) (Status: EXPERIMENTAL)

3879 Deprecating Site Local Addresses. C. Huitema, B. Carpenter. September 2004. (Format: TXT=24,142 bytes) (Status: PROPOSED STANDARD)

APPENDIX B

∎∎∎

Startup Scripts

When left to their own devices, trained professionals will invariably start working on the ultimate solution to a problem that, as far as anyone else can tell, really doesn't need further solving. A good example of this affliction is starting services on UNIX and UNIX-like operating systems: although Linux, FreeBSD, and MacOS all share the same heritage in this area, service startup has evolved and continues to evolve in different directions on each.

Red Hat Linux

The Red Hat Linux service startup mechanism was inspired by UNIX System V and IRIX. The idea is that startup scripts are in the /etc/init.d/ directory (which is actually a symbolic link for /etc/rc.d/init.d/). In /etc/rc.d/, there are additional directories that govern which startup scripts are called for which run levels, but fortunately, we don't have to deal with that directly. When adding a new service to the system, the first order of business is creating a startup script, like the one in Listing B-1, and putting it in /etc/init.d/ (well, /etc/rc.d/init.d/, really) under a suitable name, such as zebra.

Listing B-1. *A Startup Script for the* zebra *and* bgpd *Daemons*

```
#!/bin/sh
# chkconfig: 2345 60 40
# description: Zebra is a set of routing daemons
### BEGIN INIT INFO
# Provides: $zebra
### END INIT INFO

# Source function library.
. /etc/init.d/functions

[ -f /usr/local/sbin/zebra ] || exit 0
[ -f /usr/local/sbin/bgpd ] || exit 0
```

```
start()
  {
    echo -n $"Starting zebra: "
    daemon /usr/local/sbin/zebra -d
    echo
    echo -n $"Starting bgpd: "
    daemon /usr/local/sbin/bgpd -d
    echo
  }
stop()
  {
    echo -n $"Shutting down bgpd: "
    killproc bgpd
    echo
    echo -n $"Shutting down zebra: "
    killproc zebra
    echo
  }
rhstatus()
  {
    status zebra
    status bgpd
  }
restart()
  {
    stop
    start
  }

case "$1" in
  start)
        start
        ;;
  stop)
        stop
        ;;
  status)
        rhstatus
        ;;
  restart|reload)
        restart
        ;;
  *)
        echo $"Usage: $0 {start|stop|status|restart}"
        exit 1
esac
```

As usual, the first line points to the shell that should be used to execute the script. The line after that tells the chkconfig utility (see Listing B-2) for which run levels this script should be executed, along with a value that determines the relative startup ordering and a value that determines the relative shutdown ordering. The next four lines are necessary for chkconfig compatibility, and the . /etc/init.d/functions imports some functions into the script that are used later. The script then checks whether the zebra and bgpd executables exist and exits when this isn't the case.

After this, four functions are defined: one that starts the daemons, one that stops them, one that displays their status, and finally one that stops and then restarts the daemons. The daemon, killproc, and status commands are provided by the system to simplify this. Note that our status function is called "rhstatus" to avoid a conflict with the status command. Finally, a case construct tests the first argument for the script and calls the appropriate function or displays a usage line if the argument wasn't recognized.

Startup scripts are readable, writable, and executable by root and readable and executable by group and world, although it's not clear why other users than root would have to look at these scripts, let alone execute them. A chmod 755 zebra (where zebra is the name of the script) makes sure that our script doesn't stand out. You can now manually execute the script to start or stop the daemons, or list their status. But the point of the exercise is to have the script executed at system startup. The chkconfig command in Listing B-2 makes this happen.

Listing B-2. *Using* chkconfig *to Execute a Script at System Startup*

```
# chkconfig --list zebra
service zebra supports chkconfig, but is not referenced in any runlevel (run  ➡
'chkconfig --add zebra')
# chkconfig --add zebra
# chkconfig --list zebra
zebra           0:off  1:off  2:on  3:on  4:on  5:on  6:off
```

The first chkconfig --list shows that the zebra script wasn't installed in the chkconfig system yet, hence the chkconfig --add. The subsequent chkconfig --list shows that the zebra script is executed when entering or leaving runlevels 2 to 5, with arguments "start" and "stop," respectively. If you want to disable a service, do this with chkconfig zebra off, and then you can enable it again with chkconfig zebra on. You can remove the script from the chkconfig system with chkconfig --del.

FreeBSD

Under FreeBSD, the traditional way to start services at system startup is to create a startup script in /usr/local/etc/rc.d/. As you can read in "Starting Services" in Chapter 11 of the FreeBSD Handbook, available at http://www.freebsd.org/, these scripts must have a .sh extension and be readable, writable, and executable for the system (the handbook recommends a chmod 755 <file>) and react appropriately to start and stop arguments. Listing B-3 starts the racoon IKE daemon when the system boots.

Listing B-3. *Startup Script for the* racoon *Daemon*

```
#!/bin/sh

case "$1" in
        start)
                if [ -x /usr/local/sbin/racoon ]; then
                        /usr/local/sbin/racoon && echo -n ' racoon'
                fi
        ;;

        stop)
                /usr/bin/killall racoon && echo -n ' racoon'
        ;;

        *)
                echo "Usage: `basename $0` { start | stop }"
                exit 64
        ;;
esac
```

When the argument is start, the script first checks whether the racoon executable exists, and if so, it starts the daemon and prints " racoon" to standard output so an administrator sitting behind the console during boot knows what's going on. When the argument is stop, all processes with the name "racoon" get killed unceremoniously. Doing this with the aid of a pid file would be cleaner, but I'm just a long-time fan of the killall command. If the argument wasn't recognized, the script shows how it expects to be executed. The basename executable between the backticks takes the script name as its argument and strips off the leading path.

Listing B-3 is about the shortest usable startup script possible. Most FreeBSD startup scripts check in the /etc/rc.conf file whether they should run, usually through a NAMEOFSERVICE_ENABLE="YES" line. See existing startup scripts in /etc/rc.d/ and /usr/local/etc/rc.d/ for inspiration. Under FreeBSD 5.x, there is a new "RCng" mechanism that allows startup scripts to take their configuration information from the /etc/rc.conf file, rather than just whether they should run at all or not. The new mechanism also handles dependencies, so services that depend on something else are only started after the service they depend on runs. See the handbook for more information. However, traditional startup scripts still work as well.

MacOS

MacOS X has several mechanisms to start services during boot. The most appropriate for configuring a manual tunnel at system startup is a shell script in the StartupItems directory.[1] There are actually two of those: one in /Library and another in /System/Library. We should probably use the former. First, we need to create a directory for our shell script:

```
% sudo mkdir /Library/StartupItems/IPv6Tunnel/
```

---

1. For more information on MacOS startup and other peculiarities, consult *Mac OS X Panther in a Nutshell*, 2nd Edition, by Jason McIntosh, Chris Stone, and Chuck Toporek or *Mac OS X Tiger for UNIX Geeks* by Brian Jepson and Ernest Rothman. Both books are published by O'Reilly & Associates in 2004 and 2005, respectively.

The actual script needs to have the exact same name as the new directory we just created for it to reside in: IPv6Tunnel in this case. Listing B-4 shows the script.

Listing B-4. *A Shell Script to Set Up an IPv6 Tunnel at System Startup*

```
#!/bin/sh

. /etc/rc.common

case "$1" in

  start)
    ifconfig gif0 tunnel 192.0.2.1 223.224.225.226
    ifconfig gif0 inet6 2001:db8:31:1::2/64
    route add -inet6 default 2001:db8:31:1::1
    ;;

  stop)
    route delete -inet6 default 2001:db8:31:1::1
    ifconfig gif0 inet6 -alias 2001:db8:31:1::2/64
    ifconfig gif0 deletetunnel
    ;;

esac
```

As is standard operating procedure for shell scripts, the first line specifies the shell that must be used to run the script. The next line is necessary to include a number of system settings. Then, the case command looks at the first argument that was passed to the script. If this argument is start, the tunnel is configured with endpoint addresses and an IPv6 address, and a default route is set up. If the argument is stop, the opposite happens: the default route, the IPv6 address, and the tunnel endpoint addresses are removed. The final esac terminates the case earlier. In addition to the actual script, MacOS also wants to see a file called StartupParameters.plist in the same directory. Listing B-5 shows the contents of this file.

Listing B-5. *The Contents of the* StartupParameters.plist *File*

```
{
  Description = "IPv6 tunnel";
  Provides = ("IPv6Tunnel");
  Requires = ("Network");
  Uses = ("Network");
  OrderPreference = "None";
  Messages =
    {
      start = "Starting IPv6 tunnel";
      stop = "Stopping IPv6 tunnel";
    };
}
```

The purpose of this file is to provide the system with information about the new service. Apart from the obvious description and messages, this is information the system uses to decide the order in which services are started during boot. In this case, the IPv6Tunnel service will be started after the network has been initialized. This means that you won't see the tunnel immediately after startup if you use a network connection that needs some time to start, such as Airport (wireless). MacOS 10.4 Tiger is very picky about the file protection mode for the files in Listings B-4 and B-5. If you set them to read, write, and execute for the owner (root) and read and execute for group and other, they'll work just fine:

```
% sudo chmod 755 /Library/StartupItems/IPv6Tunnel/*
```

In addition to supporting the more traditional startup mechanisms, MacOS 10.4 has a new launchd daemon that replaces many other mechanisms, such as the init process and the inetd daemon. It has many very useful features, especially for starting daemons. So if you plan on running additional daemons under MacOS Tiger, have a look at the launchd man page.

Note Although none of the startup scripts listed here was directly copied from an existing one, they do resemble existing startup scripts because there are only a few ways to accomplish the desired function.

Postscript

After reading the preceding chapters, you've learned a lot about IPv6—as it is today. But IPv6 is very much a moving target. I'm typing these final thoughts from the terminal room at the end of the 63rd IETF meeting in Paris, and for me, it has been a week filled with IPv6, both inside and outside the IPv6-specific working groups.[1] A lot of IPv6-related work is still in the pipeline. The most interesting are mobility in IPv6 (MIPv6), a new way to multihome, and secure neighbor discovery (SEND). But it certainly doesn't end there.

MIPv6, SEND, and Shim6

The idea behind MIPv6 is that more and more IP-capable hosts aren't tied to a fixed location. Laptops and PDAs are an obvious example. Their connectivity changes from moment to moment and location to location. One moment, such a device may be connected to a Wi-Fi network, but the next moment, it may move out of reach and switch to a second- or third-generation mobile data service such as GPRS or UMTS. Mobile IP makes it possible to keep using the same IP address when switching network connections. There is rudimentary MIP for IPv4, but MIPv6 is much more ambitious—for instance, it supports mechanisms to optimize the routing between the mobile node and its correspondents, rather than have these packets flow through a "home agent." In most books about IPv6, MIPv6 has a prominent place, but because the specification isn't finished yet, I felt I shouldn't discuss it in this book, which is about *running* stuff that's actually available today. But mobile IP is a fairly hot topic in the IETF, and we certainly haven't heard the last of it.

Multihoming in IPv6 is a subject that I'm personally involved with. The current way of multihoming in IPv4 by injecting an independent address block into BGP won't work in the long run, especially in IPv6, where many artificial constraints that exist in IPv4 have been lifted. The recently concluded multi6 (multihoming in IPv6) working group considered this problem for a long time, and finally it was decided to go for an approach where hosts have several addresses, one for each ISP that the site gets reachability from. The idea is that when one address no longer works, any active sessions and subsequent new sessions that use the no-longer-working address are transparently moved to a still-working address. Protocols such as TCP don't have the capability to change addresses in mid-flight, so to avoid having to change all transport protocols, this new address agility will be implemented in a new "shim" layer that sits between the IP layer and upper-layer protocols such as TCP and UDP. A new shim6 working group was chartered to develop this shim layer. Because work on the shim layer just started and there is a lot to do, it will be a while before this new way of multihoming is a reality. But when it is, having two or more connections to the Internet and transparently

---

1. There are about five different working group sessions scheduled in each timeslot during an IETF meeting, so the fact that I managed to fill my time with IPv6-related work doesn't mean *everything* that happens in the IETF is IPv6-related.

switching ongoing communication from one to another will no longer be something that only medium-sized or larger organizations can afford; even residential users will be able get both a cable and an ADSL connection and enjoy increased availability.

Last but not least, there is secure neighbor discovery (SEND). IETF work on this was already concluded before the Paris IETF meeting, so SEND will likely find its way into implementations sooner rather than later. The idea is to encode the result of a cryptographic hash operation over the public key in a security certificate in the interface identifier in the lower 64 bits of an IPv6 address. Neighbors can then authenticate the certificate and see if the interface identifier matches the public key, and thus the certificate, and whether the party they're communicating with is actually the one holding the certificate. Using this procedure, it's easy to detect rogue routers and other fraudulent neighbors and reject communication from them.

It's interesting to see that the extra bits in the IPv6 address are now used to implement protocols such as SEND in ways that aren't possible in IPv4. The shim6 work will very likely use a security mechanism similar to SEND.

The IETF Attitude Toward IPv6

One reality is that the IETF is doing a lot of work on the IPv6 protocol and new protocols that assume IPv6 as their substrate. When possible, these new protocols are later "back ported" to IPv4. A good example of this is IPsec. The AH and ESP headers are obviously inspired by the IPv6 "protocol chain" notion. IPv4 doesn't have a built-in understanding of protocol chains, but with some extra effort, it can be made to work. On the other hand, a protocol like the multihoming in IPv6 shim is unlikely to find its way back to IPv4: not only does it use up extra address space, which isn't very helpful in IPv4, but it will also likely use the extra space in the IPv6 address for its security mechanisms.

At the same time, there are people within the IETF that don't believe that IPv6 will ever amount to anything. One often-heard criticism is that IPv6 doesn't solve the routing problem. That's true: although we have some more bits to play with, IPv6 routing is essentially identical to IPv4 routing. Especially interdomain routing with BGP is problematic: ISPs need to have routers with lots of memory and CPU power just to keep up with the growth of the number of prefixes that people insert into the collective global Internet routing table. The IETF has a long track record of moving forward in small steps; there is usually no "rough consensus" to make bold leaps into uncharted territory. Others claim that IPv6 tries to do too much, and that the IPng effort should have increased the address length to 64 bits and called it a day. But interestingly, most IPv6 skeptics work for businesses that have support for IPv6 in their products, even if those skeptics generally don't work on IPv6 themselves.

For the most part, the skeptics do have a point: IPv6 doesn't fix *all* IPv4 shortcomings. However, in engineering, as in many other aspects of life, there is no such thing as a free lunch. For instance, there are ways to make routing scalable, but the costs are very high: a more scalable way to do routing would impose restrictions on how different parts of the network can and can't interconnect and make traffic flow through less optimal paths. The way I see it, in general, IPv6 presents a good compromise between improving on IPv4 and limiting harmful side effects. But more importantly, IPv6 provides many opportunities for future refinement and expansion. You ain't seen nothing yet.

Index

forums.apress.com